"There is a bit of a 'loner' streak in fire. This is not an element that easily attaches itself to others for long periods of time. Fire doesn't comfortably settle into structured relationships, and even the security of enduring intimacy is not what it wants—especially if that means its freedom to spontaneously move about will be curtailed."

—from Chapter One

"Aries knows it's here to get something in motion, *now*, at this moment! All personal interests are activated by a single-minded drive to satisfy self-will. Like a bullet, Aries ejects itself into its immediate world to give whatever it targets its best shot—and sometimes its *only* shot—of adrenaline and self-starting power."

—from Chapter Three

"Describing Scorpio as intense, penetrating, brooding, and even volcanic makes this archetype sound like something that's best left alone to quietly lurk in dark, hard-to-reach hiding places. The warning is that unnecessarily agitating a Scorpion who's within deadly striking distance is a very bad idea."

—from Chapter Four

"Taurus doesn't seem to have much in common with Gemini, although it provides the sensible grounding that this sometimes flighty air sign needs in order to capitalize on its versatility. Besides benefiting from having its energies harnessed and given practical direction, the Twins also profit from the Bull's common sense and its ability to market any product of worth. In fact, this earth sign can't stand to see any talent go to waste."

—from Chapter Seven

"Part of our ongoing development in Cancer's house involves learning to deprogram negative influences from our past, especially in those areas where unexamined, subconscious fears prevent us from attaining our desires. We need to outgrow these parts of ourselves, yet it's difficult to let them go. Many of our ingrained safety needs—those that we sometimes defend against all logic or reason—are also attached to the matters of this house."

—from Chapter Nine

About the Author

Bil Tierney has been involved with astrology for nearly thirty-five years. As a full-time professional astrologer, he has lectured and has given workshops at major astrological conferences throughout the United States and in Canada since the mid-1970s. His special interest is studying the birthchart from a practical, psychological level that also encourages grounded spiritual growth. He has been a longtime member of the Metropolitan Atlanta Astrological Society (MAAS), and is also a member of ISAR (International Society for Astrological Research). Bil's work has been seen in astrological publications such as *Aspects* and *The Mercury Hour*. He has also contributed articles for StarIQ.com. His other books in print are *Dynamics of Aspect Analysis*, and the Llewellyn publications *Twelve Faces of Saturn*, *Alive and Well with Uranus*, *Alive and Well with Neptune*, and *Alive and Well with Pluto*.

Readers enjoy Bil's thorough, insightful approach to the astrological topics he writes about. They also appreciate his humorous slant and the effort he makes to teach astrology with the needs of the student in mind. He writes in a clear and easygoing style, and skillfully blends intuitive thinking with analytical reasoning in a way that makes for entertaining and informative reading.

To Contact the Author

If you wish to contact the author or would like more information about this book, please write to the author in care of Llewellyn Worldwide. **Please include an e-mail address, if possible.** All mail addressed to the author is forwarded, but the publisher cannot, unless specifically instructed by the author, give out an address or phone number.

Bil Tierney
℅ Llewellyn Worldwide
P.O. Box 64383, Dept. 1-7387-0111-4
St. Paul, MN 55164-0383, U.S.A.

Please enclose a self-addressed stamped envelope for reply,
or $1.00 to cover costs. If outside U.S.A., enclose
international postal reply coupon.

Many of Llewellyn's authors have websites with additional information and resources. For more information, please visit our website at http://www.llewellyn.com.

ALL AROUND THE ZODIAC

Exploring Astrology's Twelve Signs

BIL TIERNEY

2001
Llewellyn Publications
St. Paul, Minnesota 55164-0383, U.S.A.

First Edition
First Printing, 2001

Book design by Donna Burch
Cover design by Gavin Dayton Duffy
Editing by Andrea Neff

Library of Congress Cataloging-in-Publication Data

Tierney, Bil.
    All around the zodiac : exploring astrology's twelve signs / Bil Tierney.— 1st ed.
      p.   cm.
    Includes bibliographical references.
    ISBN 0-7387-0111-4
     1. Zodiac I. Title.

BF1726 .T54 2001
133.5'2—dc21   2001038642

Llewellyn Publications
A Division of Llewellyn Worldwide, Ltd.
P.O. Box 64383, Dept. 1-7387-0111-4
St. Paul, MN 55164-0383, U.S.A.
www.llewellyn.com

Printed in the United States of America

Dedication

I dedicate this book to Marion March,
one of astrology's shining lights,
who showed us what positive
Aquarian energy is really all about.
May she continue to be an inspiration
to astrologers everywhere.

Acknowledgments

I would like to thank Nancy Mostad and the acquisitions committee for accepting my book for publication. A big thanks and much appreciation also goes to the cover designer, Gavin Dayton Duffy, the book designer, Donna Burch, and my most helpful and hardworking editor, Andrea Neff. You've all played a major role in making this book look so good. Also, my thanks go to Tom Bilstad for his excellent proofreading skills, Lisa Braun (publicity), Amy Martin (marketing), and everyone else who assisted in the production of this book.

And last, I wish to express my gratitude to my colleague Carol Tebbs, who read a prepublication copy of *All Around the Zodiac* and submitted her comments for the back cover.

Contents

PART TWO
Sign Combinations

PART THREE
Combining Signs with Planets & Houses

Introduction

WHAT'S YOUR SIGN?

There was once a time—around the late 1960s—when asking folks to tell us their Sun signs was a charming and fun way to make initial social contact. This was especially so if everyone was wearing bell-bottoms and love beads, and was high on life and feeling spiritually connected, perhaps even going back to past lives in ancient Egypt—where else? If we actually knew something about the zodiac and the planets, people seemed genuinely fascinated and open to the subject. Many kind and gentle souls, looking a little starry-eyed way back then, were easily enchanted by the mysteries of the Cosmos—quite fitting for the anticipated "dawning of the Age of Aquarius," even if only realized in a Broadway hit musical.

Yet, perhaps all that "New Age" excitement was a bit premature. That's because at some point during the money-hungry, "dressed-for-success," power-seeking 1980s, asking a stranger such an innocent astrological question—and not at Woodstock '69 this time, but "up close and impersonal" in some chic, crowded dance club—would have risked getting a watered-down drink splashed in our face, maybe by some ticked-off Aries having a bad day on Wall Street. Actually, a disgusted look would usually suffice, as that individual would then head off to parts unknown just to escape "space cadets" like us. Gee, and all we were trying to do was to make sure we weren't attracting any more "crazy Aquarians," since we know how easily they can rattle our usually calm and steady Taurean nature.

Well, the times have changed since then. Nowadays, annoyed strangers who find astrology to be a bunch of nonsense may instead throw their business cards at us and not even walk away, but defiantly just stand there and stare at us until either *we* take a hike or else promise to network for them! It's a whole different ballgame out there. Actually, thanks to the Internet, there is reason for renewed optimism. Astrology has gotten an unexpected surge of widespread exposure in cyberspace ever since the early 1990s. Many people around the globe now have access to sophisticated astrological information that goes way beyond what's offered in newspaper Sun-sign columns. They are discovering that astrology has deeper, psychological meaning for them. It's not just a handy predictive tool to help them get an instant jump-start on tomorrow.

There are also several professional-level astrology software programs to choose from that can quickly do the tedious mathematics involved in calculating a birth chart, as well as compute a variety of other corelated charts used in forecasting techniques. This helps to make "real" astrology even more accessible to anyone interested in the subject. In addition, at the turn of this twenty-first century, Kepler College of Astrological Arts and Sciences in Washington State has opened its doors—this is a milestone event in the history of modern astrology.[1] Kepler's goal is to have qualified applicants work toward getting a B.A. in astrology, after four years of intensive study, and then hopefully to advance to a Master's degree.

Things are really changing for the better, as bright and open-minded individuals from all walks of life are gravitating toward astrology in greater numbers. It's thus a smart move to not only know what your Sun sign means these days, but also to learn about all the other key astrological factors in your chart. There is much astrological reading material available in bookstores and from online websites (even local library shelves are becoming better stocked with quality material). Whether you are a novice who's fascinated with this field of human exploration, or one who's still reading Sun-sign paperbacks, it's time to learn more about what serious students and professional astrologers already know.

Who Needs to Read This Book?

Who may benefit from reading *All Around the Zodiac*? The simple answer is, "Anyone broad-minded enough to want to learn more about astrology." Although readers are at different levels in understanding this vast subject, I think what I've written here will appeal to many—except, perhaps, one group: the Merely Curious. These are often the folks who don't want to put a lot of time and effort into looking deeply at their self-created and often perplexing life patterns. They instead seek to find quick and painless fixes for their momentary problems, usually by enlisting someone else to do the needed repair work. They typically will take marginal responsibility—if any at all—for what happens to them, and are sooner to blame others for the predicaments that dog their lives.

If this unflattering description sounds like you, I still want you to read this book, even if you're not too sure that you have the concentration and patience needed to absorb all that you're reading. Many of us feel like that when we first study astrology—there's *so* much to learn, that we don't know how we will possibly take it all in. However, if you want to get a better handle on your life and maybe turn things around for the better—so that you can be more in charge of yourself rather than feel like a pawn of fate—this book offers you fresh, eye-opening ways to look at everything and everyone in your world. It's at least a positive, self-empowering step in the right direction.

This is also a book for those more-than-curious types who already have the good sense to realize that if astrology can help us figure out the inner forces that drive human nature, it must indeed be a broad, profound, wisdom-inducing study worthy of serious investigation. Although astrology *is* a very big and challenging subject to tackle, learning all about the signs of the zodiac is a great way to begin exploring this field. People who are taking astrology classes or have already been reading astrology books for a few years will appreciate this detailed material, and even veteran astrologers—those who have probably "read it all by now"—should still be able to find some insightful information in these pages.

The Signs Are Everywhere

All Around the Zodiac is different from most books available in astrology, in that it deals strictly with the twelve signs—Aries through Pisces—and *not* from the usual Sun-sign perspective. (Although our Sun sign is a major influence describing traits central to our being, it doesn't tell the whole story of our life.) Surprisingly, there aren't many books in print that emphasize the twelve signs, since much of what is written focuses more on astrology's planets, houses, aspects, predictive techniques, and how to put all these factors together to understand an individual's chart patterns.

Yet somehow, relatively speaking, the signs get less coverage. Maybe it's an adverse, unconscious reaction to all that Sun-sign commercialism with which the media saturates the public—including ads for zodiac T-shirts, keychains, and coffee mugs. (Astrologers want people's interest to go beyond just Sun signs.) Whatever the case, astrology books that delve more thoroughly into the dynamics of the twelve signs are a welcome addition.

This book explores the meaningful ways that astrological signs describe our inner makeup and how we perceive the people and experiences we attract in our outer world. Although I won't be covering "everything there is to know about astrology," or promise that this is "the only book you'll ever need to read" on this subject, my focus will be on the character-shaping influence of these twelve signs.

While the planets will always symbolize the key energies of human nature in anyone's astrological chart—being that they are the basic drives that motivate us to act out our internal needs—the signs through which our planets were moving at the time we were born provide additional psychological material that helps flesh out the nature of our planet-associated urges. These signs suggest how we most typically respond to life, according to the inherent traits of the planet in question—and even those based on the social conditioning suggested, in part, by the times in which we live.

For example, we all have Venus—our urge to attract love and comfort—in a particular sign in our chart. That sign gives us clues about how we might generally behave when expressing our Venusian energies. Maybe our Venus is in Virgo or maybe it's in Aquarius. Virgo looks at love and life differently than does Aquarius, and so it is important to know what the basic life orientation of Virgo or Aquarius might mean to a sociable, sensual planet like Venus. Signs can be looked at, in part, as culturally induced modes of behavior that we adopt in order to further express our planetary impulses and instincts.

It's not uncommon for a beginning student of astrology to confuse a sign's general behavioral traits solely with the interpretation of his or her Sun sign. For example, the wide-ranging characteristics of Pisces are mistakenly viewed as the exclusive traits of all Sun-in-Pisces individuals. This can lead to mixed feelings, in some cases, when those traits are less than flattering. The (Piscean) student is apt to take things too personally, and typically out of context by not realizing, at first, that the addition of any planet—in this case, the Sun—immediately modifies the basic nature of the sign. That planet must have its needs met through the natural processes of the sign in question. Yet sometimes a planet and a sign don't harmonize well, due to their contrasting temperaments.

In truth, the psychology of each sign is much more full-bodied and complex than the usual Sun-sign evaluations presented in the media. Thus, when I discuss Pisces in this book, I'm referring primarily to the more abstract essence of this sign and not to those folks born from late February through the first three weeks of March. The same goes for all the remaining eleven signs. Admittedly, what I say will still sound very much like what most people are used to reading ("Gemini is this, Capricorn is that . . ."). So just realize that I'm not describing actual Sun-sign profiles.

You'll find that astrology's zodiac signs are brimming with color, plus they're enriched with psychological depth. Aries means a whole lot more that just "boldness" and "a headstrong disposition." Scorpio means more than just being "vengeful" and "suspicious," or even "sexy." Signs are as profound in their meaning as our self-awareness allows, yet they're also as superficial as our own ignorance permits.

Unfortunately, some people only express the more shallow traits of the signs emphasized in their charts. Astrology can teach us all to dig deeper to find what inner treasures of each sign lie hidden below the surface of our conscious reality.

Not a Star in Sight

Most uninformed individuals—including a majority of astronomers—assume that all astrologers use the zodiac that is composed strictly of fixed-star patterns, in the form of twelve *constellations* that have enchanted people since ancient times, beginning with Aries the Ram and ending with Pisces the Fishes. These groups of stars comprise the visible, celestial, "sidereal" zodiac that has captured the imagination of the public, as it has since long ago when astrology was in its earliest stages of development. That these stars patterns are so far away from us only adds to the magic and allure of this observable zodiac—it even implies a mysterious, cosmic dimension.

Yet, it is the grouping of astrology's twelve *signs*, rather than these constellations, that creates what is called the "tropical" zodiac. These signs share the same names as their stellar counterparts, and this alone presents some initial confusion. The tropical zodiac renews its annual cycle (beginning at 0° Aries) exactly at the vernal equinox, which is a clearly defined point marking when the apparent path of the Sun—called the *ecliptic*—intersects the celestial equator. This "movable" zodiac was used by Greek astrologers over 2,000 years ago. From the vernal equinox, the signs are evenly divided into twelve sectors of space, forming an invisible circle that is referred to (in terms of birth charts) as the Zodiac Wheel.

In a sense, the signs are twelve variations of solar light and radiation created by the astronomical relationship of the Sun and Earth during the year; these variations affect the energy patterns of all that exists on the planet. Seasons don't just measure the predictable passage of time—they are also vital to the growth of all living things. Ancient civilizations certainly depended on their knowledge of the seasons—and the heavens—to help them know just when to plant seed and when to harvest their crops. Astrology was therefore originally born of an essential, practical, predictive need. Astrology goes a step further by suggesting that the seasonal changes of the natural world parallel the seasonal cycles of our internal human experience. (Another timeless symbol of our life's outer and inner ebb and flow has been the Moon and its monthly phases.)

High-profile astronomers—who are typically anti-astrology—seem glaringly ignorant of the fact that the signs we use are *not* the same as the zodiacal constellations. I suspect that some of these debunkers actually want the public to believe that astrologers (derided for being gullible, superstitious, and misguided) are completely unaware of the precession of the equinoxes—the phenomenon where the constellations appear to move backwards gradually in time in relation to the vernal equinox point, due to the tilt or wobble of our planet's orbit. Thus, where the stars of Aries were located two millennia ago, on that first day of spring, is now where constellational Pisces is today, and where the star patterns of Aquarius will soon be seen in the near future. It's been quite a while since the *sign* Aries matched up with the *constellation* Aries at the vernal equinox—supposedly around the year A.D. 221.[2]

From that time on, the gap between the two zodiac systems has grown ever-wider until that difference is now almost a full sign apart. The authoritative-sounding criticism leveled at astrologers, then, is that we are "all wrong" regarding the Sun signs we use, since we're sadly almost one sign off, and—amazingly—we don't even know it. Well, to borrow a pet term expressed by many such skeptics—"Rubbish!" The truth is, astrologers are not the ones who are mixing apples with oranges in these matters and creating confusion.[3]

Distant star formations are not used at all in tropical astrology when determining planetary positions, nor would constellations be able to divide the ecliptic pie into equal slices (since such star patterns come in various sizes). Yet zodiac *signs* do neatly divide the ecliptic into twelve segments, each consisting of 30° of space—and thirty times twelve equals a circle of 360°. As the tropical zodiac symbolizes the Sun-Earth's yearly cycle, it further subdivides into the four distinct seasons, each of which are astrologically made up of three signs. The signs of spring in the Northern Hemisphere, where astrology was first developed, are Aries, Taurus, and Gemini; the signs of summer are Cancer, Leo, and Virgo; the signs of fall are Libra, Scorpio, and Sagittarius; and the signs of winter are Capricorn, Aquarius, and Pisces.

Motley Crew

The term "zodiac" stems from the Greek word *zodiakos*, which translates as "circle of animals." Actually, the zodiac begins with a strong-willed animal (Aries), followed by another hefty critter (Taurus), human twins (Gemini), a crabby crustacean (Cancer), a proud feline (Leo), a demure maiden holding a sheath of wheat (Virgo), an inanimate object used to weigh things: the scales (Libra), another moody critter known for its venomous sting (Scorpio), a mythical centaur (Sagittarius), an old goat that's part fish (Capricorn), a man holding a jug, out of which pours something that resembles water, yet is not (Aquarius), and finally, two fish side by side that are bound by a slender cord (Pisces). Sorry, there's no partridge in a pear tree—but still, what a motley crew we have here.

Perhaps the fact that the majority of signs depict animals of some sort tells us that the zodiac is, in part, a symbolic model of our more instinctual traits, those urges and impulses inherited from our evolution as mammals. Of course, our proud ego has us intellectually reject the notion that we're basically animals who were merely lucky to end up with larger and more powerful brains than most creatures on Earth. No, we're more than that, we claim—we're intelligent, self-aware beings who perhaps are made in the very image of God, not beast. However, the zodiac says these "animal" qualities are nonetheless essential parts of what make us human. They have a special intelligence all their own, and we couldn't survive for long without them. They help firmly anchor us to our finite, earthbound experience.

Our more distinctively human parts, aspiring to rise above the purely instinctual realm of Nature, are symbolized by three signs bearing totally human symbols (Gemini, Virgo, Aquarius), and by another that is at least half-human (Sagittarius). Two of these signs (Gemini and Virgo) excel at logic, reasoning power, and basic linear thinking. The other two signs (Sagittarius and Aquarius) deal with more far-sighted, intuitive qualities that help us process information quickly and even tap into a sense of future vision. Here, we are urged to go beyond our limits so that we may embrace the greater possibilities of mind expansion and even spiritual enlightenment. Thus, the zodiac also includes these human symbols as a major part of our ongoing potential.

Oddly enough, there is one nonliving symbol among the group. Not an animal and not human, the scales of Libra depict a more abstract life principle that goes beyond our earthly, biological experience. They hint at the impersonal laws of the Cosmos, ever at work, trying to keeps things balanced and in tune with creative harmonies that permit life to continually improve, even if all this seems to take forever. Libra's scales are a reminder that there exists a detached but vigilant and active principle in life that is always on the side of pure Truth, especially should such truth go against our more selfish desires to have our way at the expense of others (or even of Nature and its many creatures). Cosmic law—call it karma or divine retribution—overrides our will and ego, those parts of our psyche that wrongly assume that they're always calling the shots.

Final Words

This is not necessarily a book that you need to read sequentially—chapter by chapter, from start to finish—in order to figure out what's going on (although I would). It's okay to skip around and read whatever appeals to you. Heck, this is what Gemini and Sagittarius types do all the time, and look how smart they turn out to be—they seem to know at least a little bit about everything. Maybe you'll want to read some of this material, and then put the book down for a while, only to eventually pick it up to read other sections later. That's fine. After all, there is a lot to take in here, especially if you are new to the language of astrology.

Also, reading other astrology books will supplement your understanding and perhaps help you look at the signs in even different ways than I've described. Let me recommend the works of Steven Forrest, Kim Rogers-Gallagher, and Caroline Casey, for starters. These are three individualistic authors whose styles of writing won't put you to sleep.[4]

All seasoned astrologers agree that we cannot pull just one factor out of our chart—like an emphasized sign—blow its function out of proportion, and then claim that it will accurately reveal all about who we are, very much in the manner that Sun-sign astrology has tried to do for the last sixty or so years. For example, we may have several natal planets in Cancer. Yet if these planets are the Moon, Mercury, and Mars, and if they are all forming tensional patterns to Uranus in Aries in our First House, we may not seem very Cancerian in traditional ways: domestic and homebound? Hardly. Maternal and protective? Hmmm . . . those urges haven't hit us yet. Security-conscious and defensive? Perhaps most so when our freedom is being threatened by those who insist we stick to safe and predictable ways of living.

Many things can radically change the typical meaning of any feature of our chart, such as having cautious signs on the cusps of adventurous houses, or conservative signs pitted against those that dare to really live. It's best not to become rigid or overly structured in your thinking when you read this book, since many factors modify how signs are expressed. Also, effective astrological interpretation isn't about always being "right." It is more about finding helpful, insightful ways to address those psychological conflicts, ambiguities, unconscious needs, or even hidden strengths and talents of which we need to become more aware.

Well, it's time to start taking these twelve signs apart for a closer inspection of their innards, both to find out what makes them tick and to size up what we can do to get the most mileage out of their effective use. After all, we all have each one of these signs active in some area of our birth chart, to a greater or lesser extent. This fact alone is one good reason not to develop a strong, irrational bias against any particular sign (in other words, stop relating it to all the horrible people you've met who have been born under that sign). We will someday have to confront within us any sign we seemingly despise, probably to dispel the notion that it represents something we must forever reject. One more thing—I aim to have a little fun while exploring these signs, so please don't take any of my comments too personally. After all, the zodiac doesn't.

Notes

1. Log on to *http://www.kepler.edu* to find out more about Kepler College.

2. The estimated year that the constellations and the signs exactly lined up— A.D. 221—is given in Robert Powell's excellent booklet *The Zodiac: A Historical Survey*, available through ACS Publications (log on to *www.astrocom. com* for more information).

3. To learn more about how skeptics try to malign astrology unfairly, and the intelligent ways one can counter such attacks, I suggest you read the very different and enjoyable *In Defense of Astrology: Astrology's Answers to Its Critics*, written by Robert Parry, and published by Llewellyn in 1991. Parry nicely explains the two zodiacs, and why there's all this confusion about them, and also addresses other issues that those who doubt astrology's validity love to bring up time and time again—usually on television talk shows where such folks have a captive, but ignorant, audience of people who don't know enough to form their own independent opinions. For more on this book, log on to *www.llewellyn.com* or *www.amazon.com* (or check other online booksellers).

4. There are many good books out there on astrology, and if you study this subject long enough, you'll probably end up having most of these books on your shelf. I'd recommend Steven Forrest's *The Inner Sky* (ACS Publications, San Diego), Kim Rogers-Gallagher's *Astrology for the Light Side of the Brain* (also ACS Publications, San Diego), and Caroline Casey's *Making the Gods Work for You* (Harmony Books, New York). All these books describe the twelve signs and other features of astrology in refreshing ways.

PART ONE

Cosmic Sign Language

Chapter One

Signs & Elements

WHY SIGNS ACT THE WAY THEY DO

Before analyzing each of the twelve signs, it's good to first explore two prime features that contribute much to understanding each sign's characteristics: its **element** (fire, earth, air, or water) and its **mode** (cardinal, fixed, or mutable). The blend of these two factors helps explain why a sign behaves the way it does, why it's motivated to respond to life in a manner unlike any other sign, and how it goes about getting its needs met. Note that no two signs share the exact same element-mode mix:

Sign	Image	Symbol	Element	Mode
Aries	The Ram	♈	Fire	Cardinal
Taurus	The Bull	♉	Earth	Fixed
Gemini	The Twins	♊	Air	Mutable
Cancer	The Crab	♋	Water	Cardinal
Leo	The Lion	♌	Fire	Fixed
Virgo	The Virgin	♍	Earth	Mutable
Libra	The Scales	♎	Air	Cardinal
Scorpio	The Scorpion	♏	Water	Fixed
Sagittarius	The Archer	♐	Fire	Mutable
Capricorn	The Goat	♑	Earth	Cardinal
Aquarius	The Water Bearer	♒	Air	Fixed
Pisces	The Fishes	♓	Water	Mutable

Repetitive patterns can be found in these two primary sign classifications. In the element column, note that the zodiac begins with a sign of the fire element, followed by earth, and then air, until the cycle ends with a sign whose element is water. This element pattern then repeats two more times. In the mode column, cardinal energy begins the cycle, followed by fixed energy, and ending with mutable energy—a pattern that then repeats three more times. Let's explore what all these groupings mean regarding the psychology of the signs, starting with a look at the four elements.

THE ELEMENTS
Fire, Earth, Air, and Water

Before analyzing the basic features of all twelve signs, knowing each sign's element will tell us much about how that particular sign interprets its surroundings—what is its natural orientation toward life in general? What is the lens it uses to assess reality? Each element represents a basic quality of consciousness that contributes to our personal awareness—it acts like a psychological sense organ. It describes how we are apt to perceive both our inner world and outer environment. Elements are the four filters we use to interpret what's happening to us. They describe how we naturally perceive the people and things around us, as well as how we understand our internal drives and urges. Ideally, we need to partake of the insights afforded by each astrological element, even if only certain ones actually dominate our basic, day-to-day temperament.

The four elements of astrology all have equal value and are interdependent, although in a manner not always obvious at first. They also unfold in a meaningful sequence. There is an intelligent reason why—from Aries to Pisces, all around the zodiac—fire always starts each cycle and water always completes it.

The twelve signs are thus divided into these four categories. Each element is associated with three zodiac signs. The **fire signs** are **Aries, Leo,** and **Sagittarius**. This immediately tells us that these three share something in common that the remaining nine signs do not. The **earth signs** are **Taurus, Virgo,** and **Capricorn**. The **air signs** are **Gemini, Libra,** and **Aquarius**, and the **water signs** are **Cancer, Scorpio,** and **Pisces**. It is vital that students of astrology learn these four main groupings as soon as possible, which is why I am presenting them so early on in this book.

Although we could attempt to memorize a handful of traits ("keywords") belonging to, say, Aries or Scorpio, it is more helpful to first know a sign by its elemental properties. Many standard traits possessed by each sign are very much the result of its elemental makeup, especially at its core level. They reflect a sign's innate qualities, although such features can be molded, even distorted, by the constant pressures of social programming. It's impossible to find any of us doing a pure expression of any element, untainted by unconscious collective attitudes and assumptions that we've likely adopted.

Let's explore these elements in detail, starting first with fire.

The Fire Element
Flame Ride

Although all elements represent qualities that are equally valuable to our inner growth, the element of fire symbolizes a particularly dominant cultural force throughout the world. Fire is associated with "doing" rather than with "thinking" or "reflecting." It's an action-oriented element that freely moves out into life to dynamically seize the moment—think of flames energetically shooting upward and outward. Fire's "burning" urge is to experience life adventurously and with full gusto. Although not particularly organized, logical, or even considerate of others, fire motivates us to take quick, decisive action in the here and now—to strike boldly while the iron is hot and our passions are running high.

Until relatively recently, the archetypal world of fire has been the exclusive domain of traditional male behavior, reinforced by centuries of unquestioned and unbroken social conditioning. Society permits men to "do" their fire without much penalty—"boys will be boys"—that is, at least until males overdo their fiery expression and become destructively "macho."

Fire is a fighting element, ready to attack whatever tries to thwart its energy or get in its way. Applied on a mass level, this becomes warfare—a collective drama where men, historically, have released fire's potential fury by engaging in large-scale violence. Many men of today also vent their fire by being active in sports, by sexual conquest, by hunting, or by plunging into exciting forms of physical risk—daredevils are born of the fire element. Abhorring timid, wishy-washy behavior, fire is no coward when it comes to finding ways to satisfy its urges.

Women today are also learning firsthand—and perhaps cautiously—that it is psychologically and physically beneficial to own and openly express what fire represents: our *human* ability to move bravely out into the world according to the spontaneous impulses of our desire and self-will. More and more females are joining the ranks in such fields as boxing, football, soccer, weightlifting, and so on—formerly all male-dominated activities. More women are also running big businesses in the corporate world, and are taking on high political office—all due to their readiness and willingness to embrace the strengths of fire, and thus break gender-based stereotypes.

Newborn babies come into this world already displaying their raw, untempered fire drives—they'll cry a decidedly impatient and angry cry as their immediate way of asserting their being, as if claiming, "I am alive and I am here. Deal with my needs now!" Here is a purer, uncultured fire at work, accenting its customary focus on fulfilling "me" concerns. Although not exclusively associated with fire symbolism—despite the fact that astrologers relate it primarily to the Sun—the ego knows how to burn this element's volatile fuel when needing to draw attention to itself. Fire pumps up the ego's sense of commanding power. Thus, expect fire to be very self-focused and concerned with fulfilling its own desires, first and foremost. The signs Aries and Leo have very much been accused of this, but less so Sagittarius (and we'll analyze why later).

Strongly fire-oriented people can spend an entire lifetime acting as if their personal needs require urgent attention—they are not to be postponed or denied. Instant gratification is what fire wants and expects. However, in the process of exuberantly expressing who they are, fire types can deplete the energy of others. They can indulge in too much of a good thing, and in an uncontained manner. We tend to assume that fire people give of themselves in abundance—they warmly and generously radiate their light and heat—but they also need fresh energy sources to refuel themselves. It's exhausting to be around people who colorfully flare out all the time, who happily expend themselves, but then consume some of your vitality just to keep their own blaze going. Fire is thus a very demanding, even draining, force to be around for long periods of time. It can wear out other less-energetic elements—most so earth and water, who prefer cooler temperatures, anyway.

Still, it's no wonder that this headstrong, self-assured element has long been associated with natural leadership ability and royal command (especially Leo's proud and dignified, if not bossy, display of fire). Fearlessly moving ahead into the challenging world, to take chances left and right, while leaning on no one for supervision and support, fire will stand tall on its own. Yet again, once it has used up a temporary source of energy, leaving only ashes, fire needs a fresh supply to keep going. Fire can be a very hungry element, due to its huge appetite for living. "Give me more of what keeps me vibrant and active," roars fire.

So far, we get a sense that this element can come on strong and will fight to survive. It is willing to do battle to ensure that it will continue to thrive. Our capacity to thrust ourselves bravely out into life, and thereby develop a momentum for vigorous expression, belongs mainly to the fire element. Aries is a dynamic example of this. It's also a *cardinal* sign—as we shall later explore—and thus has an advantage when it comes to initiating energized action in the world. Because it's such a natural self-starter, fiery Aries proves a smart choice as *the* sign to begin the zodiac (our cosmic "Twelve Step" program for living a better, fuller life).

Although fire can foster selfishness, it's this element's somewhat innocent self-absorption that allows it to retain its streak of independence, which then reinforces its instinct to follow a self-chosen path. Pioneers and trailblazers thus honor the fire principle within them when they show guts by going off in new and even controversial directions. They don't need permission to go where they wish to in life, nor is gaining the approval of others what determines whether fire types single-handedly embark on a chosen course of action. (Sure, they'd enjoy having such support, but ultimately they don't need it to initiate a major undertaking of personal interest.) "I'm here to please myself, first and foremost," fire honestly admits.

There is a bit of a "loner" streak in fire. This is not an element that easily attaches itself to others for long periods of time. Fire doesn't comfortably settle into structured relationships, and even the security of enduring intimacy is not what it wants—especially if that means its freedom to spontaneously move about will be curtailed. (Trap fire in a tiny metal box, and eventually it's life-spark will extinguish.) Thus, in matters of close involvement, expect fire to have problems with total commitment (although loyal Leo has more staying power in this area, as long as few restrictions are imposed; this is because Leo is also a *fixed* sign, a factor that will be explained later). Settled relationships also hint at a shared life of expected behavior and routine habits, something that fire fears will prove too tedious to bear. Where's all the excitement and pizzazz of living? That's what fire craves.

Since fire isn't all that deeply absorbed in others—it's not one to merge or share—it won't allow itself to get sucked into the complicated worlds of people in need (that's more water's dilemma). Fire doesn't even feel it has to blend with the other elements in order to enhance itself (which is not true). It's too self-centered to even realize the value of exploring other ways of perceiving the world—it's much too sold on its own way of sizing up reality. Still, our growth process involves a skillful and conscious integration of many astrological factors that initially appear to have little in common, or that typically clash when combined (the old "incompatibility" issue).

Some of us may be born with a heavy fire emphasis: besides Aries, Leo, and Sagittarius, there are also "fire" planets to contend with—the Sun, Mars, and Jupiter. Since there are other signs and planets in our chart associated with the three remaining elements, we need to better combine our fire energies with these other components. This will help us develop a more well-rounded awareness of ourselves and of the world in which we live. We can't afford to take an exclusively fired-up approach to living, plus others would soon take issue with such a headstrong manner of behaving—we'd be accused of being arrogant, pushy, conceited, bossy, opinionated, or even too self-righteous.

So, when it comes to courageously living the life we were meant to live—unfazed by the attempts of others to censor us or "rain on our parade"—fire is the element that points us in the right direction. It believes in authentic self-expression and relishes displaying an upfront, spirited sense of self—and to heck with what the neighbors think! Fire has a hard time bowing down to the dictates of others. It won't blindly follow set rules of conduct, especially when they prove to be stifling. We need fire in our veins to give us the gumption required to take on the world in a lusty, passionate manner. Dramatic fire makes sure that our life won't be dull and anemic. It's good to note where our fire signs are located in our chart, for here is where we will be supported by a more robust and honest approach to people and situations.

Now let's move on to the next element: earth.

THE EARTH ELEMENT
Terra Firma

The fire element appropriately begins the zodiac with energetic Aries because this element symbolizes the vital thrust behind the "will to be" that gives rise to all action. Life means movement, and fire stirs our basic need for motion. Think of fire as representing the essential, vital spark within every seed just waiting to explode into a rush of activity that initiates a plant's growth cycle (amazingly, seeds found in the tombs of ancient Egyptian mummies have been known to come alive and sprout—their inner life force, although dormant, survives for centuries of time without weakening). Thus, all sorts of beginnings and births in life are associated with fire. Freshness and newness belong to this element. Yet at some pivotal point, fire's expansive energy will need structure and organization to be useful. Such necessary containment comes from earth, an element that logically follows fire throughout the zodiac.

We live in a material realm that imposes all sorts of constraints, yet activity on Earth requires a slower pace so that we can better deal with most issues of physical reality. The heaviness of gravity abounds, and time is ever-present, but together they help us feel securely anchored to the solid, comforting world of form. Fire is more at home with a rapid, even agitated, alteration of conditions—it's a highly kinetic force—but to undergo too much of that could prove hectic and disorienting (not to mention physically debilitating). We instead need a more leisurely pace in order to function reliably, and thus earth makes sure that fire's dynamic energy is grounded and better conserved. Humankind long ago learned the value of preserving actual fire, rather than wasting it by letting it burn itself out. Astrological earth is urging us to do the same, especially on the psychological level.

Earth is admittedly less showy and vibrant than fire. It appears passive and inactive (a clump of dirt or a log of wood seems inert and dull compared to the high drama of a raging inferno). Nevertheless, earth provides a necessary stillness and an economy of movement that helps fire's energy endure longer and thereby extend its potential.

Earth doesn't like to use things up too quickly or to run out of needed supplies prematurely. Less refueling is required by this stable element because it conserves fire's life force in smart, effective ways. Actually, earth is not so much "smart" in its operations as it is blessed with common sense—an instinctual "know-how" that is not based on mere intellectual knowledge.

As a result, earth is very savvy when it comes to understanding the material world and figuring out what can and cannot be accomplished with available resources. Earth signs all share a respectful awareness of life's inherent limitations. Fire may balk at accepting that life issues restraining orders now and then, but earth makes peace with this obvious fact and learns to function well within such conditions. (By the way, all elements have their own take on "reality," but earth's version of what actually exists—something highly dependent on what our physical senses register—seems less open to debate or subjective interpretation; at least that's how earth sees it.) Earthy reality is tied to the tried-and-true rhythms of the physical world, with its predictable, natural cycles. Earth depends on repetitive, reliable phenomena. It's obvious that this element plays a key role in the scientific disciplines, where an earthy capacity for clear-headedness, painstaking testing, and sober observation are a must.

As humans, we are so unavoidably earthbound and attached to our physical impressions of life that it's no wonder this element is so darn sure about what it regards as real. After all, the tangible proof that earth needs to function is clearly found all around us—matter undeniably exists. Earth signs steadily focus on this most evident level of experience, yet they run the risk of assuming that this tangible realm of ours is what counts the most and what truly makes up our prime reality—the only one on which we should fully depend. All else has less worth in the long run. Well, we can quickly see how this attitude may lead to narrow, materialistic assumptions concerning life's potential. Things in the outer world potentially hold more attraction to earthy types than do internal, psycho-spiritual realms of being. Earth is skeptical of anything as abstract as a soul or a psyche.

If close-mindedness and inflexibility can be avoided, then earth becomes a wonderful element blessed with the power to manifest the deeper potential of the other elements. Earth helps less tangible energies incarnate and enclose themselves in matter suitable for their purposes—earth gives spirit needed shape. We all have the signs Taurus, Virgo, and Capricorn located somewhere in our chart, indicating areas where we can express our needs and demonstrate our abilities in worldly, concrete terms. Earth has a talent for building something solid and supportive for us, and it believes in working long and hard to achieve what it wants. Patience is its virtue, and time is its friend.

And yet, because it is astrology's less glamorous element—one not given to colorful display, emotional depth, or imaginative thinking—earth is typically treated with less fanfare. It evokes a "ho-hum" response. (No one ever says, except sarcastically, "Wow, it must be *so* exciting to be born with *all* that earth in your chart!") Earth is more like a little brown sparrow, in contrast to fire's gloriously strutting peacock. Earth is as plain and functional as a "sensible" pair of shoes, compared to diamond-studded high heels. It's as comfy and familiar as an old sweater. Being highly praised as someone who's trustworthy, dependable, and humble—all earthy traits—seems less a compliment than being touted as dashing, witty, and effervescent.

Nonetheless, earth quietly makes sure that much of our ordinary world runs in a timely, organized fashion—it tries to keep things operating smoothly, day by day, and this typically involves setting up systems of efficiency. Should this conscientious element decide to pack it up and archetype itself elsewhere in the Universe, chaos on our planet would soon spread like wildfire, and we'd all be horrified at how messy life would quickly become, as everything broke down or became misplaced (nothing would stay put). Earth signs thus do what they can to keep such chaos at bay, mainly by devising and enforcing necessary rules and regulations that ensure order. Earth is the custodial element of life, dutifully straightening up the world whenever it gets out of control, while also carefully attending to all-important details, no matter how small, that help prevent future trouble from brewing.

But just so we don't pigeonhole earth as all work and no play, realize that the realm of bodily sensation also belongs to this element. Earth (especially Taurus) enjoys the creature comforts of being human. It believes that there's nothing wrong with feeling contentment in very physical ways. The body is not such a bad thing to own and satisfy. Earth wants us to proclaim, "Yeah, I'm part animal and proud of it!" Varying degrees of sensuality play a role in the life experiences fostered by this element. We shouldn't automatically think that means sex, since our earthy needs can also be met by taking a long, hot bath or even by having a professional massage—and let's not forget the satisfaction of eating a wonderfully cooked meal while in comfortable, visually pleasing surroundings.

Earth also realizes that physical well-being is very important in life, and thus this element will urge us to listen to our body's signals and know when to quit doing whatever could turn out to be abusive to our health. It's as simple as this: When tired, earth rests. When hungry, earth eats. When stressed out, earth . . . shops! (I'm only half-joking). Fire, in contrast, will keep going until it runs out of gas. It often can't even tell that it's exhausted until it collapses (and even then it expects to rally quickly). Wise earth respects its physical limits. In real life, however, people with a Virgo or Capricorn emphasis in their charts need to monitor their workaholic tendencies, since overwork and other taxing mundane pressures can drain a body's resources. I still contend that it's the fiery factors of our chart that make us never want to stay still and relax—fire always looks for more excitement, more action, more hustle and bustle.

Earth is an element that carefully plans its activities, but it needs sufficient time to do so. Nothing is to be rushed, since haste makes waste (earth is less forgiving of its "dumb" mistakes than fire and air are of theirs). Poorly organized folks depend on earthy types to get things finished, and done correctly. As a result, earth can take on more responsibilities than it should. It can carry heavy weight on its shoulders by over-obligating itself, which becomes burdensome. Remember, earth likes to have things running efficiently and will therefore see all projects to their completion, no matter how demanding (it may complain a lot, but it gets the job done). Nothing is to be left in the air, dangling. All bothersome loose ends are to be wrapped up. Earth can therefore run a tight ship, especially when a deadline is fast approaching. It's no wonder that all the other elements tend to leave poor, dependable earth holding the bag—earth is a sucker for doing "the dirty work" that no other element wants to touch. Yet earth is quietly confident that it can handle the task and successfully end up with solid results.

A common problem with earth is its tendency to hold back emotions, to restrain feelings that sometimes need proper venting. This kind of self-control makes earth look composed and mild-mannered on the surface. This also gives this element the appearance of awesome strength and composure—no wonder the weak and the easily frazzled are drawn to "Rock of Gibraltar" earthy types. Still, more animated elements (fire and air) often want to give earth a good shake, and tell it to loosen up. They feel earth needs to show what it's really going through on the inside for a change, and to start reacting to life more dramatically.

Well, sorry, but earth doesn't get fired up quickly about anything. It would rather evaluate people and situations with a degree of level-headed calmness and from a safe position if possible ("You never know who or what's going to explode in your face," warns earth). Still, earth needs to work at learning not to repress its emotionality or even its anger, in favor of playing it safe throughout life by not making waves.

Now let's change the scenery and explore the world of the next element: air.

THE AIR ELEMENT
Cool Breeze

First, brazen fire urges us to go out there and *do* it, whatever it is. Don't think about it, don't analyze the pros and cons, just act! Get your motor running, jump on the opportunity, take the big plunge, and hit the ground running—*now*, not tomorrow!—and don't fret too much about the possible consequences of any bold actions taken. Next, it's security-conscious earth, wanting us to slow down the tempo, get settled, and start to consolidate what we've enterprisingly initiated for ourselves. Sustaining our earthy focus helps us fortify our efforts better, thus enabling our accomplishments to last longer (in contrast, fire's outcomes can have a "flash in the pan" quality— sparkling and energizing, but here today, gone tomorrow). Earth is looking for permanent results, even if this takes time and demands much stick-to-it-tiveness. The earth signs advise us to ground our actions more fully in the practical world by laying down solid foundations, and by attending to all pertinent details. We can then keep our steady system of operations running as reliably as a Swiss watch.

"Whoa," gasps air, "let's call a time-out to think about all this talk about full-time commitment." Sure enough, this next element seeks a bit of breathing space. Air doesn't want to become too immersed in earth's big building projects. Creating a little healthy distance helps air get an objective handle on things—some needed perspective—so that it can think more clearly about what has materialized thus far. Air is afraid that earth will want to stop fire's momentum for good and instead remain stuck in dull, even stagnating, routines. It's air's nature to circulate and to distribute its energy broadly—air is not comfortable with becoming too settled in matter. It's not interested in tightly compressing energy into something that ends up densely packaged and immovable, so air intuitively backs off from any condition that appears time-consuming or too slow to take shape.

Instead, the realm more natural to air is that above the ground. It's obvious that the higher up we go, reaching even cloud level, the more widely we can observe the terrain below. Details may seem less sharp, but the greater our altitude, the grander the overview we can achieve. We can also feel an expansive sense of freedom. Thus, expect this element to be interested in comprehending life's bigger picture.

Air also likes to mix life's ingredients and then step back to witness the unpredictable results. This element enjoys observing how two or more things link up. It looks for apparent similarities between such factors as they combine, while noting obvious contrasts to be found as well. "If I join this with that, what will happen and why?" wonders air. This sounds like the dawning of scientific inquiry, or perhaps just human mischief in the making. Our capacity to undergo experimental, trial-and-error stages in life that hopefully enlighten us is something related to air, an element that's always eager to teach us something new.

Highly conscious and wide-awake, air is related to our ability to think and reason. It's the brainiest of all the elements, the one that loves to live life in its head and to create brilliant ideas to share with the world. Where would we be if we couldn't connect our words and thoughts in intelligent ways? We'd sound *un*intelligible, and that could lead to social isolation, something that all air signs dread.

Not a big fan of gibberish, air demands that language be clear and precise if real communication is truly our objective (air can set the standards here, I guess, because it even invented language). Yet that doesn't mean air can't have fun playing with words. It comes up with new, catchy phrases now and then; plus, lots of (hot) air produces chatterboxes at times. As air rules the wind, it's the element of windbags, talking up a storm.

Air is the one element of the cycle that keenly focuses on cause and effect: Bang head against wall, get dizzy, pass out. One condition not only influences another, but apparently can be the very cause or the catalyst of that other condition. That's basically what air notices, as it busily takes mental notes on how life appears to work—at least on the surface. Of course, it's on life's more observable surface where many superficialities are to be found, being the home turf of much that is shallow and trivial. Yet air gladly takes it all in, appreciating such things as momentary stimulations or fleeting distractions, if nothing else.

Fire can be passionately singular in its short-lived interests, while earth can be downright fixated on its long-range goals. But all air signs need a lot of variety and change; they wither from too much monotony or a life that lacks detours (or even a room without windows). Air doesn't enjoy feeling as driven as headstrong fire, nor is it as task-oriented as earth. Actually, air can adapt to these and other states of consciousness, as long as they are experienced in small doses for short periods of time. The bottom line, however, is that air is elusive and cannot be pinned down for long. It's not an easy element to grab onto and tightly control.

Highly curious air believes that life is a buffet table: Sample an assortment of whatever items look tasty, but don't pig out on any one thing and fill up too fast. Life is too short *not* to spread one's attention everywhere, and thereby mentally benefit from the open-mindedness such diversity encourages. Air types can be very cerebral in temperament. They sound smart and seem to know a lot; they even make up the bulk of life's "eternal students," forever feeding their minds knowledge. Along with such brainpower comes a cool detachment that can be invaluable when confronting life's more unsettling twists and turns. When others become hysterical during disruptive times of great chaos, those with air emphasized in their charts are apt to keep their wits about them and not abandon logic or clarity. However, this airy, cool-and-collected disposition doesn't work as well with life situations that require emotional depth and intimacy.

While it can appear to understand someone else's life predicament sympathetically, air does not empathize very easily (that's more a strength of the next element, water). There is a bit of aloofness to be found hidden beneath what otherwise seems to be an alert, inquisitive, likable nature that is eager to meet life straightforwardly. Air's cleverness at times can make it seem to be a bit of a trickster, playing loose with the facts, but by nature it's not a deliberately sneaky, deceitful element. Still, it has a hard time being real with itself and others in the realm of gut response. Air would sooner analyze feelings (preferably somebody else's) rather than simply "feel" its power at full potency. Even the previous two elements weren't equipped enough to prepare air for the powerful underground world of emotionality, since that's not their expertise, either.

Being emotionally disengaged with life is actually not a fault of air, since venting deep feelings isn't part of the job the Cosmos assigned this element to do—and we shouldn't blame one element for not behaving like another. Yet sometimes, due to air's strong ability to keenly mimic what it observes, this element can fake sentiments and emotions that seem convincing—at least for a while—but air does so more out of sheer curiosity as it attempts to figure out how others perceive reality. Air wants to understand where another element is coming from, perceptually. It's not afraid to confront experiences that it finds unfamiliar (in fact, it needs such stimulation). Air looks forward to learning more about life from fresh angles. It thus invites the environment to provide more and more information to excite the mind.

Air's capacity for intellectual breadth (especially in Aquarius) can result in innovative thinking, but it also has a talent for quickly scanning situations and spotting small movements and changes—a trait that can result in either sharp attentiveness or distractibility (the latter is most noted in Gemini). Air is also an excellent "people-watcher" element (here's where Libra excels). It's fascinated by human experience and even by the way people behave in diverse cultural settings. As the exchange of ideas is important to air (never an element to appear unsociable), finding ways to make human interactions smooth and hassle-free appeals to this element. More talking about issues and less fighting over them would be welcome, since air knows the value in "airing" those things out now that could otherwise cause trouble later. "So, can we talk about it first?" asks air.

The gift of analysis belongs to this element. Air helps us carefully consider life's multifaceted issues before finding suitable options to resolve them. Air comes up with bright solutions to life's nagging problems, but it realizes that seldom is there only one "right" way of looking at any situation. It also enjoys speculative approaches to life's puzzles, although this can border on abstract mind games that serve no useful purpose; they're just a lot of intellectual gymnastics, sounding impressive but impractical. While fire and earth can think in more simplistic, black-or-white, or even right-or-wrong terms—air allows us to recognize the shades of gray in between. It evaluates the many sides of any situation before coming up with a final and fair judgment. Obviously, the introduction of air to the element cycle suddenly makes life more complicated. Now there are no easy answers to fall back on, no cut-and-dried conclusions, no "one size fits all."

Perhaps when exploring the far reaches of the observable Universe and when gathering astronomical data needing to be systematically decoded by cool, level-headed minds, air becomes a fine tool for the unbiased evaluation of certain factual realities. Here's where accuracy counts, and where subjective impressions can often lead to erroneous assumptions. Yet when using such precision-tuned, laser-sharp mental equipment to probe the psychological innards of a human being, air fails to do the trick. Some other approach to perceiving our "inner" reality is needed, especially since the world of our unconscious self is not bound by logic or reason, nor does it follow linear time. We're not robots, programmed to respond in predictable ways to exact stimuli, again and again. An unanticipated human quality arises, the result of deeply internal impressions of life. That's something all three elements thus far have not had to deal with—mood swings coming from who knows where.

Now it's time to plumb the more mysterious depths of human nature as we delve into the hidden dimensions of astrology's final element: water.

THE WATER ELEMENT
Deep Well

If the element cycle simply began with fire and ended with air, humanity could survive and thrive, yet we'd tend to be somewhat mechanical in our responses to one another—almost like members of an active ant or bee colony: organized, industrious, teeming with energy, but rather flat and soulless in our interactions. Should a member of our human "hive" perish, we'd feel nothing but the urge to efficiently dispose of the corpse and continue on with our endless tasks at hand. No tears would be shed since we'd feel no sense of real loss regarding our dead coworker (perhaps the air in us would be curious about what caused this death and if it could have been prevented, but that's about it).

Since the element cycle *does* conclude with water, it adds one very critical facet to our human experience: the development of our feeling nature and our ability to sensitively tune in to others. Water also helps us reflect on the subtleties of our inner life. Welcome to the world of emotions—from the raw to the sublime. This most receptive of elements symbolizes powerful, invisible currents that at times stir internal turmoil for us, but that also move us to act with selfless compassion for others. That's because water enables us to feel deeply connected to all living things at a soul level, and this helps dissolve our usual sense of being separate entities. If water sounds a bit mystical, it is! This is the only element that has a true feeling for inner states of Oneness and Unity. Water allows us to become a part of all that is, as we merge our consciousness with our environment.

Merging seamlessly with our surroundings, however, does have its problems. On one hand, this fluid ability gives water a chameleonlike quality. Water excels in the art of camouflage—it loses its distinct form while blending in with its habitat—something that has proven invaluable to the survival of the fittest from an evolutionary perspective. Water is absorbed by what it contacts and thus it loses its sense of self somewhat. The boundaries become blurred. On the other hand, this characteristic of water is exactly what makes it so empathetic, so able to get under other people's skin and experience their internal realities. For example, fire may state, "I am me and nobody else!" Earth may claim, "This is mine and that is yours!" Air may realize, "I've got my own ideas, but what about you?" Each of these elements clearly retains an awareness of its own identity; a basic sense of self remains intact. Yet only water says, "I'm feeling exactly what you're going through, as if it's happening to me!" That's quite a radical shift of awareness.

In a sense, water invades its surrounding space without asking for permission to penetrate. Its instinct is to ignore all boundaries and instead to quietly seep into otherwise inaccessible places that are hidden from view. Yet feeling little need for protective barriers in relationships can prove problematic, especially when we become too absorbed by somebody who is filled with turbulent energy or is loaded with negativity. Water signs can get sucked in to this kind of dark scenario, but sometimes they become the troubled ones who pull others deeply into their vortex. A lack of boundaries can also imply poor self-preservation instincts. Water signs can be reluctant to fend off the dominating influences of others; they are not fighters by nature (except for Scorpio, who nonetheless can still feel conflicted when engaging in emotional battles). Water suffers from its passive tendency to take in other people's energies indiscriminately. It needs to learn to devise a better filtering system by borrowing a few natural defenses that the other elements use (such as fire's self-interest, earth's territorial streak, and air's emotional detachment).

One very important condition that water enables us to feel is love—not gushy romantic love, which is more a social invention, but love as a measure of caring and intimacy that reveals a deeper concern for the welfare of others. Water offers love as a uniting force to help dissolve all barriers that keep people at odds with or isolated from one another. With such love emerges many soul-refining traits, such as gentleness, kindliness, unselfishness, charity, and patience (especially the patience required to cope with the difficult temperaments of others). Water has the inner strength needed to endure external conflict, although such conflict can be very jarring initially to this highly impressionable element. Water may appear weak and vulnerable during times of stress, yet its deep, uncanny understanding of human nature suggests it has the power to withstand much turmoil before collapsing or falling apart. However, such psychological endurance can seem self-punishing at times and even irrational.

Imagination is the realm belonging to the water element. Water has a direct pipeline to our unconscious, from which a vast and colorful assortment of wondrous images can emerge whenever we are in a proper state of receptivity (i.e., when we're sleeping and dreaming). Such energies aren't always pleasant, since the underground caverns of our psyche also harbor images that are terrifying or filled with darker desires that we usually manage to keep from consciously surfacing. Our angels and demons within reside in our unconscious, and the water element therefore symbolizes a wide range of emotional states— from bliss to hysteria. Having access to our mysterious but alluring inner dimension is a must for strong water types. The rewards to be had in the external world are not enough to provide true contentment. In fact, an almost divine discontent can plague water signs when life pressures them to neglect this private reality of the soul. Emotional disturbances can crop up as well.

Historically, just as men have been programmed to channel their fire energies into being manly, women have been identified—almost exclusively in the minds of men—as possessing the qualities of water, in large part because of this element's association with maternal urges and mood swings. Women, as mothers, were viewed as tender caregivers by nature, rather than by social dictate. They also have long been saddled with the task of maintaining domestic harmony and order, suggesting (to the men in their lives) that they inherently have a stronger need to be sheltered (due to their assumed nesting instincts) and protected, as the so-called "weaker" sex. While fire-identified men were to go out to eagerly fight life's battles and even literally bring home the bacon, their women were expected to keep the home fires burning and to have food ready on the table for when these strong, brave warriors returned from their vigorous outdoor adventures. This fixed pattern of gender role-playing has gone on for thousands of years, and it has deprived both sexes of their greater human potential.

Thankfully, much of that is changing in today's transitional world regarding the sexes. The concept of men becoming "Mr. Moms" who work at home while doing housekeeping and raising kids—while their ambitious wives fearlessly climb the corporate ladder—is now a reality. Of course, it's still not something every man would consider doing (the routines of housekeeping alone are perceived as undesirably feminizing to many men). Yet modern men with a water emphasis in their charts feel a natural affinity for many realms traditionally deemed to comprise "a woman's world." They find that they are naturally domestic by temperament, and probably love the quiet joys of cooking and gardening. They also may believe that crying is a natural, healthy, human response and not just what "sissies" do when they can't cope with what life tosses their way.

Men who deny or reject their touchy-feely parts are also choking off a supply of vital, psychological fluid in ways that may later render them rigid and calcified as they age, with deadly health consequences to pay. Water keeps our soul moisturized and able to go with the flow instead of resisting the unfoldment of our real feelings with all our might. Water signs are adept at understanding people's needs, which gives them an advantage when it comes to perceiving another's hidden motivation. They are drawn to what is secretly going on below the surface of people's observable behavior. Thus, expect water to bless us with an instinctive urge to investigate the deeper mysteries of being human. Water's not afraid to go to the heart of such complexity, even though potential turbulence can be found as we descend into the underground of our unconscious.

As previously suggested, there's a logic behind the sequential order of the elements. Fire is followed by earth and earth by air, for good reason. Water not only rounds out our cycle of human experience, it also succeeds the air phase in order to ensure that our understanding of life doesn't neglect the emotional underpinnings of subjective, psychological reality. Having surface knowledge about ourselves and others is not enough to help us evolve. We must dig deeper in order to contact our soul. This is what water encourages, a journey within, where we get to uncover repressed or underdeveloped potentials whose released power can renew our total being. Water can be a soothingly restorative element, refreshing our spirit, especially if our approach to life has become too dry, sterile, or cynical.

It's time move on to chapter 2 to look at the three modes under which the signs operate. This adds yet another layer to our understanding of why each sign behaves in the manner it does.

Chapter Two

Signs & Modes

THE THREE MODES

Also called "qualities" in traditional astrology, the modes represent three ways in which astrologers categorize how energy flows. Each mode describes the characteristic manner in which such energy can be applied to all aspects of life. It depicts the style of action/reaction we adopt whenever we're dealing with people and situations we attract. Four signs of the zodiac are related to each mode, and astrologers often like to use the four seasons of the year as an analogous way to demonstrate the unfolding stages of these modes. This is appropriate, since the twelve signs are intimately connected to the seasonal cycle.[1]

It is important to note which of the three modes is dominant in our chart (especially if our Sun, Moon, and/or Ascendant are found in this mode). This will determine our most characteristic method of how we basically move out into life to achieve personal goals. Regarding our least emphasized mode (having little or no planetary emphasis), we often attract people whose charts are loaded with that quality; they show us the value of adapting to some of the ways in which that mode typically activates. This dynamic also applies to our birth chart's least emphasized element.

Let's look at each mode in detail to determine what kind of approach it takes and what can result from it.

THE CARDINAL MODE
Gotta Get Moving

The cardinal signs—**Aries, Cancer, Libra,** and **Capricorn**—all live life at a fast-paced tempo. Energetic involvement in the external world is highlighted. Cardinal energy supports taking direct action, with little hesitation or preplanning (although moody Cancer may mull things over at times when feeling emotionally insecure). Here the urge is to act swiftly, even assertively, whenever advantageous circumstances present themselves. Cardinal types won't stall or beat around the bush when something needs to be done *soon*, or when urgent, critical issues need to be squarely resolved.

This vigorous mode is psychologically built to respond to situational challenges involving quick decisions and sudden changes, those that underscore the benefits of being conscious in the "now" and of living in the moment. This is especially so for the sign Aries. In fact, fiery Aries and earthy Capricorn—the cardinal signs that seem most dynamically engaged in ambitious worldly activity—are ready to grab opportunities as they come. They both share the urge to mow down obstacles, and would hate to lose ground in life by not being ready to take decisive action. Thus, ready they are! These two signs are the more obvious go-getters of the cardinal group, the ones willing to face most issues head-on.

Cardinal energy can be confrontational, but cardinality doesn't necessarily demand a noisy clash of opposing forces—lively, open negotiation is an option. This mode is upfront and straightforward in its dealings, but it also expects fast results. However, frustrated cardinal types will stir up a little commotion, now and then, that results in a temporary crisis where something's got to give. Cardinal signs don't do well with prolonged deliberations, whereby dilemmas are drawn out. They seek a quicker release of tensions. They're also too impatient to cope with deadlocks or the foot-dragging tactics of others (even though airy Libra is good at stalling, usually when trying to buy a little time in order to come up with a better strategy for dealing with others).

Folks with a cardinal emphasis in their charts are very enterprising. They are self-starters who want to get something new going without being detoured by the interference of others. This is an "Outta my way, here I come!" mode that can show much initiative in getting personal plans off the ground. Of course, their natural sense of push can be interpreted more as pushiness. Cardinal types can appear a little too driven, and anxious to put things into motion. They do need to slow down before jumping into half-baked projects. Wired for action doesn't always mean being fully aware of the consequences that acting on impulse can sometimes bring about. Here again, it's Aries—the fiery aspect of cardinality—that has to watch out the most for not looking before leaping. However, even the remaining cardinal signs can get restless and antsy on those levels of awareness determined by their associated elements (watery Cancer can be emotionally impatient with people who won't openly commit themselves to a closely bonded relationship).

Even if cardinal signs are not all that productive and accomplished, they give the appearance of being in the thick of activity, of always being very busy and on the go. This is the mode known for hustling and bustling, where there are few quiet, still moments to enjoy before another phase of high activity begins. These signs seem vibrantly alive and driven to instigate situations in life rather than wait for things to happen naturally. They may at times jump the gun and act prematurely. Obviously, troublemakers who agitate others by being aggressive may have their share of cardinal signs, but so do the movers and shakers of the world who help society get a lot of vital social projects up and running.

Now it's time to blend the traits of the cardinal mode with the characteristics of each element to understand this group of signs better. In other words, cardinality comes in four flavors, which explains why its four signs may not seem alike on the surface. Here's a brief look at them:

Aries is a **cardinal fire** sign. There is a lot about cardinal energy that reinforces what fire symbolizes temperamentally. Indeed, all cardinal signs act like they've got their internal pilot lights on all the time and are always warmed up for action. Aries has the added advantage of fire's natural spontaneity and its courage to take chances in life. Immediate action taken is typically backed by much self-will.

Aries won't weigh all sides of a situation and thereby waste time or risk becoming indecisive in the process. This sign instead sizes things up quickly and then jumps into action, for better or worse. It does not scatter its energy, but single-mindedly aims its undivided attention toward one challenge at a time. Cardinal fire symbolizes a highly driven, motivated nature—ever on the go—that wants to move forward to pioneer new territory. This is cardinality in its hottest, most overt expression, burning with an eagerness to be in charge of here-and-now operations, with an expectation of always coming out on top of things and ahead of the game.

Cancer is a **cardinal water** sign. Just because Aries and Cancer are members of the same club (two cardinal signs) doesn't mean they naturally see eye to eye or blend well together. The main problem getting in the way of smooth interaction involves temperament: Aries' element of fire sharply contrasts with Cancer's element of water. Water is too sensitive to withstand the often rough-and-tumble treatment Aries dishes out (the Ram's brusque ways, alone, jar the Crab's more delicate sensibilities). Aries is also much too impatient with the sometimes whiny, crybaby side of Cancer that readily shows its hurt feelings (the big pout) when neglected or rejected. Strong-as-steel Aries doesn't have much respect for any sign that tries to use its weaknesses and insecurities to solicit sympathy or pity.

However, cardinal water suggests that Cancer's powerful emotions are quick to rush to the surface to make an immediate impact on the environment. Cancer can be assertive and even agitated when expressing its feelings, as it is the most demonstrative of the water signs (ol' "rubber face") thanks to its cardinal nature. It can't easily hide what it's really going through on the inside, at least not for long, unlike more inscrutable Scorpio or Pisces. When it does feel safe and secure, Cancer can energize others to openly express their own emotions in healthy, tension-releasing ways.

Actually, it's cardinality that spurs Cancer to keep emotions activated and in play. Cardinal water may not feel comfortable being too still in this area. It always likes to know what someone is feeling—in other words, do whatever it takes to get other people to react. Of course, if not handled skillfully, this need for a mutual exposure of feelings in relationships can be a source of many emotional ups and downs for Cancer, because not everyone likes to be as revealing as the Crab wants them to be (plus Cancer expects to hear only what it can handle emotionally).

Libra is a **cardinal air** sign located halfway around the zodiac, and thus it's directly opposite Aries. Air is a sociable element, curious about human interaction, and here it combines with cardinality to make for an active interest in connecting directly with people—up close and personal. Libra comes alive around others and generates a lot of dynamic energy in all its one-on-one relationships. In many ways, Libra is just an Aries who has learned how to charm others into being cooperative and willing to help this air sign get things to turn out its way.

Aries, all on its own, will fight for what it wants. Libra instead persuades others to become its valued allies, ensuring that it'll have the backup support it needs to get its objectives met—but Libra will then turn around and give as good as it gets (showing much appreciation when treated well by another, yet becoming a ready opponent when handled unfairly; indeed, if unduly provoked, all cardinal signs feel the urge to attack others or defend themselves).

Libra is also assertive in initiating relationships due to its cardinal need to push forward and get something going. Actually, this is usually done in an agreeable manner that lets the other party know that Libra's quite interested in forming a close union. Cardinal signs usually like to give and receive unambiguous signals (the exception is watery Cancer, who can send out mixed messages when unsure about its feelings).

Capricorn is a **cardinal earth** sign. This mode-element combination may seem strange at first, since cardinality urges us to rush around and do a lot of things—at least to start them—while earth wants us to stay in one place with our feet planted firmly on the ground. Earth urges us to plan our moves well and to use time and energy efficiently. Capricorn thus feels a strong drive to do big, important things in society, but it also works hard to make sure the results last a long time. This sign can be very assertive in the material world when it comes to gaining status. It's driven to manifest its goals in solid, enduring ways.

Of all the earth signs, Capricorn is the most willing to venture forth into unknown territory to take a few calculated risks, something Taurus and Virgo have trouble doing. The Goat won't take chances based on blind faith, but will move out into the world to try new things only after it has carefully evaluated the situation. Still, this is an earth sign with guts and gumption. Capricorn also has a strong instinct to climb (this is the sign of upward mobility regarding the ladder of success). It's an ambitious sign always looking out for more influential social positions to attain. It's also the only earth sign with the momentum to achieve prominence on a grand scale. The go-getter energy of cardinality is certainly behind the Goat's determination to "make it big" in the world.

Now let's take a brief look at the fixed mode and its associated signs.

THE FIXED MODE
Sticking to the Plans

The fixed signs—**Taurus, Leo, Scorpio,** and **Aquarius**—don't enjoy the relatively fast and furious pace of cardinal signs on the move. They don't at all take kindly to pushy, aggressive people (cardinal types) or high-pressured situations (although Scorpio is well equipped to handle emergency predicaments). While not necessarily slow, these fixed signs take more methodical, organized approaches to life (perhaps less so with experimental Aquarius). They need to feel that they can control what happens to them, rather than be swept up in a flurry of exciting but short-lived activity. If anything, their main interest is to pull their energies inwardly to better fortify themselves from within. Being centered allows them to tap into their internal power resources. Fixed signs consolidate such inner forces in ways that enable them to concentrate and focus long and hard on their objectives. Their attention is not easily diverted by fleeting distractions. Their interests in life are purposeful and enduring.

Stability results when applying fixed energy. Such steadiness helps these signs persevere with a true sense of goal attainment; they're less in need of immediately obtaining what they desire—they can wait, unlike the "gotta have it now" cardinal group. (Actually, Leo can sometimes have a problem with waiting to be gratified, but nonetheless, it is learning how timing plays an important role in the fuller enjoyment of life.) Patience and the ability to clearly define what they want are keys to the fixed signs' eventual success. They're blessed with stamina and will persist in all personal endeavors. Of course, this can make them the most stubborn and fixated signs of the zodiac—the ones who won't take "no" for an answer. Sometimes they win in life only because they have worn down the opposition.

The desire nature is strong in these signs. The fixed-mode signs have appetites that are not easily denied or put on hold—and that includes even Aquarius' appetite for free social expression and its desire not to follow a conventional path. These signs may not put up a bloody fight when their needs are threatened, but they will—to the nth degree—resist being dictated by others. They can't easily be forced to submit to outer authority. In short, they won't budge from any position they've taken until they're good and ready—and they typically are not "good and ready" until outside pressures back off and leave them alone to determine their own course of action. Interference from the sidelines is very unwelcome. Their motivation to change is always internal.

What's so great about the fixed mode is that its inherent staying power allows us to finish what we or others start. Cardinal energy may get the ball rolling in a high-energy manner, but fixed-mode energy quietly and steadfastly sees something to its completion. Fixed signs are the builders of life, desiring to further construct and give substance to what the cardinal signs have initiated. Thus, fixed signs are quite reliable (but again, watch out for Aquarius, who's not always great at handling the minor details of a big project, yet can often pull through ingeniously regarding those matters needing large-scale organization and smart social networking). Simply put, fixed signs are determined to get the job done. They cannot tolerate halfway measures and instead tend to give it all they've got, once motivated.

One pitfall of too much fixity, when mishandled, is its tendency to deal with life in uncompromising terms. Fixed signs can be quite unyielding, and this can lead to power struggles and no-win situations where all parties involved refuse to give in. The doggedness that fixity exhibits can cause trouble in situations where compromise and adaptability are needed most. Fixity is associated with stalemate conditions, where a battle of wills ensues. At times, this can be outright pigheadedness at work, attempting to thwart the easier solutions of others. Sometimes problems caused are simply due to being too habitual about adhering to one's daily rituals, especially at times when introducing a touch of variety would make so much more sense. (Actually, fixed signs of the earth and water variety—Taurus and Scorpio—have the most difficulty here).

Let's combine the characteristics of the fixed mode with the traits of each element to better comprehend why this group of signs behaves the way it does:

Taurus is a **fixed earth** sign. The zodiac's first earth sign is the most fixed, and thus most set in its ways of all twelve signs. No other sign is as entrenched in its attitudes as is this sign of the Bull. Yet this mode-element combo is quite steady and secure, and values stillness and serenity. Taurus is very anchored in the realm of the physical senses. It's grounded in the world of material form, from which it can attract and utilize valuable resources that sustain its life. Earth is an element that already seems "fixed," considering that, when left unaltered by other elements, it stay puts and hardly alters its shape. Those with Taurus emphasized in their charts want a calm, settled life where few changes occur—especially those that happen without warning. This is one sign that can enjoy the unvarying patterns of routine without getting bored.

Fixed earth implies utmost dependability. Fixity likes to stay on a plotted course of action, without veering off into unknown directions; earth also appreciates any consistent, uninterrupted activity that plays it safe. Taurus can thus be counted on to deliver the goods in a timely fashion, but it doesn't take such commitments lightly. In fact, it's hard to associate anything "light" with fixed earth. Purposeful Taurus is heavy in disposition, but not oppressively serious. It's more sober than somber. A big problem with fixed earth is its tendency to become too one-track-minded and unwilling to change in midstream, even when it's plainly advantageous to do so. This mulish behavior often has strong fixed-earth types tackling things the slow, hard way. Such stubbornness is an example of the deep, internal resistance this sign feels, especially when it is being manipulated by external forces.

Leo is a **fixed fire** sign. It may seem odd to think of fire as being fixed, since flames naturally love to spontaneously leap here and there, especially on windy days. But the steady glow of logs in a fireplace, where fire's flames are at least contained, becomes a fitting fixed-fire image. Fireplaces add a warm, cozy, and even romantic quality to any room. The sign Leo can be like this, as well. Its warmth radiates from its heart, and it lives the life of the eternal romantic, with all the emotional drama that entails. Fixed fire implies steady enthusiasm and long-lasting passions. Contained fire can burn more intensely and deeply (think of the fixed astronomical sun itself). Leo's fiery expression is less impulsive and more purposefully directed. It has well-defined goals to achieve and will harness all its creative power to ensure that it ends up a winner.

This is the most dependable of the fire signs, and one that is capable of great loyalty. Fixity helps Leo's fires burn steadily and longer than is typical of this element. Leo's flame is not easily extinguished once ignited. However, fixed signs can be obstinate, and fire can be willful. Leo thus has a reputation for being bossy and autocratic. It's full of pride and self-admiration, and this can lead to behavior that others find arrogant and snooty. Fixed fire means Leo's performance can come off as being inordinately self-confident (fixity feels strongly assured from within, while fire doesn't doubt the rightness of its actions). Still, Leo needs to feel utterly sold on itself in order to accomplish the great things it expects to in life. Since we all have Leo operating somewhere in our chart, it's good to know that here we have a sign that never wants us to feel like a loser.

Scorpio is a **fixed water** sign. Immediately, fixed water conjures up the image of ice. At times, Scorpio can be accused of transforming into an iceberg once it withdraws its emotional heat in its relationships. Yet its passions run deep, and thus this is a sign that is almost incapable of reacting to life in cold, aloof ways—although it may look like that, from time to time, when Scorpio is feeling deeply hurt. Since water represents the realm of emotions, fixed water suggests controlled feelings that seldom spill out and needlessly expose themselves. Scorpio's emotions are well contained—which perhaps makes them less messy —and yet, just how contained makes all the difference between unhealthy repression versus admirable emotional self-discipline.

Fixed water suggests a tendency to be very single-minded in its feelings. Such enduring interest creates an intensity that can lead to obsession. Of course, it's Scorpio's powerful instincts that compel it to probe and penetrate to the core of any matter with the dogged persistence of a bloodhound on the trail. Fixed water also means that Scorpio's feelings for others—whether loving or hateful—develop slowly and aren't easily dissuaded. There's little going on here that's superficial or fleeting. Scorpio can harbor strong feelings—even grudges—about somebody or something for a long, long time. Fixity helps stabilize water's emotionality, cutting down on mood swings and panicky reactions to outside threats. Indeed, Scorpio can appear amazingly composed in the face of impending danger. It does a marvelous job when handling crisis situations.

Aquarius is a **fixed air** sign. It appears there's always one sign of each mode that seems oddly misplaced (such as "shy" Cancer for the assertive, "in your face" cardinal signs). Aquarius is that oddball sign for the fixed group. All the other signs of this mode seem to want to hold on tightly to what they have, and can stubbornly use strong-arm tactics to get their way. Taurus, Leo, and Scorpio all can be very attached to their desires and thus too inflexible to change their ways overnight. However, Aquarius can suddenly revolutionize its behavior, given the right environmental conditions. (Besides, air signs aren't into attachments that much).

Fixed air seems like an oxymoron, since air's main interest is to circulate and spread itself far and wide, while fixity likes things to stay put. Actually, one image that comes to mind is an oxygen tank—air in a concentrated, contained form that's used to keep people from losing consciousness. Aquarius is very much interested in oxygenating society with progressive ideals that are aimed at vitalizing the social consciousness of many. Air in its fixed form suggests an intellect that is less easily distracted, resulting in stronger mental concentration. Air is filled with bright ideas that are often best applied to human situations, and here, fixity gives Aquarius the focus and patience needed to help such progressive ideas develop needed substance and durability.

Aquarius is therefore very "attached" to championing certain principles, based on Truth, that it can apply to life on a collective level—things like life, liberty, and the pursuit of happiness for all individuals. Yet airy Aquarius doesn't want to become too grounded in mundane, earthy realities that seem to limit the mind's vast potential. It must have enough intellectual freedom to breathe. Although it espouses democratic concepts with ease—especially where individual human rights are concerned—Aquarius can be a bit rigid and intolerant (fixed) in how its social reforms are to be implemented. There's a hidden dictator rattling around in its closet somewhere.

Next, we need to examine the mutable mode and its associated signs. But first:

Taking a Little Breather

I like to think of the action of the modes as a metaphor for our breathing cycle: The cardinal phase is like inhalation, where we sense an upward surge of rushing air, seemingly moving into our head—it keeps us from passing out and helps vitalize our body (being wide-awake and alert are cardinal-mode attributes).

Next comes the fixed phase, that stillness when we are momentarily not really breathing. Actually, holding our breath (fully possessing it) creates more of a static power than a gathering of energy. Hold it even longer and that power becomes more intense, with strong pressures building inside. This sounds like the inner strength of the fixed mode. (Interestingly, kids who are in a particularly stubborn mood have been known to hold their breath when defying their parents.)

At last comes exhalation, that mutable phase in which we finally release our breath and disperse its contents back out into the world. This is an act that completes the cycle of respiration, and what we are releasing at this point has been modified—it's not the same oxygen we first took in, but is now carbon dioxide. Thus, a transitional exchange has taken place—perfect symbolism for the mutable mode. Exhalation also makes room in our lungs for a new supply of air to invigorate us, allowing the cycle of respiration to repeat.

THE MUTABLE MODE
Any Way the Wind Blows

The mutable signs—**Gemini, Virgo, Sagittarius,** and **Pisces**—weaken the mighty resistances that fixed signs often put up to avoid being altered. Solid structure starts to lose its form as this process begins. Life is in a continuous state of change, even when there are periods where there's a lull in the action. Every season must come to an end. The mutable mode has the task of breaking down forces that have already peaked in expression, and that now need to be released and reformulated. The concentrated energies of the fixed mode have often become too crystallized—like a hardening of the arteries—to enhance the vital flow of the life force that was first animated by the cardinal signs. Mutability thus plays a necessary role in redistributing this energy, and preparing it for a future cycle of cardinal activity, just in time for the arrival of a brand-new season of promise.

As fixed-mode energy begins to wind down, small changes occur that signal a readiness for adaptation. Mutable signs become the agents of consciousness that allow for this needed adjustment. They are highly alert regarding where and when such alterations are required. Mutability's greatest strength is its flexible openness to change. These pliable signs urge us to stay open and adaptable to the various ways life introduces us to new paths of self-knowledge. They also try to educate us about life's multifaceted nature. The mutable mode activates our mental curiosity, whereby we sometimes are left with more questions about life than ready answers.

Nothing is quite firm and absolute in the world of mutability, because everything appears to be in a transitory state, going from one necessary phase to another. It's hard to feel settled about anything. It's not even easy to have a clear direction in life, since nothing can be taken for granted. Life is full of twists and turns, making long-range planning tricky for strongly mutable types.

Mutable signs need much variety to appeal to their decidedly mental nature, although "mental" doesn't necessarily mean cerebral in a logic-minded sense. Sagittarius and Pisces are two signs that live easily in their heads, yet they need grand ideas and visionary ideals that inspire their collective hopes and dreams. In many ways, their interests lie in envisioning unrealized potential and conceptualizing life's purpose in the broadest of terms. The other two mutable signs, Gemini and Virgo, are more turned on by facts and figures, and by all concrete matters that can be measured, tested, and confirmed as "real." They are less impressed by ungrounded, abstract thought (although Gemini is momentarily impressed by anything that sounds brilliant, however impractical). Still, all mutable signs are keenly observational—they want to better understand how life works and how its many pieces fit together.

This group is loaded with nervous energy that needs proper channeling. They can be easily distracted by everything around them, although earthy Virgo is self-disciplined enough to stay focused on details and not mentally wander (even though disorder in its surroundings quickly captures its attention). It's good for mutable signs not to be given too many options, since this leads to indecision or a wasteful scattering of mental energy—they can spread themselves too thin by trying to tackle too many things at once. At the same time, mutable signs cannot tolerate monotony (although the earth in Virgo can handle dull routines more easily than the rest). Variety is the spice of life for this mode.

With the pliability of the mutable mode comes a bonus: youthfulness. It seems such resiliency can keep us young at heart by putting a little spring in our step, a little bounce in our beat. Mutable signs certainly do not plod on, as if weighed down by gravity, but are light on their feet. They seem to skip along life's path and tiptoe around heavy predicaments (although watery Pisces has to watch out for its attraction to life-complicating, melodramatic scenarios). All fours signs help us appear chronologically younger than we are (they even have an aversion to aging). The mutable mode shows us that we can greatly benefit from keeping our mind flexible and eager to sample more and more from life, even if only in small but digestible bits.

Gemini is a **mutable air** sign. Air and mutability have much in common, making this sign the winner of the group when it comes to expressing the most obvious mutable traits. Air already likes to move about in many directions, unhampered by time or structure. It doesn't like feeling stale, which can happen when it stays still for too long. Mutability gives air plenty of opportunities for ventilation. Gemini thus has mental equipment made for exploring a wide range of interests. It sees little reason to restrain its appetite for knowledge. Information, no matter what kind, is stimulating for Gemini, who can quickly scan the environment and pick up newsy facts here and there. There's little that doesn't interest Gemini, at least for the moment. The only problem is that the Twins can suffer from "info" overload, a case where its head is crammed with an assortment of data that may be too trivial in content to be truly mind-expanding.

Still, Gemini will give anything that moves its short-lived attention—and does it ever enjoy seeing life in motion! There is a breezy side to Gemini that keeps it from getting hung up about anything that's too heavy in life, although it seeks to attain a general knowledge about such matters. Mutable air wants to cover a lot of intellectual territory. In order to quickly get the gist of something, it'll skim the surface before moving on to something new. All in all, Gemini is blessed with a versatile intellectual capacity for studying a variety of interesting subjects.

Virgo is a **mutable earth** sign. While an apt fixed-earth image is a compost heap (which takes a while to "cook" and decompose into "black gold"—a rich, fertile soil with a concentration of nutrients), mutable earth sounds more like sand, which is known for its ability to shift and easily reshape itself. Sand is a more fluid form of earth, one that is not all that solid to walk on. Virgo thus symbolizes an expression of earth that is able to yield readily to pressure and alter itself, rather than firmly resist. Virgo can bend and adapt in practical ways, while always looking for simple solutions that work well. What's not so simple is Virgo's near obsession with exactly how everything in life works, down to the finer, technical details. Mutability always stimulates curiosity, while earth gives careful attention to life's nuts and bolts. Therefore, Virgo excels in organizing its specialized knowledge of the more mundane facets of living.

Virgo likes to give attention to the small stuff in life, and wisely knows that even big, complex machinery can come to a screeching halt should nobody on the job notice one loose screw. Virgo, therefore, feels its mission is to attend to the minor, often overlooked issues of any project—it's an even keener observer than Gemini, due to earth's ability to concentrate patiently on one thing at a time. (Virgo's better at shutting out any unwanted distractions, unless it's a dripping faucet or a creaky floor.) Here we have a bright but down-to-earth intellect that seeks to get to the heart of any matter, without becoming sidetracked by nonessential issues (which is something harder for the remaining mutable signs to do).

Sagittarius is a **mutable fire** sign. If you overlook the apparent random destructiveness involved, a lightning-instigated, raging forest fire is a good metaphor for mutable fire. It's a blaze, triggered by a bolt from the blue, that quickly spreads far and wide—a form of fire that goes beyond its original boundaries to cover more and more territory, when left unchecked. (Actually, ecologists now know that Nature uses spontaneous forest and brush fires to help invigorate the ecosystems involved.) Sagittarius wants its own fires of inspiration to distribute themselves widely and to keep on spreading. Here, the enthusiastic side of fire is most easily dispersed. Sagittarian warmth and hopeful optimism can uplift many people at once, which explains this sign's urge to go out and greet the big world with its good news about life's greater meaning.

Sometimes mutability means that Sagittarius gets a little too widespread regarding its sincere beliefs—it suffers from too many sweeping generalizations about the big, important issues of life. It naturally observes and theorizes on a large-scale basis, and generously endows the human experience with almost unlimited potential—particularly in the area of mind expansion. The fires of its vigorous intellect burn brightly for this sign, but any contradictory details that crop up and challenge one's faith is for another sign (Pisces) to fret over, not Sagittarius. The Archer is convinced, with all the fiery self-assurance it can muster, that it's on the right track with its overall concepts—and that's all it needs to know.

Pisces is a **mutable water** sign. Although Pisces is more emotional than mental in temperament, it's also capable of grand, abstract overviews of life—it is *the* sign most receptive to cosmological theories that attempt to unify all that exists under one universal law (even more so than Sagittarius). Pisces' scope of cosmic awareness can be vast and profound, partly due to how well both our left-brain and right-brain hemispheres can creatively unite. This sign may not sharply analyze details, yet Pisces has a knack for synthesizing many diverse factors and arriving at a better understanding of the whole picture of life, not just its bits and pieces. As a mutable form of water, Pisces also emotionally moistens everything it touches, like a gentle mist—not like the heavy drenching common to the rushing waters of cardinal Cancer, or the blast from a high-pressured hose that typically characterizes fixed Scorpio's intensity (especially when outraged). Pisces is more a light drizzle than a torrent of rain.

Mutable water suggests a feeling nature that is able to connect with life on a broad basis—emotional sensitivity is less contained (this is a boundless, pervasive expression of water). Pisces feels what all of life feels, a result of its mystical talent for linking with others in less visible ways. All the water signs are active on these invisible levels of energy-exchange, but Pisces seems the most unfettered in its ability to flow in and out of the inner worlds of others. Mutability implies versatility, and when combined with empathetic water, it means Pisces has a universal understanding of humanity and can sensitively interact with people from all walks of life. There must be a special reason why the zodiac concludes with this mode-element combination, which certainly sounds more malleable and flowing in its life approach than does the hard-headed, cardinal-fire mix that began it all in Aries.

In chapter 3, the zodiac's first six signs will be explored in greater detail. Realize that signs—like planets and houses—can be applied to anything and everything that is a part of our existence, no matter how mundane or trivial. Astrologers can spend a lifetime trying to determine what those specific associations may be—an important task, since astrology is fundamentally a study of symbolic correspondences: i.e., Gemini "rules" motorbikes, Virgo "rules" the small intestine, Sagittarius "rules" the Las Vegas casino mentality, and so on. Since not every existing or speculative association can be included in this or any other astrology book, I will focus on the twelve signs more from a psychological, character-defining perspective, although not exclusively or definitively so.

Well, it's time to turn the page and find out why Aries cannot wait a minute longer to reveal to us what it's really all about!

Note

1. Each season consists of three months, and each month appears to reveal a different mode's energy in operation. The first stage of a season, related to the *cardinal* mode, expresses an energy pattern that describes the initial thrust or momentum that begins the season—it's a time when notable changes start to occur. A season's cardinal beginnings signal an active phase when the new qualities of that season rush in. The changes in Nature can seem like dramatic turning points.

   Whatever a season is primarily all about, its "cardinal" month and sign (starting at the equinox and solstice points of the year) reflect the energy-generating display of that season's dynamics—away with the old, worn-out reminders of the previous season, and in with fresh energy that needs to be released. The months and signs associated with the cardinal mode—starting from the first day of spring in the Northern Hemisphere—are April (Aries), July (Cancer), October (Libra), and January (Capricorn).

   Following this cardinal phase is the *fixed* mode. The word "fixed" sounds like something is to stay put here for a while and not move. This second stage (second month) of any season is when fixed-mode energy is strong. As the cardinal stage wanes—and thus a period of an initial flurry of activity and change has diminished—the season settles next into its most intense, concentrated expression.

   Any extreme conditions typical of that season are now evident during this time (such as summer's scorching heat waves and winter's blinding blizzards). Nature is at its peak during this fixed phase. Actually, changes occur less often, since consistency and stability reign (the days can seem almost boringly similar to one another). The months and signs associated with the fixed mode are May (Taurus), August (Leo), November (Scorpio), and February (Aquarius).

   The final phase belongs to the *mutable* mode. Here is when the season starts to get fickle, weather-wise, a time when nothing is all that predictable. Change is in the air, as the season winds down and, little by little, a transformation begins. Nature is in a state of transition. Those characteristics that were so vividly present during its fixed phase now start to lose steam, as the steady pattern begins to break up and give way to the adjustments needed for a brand-new seasonal experience during the cardinal month, once again. The months and seasons associated with the mutable mode are June (Gemini), September (Virgo), December (Sagittarius), and March (Pisces).

Chapter Three

From Aries
to Virgo

DIFFERENT STROKES

The zodiac's twelve signs are said to represent powerful archetypes that are universal in theme. Perhaps they've psychologically portrayed our human potential ever since those early times when our prehistoric ancestors began to socially interact—probably ever since the day that some smiley Libran cave dweller was the first to teach everyone how to stop throwing rocks at each other and instead play nice. It must have been a momentous occasion when *Homo sapiens* learned that there are at least two sides to every relationship in life. Being human thus became more complicated—what to decide on now, rocks or hugs?

Although the signs may have fundamental meanings applicable to all of humankind, we need to keep in mind that our actual modern-day experience of each zodiac sign depends a lot on our cultural background and the historical times in which we live. Certain repressive eras and social environments may not allow various signs their wider range of expression. Or when overglorified, some signs become distortions of their true essence (think of the over-the-top Arien aggression and violence shown during the fierce fighting days of Ghengis Khan, who—as legend has it—was born clutching a clot of blood).

Perhaps some are cultures are more naturally attuned than others to the life processes symbolized by some signs. Tibetans have long been enthralled by the otherworldly, mystical realms of Pisces, while ancient Egyptians were intensely fascinated with Scorpio's world of the dead and the afterlife.

So, is each sign expressed the same way around the globe? Astrologers ideally assume, for example, that Virgo's traits will remain intact for people everywhere on the planet—from Stockholm to Bangkok to Tierra del Fuego. Theoretically, folks with their Sun in Virgo who were born near the North Pole should be just as picky and detail-obsessed as those born near the South Pole. Indeed, it does appear that Virgo still acts like Virgo for citizens from Down Under as it does for people who hail from Chicago. We thus can say, with assurance, that fastidious Virgo has not—anywhere on this planet—mysteriously transformed instead into an archetype of the superslob who thrives on disorder! Likewise, we can consistently count on a certain degree of uniformity throughout the world regarding any sign's behavioral traits.

In various cultures, because of the social customs involved, some signs may be less free to be all that they can be, especially the fire signs in those countries that have long had a tradition of keeping women from showing their assertive, independent side—perhaps for fear that they might directly compete with and outdo the men (the ones who normally get to act out fire without impunity). Fire-sign expression for such women may be muted and even heavily projected onto the males in their lives—and that's not a psychologically healthy thing to do.

In contrast, nations that cherish and protect the personal freedoms of its people promote a more open expression of both fire and air—although, again, men can exhibit such traits without any problems while women have to be careful not to overdo it and intimidate the easily threatened opposite sex (that's at least the social message women get).

In cultures that place a high value on air, everyone at least gets to voice an opinion—air-sign expressiveness is seldom held back here. Actually, people everywhere exercise their air-sign ability to a degree, since every culture uses language to facilitate communication, plus societies have all devised ways to count (even bartering requires the concept of numbers). In countries where access to certain information is forbidden by the ruling parties, or where illiteracy prevails, the expanded potential of the air signs is impeded. The air in each of us evolves the more we're free to know things; censorship thus thwarts air's natural development.

In heavily industrialized nations—where a pragmatic, materialistic, even scientific intellect is highly prized—it's our water-sign experience that suffers. Water leans toward more mystical, magical, gut-knowing ways of perceiving reality—ways all deemed by left-brain-dominant authorities as "superstitious" irrationalities that threaten to take us "back to the Dark Ages" if left unchecked by the superior powers of logic and reason.

Some cultures criticize too much introspective self-preoccupation as a cause of antisocial behavior or even mental illness. Wanting to be left alone with few social contacts (water signs crave solitude) is looked on as odd and troublesome—society is quick to warn such water types that they really need to "get out" more and mingle. Of course, most people turn to television, movies, or novels to escape into worlds of larger-than-life emotionality and melodrama—a vicarious way to safely experience water-sign intensities.

Earth signs seem to reflect the common experience of all people, but perhaps most so for those intimately bound to the land for their sustenance on a continuous basis. Less-sophisticated cultures, existing in rural, jungle, or isolated settings, are highly attuned to the earth element and know how to survive in this sometimes harsh and physically taxing realm. Yet, if we live in countries where learning the ropes of survival is less critical—since industry provides our basic needs—we may be less in touch with the nurturing depths of the earth signs. Earth, instead, takes the form of manufactured goods we'd like to own.

Because of such limited earth-element contact, we may not be self-sufficient enough to know how to live off of the goods of the earth while in the woods or the wilderness, if we had to. We also live more insulated lives to avoid exposing ourselves to Nature's raw elements (even our cars come with their own climate-control technology).

It seems that nobody gets to experience these twelve signs and their modal-elemental energies in a full-bodied or even a balanced manner. Nobody's a walking, well-adjusted, living archetype of any sign! We'll always have to grapple with any perceptual deficiencies brought about by collective forces beyond our control, or so it seems. Perhaps all this will change in the centuries to come, so that more self-aware men and women will value the processes of *all* twelve signs equally and use them in more self-empowering ways.

Still, it's so darn hard to erase thousands of years of collective programming, especially that which involves traditional gender roles. The good news is that evolutionary indicators suggest we are ready to shake off social roles that have hamstrung our potential, as spiritual human beings, to be much more than just the limited byproducts of our short-sighted cultural conditioning.

Now let's look more closely at the dynamics of the first six signs, keeping in mind that the following interpretations do not necessarily reflect the traits of someone born with only the Sun in any of these signs. They are more apt to reflect the temperament of individuals who have several planets in a particular sign—especially the Sun, Moon, Mercury, Venus, or Mars.

ARIES
Party of One

Glyph: ♈
Symbol: The Ram
Mode: Cardinal
Element: Fire
Planet: Mars/♂
House: First
Motto: "I Am Me—You're Not!"

Full Speed Ahead

Of all the signs of the zodiac, Aries seems to be the most desirous of speed. Fire and air signs appreciate quick responses in life, but being cardinal *and* fire, Aries demands the fastest results and can be quite impatient when time seems to drag. Aries has a very short attention span, but that's okay, since it doesn't need a lot of time to react. Nothing is mulled over in Aries' world—either it likes something or it doesn't, either it will do something or it won't! This is a nearly instantaneous decision that bypasses careful, analytical evaluation. There's no weighing of all sides with Aries, and thus snap decisions are followed by forthright action. Actually, following gut impulse without fear allows us the opportunity to activate our fiery essence, that spark of spirit within.

Aries knows it's here to get something in motion, *now*, at this moment! All personal interests are activated by a single-minded drive to satisfy self-will. Like a bullet, Aries ejects itself into its immediate world to give whatever it targets its best shot—and sometimes its *only* shot—of adrenaline and self-starting power. It's impulse is to begin new experiences with an innocent kind of boldness that you won't find anywhere else in the zodiac—innocence based partly on Aries' inability or reluctance to self-reflect. Being reflective can slow any sign down—definitely not what the Ram wants to experience.

Thus, Arien self-interest is strong, ongoing, and fairly obvious. Its initiative and enterprise are to benefit itself, first and foremost, in ways that often ignore, minimize, or dismiss the needs of others. How this sign applies its raw, uncultured power becomes its big lesson. Life will teach Aries that it cannot live or act only for itself, nor will it be allowed to let others dominate its life. It needs to balance its energies better. Developing a dynamic sense of personal identity is a main concern for this sign. "Can I live life *my* way?" wonders Aries. Typically, the Ram doesn't feel it has a lot of time to be what it wants to be and to get to where it wants to go—cardinal Aries is certain it's "gotta get moving" before someone else gets there first.

Don't Crowd Me

Until Taurus came on the scene, Aries was utterly sure—even for so brief a moment—that it was the only archetype that Creation had designed for human consumption. "After all, what else could beat the thrill of getting all fired up by a surge of self-seeking impulse?" asks Aries. But even as the other signs soon began to multiply like rabbits and then became curious as to how they could interplay with one another—especially those last six signs—Aries could never erase from its awareness the realization that, once upon a time, it was happily all by itself, unfettered by any kind of energy-sucking relationship. There was no one else to cater to. This archetype still likes to keep some healthy distance when creating partnerships—it's not a sign that is so much detached as it is noncommittal. The Ram doesn't want its spontaneous fires snuffed out by demanding or needy types who either make all the rules or lay on heavy guilt trips. It also hates to hear how selfish and "me, me, me" it can be.

One way for Aries to avoid that kind of dreaded entanglement is to do as much as it can as self-reliantly as possible. "Don't ever lean on people, and then they'll never feel they own you," concludes Aries. Actually this sign is not so well equipped to psychoanalyze the motives of others (that's Scorpio), yet it knows that the less people involved in its act, the better. Then things will move faster with fewer obstacles in the way (people's opposing needs pulling at Aries become such obstacles). All fires signs need a lot of room to grow, but Aries will fight for its own space, and won't take kindly to anyone who's too clingy or possessive. It's not in Aries' nature to attach itself to others and thus lose some of its vitality. Although it will energetically interact with people —and often competitively so—it doesn't want to own anyone or be owned by them. It wants everyone else to be as self-reliant as it is (this sign would have a tough time being the codependent type).

War Games?

A classic image of Aries is that of the warrior, all done up in red paint and armed with spears, swords, piercing war cries, or whatever else it takes to look and sound fierce and dangerous. In real life, Aries is not all that angry or ready to do battle, plus today's world doesn't allow the Ram its destructive outbursts—those leading to physical attacks— without suffering penalizing, legal repercussions. Besides, Aries is not innately bloodthirsty and out to kill. It's not psychologically twisted enough for that.

One thing that does get Aries to see red is being denied the right to act immediately on something when it's darn ready to. When Aries' energy is blocked by others, its instinct is to scratch and bite. Yet when it's given the go-ahead to plunge into activity at its customarily vibrant pace, there's no problem. Aries then becomes an invigorating influence that heats up situations in just the right way.

While it's true that Aries is sometimes as testy as a hornet stuck on the wrong side of a screen door, it doesn't sustain its anger for long. Nothing gets to linger inside Aries and slowly build pressure. Nothing festers. Aries has a low tolerance for such pressure and blows off steam quickly. It can make an awfully noisy scene when riled, but then it'll just quit flaring up when it's had enough action (even though that's typically when its opponent is just getting started).

Cardinal fire, not known for its stamina, often does better when releasing energy in short but intense spurts, the kind that packs a mean punch when needed. Astrologers eagerly tell clients with lots of Aries in their charts to work off their energy surplus by exercising or staying active. Beware of those strongly Arien types who, oddly enough, are chronic couch potatoes—they could be human time bombs quietly ticking away, and all it takes to trigger a big blowup is to dare yank that remote control away from them!

Identify Yourself

Aries needs to develop its own identity by putting its personal stamp of individuality on everything it does. It wants to be left alone to discover its strengths on its own terms. This becomes critical for those strong Arien types who have been raised in households where they were not permitted to just be themselves, even if that meant being irrepressibly loud and overactive little kids (especially with natal Mars and/or Mercury in Aries). As Aries' natural inclination is to break the rules, trying to conform to the standard conduct expected of all "obedient" children might have been a struggle. Aries, who'd rather govern its own behavior, will resort to a little head-butting when met with opposition—it's not easily disciplined by others and hates being supervised.

In later years, when we're more on our own, our Aries energies make us wary about how much of ourselves we'll let the world control. We don't want to feel we belong to anybody—not a lover, a spouse, a company, or even a religion—who then would have the power to dictate our moves and make decisions for us. Those are two surefire ways to make us feel we're losing our identity by becoming someone else's creation. Aries will make certain that things never get that far, and one way to prevent this is by not allowing for true intimacy—nobody gets to see Aries' more vulnerable, emotional side. They instead get to witness the tough-as-nails act, the bravado, the chip on the shoulder, and the "I don't need you" routine—all protective Arien defenses used to keep potential control freaks at arm's length.

Daredevil

To see Aries taking risky chances here and there is to wonder if this sign has a secret death wish. It doesn't. It's just that Aries is sometimes like a toddler who thinks nothing of running into noon-day traffic, oblivious to its dangers. The child is simply caught up in the thrill of energetically rushing ahead and is really paying attention to little else. Aries also has a similar ability to block things out when focused on an immediate objective. It's very single-minded and determined when it wants to do something, even if that something is pretending to be Spider Man climbing up the Empire State Building. Strong Arien types are gutsy (and reckless) enough to attempt going over Niagara Falls in a steel barrel. Let's not forget that Aries is a very physically assertive sign, but one that is not very protective of its body (unlike Taurus). It is more driven by its fiery will to battle its fears and to prove itself to be ever-courageous in action.

It indeed takes courage for us to be ourselves, Aries-style, in a world where becoming what others want us to be is instead rewarded, status-wise. When we play certain preapproved social roles to perfection, never veering much from the script, society holds us in high regard and allows us a secure position in the world. We become upstanding citizens who are worthy of even becoming role models for others. Yet this all sounds too much like Capricorn, a cardinal-earth sign that Aries has trouble relating to, probably because Capricorn is so hung-up on glorifying authority (either by being one or bowing down to one). The daringness of Aries is not just reserved for death-defying stunts. It also comes in handy when trying to stand up against a social system that tries to turn people into obedient sheep, not fighting rams. Aries will defy authoritarian control in very personal terms. It must be free to be itself!

It's probably a fact that many malcontent Ariens, during turbulent historical times of political upheaval, have clashed with the dictatorial powers in charge and have lost their freedom (and even their heads). Still, where would we be without such warriors ready to fight for an individual's rights? Many planets in Aries suggest folks who won't toe the line in order to climb the ladder of success, often much to their detriment—but at least nobody owns their soul. Still, it's important to know when to stop being so headstrong and instead to submit to a few of Capricorn's virtues if we really want to be taken seriously by society—besides, earth doesn't always have to put out the flames of fire.

Simplicity

Aries is not a simple-minded sign—and never let it hear you say that! Still, it does become restless and less engaged with things that are too involved or multifaceted. Details bore Aries, yet ignoring them can get a sometimes ill-prepared Ram in hot water. However, Aries does see the value in keeping most matters in life as uncluttered as possible. Why overload experiences with nonessentials? Aries is a little like Virgo in this regard. Of course, it's hard to achieve depth-awareness when we're unwilling to handle the complexities of being human. Aries sees things in black-and-white terms—nothing vague or ambiguous: "Are you or are you not a murderer?" barks the Arien prosecutor. "Well, yes . . . I guess I am . . . but that dirty cockroach had it coming—they can make you quite sick, you know," timidly explains Virgo. Hmmm . . . Aries obviously doesn't deal well with certain subtle distinctions.

Nonetheless, Aries has an ability to get right to the heart of any matter. "What are we basically trying to accomplish here?" asks Aries, who then goes about doing it. Wherever Aries is in our chart, it's best not to beat around the bush too much. Decisive action is needed, once we view our situation in simpler terms, without throwing in extraneous considerations. That helps us become more clear about what action needs to be taken. Real life doesn't always accommodate this "keep things simple" approach, but Aries doesn't work as well when bogged down by too many unnecessary roadblocks, nor does it like to take detours due to the complicated affairs of others. Its solution: Don't obligate yourself to people or let them interfere with your personal plans of action. Wing it alone if you can.

All by Myself

Aries may be thrilled not to have others around who can slow things down and keep matters from being anything but spontaneous. Aries lives in the moment—and it can be a vigorously exciting moment— but once somebody else is involved (making it more of a Libra experience), activity has to be shared. Sharing, to Aries, means that someone else is going to butt in and try to exert their influence. Aries doesn't like to realize that others can have equally strong wills and can be just as pushy, or even aggressive, as Aries is in getting its needs met. So sharing space with another is to risk losing autonomy and the power to make one's own decisions.

It just so happens that Libra is Aries' opposite sign, and the one best able to provide the Ram with needed balance (see chapter 5 for interpretations of opposing signs). Inside Aries is latent Libra energy that needs to come out and express itself. Aries types don't recognize this Libran quality in themselves early in life, but probably warm up to the notion as time goes on—and as they realize that without cooperation and a showing of consideration for others, Aries gets nowhere . . . fast!

Still, Aries cannot afford to become too relationship-dependent or to even let others always have their way. Never being allowed to take the initiative in personal matters can eventually leave the Ram boiling inside with anger and self-disgust. This sign psychologically must call the shots rather than acquiesce to others. Those of us with a natal Aries emphasis would do well to be self-directive, meaning we need to think twice before letting others in on our pet projects—even highly competent people. Aries has a built-in sense of life as an ongoing struggle, but the Ram also realizes that its physical and psychological muscles will strengthen once it allows itself to make more of an effort to attain its goals independently.

Quality time alone is vital for Aries types. It's all right to indulge in that Arien "loner" streak from time to time and do things that don't require another's involvement. (Jogging while wearing headphones, dangerous as it can be during peak traffic hours, is probably a delicious experience for Aries—one that combines running fast, sweating hard, and shutting out the external world by listening to blaring music with a driving beat.) It is hoped that the Ram will use any quality time alone to understand why it was blessed with an abundance of energy, backed by a strong will to achieve. With Aries, we are to learn what we can do on our own, once we fearlessly take that first step.

A Blast of Mars

The planet associated with Aries is Mars, known for its spunky self-assertiveness. Fiery Mars is loaded with a burning drive to triumph in its endeavors without outside help. It likes to find out what it can accomplish on its own, similar to Aries. Both planet and sign need to be energetically doing things, as inactivity can be vitality-depleting for them. Mars is a self-focused planet and thus appropriately represents the "me-first" side of Aries. Like the Ram, Mars won't lean on others for support, but will strike out on its own to confront challenges with courage. It can be as single-minded in its pursuits as Aries can.

However, strong Mars types aren't as innocently naive about their potential strengths as is Aries, who can be a bit foolhardy when asserting itself. The Ram is spontaneously daring because it is typically blind to the consequences involved in plunging into risky enterprises— it just wants to ignite immediate action. Mars is better equipped to battle life because, while aware of the dangers involved, it is determined to fight to the end (its symbol ♂ shows that it already comes armed with its sword and shield). Both planet and sign are self-willed in action, yet Mars is more capable of satisfying its desires due to its greater staying power—it's determined to succeed at all costs, while Aries is prone to move on to something new before finishing what it had once vigorously started. The Ram is sometimes too cardinal—too impulsive and lacking in strategy—to suit the needs of Martian ambition and desire.

Closing Comments

Aries motivates us to test our inner strengths when facing life challenges that require our undivided attention for the moment—times when we are encouraged to put all our eggs in one basket and take here-and-now risks to get what we want. If we make a few Arien mistakes along the way—maybe we're too impulsive and headstrong in action—life allows us to start again without much ado. (That's certainly not the case once we get to Libra, a sign that teaches us much about the consequences of actions.) Aries attempts to do the impossible, whether it succeeds or not. It always wants to feel victorious, but more importantly, it never wants to back down from a chance to do things within its grasp. However, Aries won't really know what can or cannot be done until it takes the plunge. This uncertainty is, in itself, motivating. At work here is Aries' blind self-trust and its innate "can do" attitude, two things that pave the way for the Ram's ultimate success. Where Aries is in our chart, let's plow through any doubts and fears, and come alive in the Now!

FAMOUS ARIES TYPES (natal Aries placements listed)

Marlon Brando, actor: Sun, Moon, Mercury

Gloria Steinem, writer-editor: Sun, Mars, Uranus

Gregory Peck, actor: Sun, Mercury, Jupiter

Maya Angelou, poet-writer: Sun, Jupiter, Uranus

Joseph Campbell, mythologist-writer: Sun, Mercury, Jupiter, Mars

Diana Ross, singer: Sun, Mercury

TAURUS

The Comfort Zone

Glyph: ☉

Symbol: The Bull

Mode: Fixed

Element: Earth

Planet: Venus/♀

House: Second

Motto: "It's Mine, Once It's on Sale!"

On Steady Ground

It seems a bit odd that the speediest sign of the zodiac (Aries) is immediately followed by the slowest, Taurus—talk about slamming on the brakes! Actually, the Bull's reputation as a slowpoke is exaggerated, especially if "slowness" is to be deemed undesirable (like a slow day at the office). We should appreciate what the Cosmos had in mind at that pivotal moment when it decided, "Aries is great, but life needs more options!" Once word got out that there were more openings available, Taurus—surprisingly the first archetype on line—patiently waited to be picked. Hmmm . . . the Bull was apparently not all that slow way back then. As Taurus has always been good at quickly spotting the best seat in the house to plop down in, here it somehow knew that being the second sign of the zodiac would be one cushy position that it just had to have!

Considering only these two emerging signs, we see that Aries first whips up a firestorm of activity—sending seeds of vital, germinating energy flying every which way—and then Taurus enjoyably contains all that wild, fiery energy ready to burst at the seams; that is, once the Bull has lovingly added a little fertilizer to its basic soil mix—that richly organic, earthy-smelling stuff really helps all things take root. The life spark in Aries establishes a more settled, stable environment in which to materialize in concrete terms.

Taurus is a fixed-earth sign, suggesting a double dose of stability— something the zodiac apparently needed, soon after its combustible Aries stage, before it could sensibly diversify. Fixed energy isn't going anywhere, at least not until it has pulled together and organized all its resources. In addition, methodical earth likes to takes its time when building supportive structures that ensure durability. Thus, Taurus has little trouble planting its hooves on the ground and firmly con- necting with the world of matter—a tangible substance it knows it can count on to not rapidly change in form. Matter is appealingly solid and predictable to Taurus, a sign that needs to feel safely enclosed by protective and even permanent boundaries.

Don't Push Me

Taurus' reputation for being slow and deliberate may be the result of the Bull's cautious reaction to anything that rushes toward it. Taurus doesn't like having things that demand immediate action thrust in its face. To suit this sign temperamentally, new conditions have to ease on in at a more relaxed pace. There needs to be enough time to consider issues carefully. Having slower reflexes than Aries—and what sign doesn't?—Taurus is not very jumpy in disposition. It's also not as quick to act on impulse—unless it's feeling hunger pangs.

Like Aries, Taurus has strong, instinct-driven desires that seek sat- isfaction in very personal ways. However, the Bull will first sensibly size up any current situation before expending its energy. It is smart about conserving its strength and won't waste its vitality on activity that it doesn't value. Although less apt to first analyze conditions logi- cally, Taurus uses its powerful instincts and common sense to allow it to get a better feel for the general tone of a circumstance. It wants to know, before making an effort, what actions will best lead to satisfying

results. Its comfort zone must always be honored if Taurus is to cooperate with any unfoldment of events.

Should Taurus appear to be slow or lazy about taking action, it's
also because it often unconsciously waits for the right—even the
ripest—moment in which to invest its energies. The Bull has an uncanny sense of practical timing in most mundane affairs, especially
when it comes to getting good deals on purchases—here, its tendency
to hold back from taking action, until a later date, often pays off.

There's a big difference between waiting to take advantage of optimal timing versus plain ol' immobility—refusing to budge for less-
sensible reasons. Taurus can be entrenched in its familiar worlds of
habit and routine, to the point of being stuck in a rut. That's when the
Bull's inner stillness turns to stagnation. It's at times like this that Taurus will stubbornly refuse to be pushed into taking action, at least not
until it's darn ready, and that could be never!

Gentle Treatment

Part of Taurus' need for comfort stems from its capacity to receive
sensory pleasure from its surroundings. The gratification of the physical senses is vital to this sign, and not necessarily for hedonistic reasons. Pleasing our five senses is one way to develop them further.
(Children deprived of adequate sensory stimulation during their for-
mative years often become emotionally flat in their response to life
later as adults—very little fills them with delight.) By responding to its
own sensual urges, Taurus learns much about the ways of the natural
world. Touching, tasting, hearing, smelling, and seeing all help Taurus
appreciate life on its most basic, physical level. Unfazed by abstract,
theoretical concepts that seem far removed from real-world experience, Taurus instead wants to appease its earthy appetites regarding
the more concrete, here-and-now matters of the flesh.

It's in Taurus that we first sense life's softer, maternal side—after
all, this is the sign of "Mother Nature"—although mothering themes
are more explicitly realized in emotional terms in the water sign Cancer. Along with Taurus' protective instinct to insulate comes a gentle,
peace-loving disposition. This sign has a natural talent for being sooth-

ing. It knows how to relax and unwind bodily tension. It can settle down into more tranquil states of consciousness that also have a calming effect on its surroundings. Energy becomes evenly modulated and applied in steady, reliable ways.

All this sounds lovely—and what a contrast we have here from all that driving fire of ever-active Aries—yet this observably serene quality may mask a less desirable passivity that keeps Taurus from ever growing beyond its accustomed ways of being. Its senses can become dulled from too much monotony in life or perhaps gorged from too much self-pleasuring. Taurean types can feel too much at ease with their lack of dynamic expression in life, as their low levels of activity become bad habits not easily broken. It may all look "laid back" and restful on the surface, but the Bull may sadly be vegetating. Such folks need to be careful not to resist making even moderates changes that could bring in needed fresh energy (there's a good reason why Gemini must follow Taurus—Gemini will never let us get stuck in mindless, habitual routine).

Brick by Brick

A Taurean emphasis in our chart means we are to learn to ground ourselves in worldly reality. No other sign accepts the terms of the material realm as well as Taurus, an archetype very much in harmony with Nature. Fixity symbolizes energy that is purposefully applied in steadfast ways. Earth is the element that deals with practical, tangible issues in the here and now. Patient planning plays a role in our successful outcomes in life. Nothing unfolds quickly here. It will take a while to capitalize on our raw talents and to amass resources, but the Taurus factor within us can wait for the tide to roll in—which is something that Aries has great difficulty doing.

This earth sign's main objective is to stabilize conditions by carefully building, brick by brick, frameworks of security that will prove everlasting (although life upsets even the best-laid plans, now and then). Taurus is very hard-working, not just pleasure-seeking. It has the stamina and focus needed to plod on. It refuses to quit any project until all is satisfactorily completed. Once committed—this is a sign that isn't afraid to make commitments—the Bull will carefully organize itself so that any job at hand is effectively accomplished. Methodical in its approach, it can be a little too fixated on its habitual ways of getting things done (it rarely deviates). Taurus is not looking for a wide range of options; that's more an interest of the next sign, Gemini.

Because it knows it will finish whatever it starts—unlike Aries, who tends to abort labor-intensive missions without warning—Taurus hates to be pressured or forced to do things it really doesn't enjoy. That's basically because Taurus knows it will nonetheless put much energy into even those projects it finds unappealing, *if* they must be done. It doesn't jump ship. The Bull also won't do a careless, messy job (its aesthetic sensibilities are strong), nor will it leave things half-finished. Because of this, Taurus is wary of obligating itself to others. Deep down inside, it feels everyone should strive to be as self-sufficient as it is. Taurus tries to take care of its own tangible needs in the material world and therefore leans on no one.

Of Great Value

One critical theme of Taurus in modern astrology is the cultivation of self-value. The more Taurus is emphasized in our chart, the more pressing it becomes for us to establish a personal sense of worth—something that is not to come from external sources, such as wealth or a prestigious title. Nobody can give us what we'll need to best appreciate ourselves. It has to come from deeper, subjective parts of ourselves for it to feel truly valuable to us. Of course, once we've established such inner worth, nobody can take it away—we've earned it.

It makes sense that self-worth is something of which Taurus needs to have total control, like everything else in its life. Both Aries and Taurus instinctively push off the influence of others, seeing it as interfering with their desire to be self-directed. Taurus is more independent in action than traditional astrology has led us to believe, although sometimes bullheadedness may result. Still, a strong sense of self-appreciation helps this sign feel good about itself and its actions taken in life.

With our self-value intact, we can emanate warm feelings of inner satisfaction. Perhaps no other sign experiences self-contentment as deeply as does Taurus, especially when everything on a material level is working out—in other words, when the Bull is feeling rewarded for living in sync with the rhythms of the natural world. Working hard and then being paid well is evidence for Taurus that it is, indeed, in harmony with life. Staying healthy is another indicator.

The Bull's needs are fairly simple, although perhaps unsophisticated. It doesn't require a life of glamour and glitz (or not even great wealth) to be at peace with itself. Its appetites are certainly not insatiable nor a source of internal suffering (that's more the case of its opposite sign, Scorpio). Taurus is blessed in knowing exactly what it wants and needs to be happy. Not many other signs—especially those always hungering for newer and more challenging experiences—can claim that, since they are rarely satisfied with the status quo of their lives. But not Taurus, a sign that does take the time to both plant *and* smell the roses.

Basic Instinct

By the time we get to Pisces—the zodiac's crowning achievement—we are ready to understand how "Believing is seeing." But Taurus is sure it's the other way around. It likes to think that it always has its feet on the ground and its eyes wide open when it comes to reality, and thus it cannot be easily fooled by illusion. Like Aries, Taurus typically accepts or rejects things at face value. It's not inclined to dig deeper in search of hidden complexities in life—either something exists or it doesn't.

Taurus is especially sold on its initial perceptions of people and situations, those based mainly on surface evidence or the "facts" as they appear (rather than on intuitive hunches, since at this early stage of the zodiac, real intuition technically doesn't exist, although powerful, animal instinct does). Once it has an image of something or someone firmly planted in its head, the Bull won't easily be swayed by any updated evidence to the contrary. It sticks to its first impressions.

Maybe Taurus is not intuitive in a Sagittarian, Aquarian, or even Piscean sense (three signs that can tune in to high-frequency energies at times). Yet because the zodiac's first two signs are more primal in their instincts, Taurus can tell on a gut level when something just doesn't feel right. This is certainly not an analytical assessment or one that can even be articulated, but it's probably an awareness—shared throughout the animal kingdom—that keeps the Bull ever on the alert regarding potential threat or danger.

Taurus gets a "vibe" about something, won't take time to evaluate it, doesn't even need to know why that "something" feels off-the-beam, but protectively reacts based on what it feels, nonetheless. This can lead to instant likes and dislikes of people and things. It may not seem rational at times, but Taurus will hold tight to its initial feelings. The Bull usually benefits by heeding such strong but seemingly irrational instincts, yet at times it will need to learn the wisdom of altering such first impressions, as new "facts" present themselves in ways that would be foolish to doubt. Even then, something inside the Bull doesn't want to adjust, at least not until enough time has passed.

Territorial Critter

Taurus is keenly aware of what it owns, since the things it possesses become strong emotional attachments—even those that have great resale value. The Bull knows its territory well because it carefully creates clear boundary lines. (Heck, it's the sign that first thought of putting up fences to keep intruders out.) Taurus knows exactly what belongs to it—even where it belongs—and is never vague or confused in this regard. It'll stake a firm claim to something and will not easily part with it.

Never give heavily Taurean folks nice gifts and then dare to take them back—that will just bring out the hidden "raging bull" factor in this sign. Taurus takes its possessions seriously and expects to keep all the goodies that life gives it. One big problem here occurs when that "possession" happens to be a person, not an object. However, corrective help arrives six signs later, as Libra works to adjust that kind of faulty attitude. (Taurus quincunxes Libra, meaning that these two Venus signs have notably different perspectives on relationships. See chapter 8.)

Because Taurus feels so attached to things, and because its nature is to preserve whatever is of true worth, we can expect this sign to take good care of what it owns. It will naturally feel responsible for maintaining its goods as a way to extend their worth (although it's not as fastidious about this as Virgo, the efficiency expert of the zodiac). A problem Taurus will someday face is that it cannot hold on to its cherished goods forever—things eventually break or permanently malfunction. The Bull hates when that happens, but at least it's not as emotionally wrapped up in its attachments as is the water sign Cancer (the one more apt to be devastated by untimely losses). Taurus is practical enough to realize that newer (and maybe improved) material items can replace that old junk it loves to hang on to so much, but can learn to live without if it must. Its inclination, though, is to attempt to keep it all.

It also may help if Taurus understands, metaphysically, that it really owns nothing—it's just borrowing the physical items it needs at different stages of its growth. The underlying energy patterns that give form to these items need to be recycled at a later date—a job for the mighty Cosmos to perform (who assigns this task to Pisces). Of course, there is little about the Bull's psychology that will openly accept this notion, since personal ownership seems so real and permanent to Taurus. Still, evolutionary forces will teach Taurean types—the hard way—that it's good to enjoy what we have for now, but then freely let it go when the time is right. After all, there will always be new possessions to take the place of those with which the Bull now happily surrounds itself.

Venus without Frills

The planet associated with Taurus is Venus, although some astrologers think this earth sign is too unrefined and unyielding to be represented by a planet long known for its gracefulness and its spirit of cooperation. Venus will bend over backwards to accommodate others—sometimes for opportunistic reasons—yet stubborn Taurus often won't give an inch in relationships if it feels pressured or used. Venus often vacillates—basically because it looks for solutions that will please everyone—while Taurus has little trouble deciding that it will at least please itself (of course, neither Venus nor Taurus like to be rushed).

The Bull may have too many utilitarian traits to suit those who view Venus as cultured, aesthetic, and desirous of living a life of refinement (which can get expensive in ways that turn off frugal Taurus).

Obviously it's the earthy—rather than airy—side of Venus that better fits less-polished Taurus. This is an aspect of Venus less susceptible to socially programmed behavior. Venus loves the pleasures of the flesh, and Taurus has strong, sensual appetites. Both planet and sign seek bodily gratification. Taurus certainly is calm and gentle enough to evoke the relaxing, soothing qualities of Venus. Each loves giving and receiving affection, as physical closeness is important to both. Earthy Venus also is as beauty-conscious regarding form as is Taurus, but it appreciates a less idealized kind of beauty, one that's more rooted in the natural world. Both Taurus and Venus seek harmony in their environment and are usually even-tempered.

Closing Comments

Taurus enables us to contain our vital energies to the point whereby an inner strength develops, which is something that can help us feel securely anchored in the world. We'll learn that some measure of self-discipline and emotional control helps this process along. We Taurean types are here to both consolidate our assets and make practical use of them in the mundane world. We're here to recognize and develop any raw talents and find practical ways to materially sustain ourselves through them. It is typically where our Taurus is in our chart that we'll want to be remunerated on some level for our efforts (not just monetarily). We can't keep on giving and giving without getting back something solid in return. We need to feel rewarded for our efforts.

Although seeking gratification, Taurus can also delay satisfaction until the timing is just right—this is something impatient Aries will not readily do. There will be other human experiences, represented by the upcoming signs, whose success will require the Taurean ability to wait, be still, and remain calm before taking action (especially since life gets more complex the further into the zodiac process we get). Taurus has a gift for turning energy into viable forms. Still, we will need to recognize when forms have outgrown their purpose and are no longer useful, since that's when they start to become burdensome.

FAMOUS TAURUS TYPES (natal Taurus placements listed)

Andre Agassi, tennis pro: Sun, Mercury, Saturn

Glenda Jackson, actress: Sun, Venus, Mars, Uranus

Liberace, pianist: Sun, Mercury, Mars

Katharine Hepburn, actress: Sun, Moon, Mercury

Karl Marx, philosopher: Sun, Moon, Venus, North Node

Jessica Lange, actress: Sun, Mercury, Venus

GEMINI
Two for the Road

Glyph: ♊

Symbol: The Twins

Mode: Mutable

Element: Air

Planet: Mercury/☿

House: Third

Motto: "I'm Interested, So Let's Talk about It Some More!"

Wind Gusts

It seems every time the Cosmos comes up with a fresh concept—embodied in a new sign—it can't help but boast, "Now there's a needed improvement!" Life has biologically functioned for eons on this planet by running exclusively on raw Arien and Taurean energies—two signs blessed with savvy, animal instinct. Their main concern is self-preservation: the survival of the fittest—or even of the fattest, where food-worshipping Taurus is concerned. As long as their basic "me-first" needs are provided, these two signs are satisfied. The ever-wise Cosmos knew that the zodiac still had to include more options to make human life interesting. Hmmm . . . how about some brainpower? While all signs offer us their native intelligence, what Gemini brings to our awareness is quite unlike what has already manifested thus far.

Staying alive involves a lot of little things we must learn to do repeatedly. Instinct is great, but it can't really plan ahead or analyze past mistakes. Simple, organized thought becomes the key to accomplishing life's necessary tasks on a day-to-day basis. Observing cause and effect in action—and taking mental notes—helps us learn how to understand things better. It seems that in the astrological scheme of life, Gemini *has* to follow Taurus if we are really to get anywhere, mentally and even literally, since Gemini was born knowing how to drive and use a cell phone at the same time!

Apparently, Gemini—showing an interest in being the zodiac's third sign—knew just how to catch the Cosmos' attention and sell itself by coming up with its own little gimmick: talking Twins—two minds for the price of one. What a novel idea—mental energy split in half, with both sides equally stimulated but headed off in opposite directions. This clever trick was something that neither the Ram nor the Bull could ever concoct, yet coming up with smart ideas is essentially what the Twins are all about. Being both mutable and airy, Gemini is the most adaptable sign of the zodiac. It's like the wind in a playful mood, with air currents changing their speed and direction at whim, from a light, refreshing breeze to a sudden, mischievous gust—the kind that loves to scatter important papers all over the place.

Off Course

Mutable air has little of the driving force of Aries or the physical stamina of Taurus. Lacking the impetus and focus needed to push hard in any one direction, Gemini follows no fixed course of action. Aries energy first propels itself outward into life and assumes it will never stop rushing forward. But then Taurus slows things down—it even stalls for time—so that it can gather its power and build on itself further, until its foundation is rock solid. And now, in airy Gemini, mutable energy decides to take a few experimental detours by sharply moving sideways, or diagonally, or in any direction that allows it to view life from different angles.

By the time Gemini came onboard, Taurus was already becoming oppressively predictable, since it's a sign that rarely ventures off the beaten path (the Bull is seldom ready to face life's unknowns). Entrenched habits, although they keep things safe and stable up to a point, eventually become tedious due to a lack of variety—same old stuff! Yet life thrives on unpredictable change, even if in only minor, transitory ways. Gemini's function is to keep energy in a variable state so that nothing grows stale or limits us. The Twins open the door to refreshing activities that deviate from Nature's established patterns, and this helps quicken evolutionary progress.

Besides moving sideways—an urge perhaps triggered by momentary distraction—Gemini is also eager to rise into the air and spread itself over an expanse of local space. This sign will elevate beyond ground level in order to scan a wider territory, one that offers a broader view of things. Gemini is less locked in by the dense boundaries that Taurus has structured, plus it can rekindle the flames of adventure in Aries (Gemini and Aries feed each other in complementary ways). Taurus may feel unsettled with the Twins' apparent lack of direction, purpose, and staying power, but Aries senses that Gemini helps life branch out further in ways that require fiery vitality. Gemini is willing to explore the unfamiliar, something that excites Aries. However, to offset Arien intensity and Taurean heaviness, Gemini introduces a little needed lightness (we can thank Gemini for allowing biscuits in the oven to rise and turn out fluffy). Perhaps the secret to staying light and airy is to get things off our chest by talking about our problems, Gemini-style, before stress gets the best of us.

Can We Talk?

Gemini probably started out talking to itself first in order to practice the art of gab (besides, it couldn't get much out of tight-lipped Taurus—and Aries, naturally, was more action than talk). The Twins soon realized that mere chatter transforms into real communication once a creative exchange of ideas is involved. Gemini is thus astrology's first sign of social dialogue. Here is symbolized a lively interplay between minds that seldom see issues the same way. Gemini enjoys the contrasts and contradictions in life that provide us with different ways to look at anything. The first two signs of the zodiac see this new air trend as somewhat of a complication, since single-mindedness is now no longer the only way to tackle life. Gemini refuses to overconcentrate its energies on any one interest, especially since casually spreading itself all over the place is much more satisfying.

However, at this early stage of communication—which is not as refined a process as it will later become—Gemini is more prone to talk *at* someone than talk *with* someone in any kind of a balanced, give-and-take manner. The first three signs of the zodiac are still very "me-oriented" in attitude. Gemini, obviously enthused and charmed by its clever ideas, tends to talk too much and unwittingly hog the conversation, although entertainingly so. It's a sign that needs to realize how much can be learned about life and people by simply being a good listener (something Libra is skillful at doing). Otherwise, Gemini becomes much too stimulated by the workings of its own active mind, and when all this is verbally expressed, everyone else eventually becomes bored—not so much with the information the Twins deliver as with their style of delivery: nonstop yak yak yak! Who can get a word in edgewise when Gemini's mind and mouth are going strong?

It would seem that Gemini, delightful as it can be, expresses the mentality we see in toddlers who are learning language and using words for the first time. They babble on as they dart quickly from topic to topic, while never pausing to reflect. Of typical interest to a young mind is "why" things are the way they are. Gemini is highly curious about the "whys" behind the "whats" in life. It quickly notes how one thing in life can link to another (Gemini can happily spend a lifetime observing or even creating such connections). Its flexible mind is one reason why Gemini stays so youthful. Wherever Gemini is found in our chart, we need to keep from becoming too serious and too adultlike in our disposition, if doing so means becoming stiff and unimaginative in our ways. Instead we need to loosen up, remain pliable, and forever be willing to try out new ideas, even if for only short periods of time.

Skimming the Surface

So far, the first three signs of the zodiac seem comfortable living in the here-and-now world. They deal consciously in the present and operate directly on the surface of life. Although Gemini introduces a multilevel way of viewing reality, none of these signs are truly complex in their makeup (things get much more complicated for the zodiac's last six signs). Gemini's orientation is a major departure from the strongly instinctual ways in which Aries and Taurus relate to the physical world. It's also the first sign whose image involves human figures, instead of an animal. The Twins could have aptly been portrayed as two chattering magpies, but the human element depicted here instead is intentional and significant. It suggests that Gemini symbolizes a handful of character traits that are only to be found in people, even though all of life's creatures have ways of communicating with one another. One of those human traits is humor, especially of the witty variety. Gemini likes poking fun at everyday life.

Also, what Gemini adds to the communication process—something more than just grunts, whistles, and body signals—is the ability to reason. Logic and reason have long been deemed as distinctly human skills, although some researchers suspect that certain mammals (such as apes, elephants, and even dolphins) may share these abilities, at least on a simple level. Reason, alone, ideally helps us learn from our mistakes, as we evaluate our actions and seek explanations for what went wrong. Our thinking may not really be all that logical, but we do want to know how to avoid repeating unpleasant experiences.

Gemini teaches us to study the outcome of actions taken by others and then learn from their situations. Gemini is smart enough to realize that it doesn't have to undergo such events firsthand to benefit from any knowledge gained. Let old Aries and Taurus play the role of crash-test dummies—learning things the hard way—while the Twins, cool and collected, stand back and take mental notes on what results.

Always a quick study, Gemini is ever-curious about how things work, as long as the details involved are not too grueling. Air usually prefers to have a clear, concise, overall picture of something rather than to be given precise, blow-by-blow descriptions (which are of more interest to Virgo). "Keep all answers short and to the point, since we have a lot to cover," advises Gemini, even though this sign does have its own windy days when it becomes much too talkative. For the most part, Gemini doesn't care to get too deeply into anything. That's not its function. It can be brilliant, yet seldom is it profound. Comfortable with trivial but fascinating information, Gemini doesn't delve into life's more imponderable issues. Obviously, its intellect can be glib, and quite bright, but a tad superficial. Intellectual breadth is not its forte. However, the Twins enjoy every minute of observing their world from less intense mental perspectives.

What Am I Feeling?

"If you have to ask, something's wrong!" says Cancer, the water sign that follows Gemini. Water signs typically know what they're feeling, even when they are not in touch with why they are in the mood they're in. When Gemini, like all air signs, feels a little emotion stirring within, it quickly wants to take its feelings apart to figure them out—anything to avoid merely *feeling* feelings on their own terms. The world of emotions, being a nonverbal one, baffles and even frustrates Gemini. Of course, the Twins, as excellent mimics, can display any human response after first studying it in others, but can they genuinely feel emotion on a gut level? Probably not.

The Twins are not cold-hearted—and thank goodness they're not cynical—but they are on the cool-headed side. Technically, the depths of emotional reality have yet to be acknowledged at this early stage in the zodiac process (although the next sign, Cancer, remedies that). Gemini types need to talk out their feelings, hopefully to those who may have insights to offer (air signs like to share their experiences). But generally speaking, this particular mutable air sign is uncomfortable with the delicate and often sticky realm of personal feelings. One big reason for this is that emotionality can seem so irrational and perplexing. Gemini wants to back off and turn its attention to matters of a more coherent, cerebral nature.

As previously stated, we shouldn't fault a sign for not doing another sign's job. Gemini is not temperamentally suited to be ultrasensitive, in touchy-feely ways, to the inner workings of others. It doesn't enjoy reading into things that deeply, but would rather have human motivations plainly spelled out. It seeks unambiguous, clear-cut definitions. Yet, the world of emotionality is loaded with hard-to-define, inarticulate moments. How does an air sign handle all this murky, internal business? It detaches and creates a little distance. Emotionality can prove suffocating, and air needs space to breathe.

Mind Journeys

Gemini is associated with our mind's ability to comprehend all sorts of topics that educate us about the world in concrete ways. The information Gemini seeks musn't be too abstract or esoteric. While Gemini doesn't always demand useful knowledge—since it enjoys studying oddball stuff as well—it does appreciate anything that it can quickly apply to its life. It likes to have the answers it needs at its fingertips, and thus gets antsy when such information takes too long to obtain (that's when Gemini changes its mind and decides it really doesn't need such information after all, since its intellectual interest has suddenly shifted).

What mutable air offers us is the concept that our minds are free to roam wherever they wish, and free to make sharp detours and head elsewhere if we don't like where our journey is leading us. The mind's unrestricted development is what Gemini supports. The Twins do not wish to be protected from exposure to any subject, just because others find such topics to be controversial or provocative. Like Aquarius, this sign detests censorship.

Frankly, because the Cosmos hasn't even dreamed up high-minded Sagittarius yet, Gemini doesn't reject anything based on moral beliefs—it's an amoral sign. It has a budding awareness of life's duality (which includes the concepts of good and bad, right and wrong), but Gemini certainly isn't in an all-knowing intellectual position to offer final answer on such matters. It even enjoys the juxtaposition of shadow and light—it's too much of the same that Gemini finds boring.

In this regard, Gemini makes a wonderful "devil's advocate," intellectually swapping sides just to keep things lively in discussions and to exercise more than one viewpoint on any subject. It's all done for fun and perhaps as a way to show off the Twins' mental agility. Mutable air can convincingly adopt any position for a short period of time. It has the ability to sell anything to anybody by knowing how to use the right words to get its message across. Folks with a strong Gemini emphasis in their chart need to be active in verbally expressive fields where they can use their powers of persuasion. They like to turn people on to new information—Gemini's a natural teacher—but then they wish to move on to explore new subjects themselves.

Travel Bug

What Gemini can't afford to do too much is to stay still. It must be mobile on some level. While its active mind is always clicking away, never at rest, Gemini also likes to make the rounds to check out the comings and goings of its local environment. Of course, it's not limited to its neighborhood, and can happily explore all unfamiliar territory. The need to move about and enjoy a change of scenery is essential to Gemini's well-being. For this reason, it's called the butterfly of the zodiac. Butterflies are carried aloft by the shifting winds, as they flit from flower to flower. Even when it finds a delectable blossom, a butterfly won't linger—suddenly, it's ready to take off again. Gemini is very much like that, too—it's here, there, and everywhere!

What travel affords Gemini is proof that human diversity exists in a world of different strokes for different folks. The farther away from home the Twins venture, the more that things look different (this fact is empathetically realized by the time we get to the sign of culture shock, Sagittarius). Urbanites who spend a recreational weekend in the mountains get to briefly experience the Gemini joy of travel. Rural folk who spend a few days shopping in "the big city" are also relishing Geminian energy. The key here is that our environmental changes are to be brief, stimulating, yet not that demanding of an adjustment. Gemini's energy is carefree and ephemeral, not intense and dramatically life-altering.

Mercury Behind the Wheel

Mercury is the planet associated with Gemini. Both planet and sign share many qualities in common, including mental agility, quick reactions, restlessness, curiosity, and a need to be in constant motion.

However, Gemini may be too flighty at times for Mercury, a planet more capable of studying—not just scanning—whatever it finds interesting. If given the right subject matter, Mercury is less apt to be bored. But Gemini, by temperament, does not want to stay glued to anything for too long, since this sign is more easily distracted than Mercury. However, both are skilled at verbal self-expression.

Gemini is probably also more flexible than is Mercury, a planet that has a harder time adapting to change when in fixed signs, or focusing its mental powers when in mutable signs. Unless Mercury in one's chart is in Gemini, the natal sign it's in greatly influences its expression. Should this be an earth sign, Mercury won't seem very much like Gemini at all, since the mind described here is careful, methodical, plodding, and less likely to invite change just for the sake of change. Still, the airy side of Mercury and mutable Gemini are well matched.

Closing Comments

Wherever Gemini is in our chart describes where life doesn't want us to feel stuck in a rut. We shouldn't seek total, everlasting security, since Gemini is instead teaching us to adapt to frequent change. We thus need to not hold on to experiences here too tightly. Gemini helps us step back and look at our situational conditions dispassionately, without emotional biases clouding our judgment. The Twins want us to take advantage of opportunities in the present, and to perhaps also get a little excited about the potential of the near future, but never to wallow in the past and rehash the painful steps that led us to any failures—unless we can truly learn something from the experience, and then move on. Let's not get too emotionally worked up while we're doing this. Be enthused about life, but let the head rule the heart in most matters. Meanwhile, if we have something brilliant to offer the world, by all means, let's find out how best to get our ideas out there. Gemini doesn't enjoy being silent for too long. We'll need to find a variety of smart ways to express our thoughts.

FAMOUS GEMINI TYPES (natal Gemini placements listed)

Isadora Duncan, dancer: Sun, Mercury, Venus

Bob Dylan, musician: Sun, Mercury, Venus

Marilyn Monroe, actress: Sun, Mercury

John Denver, musician: Mars, Saturn, Uranus, Ascendant

Steffi Graf, tennis pro: Sun, Moon, Mercury

Patti Labelle, musician: Sun, Saturn, Uranus

CANCER
Call Me Mama

Glyph: ♋

Symbol: The Crab

Mode: Cardinal

Element: Water

Planet: The Moon/☽

House: Fourth

Motto: "It Hurts to Say Goodbye—So Don't Go!"

Ties that Bind

The Gemini stage of life teaches us to not get bogged down in anything for too long. Let's not try to nail material security to the floor in hopes of enjoying it forever, since we live in an ever-unfolding Universe where change is the only constant—and change permits our awareness to expand, even while it periodically shakes us up. It's best that most life conditions do not remain permanent, forever unaltered by time. Gemini enables small, continuous changes to occur—life's little detours—that eventually result in large-scale, evolutionary innovation. The time comes when DNA finally gets restless from boredom and decides it's just not going to faithfully reproduce what has predictably come before. Gemini instead encourages life to juggle something different, for once, something that puts the cosmic zing back into living.

Now, if the zodiac process were to abruptly quit after this stimulating Gemini phase—something the Twins even once suggested the Cosmos consider, since they couldn't imagine what else could be missing from life that would be more exciting than an active intellect—we could still survive, but without any real sense of deep connection to one another. The human race certainly wouldn't seem like one big family, and nobody would feel in their gut that they just *had* to go home for the holidays! Even worse, television soap operas would fail miserably due to a lack of sympathy in viewers (or maybe because the characters and subplots would seem on the dry side).

Friendly Gemini helps us interact with one another, although not intimately so. Smiles, handshakes, and even witty remarks abound as everyone's talking up a storm. Still, this air sign prefers to keep a healthy emotional distance from others while it shares its mental energies (of course, Aries and Taurus are not convinced they even *want* to share what they've got with smiley, chatty strangers). Unknowingly, Gemini sets the stage for Cancer to emerge, by demonstrating how much fun it can be to intermingle with those we find interesting—the concept of informal sociability is thus born in Gemini.

Legend has it that Gemini even first taught Cancer how to hug and kiss. This was something the Twins spontaneously came up with as an odd but amusing way to pass the time: Let's hug and kiss, kiss and hug—ha ha! (The Twins love to dream up "silly" stuff to do when bored.) But then when they each tried out this routine on the lonely-looking Crab, who was tightly clutching strands of seaweed on some desolate beach, suddenly the poor crustacean burst into tears! At first, the Twins nervously thought the Crab had sprung a fatal leak—what else could it be? But teary-eyed Cancer later confessed that it cried because it had never been shown such kindness and concern, leaving the clueless Twins to scratch their heads in puzzlement. "Whatever!" they muttered, as they realized their little "hug and kiss" game was now getting too intense for them to enjoy—it's no longer a kick for Gemini if someone becomes too choked up to talk!

Anyway, what Gemini innocently started turned out to be one of the most powerful forces ever to take hold of humankind—raw, gut emotion. This was something beyond mere instinct, as all three previous signs concluded. It was even a little scary to behold, yet it was also a very compelling power that seemingly came from deep within. Cancer is the zodiac's first sign to put us in contact with our soul, which is a different entity than the fiery spark of spirit that Aries embodies.

While Cancer may not be all too clear about what "soul" means, it nonetheless senses that something potent inside itself moves it to want to protect all in life that is vulnerable and in need of shelter. This is also the first zodiac sign to poignantly feel both love and sadness for the human condition. Cancer worries that the often indifferent outer world, which cannot easily fulfill our inner needs, doesn't even have a notion of who we really are deep down inside—plus, we're typically reluctant to show others our most private selves.

Moody Waters

It didn't take much time before Gemini observed touchy Cancer in action and sighed, "Life's gonna get messy—no more fun. Now we have to watch what we say!" Cancer is a cardinal-water sign, and so it is very active and sometimes pushy in the expression of its feelings. Just as Aries cannot easily turn off its dynamic, fiery energy and rest for a while, Cancer has difficulty shutting off its emotional faucet. The water always seems to be running forcefully. This is a highly reactive sign driven by its surging feelings. The Crab was born with an amazing sensitivity that allows it to absorb what's going on inside others—stuff that's kept hidden from surface exposure (all three waters signs have this ability).

Cancer, always alert to the unspoken feelings of others, somehow thinks it is obligated to offer its sympathetic support to those in need. People's neediness arouses its maternal instincts. The problem is that it doesn't always wait to be asked to help. It feels compelled to mother people—once it picks up on their distress signals—and thus intrudes on their emotional space. Yet the Crab sees itself more as being timid and shy—though this is not so (remember, cardinal energy can be quite assertive).

Actually, how Cancer responds to its surroundings is as varied as the phases of the Moon, its planetary agent. Some see such changeability of temperament as moodiness. The Crab would instead say

that it's only reflecting the invisible currents in the psychological atmosphere of the moment. Cancer readily sponges in the environment,
and often without using protective filters. It's typically only after the
Crab has taken in too much "negative" emotional discharge from others that it learns to build a hard shell to ward off further invasion.

Along with such armor comes a crusty, crabby disposition that be-
lies Cancer's softer, gentler side. It's a needed defense that keeps antagonistic forces at bay—learn to snap at others and be grouchy, and then
maybe the world might back off and leave you alone! Note how real,
live crabs on the beach have that one huge claw they love to thrust out
at whoever approaches uninvited—as if to menacingly say, "Ya see
this?" Apparently, Cancer can already start off with a bad attitude
when feeling insecure about dealing with new situations.

Sometimes Cancer's mood swings are how it deals best with its
own feelings in flux—its internal high and low tides. Nonetheless, the
Crab is the first sign to introduce a warmer kind of caring that goes
deeper than the comforting energy of Taurus. Cancer envelops others
in its protective aura as it tends to their needs, although it attaches itself in ways that feel suffocating at times. It's not objective enough to
realize how oppressive this can be to others—it doesn't pull back and
create healthy, needed space.

The mothering side of Cancer also unconsciously refuses to let
anyone it loves grow up and exercise independence. Should they no
longer need to be parented, loved ones might one day say goodbye
and walk away, leaving Cancer all alone—and being left alone is one
of the Crab's worst nightmares. The fear of abandonment wouldn't be
such a big theme for Cancer if it weren't able to connect with others as
deeply as it does.

Perfect Nest

There's little that is shallow about the Crab, although Cancer can be
preoccupied with the immediate, surface reactions of others. It's too
quick to let itself be triggered emotionally by someone else's body language, especially facial expressions—for example, you can drive Cancer crazy by remaining stone-faced and still; this sign thrives on active

human response. Laugh, cry, get angry—but show something! The Crab will try to look for even the subtlest of signals in people that spell rejection. All this can often make Cancer a temperamental sign to live with—unless you enjoy walking on eggshells, never knowing if your actions will be taken the wrong way.

Actually, Cancer has more emotion invested in creating and sustaining a calm and peaceful home, one where all relationships reflect deep and sensitive bonding. It's not a sign that handles fights and disagreements well, which is one reason why it receives a frictional square—often an aspect of blockage or resistance—from both combative Aries and potentially argumentative Libra (read more about signs that square one another in chapter 5).

Domestic tranquility is vital to Cancer, since—besides shelter—a home is a place where our ability to nurture ourselves and others can be developed. Being able to nourish all living things is important to this tender-hearted sign. Water is an element that wants close, human contact. Yet Cancer can be aggressively attentive (cardinal) in how it cares for whatever it looks after. Such smothering attention could be misread as being bossy and controlling. It's just that Cancer holds on too tightly due to its insecurities and its fear of loss. However, the Crab would instead say that it's only protectively watching out for the welfare of others, and won't hesitate to do what has to be done to ensure their ultimate safety.

The "perfect" home environment allows Cancer to retreat happily into its private world (although cardinality can also motivate the Crab to secure a safe haven in society as well, most so regarding one's professional interests—Cancer's opposite sign, Capricorn, plays a role in this, as we shall see later). As the Crab has a need to feel "at home" wherever it goes, it thus tries to quickly establish an emotional rapport to help it adjust to new places and new faces. This doesn't mean Cancer is overtly friendly, but it does look for signs of receptivity in others. (When traveling to parts unknown, some Cancer types may even bring their family photos to share with others they meet, just to feel more comfortable when far away from their home turf!)

Acting Loony

Cancer is the first zodiac sign to activate imagination, although Gemini also pokes around here a bit. The Crab is able to draw upon unconscious resources that tie into humankind's collective memory bank. This is one reason why Cancer is so rooted in the past and is comfortable with the strangely familiar world of times long ago—it's a sentimentalist at heart, one who loves to reminisce about bygone days. Of course, selective memory is at work here, since many not-so-pleasant things make up part of everyone's past. Cancerian nostalgia chooses to dwell only on the good stuff that happened.

However, the unconscious can also be home to the dark side of being human. Cancer can suffer from a brooding, negative kind of imagination that allows fears to loom too largely. It is the fraidy cat of the zodiac, the one who's scared that it may bump into its own (Jungian) shadow. No wonder Aries has trouble respecting ol' chicken-hearted Cancer, at times, since this water sign worries too much about the threat of a potentially shaky future. The Crab can sometimes be so spineless.

Worse than that, an emotionally out-of-sorts Cancer tends toward pessimism, a general distrust that the world's basically a selfish and cold-hearted place. Cancer types who get like this are too easily discouraged when their lives takes a bad turn and things seems to fall apart. Suddenly, everyone else is at fault and Cancer is the poor victim—that's how the Crab sees it. Nobody seems to be able to help Cancerians gain the perspective needed to feel better, once they start to go loony like this. They willfully insist (cardinal) on creating much overblown, psychological drama for both themselves and whomever else they latch on to in desperation. No other sign can drown in its own sorrow as intently as Cancer.

When Dark Skies Clear

After the rainstorms of life have passed and the sun comes out again—assuming Cancer has survived the ordeal—the Crab is ready to build a new foundation for itself as it once more starts to feel that it belongs to the world and is needed by many. Luckily for Cancer, life is full of people who are hungry for this sign's soothing, reassuring energies. Still, the Crab has a memory like a steel trap, and can never innocently begin its life anew if past disturbances have not been completely forgotten or forgiven. It will feel like it still has to watch out about getting hurt again by similar life disappointments. Cancer will thus remain guarded and self-protective (and can physically gain a lot of insulating weight—a buffer zone of fat and retained water—as a result).

A formerly wounded Crab tends to build protective walls around its heart, and only traffics in safe relationships that cannot cause much emotional damage. These relationships may not be intimately fulfilling, but they do allow Cancer to give deeply of itself in ways that can feel healing to all parties involved (as in doing volunteer work for the disabled). If Cancer has suffered repeated abuse and rejection, it can seem coldly remote for a while (as it is symbolized by a cold-blooded creature, it can expertly turn off its feelings). Yet, its truer nature is to be warm and maternally giving, for that's when it comes alive most and feels empowered.

Steamed Crab?

Cancer can be cranky, irritable, and capable of lashing out when it's feeling stressed. It may seem odd to discover that it's also terrified of losing its temper, for fear that doing so will permanently drive loved ones away forever (it anticipates isolation as its punishment for venting conflicted feelings). Ironically, when Cancer does get angry, it can go ballistic with a totally blind, irrational rage that can be destructive in its full release. This overwrought display of fury happens because the Crab lets its emotional tension build and build to levels of dangerous, pressure-cooker intensity, and then it blows like Mount Etna! The floodgates open wide, as a river of boiling emotion rushes forth. The Crab is then aflame with heated grievances and burning resentments (as there is something inherently fiery in cardinal energy).

Scorpio has this problem as well—the slow, steamy build-up routine—except Scorpio is usually quite aware that it's becoming enraged long before it finally erupts (it can even plot the grand finale). However, when ticked off, Cancer may instead plunge vigorously into heavy-duty housework (or child rearing) and doesn't suspect it has a growing problem with stored-up hostility that needs serious attention.

When its attack of fury is over, the Crab is as stunned as anyone that it let itself get so emotionally out of control. That's when it wants to go back into its shell and pretend it was all a bad dream. What it really needs to do is to own up to its anger, vow not to turn its fired-up feelings back on itself—only to suffer bodily inflammations or infections—and instead face the fact that being human sometimes means confronting those who make us see red. We have to blow off a little steam when pushed to our limit, just to let folks know how we really feel.

Baby Me

Cancer assumes it's born to play the "mamma" role in life, but the fact is that it also never got over its quality time in the womb. Thus, the baby within the Crab's psyche is still alive and kicking, almost as if it has prenatal memories of it all. As a result, some Cancer types feel they need a lot of pampering and tender loving care from those they get close to. There may be a degree of emotional immaturity to deal with when the Crab doesn't get fed what it wants from others. Nevertheless, Cancer enjoys affection (let's play "huggy-kissy") and can especially lavish sweetness on young animals and infants (the Crab is aroused by anything that seems helpless and dependent). Still, when the needy baby is actually a Cancerian adult who's way past the midlife crisis years, perhaps therapy is in order—primal scream, anyone?

Moon Glow

The "planet" associated with Cancer is the Moon (yes, astrologers know it's really a satellite of Earth, but from a horoscopic point of view, it operates like any other planetary archetype). Changeable Cancer sounds much like this planet, famous for its monthly mood swings. Both planet and sign instinctively adapt to their surroundings, although insecure Cancer can put up much resistance at times if changes are imposed too quickly or insensitively. The Moon's power stems from its willingness to protect life by making things feel safe—it thus appears less fearful of uncertainties than does more anxious Cancer. Astrologers don't usually view the Moon as hiding behind a hard shell for the same defensive reasons that Cancer does. Still, it is a planet that likes to feel insulated from life's harsher elements. Insulation also provides a nurturing kind of warmth when the emotional climate starts to turn chilly. Under certain conditions, an upset Crab can even turn stone cold and emotionally distant (as can all water signs).

Both planet and sign are responsive to human need. They offer tender care that helps people feel nourished. Both dwell in the world of our subconscious, where a gut-reactive awareness is at work, picking up on subtle information from life. The Moon is just as much a sponge as Cancer, absorbing everything that touches its emotions. Yet letting things go or even releasing the past can be tricky for both of them. A maternal streak is another strongly shared trait, although the Moon is more apt to mother others, while Cancer can revert to the helpless baby who always hungers for love and attention. Cardinality drives Cancer to reach out assertively for a support system, while the Moon is more likely to go within to create a secure, inner home base.

Closing Comments

Wherever Cancer is in our chart points to a need to let our emotions flow more openly into the world. Let's be upfront with our feelings and deal with them honestly, in the moment. Water signs—when repressed for long periods—suffer psychological damage, as their injured parts sink deeper within to slowly fester and become toxic. The results can be very harmful to our physical and psychological health. Cancer, a surprisingly headstrong and willful water sign, thus pays a heavy price when it refuses to exert needed emotional self-discipline. The Crab often gets itself much too worked up over various things— both big and small—that are beyond its power to control. Where our natal Cancer parts are found, we need to stop busting a gut over what we cannot change or fix in others. On the plus side, don't forget that we can be very imaginative in using our Cancerian energies, and should nurture all creative outlets that grab us emotionally. Maybe then we can mother budding talents that we *can* control, with the blessing of the Cosmos.

FAMOUS CANCER TYPES (natal Cancer placements listed)

Tom Hanks, actor: Sun, Moon, Mercury

Meryl Streep, actress: Sun, Venus, Uranus

Robin Williams, actor-comedian: Sun, Mars, Uranus

Phyllis Diller, comedian: Sun, Moon, Mercury, Pluto

John Glenn, astronaut-politician: Sun, Mercury, Mars

Elisabeth Kübler-Ross, psychiatrist: Sun, Moon, Pluto, North Node

LEO
Hear Me Roar

Glyph: ♌
Symbol: The Lion
Mode: Fixed
Element: Fire
Planet: The Sun/☉
House: Fifth
Motto: "The Show Must Go On—Starring Me!"

Getting Noticed

The Cancer stage of being—with its emotional highs and lows—can be a bit of a drain, since it's exhausting to cater endlessly to people's internal needs (no wonder the Twins warned us that things could "get messy" once the Crab became a bona fide member of the zodiac). Still, with Cancer comes a deeper awareness that we're all brimming with potent energies that enable us to impact one another strongly. We can arouse hidden feelings in people that simultaneously help us get in touch with our own feelings. It thus benefits us to reach out sensitively to others in an attempt to understand their personal lives, since their needs often mirror our own.

Water ignores—even as it penetrates—the barriers deliberately created by the ego to keep everyone apart and unattached (such ego defenses probably took effect way back when Aries was the only game in town). Cancer's watery phase gives us a sense that—although we may appear to be separate individuals contained in our own private space—we're invisibly connected to one another by way of an inner realm we all share. There is unseen, psychic networking going on at all times, as we all swim in the same river of energies. This development of a special sensitivity to one another prepares us for Leo's energy, since the Lion also wants to have a huge impact on others.

This fire sign realizes that it can energize people by its dramatic self-presentation, and so it learns to become larger than life in its actions and behavior. Leo is a strong individualist who has a clear sense of self, thanks to the ego-building experiences provided by all four previous signs. This second fire sign also belongs to the fixed mode, suggesting that its flame is steadier and more enduring than what cardinal Aries produces. The Ram constantly fights the containment of its blazing fire, while the Lion learns to make such containment work to its advantage. It offers the world a more reliable, radiant heat that warms the heart while it also lights up the stage. It's an appealing, charismatic form of fire that knows how to get noticed. Leo is determined to receive positive attention and desired rewards from an adoring world.

Full Esteem Ahead

The Lion doesn't spend a lot of time wondering what's wrong with itself, since it's rarely plagued by insecurity or self-doubt. Fire doesn't hold itself back from taking gambles in life, even when success cannot be guaranteed. Leo's confidence in its abilities is usually strong. Such self-assurance leads to inner pride and dignity. We expect this much from fixed fire. Yet Leo's feelings of self-honor aren't necessarily earned solely through its achievements. The Lion feels it was born to shine brightly and enjoy elevated status. It behaves as if first-class treatment from the Cosmos is its birthright.

This is the first sign to think about its place in society, although not with any real perspective regarding collective needs. Leo still knows that, at this stage, "It's all about me!" The ego is very comfortably entrenched in this sign and sees no reason to release its tight grip anytime soon. However, fire represents the start of a new elemental cycle, and in this case, we are learning to feel more important to those around us who need our dynamic involvement, even if in a leadership capacity. Therefore, Leo cannot live and breathe only for itself. It must pour its vitality into others—preferably an audience of loyal fans—to help them enliven their own creative energies and thereby raise their spirits. Leo, a wonderful morale booster, is a shining example of one who has great faith in itself and has the will to accomplish much.

What's happening at the Leo stage of life is that we are starting to become more socialized.[1] At this blossoming stage of social interplay, the Lion soon discovers that it needs applause, but also that its goals will never be satisfactorily met if it only basks in its self-created glory. To get a lot out of life, you've got to give a lot in return. With Leo, we learn to be generous with others regarding our spirited energy and positive outlook on life. If we can pump people up and make them feel good, they'll turn around and inflate us with joy, as well. Leo will consciously play this game because it wants to feel big and important.

Snob Story

Feeling like a divine child favored by the gods, Leo can sometimes act like an obnoxious Very Important Person by displaying a few unappealing traits, those stereotypically associated with privileged rank. Arrogance is something this fire sign can indulge in, often without realizing it (as Leo won't give itself bad reviews). Acting smug can get the Lion in trouble with others, who would then love to dethrone this sign for being so full of itself—so full of it, period!

A stumbling block to true social integration for Leo is its tendency to feel superior to others. However, even though Napoleon and Mussolini were such Leos, most Sun-in-Leo people shouldn't automatically be seen in this light, since they have a host of other modifying astrological factors to offset the Lion's potential to be a royal snob. Still, any egotistical sense of self-adulation for feeling special—in a kingly or queenly manner—comes from the essence of Leo. Thank goodness nobody is a pure, living, overblown archetype of just any one sign.

Being a member of the same element, Aries feeds the fires of self-interest in Leo. The Ram's way of looking at life appeals to Leo, who'll easily draw on Arien energy when needed. Gemini stimulates Leo to be creatively versatile while it encourages playfulness. It's Taurus that poses a problem for the Lion, since these signs square each other (they share the same mode, but involve less compatible elements).

Part 2 will analyze all sign-to-sign relationships in detail, but here it's safe to say that the quiet humility that comes naturally to less-assuming Taurus is not what Leo thinks will help it make its big splash on Broadway! Maybe a slice of humble pie should be on its plate, yet the Lion would rather roar its way to stardom, just to let everyone know its alive and here to dazzle the world. Don't tell Leo to tone it down just so others can feel better about themselves and less intimidated by such an overwhelmingly fiery force. The Lion is only interested in showing off its greatness in an honest, self-validating manner. "Don't dare try to put out my eternal flame, especially when the cameras are rolling!" says Leo.

Forever Young

Leo may seem bold yet brassy to those who find such self-glorifying behavior annoying. Yet others are enchanted by the Lion's ability to enjoy itself wholeheartedly in all its endeavors. This sign has managed to shake off the sometimes crippling fears and inhibitions that make the Cancerian phase of life so painful at times. Maybe it pays not to worry too much about what others think. Let's just let our hair down and have fun adding color to our personality. Leo wants to engage in a robust life adventure without anyone or anything dampening its spirits. Thanks to the fire its exudes, it does a good job retaining its youthful vitality—if it could, fixed fire would love to burn brightly forever. The Lion has a knack for staying young and vibrant, partly because it doesn't allow itself to grow up completely and burden itself with somber outlooks. Capricorn-style "maturity" may curtail Leo's joy of living a more carefree life of self-admiration.

Another youth-ensuring trait is Leo's willingness to face its future with optimism and enthusiasm. Although not deeply philosophical, Leo is an idealist who believes that we can make fabulous things happen by allowing a sense of high self-regard to empower us. The Lion refuses to think little of itself. It is sure that the Cosmos didn't put us all on Earth just to suffer, by being denied our rightful opportunity to show off our special talents to the world. Like the spirit of youth itself, Leo willingly takes chances to get what is wants. It's blessed with courage and a unfaltering belief that the Universe will grant it its heartfelt desires.

At times impetuous and too strong-willed, the Lion is willing to risk all on a golden dream, never foreseeing anything less than a glorious outcome. When failure or loss occurs instead, Leo is crushed and heartbroken (it may roar with hurt and anger when it doesn't win the top prize it seeks). Still—unlike emotionally immature youth—the Lion is big-hearted and self-assured enough to know that its competitors also need to feel like winners, now and then, and thus Leo—after swallowing a little pride—can allow others their moment of glory, as long as the Lion doesn't remain out of the spotlight for too long.

Love from the Heart

For Leo, the principle of love—which first began to develop in family-oriented Cancer—is not universal in scope, as this sign's steady ego focus is on personal fulfillment (the world is to revolve around the Lion, who acts as if it's in charge at the center of it all). Yet to evolve, we do need to learn about the importance of self-love and of being genuinely good to ourselves, without guilt or apology. Leo symbolizes the stage at which we're allowed to have a romance with the creatively dynamic person we're becoming (this is a sign that naturally excels in high-visibility, self-promotional activity). In doing so, Leo is listening to its heart when it says, "Give all that you've got if you truly want to be loved." Thus, don't hold back on being your radiant self if you wish to be filled with the admiration of others. Love what you do, do it with all your heart, and others will then love and honor you, too. Hmmm ... it might just work!

Leo could actually be saying to its throngs of autograph-seeking well-wishers, "I love you for helping me love myself so well." It's not too clear if the Lion sees others as anything but extensions of itself, sort of like props on a stage. Leo may think, "Everyone's supposed to make me look good, and those who do so best get my love the most." Love does come straight from the heart for Leo, a brightly burning kind of love full of idealism and high expectation.

Romance is also a very special state of being for the Lion, whose generous emotional nature easily reveals itself whenever it has fallen passionately for someone. Leo is a sign that puts all its eggs in one basket and won't play it safe when it comes to such heartfelt matters (even if it is actually romancing a breakthrough scientific theory that it has lovingly crafted). No matter who or what is the recipient of its attention, Leo will give what it loves its *all*, while in a high-level state of vitality. It won't even consider remaining involved if it can't keep up this degree of elation, plus love also has to be deemed to be a fun and even recreational experience. Expect Leo to be thoroughly committed to having a grand time when in love with a person, a project, a concept, an ideal, or a dream it knows will someday come true.

Ego in Bloom

A simple, uncomplicated display of ego-in-the-making is found in Aries, who's often unaware of how totally self-absorbed in action it is. The development of our individuality depends a lot on the strength of our ego. Yes, it's true that "ego" has been seen as the eternal enemy of that blissful state of Oneness mystics talk about (although they then turn around and assure us that the ego's power is illusionary). Aries has highly personal needs that override anyone else's—and it's too bad if that appears selfish to others. Aries is driven to survive at all costs, and thus the Ram will first look out for its own well-being in most situations. However, without Aries, we wouldn't have the fire in our belly—and that innocent sense of daring—that spurs us to go out into the world to test our strengths and conquer our fears. And so, for Aries, ego arousal is a good and most necessary thing.

By the time we get to Leo—where fire begins to operate in a new mode (now from cardinal to fixed)—the ego has polished itself up a bit and has developed more backbone. It becomes a consolidated force. Theoretically, Leo's ego power is at its peak performance level in terms of how it serves our individual needs. This is a turning-point stage in the zodiac process, when both our will and ego are sufficiently developed so that we can now cope with the demands of the bigger world around us. Leo provides us with a solid inner center, a core sense of self that helps us become involved in increasingly collective circumstances, without losing our hard-earned identity. This is important, since once we get to Sagittarius and beyond, ego identity is challenged by more transpersonal ways of being. But for now, Leo needs to enjoy its self-importance and its ability to unabashedly celebrate its attention-grabbing individuality.

Wanna Be a Rock-and-Roll Star?

Although fame and acclaim becomes a serious quest for Capricorn (another go-getter member of the cardinal group), Leo is the first sign to care about being favorably known and even idolized by others. It seems that once we feel secure at the root of our being (Cancer at its best), then we're ready to fearlessly express ourselves to an audience larger than just our family. The Lion anticipates, long before it has ignited its ambitious nature, that someday it will make a name for itself in society. It observes people who have already made it big in the world, and it knows that it, too, wants to enjoy an equally distinguished life.

Fixed signs have the ability to work long and hard to reach well-defined goals. They are determined to unfold their lives in a purposeful manner—they just don't "go with the flow" and wait to see what happens. They instead attempt to take charge of their destinies, being the control freaks that they are. Supremely confident Leo may make all this look like loads of fun, but the Lion is nonetheless serious about taking on prestigious roles of great social influence. Leo aims to be a superstar, the one to outshine all the rest.

The entertainment field magnetically draws Leo in, as this fire sign was born to please a crowd. Hollywood is crawling with Leo types.

Many of them, sadly, may never receive the accolades (or even the Oscars) they deserve, because of the highly competitive nature of the film industry (a business where luck and connections play an even greater role than talent alone). Even in jobs that aren't meant to entertain us, Leo still exhibits a flair for being expressive and even a bit showy (think of Leo types happily working at Tiffany's or selling Jaguars in fancy showrooms—the Lion has a thing for luxury items).

If Leo doesn't ever see itself on the silver screen—even though acting comes easily to this sign (Dustin Hoffman and Peter O'Toole are both gifted Leos)—another venue can be the Broadway stage or the equally theatrical music industry. Wowing and dazzling a mesmerized crowd of fans—and Leo knows how to work a room—is a dream come true for the Lion. Being a natural exhibitionist, Leo will do whatever it takes to pour its creative vitality out into the world to solicit an enthused, high-energy response. Due to its childlike awe of itself, Leo loves to make a big fuss when it announces, "Hey world, look at this fabulous thing I've just done!"

Here Comes the Sun

The Sun is the "planet" that astrology associates with Leo (of course, the Sun is really a gloriously shining star of primary importance to life, much like the Lion fancies itself to be). Both planet and sign have something to say about our ego, our willpower, our need for recognition, and our ability to be vibrantly self-expressive. Both are astrological symbols of warmth, of heat that steadily comes from our creative fires within. It's hard not to notice the Sun once it has risen; the same goes for the Lion, once it has climbed the ladder of success. The astrological Sun also relates to our integrity and our pride. Leo is a sign very much concerned with self-dignity and getting respect from others.

Actually, the Sun is less able than Leo to laugh at itself and to become a little kid having fun. Strongly solar types are not necessarily gleeful, and they view themselves more as authority figures in commanding positions. Being held in high esteem is important to the Sun (as it is for Leo), and thus it's a planet that will seldom clown around in the amusing manner that Leo does to steal the show (think of comical Leos like Lucille Ball and Steve Martin).

The Sun is the "big cheese" of the solar system, with all the planets—like loyal subjects—revolving around this central power source. Leo shares a bit of this attitude, as well. Knowing how to flatter in order to get its way, the Lion is probably better at engaging the cooperation of people than is the Sun, who'd probably rather take control of matters without assistance. Leo wants to direct a big project, but it must have a loyal crew to help out with all the necessary details that ensure a successful performance. This fire sign thus learns how to keep everyone happy within their roles. Yet spreading cheer and goodwill doesn't sound as much like the Sun, a planet that's even more self-directed in action than Leo. Still, this planet underscores much of what vitality-exuding Leo is all about.

Closing Comments

Wherever Leo is in our chart points to where we need to give in to our urge to show off our talents. We are to let others see how individualized we are. Leo is a sign that remains true to itself and won't accept being told by society what to become just to blend in better. Leo doesn't want to get lost in a crowd. ("Always wear something in bright red," advises Leo, "that way they can't miss you.") The fixity in Leo helps us recognize our limits regarding how much of ourselves we dare release to the world before we begin to overwhelm others (such unchecked fiery output can consume too much energy from others, who eventually suffer exhaustion from overexposure to Leo energy— it's like getting a nasty sunburn).

Actually, we can start off feeling self-conscious wherever our Leo energy is in our chart. Our goal, as we mature, is to develop enough self-esteem to shine in front of others without being the first ones to give ourselves bad reviews. Without sufficient self-confidence, Leo's energy quickly burns out. What we present here must come from our heart as an expression of our essence. Honoring its individuality is as important to Leo as remaining playful in life (together, these will help all Leo types stay young at heart).

FAMOUS LEO TYPES (natal Leo placements listed)

Stanley Kubrick, film director: Sun, Venus, Neptune

Martha Stewart, entrepreneur: Sun, Pluto, Midheaven

Andy Warhol, artist: Sun, Mercury, Venus, Neptune

Kathleen Battle, coloratura soprano: Sun, Mercury, Saturn, Pluto

Bill Clinton, U.S. president: Sun, Mercury, Saturn, Pluto

Kathie Lee Gifford, television personality: Sun, Mercury, Mars, Pluto

VIRGO
Tidying Up

Glyph: ♍

Symbol: The Virgin

Mode: Mutable

Element: Earth

Planet: Mercury/☿

House: Sixth

Motto: "I'm Making a List—and Checking It Twice."

Let's Get to Work

The Leo stage of life—as joy-filled and exuberant as it is—is much like an overexcited child tearing open birthday presents, left and right. While the kid is totally self-absorbed in such excitement, all kinds of things are carelessly strewn about, instantly making a big mess. In fact, most festive parties are like this—especially those superblasts that Leo likes to throw—but ultimately, there's always lots of clutter and trash left for somebody to clean up afterwards. The Lion is not particularly interested in doing what's required to restore such order. The zodiac's specialist for that job is conscientious Virgo. This is astrology's second earth sign, meaning that it symbolizes another aspect of practicality— the mutable side of earth.

Mutable energy allows earth a degree of needed flexibility, something that astro-archaeologists still have not been unable to uncover in fixed Taurus—keep on digging, folks! Think of mutable earth as potter's clay—it's solid and somewhat heavy, but malleable. Clay can be fashioned into a variety of shapes, even molded into many useful items (such as that big water jug Aquarius holds). Virgo is a sign that adapts to all pressing needs imposed by necessity in the here and now. Life demands constant (but usually minor) adjustments that require level-headed thinking and common sense. The Virgin (whom I prefer to call the Analyzer) supplies all this in carefully measured amounts. It's a sign that tackles life as if it's a high-maintenance job requiring much patience and thoughtful planning.

Putting life in working order is a must for Virgo—literally astrology's neatest sign. The Analyzer wants to get busy finding smart ways to spot and solve problems before disaster strikes. Why wait for a situation to spin hopelessly out of control? This sign tries to analyze the little things that can go wrong, sometimes long before an actual crisis looms.

Details Galore

Leo sees its life as a bold but beautiful adventure in self-discovery. However, the Cosmos has enough wisdom and foresight to know that we need to figure out how to best turn our Leo-inspired creativity into productive assets that will enable society to reach more organized levels of complexity. This involves paying keen attention to the details of daily living.

To do this, Virgo draws partly from Taurus' patient, steady focus (the Bull's message to Virgo is that a job well done takes time—slow down and do things right). Virgo rejects the speedier, less-prudent methods favored by Aries and Gemini (although as least the Ram will start a project, while the Twins can be aggravatingly noncommittal—sometimes all talk, plenty of options, but no action taken). Virgo shares Cancer's urge to nourish life in a careful, caring manner, but the Crab's emotionality gets in the way of making hard, pragmatic decisions. The Analyzer finds its own sedate demeanor to be the most appropriate and effective, since it realizes that even Leo's extravagant behavior is ill-suited for the humble and not-so-glamorous tasks that mundane life demands (like taking out the garbage every day). Leo doesn't like to do "dirty" jobs or ordinary tasks that demand keeping a low profile.

One way to know the details of something firsthand is to first take it apart. Doing this is of great interest to Virgo—a sign that loves to break things down into their many interrelated pieces, and then study each piece intently while learning how that particular part is meant to function. What practical purpose does it serve, and how is it constructed to do its job? Next, Virgo studies how these pieces interact, as it puts everything together again in hopes of restoring things to their original wholeness.

The Analyzer also learns what can happen when certain parts don't interact well, and how this itself can lead to an overall malfunction. Virgo is the first sign to note the consequences of such disharmony—a theme carried over into Libra and even Scorpio, the next two signs to follow.

If details are that important to the understanding of how life works, Virgo's mind needs to be forever organized to enable it to weed out nonessentials. Gemini finds all information temporarily stimulating, but regarding such data, Virgo devises a rating system in terms of relevancy. The Analyzer's challenge is learning not to become overwhelmed by trivial issues—don't sweat the small stuff, in other words. Fussing with less-important details can sidetrack our main objectives and fail to help us build the momentum needed to successfully move forward in life. We find ourselves stuck in irrelevant matters that nonetheless eat up our time and energy. Virgo's job is to discriminate, to know what needs attention versus what can be put aside for the moment. Thus, being selective about what to focus its mind on is one of Virgo's big lessons.

Like a Virgin?

This is a good time to clear up one misconception: the Virgin is not necessarily virginal in a sexual sense, even though many Virgo types are cautious about the private, physical intimacies they share with others. Thus, Virgo may refrain from giving in to its sexual impulses in pressured, careless situations. Yet being earthy, Virgo knows there's a proper time and place for sexual activity. This sign is not the big prude that it has been made out to be—especially by those friskier fire signs, whose policy is to have sex whenever the impulse hits. Virgo also knows that unplanned sex can later prove to be problematic (unwanted pregnancy, venereal disease, even wrinkled clothes on the floor). "Why let momentary passion invite such complications into one's life?" Virgo reasons. So the Analyzer lets its head rule its hormones in this regard.

Actually, the label of "virgin" more accurately implies that this sign strives to remain true to its essence—keeping its honor and virtue intact—rather than to allow itself to be penetrated and thus corrupted by the baser energies of others. Heck, Virgo doesn't even feel easy being around people who cough or sneeze, as if to say, "Don't pollute me!" Inner purity is valued (think of it as the desirable purity of "extra virgin" olive oil).

Virgo—following a phase of theatrical Leo behavior—wants to retain its real, unembellished nature. Remaining self-possessed is one way to help make sure this sign will stay relatively uncontaminated. Virgo obviously pays attention to those times when publicity-crazy Leo sells parts of its soul to the world in return for temporary notoriety. The Analyzer doesn't want to be owned by anybody or anything, and has qualms about becoming too public a figure. In this sense, Virgo is less socially accessible than Leo. In fact, much of what the Analyzer is all about seems to be an adverse reaction to Leo's self-promotional excesses. Of course, maybe it's better to say that Virgo seeks to refine (even redefine) much of how the Lion expresses its ego.

At Your Service

Before Virgo came onboard to give the zodiac a close-up inspection and a ratings review, all five previous signs (Aries to Leo) felt they had unconditional freedom to express themselves in any way they wanted to—warts and all. Now, their shared lament is, "Why did the Cosmos feel it had to hire this 'outside' efficiency expert to do a productivity check on us?" The Analyzer obviously makes these signs nervous, even more so by always carrying along its own regulatory manual of techniques guaranteed to improve day-to-day functioning.

This sign thinks it knows better ways to do just about anything, methods that it's willing to teach others to perfect. It plainly feels that the current state of affairs needs immediate correction before the zodiac can efficiently progress any further. After all, Virgo believes there are things that all the previous signs have mishandled in life, although the Analyzer believes that at least Gemini can be easily reeducated.

Surely, thinks Virgo, these five signs can try to do a better job at channeling their resources, and in more meaningful ways that not only benefit themselves, but even others in society. So why aren't they doing it? Virgo concludes that it's here to teach all the signs a few new tricks. The Analyzer just hates to see any constructive potential being wasted due to laziness, ignorance, or a lack of training or discipline. Virgo also brings to our attention a new life concept—the theme of willingly serving others. We can't all be selfishly preoccupied and still expect the bigger world to run like it should. There are many small jobs for all of us to do, and attitude adjustments will be required to perform those tasks uncomplainingly.

Cancer has a positive gut feeling about this new idea of "service," although it has never looked at the nurturance it instinctively gives to others in that light (to the Crab, it's more an act of love, not duty, of caring, not efficiency). Yet the other signs most likely think that Virgo has the makings of a pesky busybody, and they could be right! Virgo naturally plays the role of a censor attempting to suppress or eliminate what it finds to be objectionable (and the Analyzer—adopting a watchdog attitude—can readily object to many things in life). Its main motive, however, is to be helpful and useful.

Social service is somewhat an act of healing to the Analyzer, since it tries to do things that help make life better for all. This is a sign that thinks mainly of what will provide the best practical results for many people, not just for itself. In some ways, Virgo represents the zodiac at an interesting turning point in awareness—from a "me" to a "we" orientation. However, unlike Libra, Virgo doesn't feel equal to others, nor does it easily identify with its peers.

Fusspot

Virgo types claim never to be truly angry about anything—they're just peeved. A messy world can be so vexing to the Analyzer. Why do folks willingly do things the dumb or inconsiderate way? Why can't they take the time to do things right? (And who left this sticky gum wrapper on the floor?) What Virgo doesn't always recognize is how irritating its perfectionism can be to those who don't want to be flawless in all that they do. After all, making a mistake isn't the end of the world. ("Maybe," responds Virgo, "but making that same stupid mistake again and again is unpardonable.") Virgo believes in looking before leaping, and is amazed at those signs who either disagree or simply don't care. Don't we all want to know exactly what we're getting into before we're caught up in the thick of it? Isn't is always smarter to be fully prepared for what can go wrong before taking action?

Maybe so, but Virgo sometimes has a nagging way of getting its cautionary message across. People can feel scolded by the Analyzer, who always seems to have the right answers to everything, making this sign sound like a "know-it-all" (of course, Virgo may seem all-knowing because it studies life scrupulously). Virgo assumes that it's basically dealing with an incompetent world, and thus it doesn't trust that others necessarily know what they're talking about or doing.

The Analyzer will therefore test that assumption by asking a list of questions about the subject matter of concern. Virgo doesn't do well with vague or generalized responses, but perks up when someone has truly done their homework and it shows. This sign has a high respect for knowledgeable people. Still, others find Virgo's style of questioning to be annoying, as if they're undergoing an examination. The Analyzer seeks concise, precise answers, and doesn't tolerate rambling conversations or inarticulate responses.

Wherever we have Virgo in our chart is obviously where we want to deal in realism and clarity, yet we leave the door wide open for disappointment when we expect others to neatly package the information they give us. We feel almost compelled to establish order, but actually may unduly spend time attending to inconsequential matters that we find to be so irksome. Of course, the more imperfect something is, the more our Virgo energy gets a chance to analyze the situation and hopefully fix that which is in need of repair.

Staying Fit

Every fire sign is followed by an earth sign. Perhaps fire's expression reaches a point where it becomes overenergized in dangerous ways that run rampant. Fire then becomes a destructive force. Earth acts as a necessary protective container that harnesses fire's flames. If the zodiac were to quit after the Leo phase—"Great idea, let's end on a high note," says the Lion—we'd all become burnt out from the fiery kind of high-charged, nonstop activity that always leads to self-exhaustion. Virgo follows Leo to teach us instead to replenish our precious physical, emotional, and mental energies. We do this by getting proper rest (fire signs hate to do this), nutrition, sensible exercise, and quiet time alone.

Everything in Virgo's world is to be done in moderation. Life cannot afford to have its brightest lights always turned on at their highest wattage. Virgo thus designs a dimmer switch that will help tone things down (and save energy from being wasted). Virgo's job is to regulate the body's various systems so that none of them become prematurely worn out from unhealthy overstimulation. The earth element is always trying to teach us when to stop doing something that can otherwise harm us. Naturally, fire signs find earth signs to be classic party poopers, but earth signs demand that we shut down for a while to conserve our vitality.

Virgo types seem to know that staying fit is very important to enjoying a satisfying life. And considering the workload that the Analyzer normally handles, good health is imperative. Sharing Leo's independent spirit, Virgo doesn't relish the idea of being beholden to anyone just because it's in poor physical shape and can't take care of itself. After all, Virgo is supposed to be the expert healer who learns which medications can relieve symptoms and restore health. This sign won't allow itself or anyone else to remain sick.

Wherever our Virgo is found in our chart, we are concerned with keeping things working as well as they can, even if periodic tune-ups are required. This is seldom an area of neglect (and when it is, we suffer in obvious ways). Perhaps our Virgo qualities are also evident whenever we appear a bit too nervous about the well-being of something or someone. Still, here is where we believe in using preventative measures to avoid major hassles later on.

The Studious One

Whatever Virgo does for fun will seldom involve other people. This sign observed the frenzy of attention that poor Leo received from spending too much time in the limelight, and decided that this wasn't the route it was going to take. Being modest and humble has its advantages. Virgo discovers that it's okay to be alone. It insists it will have its privacy, and one way to ensure that is to act with discretion in all matters. Don't try to stand out among the crowd or demand to be the leader. Blend in and disappear at times, and then nobody bothers you. Virgo would rather spend quality time learning how to develop a variety of useful skills than be socially out and about.

This sign would also love to be able to fix anything on its own rather than depend on hired help. To do this, Virgo teaches itself whatever it needs to be self-sufficient (remember, it doesn't trust the so-called "expertise" of others, so a "do-it-yourself" approach is appealing). It will work hard to learn how to do things well, painstakingly so, if need be. Like Gemini, Virgo learns much by asking questions—the "right" questions, that is. Since it's not willing to be as verbal as the Twins, Virgo seeks out reading material that is lucid and educational, written by those blessed with common sense, as well. All in all, Virgo likes to keep its mind sharp and in active pursuit of timely, pertinent information. It likes to have concise facts at its fingertips.

Mercury the Organizer

Mercury is Virgo's traditional planet, but here Mercury behaves less restlessly than it does in Gemini. The influence of earth helps this planet stay more grounded and thus better able to concentrate for longer periods of time. This Mercury is discerning regarding the information it gathers (Gemini's airy Mercury, being less systematic, doesn't organize data as easily, and may get its "facts" from questionable sources). Flexibility is reduced when any planet is in an earth sign, but Virgo is nonetheless excellent at adapting to change in sensible ways (Gemini is more prone to scatter its mental energies when adjusting too impulsively and indiscriminately). The Virgo side of Mercury thinks things through logically, and then makes its final decision. It doesn't like dealing with too many options, which cannot be said of Gemini's Mercury.

Related to either sign, Mercury remains alert and observant of life's many pieces. Still, the earthier side of Mercury is better able to retain the most relevant information, while discarding the rest. It estimates what data will prove to be the most useful, and won't let its curiosity create needless intellectual detours. Virgo's Mercury stays better focused on its subject.

One problem here, however, is that this Mercury can become mired in too many details—a result of its ability to keenly observe the smaller things in life. Its gift of analysis makes it a sharpshooter when it comes to problem-solving (whereas Gemini's Mercury doesn't care to analyze anything too deeply, and only offers quickie solutions that may not get to the heart of the matter). Still, Virgo's Mercury has to be careful not to overresearch anything it finds interesting, as information overload results. When well managed, earthy Mercury knows the value of eliminating the superfluous and instead sticking to the most essential facts.

Closing Comments

Wherever Virgo is in our chart points to where we are learning to sharpen our critical faculties so that they can help us realistically assess existing conditions. Virgo is the enemy of faulty thinking and delusion. It favors down-to-earth solutions to life and shuns anything too abstract or impractical. The Analyzer is only interested in what is workable. It deals with what is evident, not speculative. At times, our

Virgo parts overreact negatively to disorder, fearing that we will be overwhelmed by chaos. This implies that Virgo is uneasy with the outpourings of our irrational unconscious, which can often seem uncontrollable.

Still, we can't expect to grow in self-awareness if we try to suppress this powerful, sometimes transcendent dimension of our inner world. Even emotionality can scare Virgo, probably because it's unpredictable (the unknown makes our Virgo side anxious) and also because it's harder to classify (plus emotions can makes relationships messy). We'll have to work harder with our Virgo energy to recognize that freely ventilating our feelings is as important to our health as making sure we get enough daily vitamins and minerals in our diet. It's also important to be less critical of ourselves and others whenever we have Virgo emphasized in our chart.

FAMOUS VIRGO TYPES (natal Virgo placements listed)

Sophia Loren, actress: Sun, Venus, Neptune

Sean Connery, actor: Sun, Moon, Mercury, Neptune

Chrissie Hynde, musician: Sun, Mercury, Venus

D. H. Lawrence, writer: Sun, Mercury, Jupiter

Lily Tomlin, comedian: Sun, Venus, Neptune

Leonard Bernstein, conductor: Sun, Mercury

Note

1. The Gemini stage of life gives the appearance of being socially oriented, since the Twins like to pick people's brains and find out everyone's opinions about everything. Gemini loves to feed its mind all sorts of interesting information. Still, it's main concern is intellectual self-stimulation—and if others learn something from Gemini's communication process, more power to them! Gemini is more self-involved with its knowledge-gathering than are the other air signs. By the time we get to Leo, we learn to risk creatively extending ourselves more publicly to others, who then either praise or criticize our "performance." Thus, other people's reactions matter a lot to how Leo sees itself, which creates an ego vulnerability that is less a problem for detached Gemini.

Chapter Four

From Libra to Pisces

LIVING IN TWO WORLDS

The zodiac's first six signs (Aries to Virgo) enable us to build a solid concept of personal self that will prove indispensable to our ability to function on an individual level. One of the most important results of this process is the development and fortification of our ego, the seat of our "I" consciousness primarily in charge of our will to be. Interestingly, two out of astrology's three fire signs are found in this first half of the zodiac, emphasizing the importance of exercising will and ego early on in our development.

If most of our planets fall in these first six signs, we'll need to focus more directly on ourselves, to discover our strengths and weaknesses, before we can effectively go out and challenge or change the world. We'll have very personal issues to address that override our engagement in broader, collective concerns. That doesn't mean we should avoid altruistic pursuits until we first know who we are inside. Real life doesn't work like that. Yet it does suggest that we'd best avoid trying to escape from who we are by instead pouring all our energies into impersonal, global issues. (Let's not devote a lifetime to saving the rain forests from destruction until we have first taken a cold, hard look at our own unresolved problems—the psychological jungle inside us.)

Avoiding our internal reality won't keep us in good shape, no matter how much we appear to contribute to society or how many honors we publicly receive for our unselfish, humanitarian efforts. The day will come when intense self-confrontation is forced on us, a time when our personal life may become quite disruptive and filled with inner turmoil. We then are made to turn our attention to our inner self in an attempt to sort out our interior conflicts. Remember, all this is necessary only if we've spent decades trying to run away from those private dimensions of our personality symbolized by the first six signs.

With undue attention paid to life matters related to the first six signs, we can become too entrenched in self-interest to the point that what happens to others on societal levels matters less to us. We're so wrapped up in our own little world that we truly don't care much about the pressing needs of humanity. We don't feel ourselves to be a part of life's bigger picture. To remedy this tendency, the zodiac continues its process with six new signs that can help us realize how much we need to willingly support society's larger frameworks. We can play more meaningful roles in the social evolution of the collective.

Society needs its reformers and social enlighteners to show the rest of us better ways to coexist in peace and understanding. These next signs put us in touch with expansive worldviews, where we shift attention from the exclusively personal to the impersonally social, and even to the transpersonally cosmic. Each of these signs also challenges the status quo of the first six signs. Suddenly, we feel we are trying to live in two worlds, and this requires balanced participation. How do we integrate our private needs with our public involvement? Life obviously gets more complex as we move from Libra to Pisces, yet the Cosmos knows full well that our spiritual self is up to the task of expanding our consciousness and allowing us to enjoy lives of fuller self-understanding.

Let's now examine the dynamics of these last six signs, keeping in mind that the following interpretations do not necessarily reflect the traits of people born with only their Sun in any of these signs. These descriptions are more apt to reflect the temperament of individuals who have several planets in a particular sign—especially the Sun, Moon, Mercury, Venus, or Mars.

LIBRA
Taking Turns

Glyph: ♎
Symbol: The Scales
Mode: Cardinal
Element: Air
Planet: Venus/♀
House: Seventh
Motto: "We're in This Together—So Let's Share!"

Two-Way Street

Virgo, perhaps without even knowing it, sets us up for a major reori-entation in consciousness—the Libra stage of life. The Analyzer knows it must tone down the egocentricity of Leo if people are ever going to be able to work together effectively (plus we can't have all leaders and no followers). In fact, Virgo seeks to refine or redefine the qualities of each sign that came before it—those first five that basically make up our individualized being. Analytical Virgo has determined that some signs have traits that are better applied to certain circum-stances, although not to others. The Analyzer realizes that there is an appropriate time and place to do just about anything. We simply need to develop greater discernment, based on a careful, practical study of the issues at hand, rather than relying on intuition or gut instinct. Virgo is a cool-headed sign not given over to impulse.

To be able to even get this far in its awareness of life suggests that Virgo can pull back and evaluate conditions more objectively than any other sign has done thus far. It's also learning how to deal with those pieces that don't fit so well together—a problem that definitely captures the Analyzer's attention—and thus, this sign is learning how to deal with dissimilarities (things that clash typically jar Virgoan sensibilities). It is a sign that seriously studies life's contrasting features. Libra, starting where Virgo leaves off, explores this theme even more intently: Can any two things (or people) that are unalike still join forces and work together cooperatively? Or are they forever incompatible?

At this Libra phase we learn to cope with factors that are different from one another—different, but perhaps complementary. Both Virgo and Libra seem to have a talent for arranging things to form more harmonious relationships. Virgo does it to satisfy a need for order and functional improvement, while Libra does it for more aesthetic reasons—harmony is a thing of beauty for Libra, not just a sensible way to make matters run smoothly. With this cardinal-air sign, we learn that there are others in life with whom we can form unions based on equality. This concept, of two or more people being on equal footing, had not been put forth before by the first six signs. It becomes a whole new way to view life, but not a simpler way. Two-way streets invite more traffic, and now we need to look both ways before crossing.

Alone No More

Libra (whom I'll call the Balancer rather than the Scales, which sounds too impersonal) seeks out others with whom it can mutually share life experience. This means more than just wanting company to avoid being alone (although that is partly the motive). Shared experience usually implies there'll be at least two different viewpoints to contend with, since people rarely see eye to eye in every matter (and Libra wouldn't enjoy that kind of union, anyway). But what if this entails two completely opposite opinions—like "Let's buy a used Chevy" versus "How about leasing a new Porsche?"

The Balancer ideally would love to reach an amiable agreement after hearing both sides and hammering out a solution—perhaps a compromise—that all parties involved can live with. Apparently, Libra is skilled in the art of negotiation. The airing out of contrasting ideas is important to the Libran growth process (all air signs must get their thoughts out in the open, and cardinality is certainly not going to sidetrack issues—it pushes them to the forefront). Libra clearly wants to get things off its chest, but it prefers venting to a committed, trustworthy partner rather than to a bathroom mirror, especially under harsh lighting!

Libra comes alive when it can interact with a partner, whether love or war is in the air. Yet achieving just the right balance of give and take is not easy, since Libra also wants to be the recipient of all that it happily gives to its partner. It's not a doormat and it won't allow itself to be used, although it takes a while to decide to put its foot down and say, "No more!" The key to its true inner contentment comes from Libra's ability to make a marriage within itself, to harmonize its inner parts in ways that lead to peace of mind—the kind that cannot come from any relationship, no matter how intimate a couple appears to be. If the Balancer is secretly *out* of balance with itself, its partnerships emphatically reflect this discord.

About Those Scales

It may seem strange that Libra's symbol—the Scales—is the zodiac's only inanimate object. Libra introduces the impersonal concept of justice, an ideal that reflects the nature of cause and effect on moral and legal levels—"As ye sow, so shall ye reap." Those unfettered actions taken by innocently self-seeking Aries are now shown to have social consequences at this Libran stage of unfoldment. What is clear here is that we can't just do whatever we please, at least not at the expense of others. Their needs are to be considered now as well. We're learning to see both sides of a relationship, not just our own.

The scales of justice don't allow for special treatment in this regard. All who break the rules of proper conduct—including fair play and common decency—will suffer penalties. What goes around, comes around—hmmm ... this sounds like karma in the making. Now we get to realize that inconsiderate action can have repercussions. Libra is a sign of potential backlash regarding selfish behavior on our part (and it only gets worse in Scorpio). At this point in the zodiac, we realize that willful misbehavior will be punished—if not immediately, then at some timely point in the future. The zodiac has now made us aware that a day of judgment awaits.

What this also suggests is that normally sweet, charming Libra—on some deeper level—is immune to dramatic emotional pleas, clever rationalizations, or brilliant intellectual arguments when it comes to a violation of rights. The Balancer has been wisely dubbed "the iron fist in the velvet glove," suggesting that it can be "one tough cookie" who's surprisingly unyielding, even under strained conditions. True justice is not vulnerable to human manipulation. No one is above the law. This explains why Libra, when oppressively backed up against the wall, would sooner die for its principles than compromise under tyrannical pressure and lose its integrity.

This doesn't mean, once we get past its pleasing, social veneer, that Libra is a cold-hearted sign. The Balancer tempers justice with mercy. Yet it wouldn't be able to do so if it didn't understand human nature very well. Remember, Libra can see and understand many sides of an issue. Nothing is to be judged in rigid, black-or-white terms. A careful weighing of diverse factors is required.

Virgo provides us with an opportunity to try to figure people out, especially regarding why they sometimes do the dumb things they do. Libra goes further by sharpening its understanding of human psychology (while in Scorpio, we finally plumb the darker depths of the psyche to determine what needs a total overhaul). Libran types appear to be more understanding of social misconduct because they can recognize conflicting motives in operation that result in such behavior. Yet if aggravated enough, the Balancer will chillingly say, "Let the ax fall so that justice is served!" Libra then becomes an agent of karmic retribution.

Have a Nice Day?

Libra is very sensitive to the current atmosphere it finds itself in, especially wherever people congregate. Observing society in action is stimulating for this sign. While Gemini is also a "people watcher," it's not always willing to participate in relationships as fully—mutable energy doesn't urge us to plunge into experience in the energetically assertive way that the cardinal mode does (the one mutable exception is Sagittarius, due to its irrepressibly fiery nature). Libran types must have harmonious social contact on a daily basis and are quite unnerved when something enters the picture to spoil an otherwise pleasant exchange between people. It's a sign that believes in the cultural importance of courteous interactions.

Since Libra is also learning about disharmony—the other side of the coin—invariably somebody comes on the scene to cause a little friction that tips the scales, typically leaving the Balancer feeling quite out of sorts. (Virgo isn't keen on such disruption either, but then, this realistic earth sign doesn't harbor idealistic expectations about other people's behavior—it anticipates that they'll eventually screw up.)

Libran types need to be careful not to express too much sweetness and light, since it becomes very hard for them to sincerely sustain such an aura of peace (and some who try to do so are probably suppressing a lot of darker elements that then get projected on to antagonistic people in their lives). Libra can forever play the "smiley-face" game and pretend everything is beautiful, as long as nobody makes any waves or touches a raw nerve.

The ability to handle the downside of being human is also important to the Balancer's inner growth. Libra even has to learn to be a fighter, and not just of social causes. It needs to learn how to defend itself against direct, personal attack. The key is to fight fairly and intelligently (something Aries doesn't always do). Doing battle can be upgraded to an art form, and indeed, military strategists benefit by having natal planets in Libra.

It's okay to be kind to others and to show consideration, but it's not so hot when Libra feels it's always the one bending over backwards to please those who'd never think of returning the favor. Why risk getting hurt again and again by expert abusers who only look at relationships one way—their way! The Balancer needs to lovingly permit itself to give back as good as it gets, and to hell with having a nice day!

(Scorpio decides it's going to give back even more than it gets to those who really have it coming, as we'll soon see.)

Looking Good

Virgo is a sign that praises the virtues of good grooming—staying clean and looking neat and presentable require a degree of organization. How freshly things smell seems to concern this earth sign (it knows that anything with a rotten odor is probably not in a healthy state). Libra carries this theme of being well-groomed to a more ideal level—looking marvelous is sometimes even more important than actually feeling great. Appearance means a lot to the Balancer, and maybe that's because when we look our best, we attract the "right" people. Yet when we look like a skid-row reject, we repel them.

Libra feels its life will run better if it takes time to doll up and package itself as a class act. It's a sign whose more cultivated, polished image becomes a magnet for social approval. It's easy to see the shortcomings of only being impressed by things having such surface appeal. Yet Libran types aren't bothered by this because they know they're not shallow at heart. They just prefer to look at things that are pretty. Why tolerate ugly conditions? Let beauty and grace come to the rescue of weary souls everywhere!

The Marrying Kind

Libra is more than just the sign of one-on-one relationships, which can also imply those of an adversarial nature. It's a symbol of committed unions, and thus it governs the traditional state of matrimony. In this area, the Balancer seems most comfortable with the conventional, legal set-up—polygamy will never do (nor will that "group" marriage experiment that nonconformist Aquarius sometimes talks about). Regardless of sexual orientation, Libran types want an intimate partnership that society will endorse, and the Balancer is not ashamed to admit that it *does* care what others think (it's like Capricorn in this regard).

However, Libra also knows how unfair society can be whenever it tries to regulate the private lives of its members (perhaps here, Libra is at odds with rule-enforcing Capricorn for this reason). Air believes in freedom of expression for all, and therefore adopts a "live-and-let-live" policy. But for itself, Libra would rather that its blessed union be bound by law, if possible—so where's the ring?

The ideal arrangement in Libra's mind would be for two people in love, who have much respect for each other, to join forces as self-determined individuals, each with a healthy ego intact. That's a situation the Balancer would value the most. Libra wants a marriage of equals (no previous sign thought of that possibility). This suggests that no one is to play a parental role, or one of a helpless child. Nor is one person to dictate the actions that another is permitted to take. Libra doesn't believe that partners own each other, just because of a marriage contract, and will balk at the thought of being unfairly controlled or dominated.

The problem is that Libran types can have stormy dialogues inside their heads that they dare not verbalize in any ongoing, difficult relationship, at least not for a while. Eventually the tables turn, as Libra unleashes pent-up anger and outrage over being poorly treated. A colder side emerges (those scales are made of hard metal) as the Balancer addresses all grievances it has suffered. It's nearly impossible to appeal to Libra's sweet side once this level of alienation has been reached. Yet until that day occurs, Libra is apt to forgive its loved one again and again (but it never forgets abuse, as it's always keeping score and will wait for the right time to issue an ultimatum, or else leave the union for good). Actually, at heart, Libra wishes that the honeymoon could go on and on . . . so why can't two people in love just try to get along?

Lazy Times?

It's hard to understand why Libra goes through its lazy spells, those usually reserved for that other Venus sign, Taurus. (Of course, the Bull can be one of the hardest-working archetypes the Cosmos ever created, and so it doesn't consider its rest periods to be akin to real laziness.) Libra is a cardinal sign, and cardinality wants to stay active and on the go. Being idle is not appealing to cardinal types. Also an air sign, Libra doesn't like to stay still for too long. It prefers to socially circulate. Maybe Libra isn't as lazy as it may appear at times (heck, Leo could win the top prize here, since it will put off doing dull, menial chores when there's fun to be had elsewhere).

Libra is a sign that deliberates before making a move. It may even prod others to initiate daring activity instead, so that it can sit back and evaluate the results by weighing the pros and cons. Yet for itself, the Balancer will refrain from doing things until everything feels right, and who knows how long that will take? When we perceive so many facets of any situation, we probably have a harder time recognizing the one thing that we must first do to initiate action. That infamous Libran indecisiveness takes hold, and we seem to be stalling for time. Then, when we don't take effective action when others think we should, we can appear to be lazy procrastinators.

Actually, if being a little lazy is pleasurable ("I've earned this goof-off time," says Libra), then it's not such a big deal. It's probably even what helps keep the Balancer so even-tempered. Libra cannot handle prolonged stress without having needed tension-releasing breaks to balance out its energies.

Venus in Style

Venus is Libra's publicity agent, always out to make this sign look good. Yet it's a Venus that—while seemingly sophisticated—can appear contrived at times. Taurus' Venus goes for a more natural look of beauty, something that's not so perfectly chiseled and flawless. But airy Venus needs a little makeup and a stylish wardrobe to create just the right allure. The props that ensure beautiful results are important. In some ways, this is a more seductive Venus that literally can charm the pants off of someone, even though Libra's Venus likes flirting more than it does having sweaty sex (leave all that erotic sensuality to Taurus' Venus). Airy Venus believes that good taste must be cultivated. This side of Venus is more conscious and thoughtful in its development, which fits air's mental nature well.

Whether associated with either Libra or Taurus, Venus is a lovely, comforting energy to wrap ourselves in. In Libra, it is simply more a relationship-oriented and less an object-related influence. That doesn't mean Libra won't enjoy being surrounded by works of art (it even can create such fine art); but people are its greater interest. Libra is more open to combat, when necessary, than is Venus (partly due to the pull of its opposite sign, feisty Aries). The Balancer can be argumentative and is stimulated by rousing debates, while Venus shies away from anything that comes close to saber-rattling or the need to raise one's voice in protest. Still, Libra loves to enjoy the good things in life and love, at least enough to satisfy Venus' refined tastes.

Closing Comments

Wherever Libra is in our chart describes where we don't wish to live for just ourselves. We'll want to include someone else in our personal activities, perhaps so that we can benefit from that person's feedback. The Balancer has a mind of its own, but it does like to field the responses of others before deciding whether it's on the right track. And if it's off the beam, Libra will modify its plans by incorporating the best advice it has received. It is a reasonable sign when it comes to accepting sound suggestions, but only from those it deems to be honest and level-headed. It's good that Libra can be as discerning as Virgo is, at least when making sure that emotions (often someone else's) don't get in the way of the mental clarity it seeks.

The more Libra is emphasized, natally, the more likeable we are—or want to be to others. We'll put our best foot forward to make a wonderful impression on those who, we hope, will then turn around and support our objectives. Sometimes that means we'll flatter people just to get them to join our side and share their talents, but perhaps we'll regret we did so later on, when some of these people prove to be more trouble to deal with than they're worth. Libra is a bit of a manipulator, an opportunist who justifies such behavior by thinking it's coordinating a project that hopefully will reward everyone who happily contributes their share. "You'll appreciate getting involved with me!" persuasive Libra says convincingly.

FAMOUS LIBRAN TYPES (natal Libra placements listed)

Matt Damon, actor: Sun, Mercury, Uranus

Gwyneth Paltrow, actress: Sun, Mercury, Uranus, Pluto

F. Scott Fitzgerald, writer: Sun, Mercury, Venus

Sigourney Weaver, actress: Sun, Mercury, Neptune

T. S. Eliot, writer: Sun, Mercury, Venus, Uranus, Ascendant

Christopher Reeve, actor: Sun, Mercury, Venus, Saturn, Neptune

SCORPIO

All or Nothing at All

Glyph: ♏

Symbol: The Scorpion

Mode: Fixed

Element: Water

Planet: Pluto/♇

House: Eighth

Motto: "Trust Me—You Don't Really Want to Know My Secrets!"

Heart of Mystery

Scorpio is a fixed-water sign with an overblown reputation for being difficult to relax around. At first glance, it's definitely not the chummy type. Describing Scorpio as intense, penetrating, brooding, and even volcanic makes this archetype sound like something that's best left alone to quietly lurk in dark, hard-to-reach hiding places. The warning is that unnecessarily agitating a Scorpion who's within deadly striking distance is a very bad idea. Well, there is some psychological truth to this, but Scorpio surely doesn't see itself as the terrifying Beast of the Abyss.

Being a water sign, the Scorpion views itself more as a sensitive soul who's commonly misunderstood by others. Why misunderstood? Because Scorpio doesn't want to reveal what it's feeling in any simple, forthright manner (leave that to Aries). If anything, it only seems to generate a smoldering intensity that warns others to back off—don't dare get too close . . . not yet, or maybe not ever. Scorpio keeps its power-packed emotions under lock and key, and that alone can make others feel suspicious and uneasy (things that Scorpio assumed it was the only one feeling). Just who is this masked stranger dressed all in gothic black? Scorpio's not too sure if it really wants you to know.

Fixed water sounds like a block of ice, which can be treacherous when in the form of an actual iceberg, whose imposing mass below the ocean is hard to detect at sea level (here, what you don't see can be more dangerous than what you do). Ice is also the hardest, least-fluid form of water there is. Likewise, Scorpio can be fixated in its focus and unable at times to just "go with the flow." It doesn't melt easily. Interestingly, this sign is a symbol of that which is either lava hot within us, or as frozen and impenetrable as the Arctic tundra in winter. No wonder Scorpio is considered a sign of behavioral extremes.

The Scorpion—probably as a reaction to Libra's friendly openness to people—realizes that, while intimacy can heal, it can hurt as well. Exposing our psychological innards to another involves utmost trust, and when we don't use good judgment regarding the partners we pick, such exposure of our private selves can result in criticism, ridicule, abandonment, or worse—betrayal. All water signs know they are quite emotionally vulnerable, but Scorpio, hating that fact, will do whatever it takes to hide such hypersensitivity. It makes the mistake of equating vulnerability with weakness (and, like Aries, Scorpio despises weaknesses detected in itself and in others).

So, while often appearing stone-faced and always in the iron grip of self-control, Scorpio becomes too emotionally cryptic and unapproachable for its own good. (Hey relax, Scorpio—not everyone's a trained bloodhound, just dying to sniff out your most guarded mysteries.) In spite of this standoffish behavior, Scorpio wonders why it so often deeply feels all alone, cut off from most social rituals it sees others happily engaging in all the time. (Gee, how come *they* aren't so paranoid about revealing themselves to others?)

Pride and Passion

All fixed signs seem to have an inborn sense of pride. Fiery Leo beams with obvious pride in its dynamic self-expression; less-showy Taurus is quietly proud of its ability to spot true value in the material world, and even without having to pay a premium price!—it's proud of its bargain-hunting skills; Aquarius is proud that it is brilliant and free-spirited enough to avoid following conventional wisdom or partaking of anything designed for mindless, mass consumption. But the source of Scorpio's hidden pride is harder to track.

The Scorpion can be riddled with deep insecurity, the kind that makes its world appear untrustworthy. Yet, just try to deliberately humiliate a Scorpio—and then watch for signs of barely contained rage. Scorpionic fury may be felt even before a sense of shame sets in, if it does at all. (Here's when Scorpio transforms into a screaming eagle, shrieking "How dare you?" at the poor soul who was stupid enough to outrage this emotionally volatile sign, especially if in public.)

The bottom line is that Scorpio will not allow itself to be teased, toyed with, scolded, or even threatened in demeaning ways. Leo may indulge in its dramatic, royal pout when its pride has been wounded, but Scorpio aims for the jugular, at least on those psychological levels where it knows it can do more permanent damage. It's not too sure if it can ever "play nice" again once violated by another. But what about passion? Any sign capable of rage and fury is naturally loaded with passionate feelings.

In Scorpio, passion is even more intensified because it is often restrained or suppressed. Deliberately holding something back often only strengthens it, yet when it does finally come out, the Scorpion's passion can become too strong and uncontrollable a force. Scorpio types need to learn to release their heated emotions more often, before they build up and become too hot to handle.

Total Commitment?

The commitment theme that Libra first proposed can be taken to the nth degree in Scorpio. Libra thinks it knows how to establish healthy boundaries in relationships—as air needs its space to breathe—and it even welcomes another's individuality and willingness to dialogue. (It could be said that Libra prefers a significant other who acts more like a self-honest Aries, although one who's not as rough around the edges.)

"I'm this and you're that, so let's enjoy our differences," says Libra. "Let's blend our dissimilarities in mutually beneficial ways."

"Well, enough of that nonsense," mutters Scorpio. For perhaps unfathomable reasons, Scorpio types are uneasy with any partner who is too independent and self-willed. Maybe this is because it's harder to merge intensely with another who behaves like that. Scorpio also senses that such a person can and will be confrontational, the last thing this secretive water sign feels it needs in any long-term union.

The truth is, the Cosmos demands that Scorpio types become embroiled in periodic confrontations that help them peel away layers of secret motivation and unrevealed desire. There's so much cooking emotionally inside Scorpio that others never get to see, and this puts them at a disadvantage. Hmmm . . . what happened to Libra's ideal of fair play? Has its two-way street of communication now become a dead-end road of silence?

Scorpio is capable of putting up many psychological barriers, designed to forbid easy access to its underground world. Yet, unfairly, it demands total candor and commitment from anyone it chooses for a partner. That means others are always expected to come clean regarding *their* private, internal life—no secrets are to be kept from the Scorpion! And if needed, Scorpio will trespass on another's territory to get at any "top secret" information is feels it must have to stay in control.

Fixed water implies that this sign can hang on tenaciously to a few, select "others" for its emotional security, and thus has a difficult time letting go psychologically. (Gee, and we thought the Crab had a big problem here, but it seems Scorpio is even more obsessed about its attachments!) Others may not feel the depth of commitment that steadfast Scorpio does, nor do they ever wish to. If Scorpio wasn't such a control freak, maybe total commitment could feel like a warmly devotional state of caring. However, this sign is notorious for trying to do unwanted makeovers on people, from head to toe, inside and out. Others may not wish to be part of such a manipulative situation.

It's true that the Scorpion has a knack for picking up on other people's hidden potential—their buried treasure—but the measures it takes to tap that potential is what others find so intrusive and coercive. "I won't be satisfied until *you* become all that you were meant to be," is something we might expect to be told while training with an Olympics coach, but not from a parent or a spouse. If this is what total commitment really means—a kind of slow suffocation—then it's time for "loved" ones to bail out and leave Scorpio all alone, once again, to ponder why.

Deep Therapy

Scorpio observes Libra in action, and appreciates how sharply perceptive this air sign can be regarding the human condition. Libra is able to understand people's mental frameworks, which thus helps it view things the way others do—but it can't necessarily get under their skin to uncover more. That's where Scorpio comes in. This sign is gut-sensitive to the unseen, unspoken energies that are constantly being transferred in close, emotionally charged relationships. The Scorpion can pick up on the scent of trouble subterraneanly brewing between people, and it will follow any darkly lit trail until it finds the hidden source of such tension. It will then offer transformative ways to resolve the problem, or else it will take drastic measures to eliminate the conflict altogether. This is at least what it would do if stuck in such a predicament—fix it or dump it! (Libran indecisiveness is maddening to Scorpio, who'll instead pick at a problem until a crisis imposes a resolution of the matter.)

Self-aware Scorpio types are dedicated to the exploration of the mysteries of human complexity. They seek out knowledge, and perhaps wisdom, regarding the nature and power of our depths within—that realm where we undergo the beginnings of metamorphic change that later erupt to alter the entire landscape of our outer world. The more interior parts of our subconscious are where we keep well-shielded secret fears, hatreds, lusts, compulsions, and other discomforting feelings. Yet they'll continue to consume our energy and drain our soul if left in their toxic states.

Our Scorpio challenge is to discover how to stop being devitalized—or sometimes monstrously overenergized—by darker facets of our psyche that need to see the light of day. When we can't find personal ways to accomplish this, alternative forms of therapy await those of us brave enough to explore such inner darkness. Scorpio discovers that it can see quite well in the dark, and thus can learn much about itself while descending deeper into its shadowy underworld.

Feeling Sexy?

The Cosmos once warned Scorpio that its archetypal assignment would be a tough but critically important one, and that this sign may at times feel cursed by those same powerful energies it seems to love the most. Sexual energy is one such mixed blessing. Taurus actually got the sex thing going a while back and found it a pure pleasure. (Apparently, the Bull doesn't think twice about a casual roll in the hay. If it feels good, do it—and then maybe make a sandwich and take a nap later.) Sex tends to be more of a fertility rite for body-loving Taurus, who feels something fruitful could come out this natural, earthy experience. It's at least relaxing.

However, things get more complicated for Scorpio, who knows it'll use sexual conquest to get at something else in another person, to perhaps dislodge some concealed emotion. Sex thus is used to provoke, as well as satisfy, a partner. Sex also helps the Scorpion release its own enigmatic intensities, helping this sign come alive in rejuvenating ways. Mere erotic pleasure is sometimes the last thing on Scorpio's mind—it instead seeks a total upheaval of the senses, perhaps triggered by a powerful orgasmic response, as Mount St. Pluto blows its lid!

It's odd that the zodiac's "sexiest sign alive" is also one that can suffer from intimacy hang-ups. Scorpio is more self-conscious about sex than folks would realize (it's a highly introspective sign and one plagued by a perfectionistic streak—something it "borrowed" from Virgo when it wasn't looking). The Scorpion fears being exploited for its sensuous appetites, yet it also dreads being overlooked or even underrated as a sex object—"What, you *don't* find me sexy?" And it's more performance-sensitive than it cares to admit. It's also hard to truly relax when you're this much of a psychic sponge, constantly soaking up other people's hidden feelings. Scorpio typically processes too many conflicting energies at once, and thus has a hard time losing itself even in the moment of sexual surrender.

Death Wish

Scorpio is the sign of death and permanent closure. None of the previous seven signs ever thought much about dying until Scorpio came along (actually, Leo worried once about possibly blowing its lines and "dying" on stage—but it never contemplated physical death, the final extinguishing of waking consciousness). In Scorpio, we become aware that, as mortal beings, our life clock is ticking away. Each of us is allotted only so many ticks until our earthly sojourn is over. Scorpio has made peace with this, probably because it wisely senses that a different dimension of consciousness awaits us after our body dies. Scorpio knows that many invisible levels of awareness exist, simply because it traffics in them daily. Although Scorpio may fight the death process (it's even a medical "cat with nine lives" who exhibits amazing recuperative power), at some point it will need to willingly release such control and resistance, and allow for this final transition.

Meanwhile, the Scorpion realizes that it must undergo many other "deaths" in this lifetime. Not all of its fixations turn out to be magnificent obsessions. Much inner darkness must be dispelled for those Scorpios types who choose to deal with life's slings and arrows by vengefully retaliating. Toxic hostility, resulting from long-term, seething resentments, needs to die. The urge to destroy others who have emotionally wounded Scorpio needs to die. And the poisonous flames of jealous rage also need to be snuffed out for good. Anyone seeking deeper self-understanding would wish for the deaths of these troublesome psychological complexes.

Actually, this sign has little choice: Redeem all of that darkness or suffer in isolation. Scorpio can easily turn even its destructive energies within, stinging itself again and again, whenever it feels ultimately powerless to control things in the outer world. This self-defeating instinct must also be killed off if the Scorpion is to psychologically survive its trials in life and become truly empowered in all the best ways.

Back to Life

Scorpio is pressured to resurrect itself during those grueling times when it has emotionally bottomed out (devastated Scorpio types can feel depressively low about themselves in self-punishing ways). No other sign, except perhaps for Pisces, can reach such gloomy inner depths of pain and remorse. Of course, no other sign learns to grow as much from such difficult, emotional states. Anyway, this is not where Scorpio is meant to stay trapped forever. It's hard-wired to soar like an eagle, once it vibrantly brings itself back to life (note that Scorpio's stinger, pointing upward, resembles Sagittarius' arrow—implying that the concentrated energy in that stinger must be transmuted and aimed in the right direction before it can become a power source of inspiration).

Being one of the final six signs, Scorpio is interested in the welfare of society. It's no saint—and it even acknowledges the educational value of sin—but it is aware that true social transformation involves healthy human interconnections. Libra provides a few guidelines that Scorpio takes a step further. Libra's focus is on the outer packaging of harmonious, stress-free relationships. It tries to stay on the wholesome, upbeat side of human contact. Yet with Scorpio comes an unsettling awareness of the shadow elements of deeper relating, those less-observable energies underpinning any close, complex union. The Scorpion is sensitive to what is problematic in partnerships, to what needs fixing (even surgery). It therefore has an understanding of all people who are having a difficult time relating to others in life.

One result of this sensitivity is Scorpio's magnetic attraction to psychology in all its ramifications. What makes anybody become twisted and bitter enough to ruin their chances for intimacy and happiness in relationships? That's what the Scorpion wants to know, as well as why some people feel like losers, loners, outsiders, undesirables, outcasts, and other social rejects. (In contrast, Pisces doesn't need to know "why"; it just accepts and loves these folks, regardless.) Scorpio does feel empathy for those who don't neatly fit society's definition of "normal." The Scorpion suspects that if it really were to spill out all its own secret feelings and desires, it could become a prime target for social rejection, as well.

Pluto's Heat

Pluto is a planet that never takes the easy way out. It's as good at complicating life as its associated sign, Scorpio. Both planet and sign will deeply probe into the human condition, searching relentlessly for qualities and traits that need to be overhauled—except that Pluto *really* means it! Scorpio battles between defensively holding on to its shadow stuff versus blasting it all to smithereens—at least those parts that refuse to be creatively recycled. Pluto shows awesome determination when fearlessly enforcing major change (stubbornness and insecurity are not Plutonian characteristics). Yet fixed Scorpio resists being pressured to totally alter itself, unless the final orders come from within.

Superficialities turn off both Scorpio and Pluto. What does interest them—which they then pursue obsessively and enduringly—are subject matters that most people find uncomfortable to explore. These two intense astrological influences describe individuals who have a gutsy boldness and a need to know the gritty, uncensored realities of life, dark as they may be. Pluto and Scorpio can also appear calm or at least restrained on the outside, which is deceptive. Their still waters not only run deep, but can transform into a constant state of boiling that can psychologically scald the unsuspecting. A challenge for Plutonians and Scorpio types is to keep their emotions from becoming too concentrated and overpowering. The more such feelings are held in, the more forcefully they erupt when provoked.

Closing Comments

Wherever Scorpio is in our chart describes where we best not take things at face value. Life will give us good reasons to dig deeply here to uncover those unseen elements that control our situations more than we realize. Naiveté, on our part, can ultimately do us in. We'll instead need to be more watchful and observant of subtleties in others (the ol' eagle-eye approach). We will also need to be less obvious about our own intentions, since we are learning about the value of remaining silent. It's good to hold back somewhat and quietly study the situa-tion, wherever our Scorpio is. Others may scrutinize us here as well, yet we shouldn't make it so hard for them to contact our deeper side. Typically it's our job to pay keener attention to what's happening in our relationships, even if doing so makes us feel unsettled or angry about what we're unearthing.

Sometimes, too much Scorpionic self-control gets in the way of healthy emotional growth, as we bottle up feelings that later blow up and make a big mess in our lives for a while. But maybe that's how all-or-nothing Scorpio likes it—hold emotions in, then violently explode, clean up the debris, clear the slate, and start freshly empowered all over again! Indeed, Scorpio symbolizes a process often requiring that we separate from our past—sometimes by force—and then bravely learn deeper self-sufficiency by embracing a new life, where every-thing seems different and yet compelling to us. A force within our soul is now strong enough to handle whatever the Cosmos has in store. We're a survivor who's enjoying a well-needed rebirth.

FAMOUS SCORPIO TYPES (natal Scorpio placements listed)
Grace Kelly, actress: Sun, Mercury, Mars, Ascendant
Pablo Picasso, artist: Sun, Mercury
Marie Curie, physicist-chemist: Sun, Mercury, Venus, Mars, Saturn
Martin Scorsese, director: Sun, Mercury, Venus, Mars
Jodie Foster, actress: Sun, Mercury, Venus, Neptune
Robert Kennedy, politician: Sun, Mars, Saturn

SAGITTARIUS
Big World Out There

Glyph: ♐

Symbol: The Archer

Mode: Mutable

Element: Fire

Planet: Jupiter/♃

House: Ninth

Motto: "I Believe We're All Here to Do Some Good!"

Endless Journey

It's time to loosen up, since we're now moving from Scorpio's compressed world of emotional introspection to the high adventures of mind and soul sought by a spirited fire sign who loves celebrating the grander designs of life. Scorpio feels compelled to plumb its depths in darkness, but Sagittarius instead seeks the sunniest of days to explore the immensity of human experience on a global scale. This easily inspired sign feels like it's on some big mission of great collective meaning. In some ways, Sagittarius represents the wondrous fruits of soul resurrection achieved by Scorpio—it thus takes joy in the unfoldment of the future. Here we happily take to the expansive skies of a higher consciousness, one that allows us broader visions of what is and of what can be. The Archer enthusiastically views life in this wide-angled manner, and tries to uplift the rest of us so that we'll do the same.

Mutable Sagittarius represents fire in its most restless expression (which means something more than just being overactive, like Aries). The boldness of fire suggested here is less physical than intellectual, and the journeys to be taken are more geographical than psychological. The Archer does not easily internalize its energies—it figures, "Haven't we already had enough of *that* in Scorpio?" Sagittarius may believe in the hellish dimensions in which Scorpio has sometimes found itself trapped, but it surely doesn't want to go there any time soon. It's packing its bags for other trips to take—the fun kind filled with awesome discoveries.

Wherever we have Sagittarius in our chart, we'll need to wander far from our familiar, comforting security symbols, the ones typically reinforced by our family conditioning. Travel, alone, puts us in contact with what is different from our background. The Archer realizes that, ideally, we humans are all the same—but culturally, we certainly are not! Mutability lends a curiosity about how people and things work, and the pioneering spirit of fire helps Sagittarius feel it's on a quest—in this case, a quest for understanding the world at large. The Archer hopes its journeys will never come to an end.

Community Spirit

This is the third and last fire sign of the zodiac. Fire always seems to usher in new experiences, and here it can be said that Sagittarius exposes us to more inclusive levels of human interaction. It's interested in how society, for better or worse, impacts the lives of many and not just of the few. Confronting "the big world" implies dealing with strangers, and not necessarily on a close, one-to-one basis. Sagittarius finds itself concerned with what's happening "over there," any place far away, even on the other side of the world. The Archer is learning to develop an international awareness of how varied all societies can be due to their cultural interests, their moral standards, their art, their language, and even their honored religions. Sagittarius find itself enthralled with all the facets that make each society unique.

Even closer to home, the Archer seeks to move beyond the personal dynamics of family life and into the broader fields of community involvement. This is the first sign to want to encounter people from all walks of life. It's not afraid of strangers or strangeness in others, which helps it warm up to matters of universal interest; Sagittarius supports human diversity. Thus, the thought of reaching out and connecting with people, in an attempt to create a more ideal society, is very appealing to this civic-minded sign. Sagittarius is the "do-gooder" of the zodiac, the one always trying to drum up good cheer between people. It tries to promote ideals and visions that will fire others up, so that they, in turn, will enthusiastically contribute something of social worth that raises the awareness of many.

The Archer's mutability indicates that its growing mental interests keep changing. This sign doesn't seek to build enduring structures that result in entrenched traditions (even though it's the sign associated with organized religion). Sagittarius instead takes on the role of a social prophet, the one to show others "the light" in hopes that something big and beautiful will come out of any revelations that this sign upliftingly offers. The dream of a model society—one that honors individuality and freedom—is what Sagittarius has in mind. Of course, it's a naive vision that doesn't take into account the need for rules and regulations (Capricorn takes over those necessary parts of society-building).

If everyone was equally high-minded, honest, and decent—as the Archer feels itself to be— then perhaps few, if any, laws would need to be made and enforced. We'd instead always be doing the right thing in ways that benefit everyone. Lofty, idealistic Sagittarius doesn't always understand why society's ironclad codes are so inflexible, and thus it fights against all authoritative restriction while thinking, "These dumb laws don't apply to me!"

Gotta Have Truth

The concept of Truth may seem abstract and arbitrary to some signs, but it is of vital importance to the Archer. A world of theoretical possibilities opens wide for this ever-expanding sign, who's in hot pursuit of knowing what the Universe is really all about. Is there one overarching Truth that determines the "real" nature of all else that exists? Is this what God is all about, or even what physicists have named "unified theory," which speculates on the possible—and as yet unproven—existence of a single, determining law that can explain *all* fundamental energy interactions in existence? Leave it to Sagittarius to ponder the workings of life on even this cosmic a scale. The big picture can get mighty BIG for this sign!

One problem here, in defining Truth, is that fire signs are not all that objective about anything they feel strongly about. Sagittarius especially wants to plainly see that which it already believes to be true, in its heart. It claims to seek the ultimate reality underlying anything, but it has a gullible, credulous nature that keeps it from recognizing life's less glorious side. The Archer is not realistic or detached enough to handle life's more depressing truths.

Whatever it wholeheartedly believes in is something that it deems to be absolutely true and right for all, not just for itself. That's when it is more than willing to get on its soapbox and proclaim stuff like, "Everyone will need to become a vegetarian before they can find true inner peace!" It's typical for Sagittarius to make such flat-out statements that sound a bit on the dogmatic side. There is a "know-it-all" quality to this sign that suggests it doesn't easily recognize all sides of any issue, just the one it preaches—it feels it's correct about its beliefs, and everyone else is a poor, unenlightened soul needing to be shown a higher path in life.

The Archer puts much stock in universal principles that guide humanity's development. It has faith in all unseen influences that benevolently help shape the course of human destiny and even the fate of nations. Sweeping assumptions about how things "really are," in terms of universal energies, are fortified by the Archer's certainty that its visions reflect clarity and purity, leaving little room for distortion. (Sagittarius was undoubtedly the first sign to utter these words, "God has spoken to me, and He said . . .") It's nearly impossible to convince Sagittarius, once inspiration has taken over its entire being, that it could be all wrong about its cherished beliefs.

Jolly Saint Nick?

Sagittarius represents a part of human nature that is willing, in most cases, to give more than it gets back from others. Not even normally gracious, agreeable Libra is willing to do that (and when it does, it often backfires for the Balancer). Yet it seems as if the Archer has an inborn sense of abundance and a surplus of goodwill that allows it to be generous in spirit. It never feels like it's a loser—at least not when it still can freely give of itself to a world in need. Sagittarian emphasis in our chart shows where we can be like Santa Claus, ready to hand out bag loads of gifts for the happiness of all. These are typically gifts of the mind and spirit that we offer. The Archer, like Leo, has a big heart, but is driven to give for less-egocentric reasons, and isn't as prone to dictate how others are to use its gifts, except as joyously and un-selfishly as possible.

Sagittarius is a firm believer in the importance of doing good works. It knows the big world has big needs that only those blessed with ongoing hope and optimism can fulfill, but certainly not cynics and misers. Sagittarius gets as far as it does in life because it really likes people. This is probably the zodiac's most gregarious sign, one that doesn't seem to mind at all who it gets to rub shoulders with—the more the merrier—as long as the energy level remains high and every-one's feeling full of pep and enthusiasm. Plus Sagittarius can be quite boisterous. Still, even if sometimes too loud and going overboard with glee, the cheery Archer is only trying to bring a smile to others and get us all to laugh ("Ho, ho, ho"), and maybe even teach the world to be thankful for its blessings.

Nature Trail

Sagittarius actively enjoys the great outdoors, perhaps more so than any other sign. Of course, Taurus loves Nature's quiet, maternal side, especially from the security of the Bull's own backyard. Taurus not only likes to patiently grow plants from seed, it also desires to stay protectively close to its well-tended garden patch, where it can watch the vegetative process slowly unfold. As Taurus relaxes in its familiar natural settings, it is soothed by the animal sounds that abound, by the fragrant scents in the air, and by the comforting warmth of the sun's rays—things that are all pleasing to the senses. For the Bull, the living is easy when Nature is at its most green and fertile stage. However, the kind of nature experience that the Archer gets excited about goes way beyond the birds and the bees.

Climbing Mount Everest is more a robust Sagittarian interest than potting pink petunias. For the Archer, the natural world is something to be adventurously explored rather than just appreciated for its beauty while we rest in a hammock on a lazy, summer day. Fire is forever on the go, burning up its energy with vigorous activity. Mutability doesn't like staying still for long and will take off in many directions. Thus, Sagittarius is happy when running, riding a bicycle, flying a plane, sailing a ship, taking a train, or hiking on a nature trail.

Sagittarius therefore likes to be in movement while it's enjoying Nature. And it loves to combine the outdoors with elements of risk and excitement, resulting in activities such as skydiving, hang-gliding, skiing, big-game hunting, and white-water rafting. There is obviously a reckless side to the Archer, who seldom feels it's in mortal danger—after all, how could something that's so much fun be perilous? Sagittarius reminds us, "You gotta have faith that the angels are always watching out for you!" Amazingly, such a trusting attitude works well for this sign, perhaps more than is warranted.

Faith Healing

A refinement of the ego is what mutable fire suggests. Aries and Leo can be fairly self-centered in the pursuit of their goals—especially the Ram—but Sagittarius' ego satisfaction is tied to the role it plays in helping society improve. Sagittarius is not a power freak (although it is sandwiched in between two signs—Scorpio and Capricorn—that have the potential to be so). The Archer wishes for great things to happen to all people, not just to itself, and thus is less self-seeking in its aspirations.

Fire usually believes in its own ability to direct its life, without outside interference. Aries and Leo have no trouble doing that, but Sagittarius is flexible and open-minded enough to yield to outside authority—that is, a supreme authority: the vast, underlying Creative Intelligence that ensouls all that exists. Whether called God or Spirit, this boundless concept of divinity at work is thus born in Sagittarius. Great faith is placed in an unseen, protective guidance that benevolently helps the Archer along on its life journey.

Relying on faith to get what it wants—instead of sheer ego assertion—is what puts Sagittarius in a category all its own. No previous sign had ever looked for inner support from spiritual sources, although Scorpio felt close to doing so at times when its own darker moods led to desperation and despair. No sign, until now, has considered the possibility that a Universal Mind exists. Sagittarius is not a mystical sign (that's Pisces). It does like to have its spiritual beliefs backed up by more concrete frameworks (perhaps a venerable holy book, if not an actual visionary leader to provide the answers). There is a surprisingly orthodox side to the Archer that seeks to uphold even ancient traditions and rituals. Whatever its beliefs, Sagittarius attests to the healing power of hope and faith, seeing them as forces for good that can move both mighty mountains and human hearts. Without Sagittarian faith, life may seem bleak, meaningless, and much too worldly in heavy, oppressive ways that wear down our souls.

Luck of the Irish?

Less-philosophical Sagittarian types—those who choose not to depend on divine guidance—still can't help but note that they can be pretty darn lucky throughout their lives. They've seen a few times when situations could have turned out much worse than they did, all because of fortuitous, last-minute events (these are the folks who, due to an unexpected traffic jam, fail to catch a plane, only to hear later that it crashed minutes after takeoff). Is this dumb luck? Maybe so, but Sagittarius will eventually want to know why it's been singled out for protections that others apparently never receive.

Even nonreligious Sagittarian types—when things are going a little too well—will find themselves looking upward, wondering, "Thanks, but why me?" It will be a test of the ego to see if this sign's famous lucky streak will make the Archer assume that it's *always* going to be the privileged one who's never slated to undergo hardships in life. Sagittarius may arrogantly believe itself to be immune to ordinary, human limitations.

Luck may be well deserved. Its source—not necessarily something magical or angelic—may stem from the state of well-being dwelling inside good-natured Sagittarius. Fortunate outcomes become the result of the Archer's deep acceptance of plenitude in life. Positive thinking acts like a magnet, drawing in advantageous conditions. This sign acts as if it was born with a Master's degree in prosperity consciousness. It is preprogrammed to expect gain, not loss, to anticipate the best, not the worst. It trusts that life unfolds with basically good intentions, and that the future looks promising, not dismal. All this adds up to create powerful energy currents that manifest as lucky breaks in life. This isn't dumb luck at all—it's the smart kind!

High-Spirited Jupiter

Jupiter is the planet associated with Sagittarius. The solar system's biggest member finds itself at home with a sign that loves to keep enlarging its perceptions of life. Both planet and sign show an interest in stretching our mental potential. They urge us to increase our ability to know all about the world around us, especially in terms of understanding its larger patterns of meaning. Jupiter is buoyant enough in attitude to relate to equally exuberant Sagittarius. Together, they promote an upbeat philosophy of living that helps our spirit soar to greater heights of awareness.

Fiery Jupiter shows the same infectious enthusiasm that the Archer does, but it is able to sustain its exhilaration for longer periods of time, due to its greater devotional streak. It's less restless for change than is Sagittarius, a sign as notorious as Aries for its short attention span (that's probably because the Archer knows there is *so* much in life to which it wants to become exposed, and yet there is so little time to do it all—whereas Aries' lack of enduring attention is more a case of disinterest).

Sagittarius, being mutable in disposition, is prone to waver, waffle, switch sides, weasel out of things, pass the buck, or renege at the last minute—especially when it's starting to feel trapped by a commitment (mutable signs always think they have a perfect right to change their minds, no matter what they've previous promised—and this is doubly the case for the fiery Archer). But all the fire planets (Sun, Mars, and Jupiter) are filled with the drive and courage to blaze on, as if impervious to obstacles in their path. Jupiter would rather think it will succeed in its endeavors than fail. Why bail out when you know you're going to end up a winner? Of course, both Sagittarius and Jupiter can be victims of poor judgment (maybe more so overconfident Jupiter). They lack the power of discrimination found in Virgo and the earthy side of Mercury, and thus they'll need to pay closer attention to life's smaller but critical details.

Closing Comments

Wherever Sagittarius is in our chart describes where life is trying to show us how good things can be, if only we'd just have more trust in ourselves. Fear or narrow-mindedness never works in our favor here (or probably anywhere else). Yet sloppy thinking, based on a reluctance to apply a little logic and reason to our circumstances, can result in big disappointments. We overestimate our potential, or misjudge what our environment can offer us. Also, the grass is not always greener elsewhere, so let's be careful not to literally run away from any current problems needing to be squarely addressed (those same problems will crop up in our new locale). Actually, if we try to get in better contact with our spiritual self—our trusty inner guide—situations can turn out very well for us. Our faith can create a few miracles, within reason. But procrastination or unrealistic expectations keep us from feeling rewarded by life.

Our Sagittarian parts also urge us to get beyond our petty, small-world concerns by volunteering to do something noble and inspirational to help society raise its consciousness. Give us big, important social projects to energetically crusade for, ones that promote the welfare of others on broad, humane levels. Yet Sagittarius doesn't want to be all alone championing such campaigns. It needs to network with people of good faith and honorable intentions. (However, Libra is willing to teach the Archer about the art of tact, since one of Sagittarius' less-attractive traits is that it's too blunt in its observations and judgments about society's shortcomings. Libra suggests dipping into diplomacy's honeypot to sweeten the Archer's fiery rhetoric.) Sagittarius points out where we have a talent for spreading the right vibes needed to boost team spirit, the kind most necessary for fulfilling high-minded goals.

FAMOUS SAGITTARIAN TYPES (natal Sagittarius placements listed)

Noel Coward, songwriter-actor: Sun, Mercury, Saturn, Uranus

Margaret Mead, anthropologist: Sun, Mercury, Uranus

Mark Twain, author-humorist: Sun, Venus, Mars

Tina Turner, singer: Sun, Mercury, Venus

William Blake, poet-artist: Sun, Mercury, Jupiter

Bette Midler, singer-actress: Sun, Mercury

Capricorn
A Slow, Steady Climb

Glyph: ♑

Symbol: The Goat

Mode: Cardinal

Element: Earth

Planet: Saturn/♄

House: Tenth

Motto: "Life Makes Me Wait—But I'm Worth It!"

Let's Get Serious

The initial spark of personal self-interest—symbolized by Aries—has by now gone through a major process of maturation by the time we arrive at the Capricorn stage of development. One result of this is an awareness of our individual responsibility to help build a strong society based on enduring collective values. Social structure on a large scale is what interests the Goat. Sagittarius gave us the vision and the ideals needed to theoretically improve the human condition, but Capricorn provides the organizational know-how to make worthy social dreams come true. The Goat is ready to deal with the masses on a serious, committed basis, typically by taking on offices of leadership and responsibility. This cardinal-earth sign is a dynamic mix of duty (earth) and the push to make things happen (cardinal). Capricorn can be assertive in how it tries to take control over societal matters, and is ambitious and eager to merit approval from those already operating from high positions.

Capricorn vows to make society a safe and orderly place for its hard-working, law-abiding members. One way to ensure this, at least in Capricorn's eyes, is to set up rules and regulations designed to keep the masses from creating instabilities that could lead to anarchy—the Goat's worst nightmare is a lawless world run amok. Someone's got to be in charge of it all! Thus, the roles people play in life—especially our professional roles—are very important to Capricorn. Everyone must serve a needed social function and be productive if society is to keep from falling apart.

Capricorn is aware of Sagittarius' many inspired social theories, but the wise Goat will only implement those few broad-based concepts that have practical, timely value. This is perhaps the most realistic, no-nonsense sign of the zodiac, and one that doesn't want to waste its energy in the pursuit of unworkable objectives. Capricorn has a healthy regard for things that endure, things that start off having a solid framework. Dealing with such worldly issues is serious business to the well-organized Goat, who truly feels its mission in life is to help chart the course of collective development in sound and sane ways. (Starting with Sagittarius, the life themes of the last four signs become increasingly people-oriented on more impersonal levels. The needs of the masses are considered more important than those of the individual.)

Born Old

It has been commonly observed that Capricorn enters the world possessing a wisdom normally reserved for the elders of any tribe, not its youngest members. It's not so much what the Goat says at an early age that gives this impression of being a sage—since Capricorn tends to be reserved in youth and may not even flow with words—it's that this sign has a savvy way of sizing up adults in a manner that allows it to partake of their world much earlier on than the other signs. Capricorn studies power roles in society and finds the benefits of all prestigious positions quite appealing. It is thus willing to behave in the self-disciplined, obedient manner needed to claim such power and privilege for itself—amazingly, many Goat types understand all this by the time kindergarten rolls around!

Young Capricorn types know that grownups are suckers for a well-behaved child, one who also just so happens to be an expert at "kissing up" to authorities to gain their respect and admiration. This may sound opportunistic, yet it's not due to being phony, since Capricorn naturally excels in calculated behavior, a byproduct of its cautious disposition. It doesn't like feeling out of control, and shows unchildlike restraint and composure. It also aims to please, although not in a Libran sense, where the specific goal is to be loved and liked.

The Goat instead caters to the expectations of others in hopes of making a good impression, one that later pays off when embarking on the road to worldly success. (Capricorn, very concerned about its reputation, will work hard to make sure its credentials are impeccable—how can it expect to enter society's upper echelons without them?) Even at a tender age, this sign knows it has dues to pay before it will be allowed to become somebody important in life—nothing comes for free in the Goat's world, and certainly not without dedicated effort.

Sterling Citizen

Much has been made of Capricorn's tendency to be so one-pointed about its ambitions that it can become cold-hearted, ruthless, and power-driven. In real life, most Capricorn types know, historically speaking, that brutal dictators in society eventually fall from power in a state of disgrace, and are forever hated for having suppressed the masses. This is *not* what the Goat wants for itself—a humiliating ending and a permanent stain on its standing in the world.

Still, in professional matters—when operating in the seat of command—Capricorn can appear as the stern parent who's always ready to crack the whip or lay down the law. It demands focus and efficiency from all involved. ("Work as hard as I do if keeping your position means anything to you," warns the Goat authority in charge.) Capricorn can thus become a hard taskmaster who can intimidate weaker souls or those who lack direction. It's not trying to scare anyone needlessly—it simply wants the best performance possible from those it employs or does business with. There's a low tolerance for incompetent folks who mess up and indirectly make the Goat look bad.

Yet behind this apparent bossy streak—and this need to socially advance—is this sign's underlying belief that its destiny involves contributing something meaningful and lasting to society. It knows it's not here to live merely for itself, but instead to help build something that is of social worth to many, something that benefits the world. Capricorn knows its goals require it to keep climbing the mountain of ambition until it reaches the summit. It's only from this peak that it can demonstrate its expert skills of management and organizational enterprise. And it is driven to act in honorable ways that earn society's praise. It may seem tough and determined when achieving its set goals, but integrity is on its side. The Goat's humility is not always apparent, but it keeps this sign grounded, no matter how successful its life turns out.

Fame

Capricorn also has a side to it that wants to be recognized as somebody special, except that it is not always sure if it's worthy of such elevated status. Leo never doubts that it's a born superstar, but the more down-to-earth Goat frowns on those who unnecessarily show off their greatness. It also believes nothing in life is to be given freely on a silver platter. If anything, Capricorn's early introduction to the limitations of the world left an indelible impression: Climbing to the top in society requires constant struggle and perseverance—and most of all, sure-footedness.

Bouts of self-doubt and discouragement plague the Goat, yet surges of inner strength and fortitude compel it to become a high achiever, one who can surpass all former limitations. None of this comes about because of sheer will. Capricorn works unendingly at whatever it eventually becomes famous for (and being a cardinal sign, it always feels it needs to accomplish more and more. Cardinal signs sometime never know when to quit pushing.).

Not all Capricorn types are born to experience fame—at least not in a glamorous, Hollywood sense—but they do need to feel sincerely

recognized for their dedicated efforts within their chosen fields of social contribution. Career status typically becomes important, as do all
the perks that come with social prominence (like Leo, the Goat demands first-class treatment, but only once it has earned it). Yet if all
this is apparently not forthcoming—and the Goat will patiently wait
before finally giving up—a sense of being defeated by a cold, uncaring
world can create bitterness and a slump of depression (even reaching
the top and then disappearing from the spotlight, due to events beyond the Goat's control, can prove devastating). Smarter Capricorn
types sense that fame may come at a steep price, so they're careful not
to want it too much—but if the Fates and the public insist, well, that's
another story!

Getting Chilly?

Maybe due, in part, to its association with the winter solstice and Saturn, Capricorn represents things that are on the chilly side. Coldness at
least suggests a lack of surface heat. The Goat may not appear warmly
emotional, and can seem a bit icy in temperament—especially when it
has been humiliated in public and its first instinct is to withdraw (even
if it instead stands firm and aggressively defends its honor).

Yet, like Pisces, the Goat can be a chameleon, in that it easily slips
into socially appropriate behaviors that others expect under certain
conditions (meaning that Capricorn can effectively appear convivial in
social circumstances that call for an engaging outgoingness). Capricorn
doesn't feel it's faking anything here. It is simply adapting to the re-
quirements of the moment in ways that give it the advantage needed to
succeed in its ambitions. This, again, is not considered phoniness on
Capricorn's part—it's a strategic move. The Goat always has darn good
reasons for behaving the way it does, yet seldom is it ever truly caught
off guard in a manner that exposes its hidden vulnerabilities.

Still, its cool and reserved side can lead others to assume that
Capricorn is uncaring (the same could be said of its opposite sign,
Cancer—at least on those moody days when the Crab uses its shell as
a shield). The Goat seems to be "all-business" in its demeanor, leaving
the impression that—although crisp, efficient, and tightly organized

—it is somewhat flat in its feeling nature. Earth signs never go too crazy with the expression of emotion, yet Capricorn is such a traditionalist who's sentimental about things of the past that it can get awkwardly misty-eyed. That's how we know the Goat's heart is not made of tin. It's just that Capricorn normally sees the world as a place that can hurt those who forget to wear their protective suit of armor in public, and thus the Goat's soft and cuddly parts are guarded and seldom exhibited.

The Parent Trap

Capricorn is one of two signs that astrology associates with parental attitudes—in this case, paternal ones (it's the sign of the father archetype); Cancer—the other sign—deals with the archetypal role of mother and other related maternal themes. The Crab needs to move deeper into the heart of the family dynamic in order to trigger its feeling nature and to establish an inner foundation of personal security patterns. On the other hand, Capricorn seems pressured to initially move away from anything that offers Cancerian, womblike protection. It instead tries to make the busy, outer world its home. (For the Goat, the ideal of domestic bliss doesn't hold a candle to the satisfaction of wielding executive power.)

While parental roles have changed dramatically in the last several decades, the functions of a mother and a father were, at one time, unmistakably clear-cut, especially in the first half of the twentieth century. Mothers stayed home to protect the nest and lovingly raise their offspring (moms also helped teach their children to feel both inner and outer security on elementary levels). Dads, hardly ever at home, went off to conquer the world and establish their place in the larger social scheme of things (dads taught their kids about dutiful commitments to nonfamily members). Mothers were close, accessible, and responsive to their children's emotions; fathers were far away, unavailable, and less aware of their children's inner lives.

Cancer and the Moon thus made symbolic sense when describing the intimate maternal side of life, while Capricorn and Saturn suited a child's impression of the more impersonal paternal experience. However, in today's world, traditional parental functions are less rigidly defined. Ideally, both parents now play out Cancer and Capricorn roles for their kids.

Like watery Cancer, earthy Capricorn is very protective, although more in the no-nonsense manner of a security guard on patrol. The Goat has to be careful not to overcontrol people in its attempt to provide them with safer and more structured ways to live. Capricorn types, no matter what their age, may try to take charge of others (even the younger ones may want to parent the adults in their lives, especially emotionally immature adults who behave irresponsibly). The Goat feels responsible for instructing people in how to conduct themselves. It tries to curb social behavior that it deems to be inappropriate or even a threat to conservative society—Capricorn targets not just lawlessness, but any actions it finds immoral (Sagittarius—a sometimes opinionated sign willing to pass judgment on others—first got this morality thing going during its fiery search for what "right" paths in life to take.)

As folks with lots of planets in Capricorn feel duty-bound, they can feel guilty when another side of them instead wants to feel free from obligations and less weighed down. However, early life has taught the Goat to be tough and not complain about what life doles out. Capricorn somehow knows that adversity and uphill climbing will only help its character grow stronger and become more resilient.

Saturn's Steady Hand

Saturn is the planet with which Capricorn is most comfortable—the Goat probably likes the security of this planet's famous rings, resembling protective moats surrounding a fortress. Saturn's earthy sensibility appeals to pragmatic Capricorn. Both planet and sign are quite reliable and are willing to work hard to attain their well-defined goals. However, cardinal Capricorn really doesn't care for the slow, deliberate pace that seems natural to Saturn (cardinal signs are the "ants in the pants" group, always eager to take action). If anything, life forces the Goat to wait, and not rush into experience, which later ensures that this sign is expertly prepared when its time has finally come.

While Capricorn hustles and bustles to make a name for itself, as it elevates its social standing, sober Saturn quietly plods on, often unnoticed. Capricorn more actively creates the right climate for the recognition it craves, while conscientious Saturn does good work but shies away from the limelight (Saturn is monkish in behavior and is in need of silent retreats, more so than the attention-seeking Goat).

Both Saturn and Capricorn are willing to be held accountable for their actions, a thought that causes them little anxiety, since their actions are typically honest and law-abiding (these are not the rule-breakers of astrology). The Goat—perhaps in its need to appeal to those of celebrated status—is more lively and socially adept in behavior than Saturn, a planet that seeks an ordinary lifestyle with less fanfare, and one with fewer people involved. Capricorn, while not gregarious in a Sagittarian sense, does thrive on social interaction with those who are going places and doing important things. Capricorn created the concept of the "in crowd," made up mainly of those on the Goat's private "A-list" of most desirable contacts—but as this sign is status-conscious, it has to watch out about becoming too snooty and elitist. Saturn is better able to relate to decent, everyday, plain-living folks who are just trying to stabilize their world and survive life's harsh realities. Saturn is more of a hard-working, blue-collar planet.

Closing Comments

Wherever Capricorn is in our chart describes where we may feel we're given tests in life that require our stamina and patience. We have purposeful needs here and we want solid results. Yet things will take time to ripen. It's common for us to use our Capricorn assets to advance our professional goals, and to help us garner social praise and respect. If the Goat's conservatism gets the best of us, we may come off here as a little too stiff—even rigid—in how we handle our duties and our social relations with others. (Sometimes Capricorn and Libra can become maddeningly proper and polite in demeanor, and much too formal for certain occasions.)

Capricorn's driving ambition helps us attain positions that allow us to feel self-important—and immensely useful. Being more than just an ego boost, this awareness of having personal significance motivates us to help strengthen society's foundation and keep its structure intact. Capricorn obviously supports the status quo and enacts needed reforms slowly, after much careful consideration. If we apply this to our personal life, we may find that a fear of change creeps into the picture, and even a dread of the unknown. Upholding the status quo may thus be done for defensive reasons, not simply for the purpose of stability.

Let's not forget that since Capricorn is cardinal in nature, we're less able to get stuck in ruts wherever this sign is emphasized in our chart (unlike fixed Taurus). Life forces us to devise sound solutions to remove whatever obstacles are temporarily blocking our path, and then we're to get on purposefully with our lives. Our Capricorn parts teach us to wise up about the ways of the world. Adopting a pragmatic outlook is valuable, as long as it doesn't convince us to suppress our creative juices, vivid imagination, or flights of fantasy. We don't need to be as grounded as a lead balloon, but simply anchored enough in practical realities so that we can build worthwhile material structures for ourselves and our society.

FAMOUS CAPRICORN TYPES (natal Capricorn placements listed)
Aristotle Onassis, business magnate: Sun, Mercury, Venus, Uranus
Dolly Parton, singer: Sun, Mercury, Venus
J. Edgar Hoover, FBI director: Sun, Mercury, Venus
Joan Baez, singer-activist: Sun, Mercury
Elvis Presley, singer-actor: Sun, Mercury, Venus
Marlene Dietrich, actress: Sun, Mercury, Mars, Jupiter, Saturn,

AQUARIUS
Breaking the Rules

Glyph: ♒

Symbol: The Water Bearer

Mode: Fixed

Element: Air

Planet: Uranus/♅

House: Eleventh

Motto: "I'm a Round Peg in a Square Hole in a Curved Universe!"

Freedom Fighter

My off-the-wall motto for Aquarius should instantly suggest that this sign applauds anything that's different—plus it's a real "original" itself. Still, as it's also a fixed-air sign with very strong collective leanings, the Water Bearer doesn't want to become so individualized—or so weird— that it feels isolated from the society it instead wants to help improve. But it does hope that its so-called "strangeness" will be accepted, since its fixity makes this sign less willing to change its nature in order to suit others. Air must have intelligent, social dialogues, and thus Aquarius is not out to needlessly alienate people. It is very fond of observing the workings of the world, especially from a sociological view, one implying an impersonal, cerebral perspective. However, Aquarius assumes that human feelings get in the way of clear perception. The Water Bearer thinks that emotionality tends to cloud or distort the truth in a manner that a detached, objective mind never would (although that's debatable).

Following Capricorn, Aquarius takes us to a different level of relating to society, one that allows room for greater cultural experimentation. Capricorn expects everyone to toe the line in ways that keep the community homogeneous—it distrusts "outsiders" or those who threaten cultural cohesion. Yet this next sign says it's time to bend a few of the Goat's time-honored rules and witness what happens when people are given a taste of greater freedom of social expression. Uniformity goes out the window as Aquarian types—who dare to be different—intentionally jolt society, from time to time. This sign's energy seems rebellious and willful, yet the Water Bearer is trying to fight for the right of all people to be themselves, rather than to bow mindlessly to authority and blindly obey the System. Aquarius urges us to break away from any limited mindset that allows others to determine the lifestyle we live.

Oddball

Aquarius in olden times was associated with Saturn, a planet who knows how hard it is to get anything accomplished within a group that lacks organization and steady commitment. Some Aquarian types do express Saturnian conservatism when involving themselves in larger social concerns. They want collective progress to be made carefully, at a slower pace, and are fearful of any radical change that could abruptly shake up established, workable frameworks—even those that at one time were considered to be progressive or even radical.

Such Saturn-dominated Aquarians put promising social reforms through endless committee evaluations before accepting or rejecting them. Yet the revolutionary spirit of Aquarius is better exemplified by Uranus, a planet of innovative thinking and unbridled truth-seeking. This is the side of the Water Bearer that cannot tolerate social restraints based merely on majority-rule decisions or stale, unchallenged traditions. This is the "rebel with a cause" aspect of Aquarius, ready to tear down the walls of conformity.

Aquarius is not a social misfit or a malcontent eager to destroy the Establishment (disgruntled Uranians are more prone to be like that).

The Water Bearer is actually a farsighted idealist who can envision better worlds of tomorrow for all. It is blessed with a progressive intellect that enables it to brainstorm brilliant solutions that help make our collective lives more interesting.

Also a bit of a techno-freak, Aquarius loves to explore innovative ways to make everyday life read more like a science-fiction novel. In its Uranian mode, the Water Bearer is a wild-eyed genius who lives in an energized world of abstract thought that traffics in theoretical concepts about reality's mentally fluid nature: Intuit it and it shall be possible. "Never stop being inventive," says Aquarius, who has no trouble telling all narrow-minded skeptics to go take a hike!

Due to all of this, some Aquarian types are dismissed as oddball eccentrics who are too way-out to be taken seriously, unless they start causing trouble in the ranks (and then they must be stopped). Otherwise, their harmless and even entertaining futuristic ravings are tolerable. Luckily, Aquarius is detached enough—not being all that emotionally vulnerable—to brush off the ridicule of critics. It remains determined (fixity) to formulate a social vision that is way ahead of its time. That's not to say that a few Aquarian types don't flip out and become disturbing to the community—as some do go wacko—but, behind any apparent madness, their intention is to foster respect and appreciation for human diversity. They want everyone to feel liberated from timeworn social rituals.

A Friend in Need

One of the main themes associated with Aquarius is friendship, yet not that of the bosom-buddy variety. Aquarius is too democratic—and too varied in its tastes—to ever think it could choose only one person to be its best friend in the whole world. The Water Bearer wants to be friendly and sociable with lots of fascinating people, and it does this by forming looser bonds that do not require high maintenance or heavy, one-on-one involvement (as if that's something a sign claiming to have about a hundred or so "close" friends need worry about).

Aquarius likes to keep its ties on the casual but stimulating side. If pals unpredictably pop in and out of the Water Bearer's life, everything's cool (it won't tolerate being possessed by others and it often needs to relate to new faces, much like Gemini). Aquarius doesn't want relationships that are too demanding and time-consuming, so this is not a sign that lets itself get too attached and committed in its social contacts. It tends to breeze in and out of the lives of many, and is happy to be able to relate to a wide range of interesting folks.

Although Aquarius may seem aloof and emotionally detached, its unpossessive attitudes are just what it needs to grow and develop. Freedom of movement is important to the Water Bearer, which is harder to actualize when involved with people who are clingy or needy (especially friends who hardly have a life of their own and who crave Aquarius' company much too much). Air needs space to move about, to ensure it stays well ventilated. It likes groups, but hates to feel crowded. It needs as much elbow room, socially, as does Sagittarius.

Still, altruistic Aquarius will volunteer its time to help out friends in need, especially when something unusual is happening in such people's lives. As long as the same pals don't hit on them too much to do little favors—and the Water Bearer sizes up such "users" pretty quickly—Aquarian types are willing to pitch in and assist without expecting anything in return. (Compare that to Capricorn and Libra, who would both keep track of all favors asked and later expect others to reciprocate—especially the Goat.)

Mind Flashes

Aquarius is given to unusual mental patterns—perhaps erratic brainwave activity—that enables it to flash on ideas at lightning speed, and even to suddenly have the answers it's looking for. The Water Bearer is able to tap into the future and bring such images into the now, for at least a brief look. Its intuition may come and go, but when it feels zapped, it "knows" its on the right track and will follow its strong hunches about people and situations.

However, being an air sign, Aquarius will also want to come up with a theory explaining how it knows what it knows. This is a sign with a talent for designing thought systems that are brilliant but complex. For Aquarius, flashes of insight often contain an instant overview of the total picture. All the Water Bearer has to do is intellectually structure and flesh out its grand vision, while adding even more to it, as one flash of insight sparks another.

What may be the Water Bearer's biggest obstacle, in selling its futuristic concepts, is its obvious impatience with slower minds that are too fear-based to take bold chances. Aquarius lacks the persuasive skills of diplomatic Libra, and it can explode when rejected by those who refuse to hear what genius really sounds like. ("But I've found *the* answer!" pleads frustrated Aquarius.) Not all Water Bearers are geniuses, of course, but they are quite bright and open-minded enough to keep their brains well exercised. Their gift is to be able to look at any problem from an unusual slant, and usually one that draws opposition from conservatives. Aquarius will need to develop common sense and stay calm when urgently trying to pitch its visionary ideals, especially those Uranian Aquarians who demand that reform happen overnight.

From the Heart?

Aquarius is cool-headed and, in its estimation, highly rational. Everything in the Water Bearer's world needs to make sense, which is why it takes a dim view of purely emotional interpretations of life. The watery world of feelings is murky to Aquarius in ways that are blinding. Being one to avoid mental fogginess, the Water Bearer supports intellectual clarity. Emotions also put us in contact with personal matters of the heart. Aquarius is very brainy and doesn't always relate well to even its own strictly personal, heartfelt needs (those apart from its future hopes for the collective). And it's surely not the sentimental type.

The Aquarian ego has a hard time focusing exclusively on self-fulfillment in ways that evoke a personal sense of being special and better than others (no wonder this sign is as far away from Leo as a sign can get). The Water Bearer is too quick to divert attention away from itself and instead on to those with whom it networks. The truth is, if it has such a tough time warming up to itself—even for all the right reasons—it's no wonder others sometimes feel that friendly Aquarius also has a cold side to its nature that makes its heart seem unreachable.

This sign, however, is part of a group of signs (Sagittarius to Pisces) that are trying to develop a more transpersonal awareness of life. Therefore, Aquarius thinks that the smart thing to do is to not allow itself to be dictated by its heart or by the emotionality of others. Still, one way to unify the world is to feel truly for one another, to put ourselves in someone else's shoes long enough to empathize. Aquarius is a sign that learns early on not to expect stability, and thus not to get too attached to people and things—since that only leads to deep disappointment and (gulp!) emotional pain.

Yet, if the Water Bearer is the adventurous, social experimenter it claims to be, why not plunge into the unknown depths of feeling and see what happens? How bad can it be to evoke a few tears or even an illogical fit of rage once in a while? Aquarius may find that studying quantum physics is a far easier task than turning on its emotional valve and letting raw feelings flow. Nonetheless, the Water Bearer needs to approach life, at times, straight from the heart and not panic if doing so goes against its mind-glorifying ideologies.

Team Player

Cerebral Aquarius is so interested in exploring the unusual in life that it could probably entertain itself forever with its eclectic studies and human observations, even if it had nobody else with whom to share this experience (all fixed signs can be self-contained, although Leo and Aquarius really need people). However, the Water Bearer knows that its own progress depends on how effectively it fraternizes with all members of society, in its effort to enlighten people about better ways to raise their consciousness and heighten their social awareness. Maybe because the ego is not as pronounced in this sign, Aquarius has less trouble being a team player. Actually, the nature of any planet found in Aquarius at birth better determines how open we are to engaging in group activity—Mars, Uranus, and Saturn here seem to be less cooperative and adaptable.

Aquarius typically believes that much can get done with the right kind of social cooperation, but it doesn't consider the varying needs of each individual that makes up the team. It figures that to stay democratic, everyone is entitled to the same treatment—no special privileges for anyone. This is somewhat paradoxical, since Aquarius champions human individuality on one hand, but then it believes in universal principles that should apply to all, unconditionally. The Water Bearer doesn't care much for prima donnas who think they're better than the rest (no wonder this sign can be an enemy of royalty and aristocracy). Still, Aquarius needs to understand—perhaps by working more on its emotional development—that not everyone is psychologically equipped to do well in groups or to enjoy exchanging energy on that impersonal a level.

Rockin' with Uranus

Aquarius' modern agent of social enlightenment is Uranus, a planet with a zest for inventive living. Called the Great Awakener, Uranus is no friend of the status quo. It is a galvanizing force that stirs dynamic and rapid collective growth, the kind that's not easily assimilated by the masses until the shock wears off and changes are later seen as excitingly progressive. Aquarius would love to identify itself with such a planet (and both surely know what it's like to be misunderstood by society).

Although Uranus can be obstinate—so sold on the rightness of its brilliant vision that it won't adopt any other outlook—it's not really all that fixed in its disposition, unlike Aquarius. The Water Bearer can be very set in its ideals—it won't compromise regarding its principles—and can at times be accused of trying to force reformative measures onto others (Aquarius can be more dictatorial that it realizes). Uranus, although explosive in its urgency to change things, doesn't want to sustain any social campaign for too long, especially when alternative routes are suddenly made available. But Aquarius' odd stick-to-it-tiveness can make it appear reactionary and less willing than Uranus to change with the times. That's when its true fixed nature comes out, loud and clear.

Uranus is more sporadic and erratic in nature than seemingly better-focused Aquarius. Uranus is more fiery in temperament—sparks-a-flying—than the cool-headed Water Bearer, although this sign can be passionately supportive of unpopular or controversial causes. Uranians protect their own freedoms first, and may even seem insensitive to the plight of others (remember, the Saturnian side of Aquarius finds a lot of what Uranus stands for to be destabilizing and not in the best interest of the public). Yet the intuitive grasp of this planet, and its courage to dive headlong into the unknown, appeals to Aquarius, who likes to assume that one's mental powers are only as limited as one's doubts, fears, and ignorance.

Closing Comments

Wherever Aquarius is in our chart describes where we're allowed to take sharp turns and veer away from any conservative programming we've received from the preservers of traditional society. We may find ourselves resistant to authority, especially the kind that intimidates our ability to think for ourselves and arrive at original conclusions. Our life may not be a smooth and steady experience wherever Aquarius is emphasized, since sudden changes can point us in unexpected directions—yet often advantageously so. Adaptability is important, even though we may attempt to force outer conditions to yield to our ideals, with mixed results. Aquarius urges us to come up with ingenious solutions rather than to stay stuck in a rut. Life may open many doors by surprise, those that allow us to enter freely and partake of new ways to create a better reality for ourselves and others.

Perhaps Aquarius is teaching us to become more gregarious and willing to find out about people who are blatantly different from us. Humanity is made up of a wide assortment of colorful folks who can help us feel more like universal citizens. (Aquarius needs to go on a trip around the world with Sagittarius to learn about how much fun cultural diversity can be.) Actually, Aquarius is where we are apt to dare ourselves to break down social barriers, and live life a bit on the wild and crazy side, in fun, self-expressive ways.

It's hard to hang on to security wherever we have Aquarius, since our life situations may constantly promote change, not stability. But the one thing that we can count on is an exciting time, once we let go and stop trying to live the life that others have already mapped out for us without our permission. Our time on Earth is too short to be wasted by fulfilling somebody else's shortsighted definition of our "true" role as a member of society.

FAMOUS AQUARIUS TYPES (natal Aquarius placements listed)

William Burroughs, novelist: Sun, Mercury, Venus, Jupiter, Uranus

Oprah Winfrey, television celebrity-actress: Sun, Mercury, Venus

Thomas Edison, inventor: Sun, Mercury, Neptune

Helen Gurley Brown, publisher: Sun, Mercury

Wolfgang Mozart, composer: Sun, Mercury, Venus, Saturn

Carole King, singer-songwriter: Sun, Mercury, Venus

PISCES
The Art of Dreaming

Glyph: ♓

Symbol: The Fishes

Mode: Mutable

Element: Water

Planet: Neptune/♆

House: Twelfth

Motto: "With an Open Heart, I Swim the Deepest Cosmic Waters!"

The Final Magic

Starting with Aries, each sign becomes progressively more complex in its psychology. This really becomes apparent by the time we arrive at Libra, who—along with the remaining five signs—takes into account the rights and needs of all others, not just of any one individual. The juggling acts thus required can make life more difficult—but perhaps more intriguing—yet these signs are well built for such interpersonal challenges. Aquarius embarks on an exciting course of authentic living that reflects its broad concern for collective growth, although its focus is mostly on an intellectual level. Its social theories and abstract principles are expected to yield the answers needed to improve the human condition—*if* everyone goes along with the program.

Aquarius intuits humanity's untapped higher potential. It will march in the streets, if it must, to protest undue governmental control and to advocate a freer, illuminated society—one that sparks the creative originality in people everywhere. "Let technology help us get there quicker," advises Aquarius. "Don't be afraid to experiment with what sounds too incredible to be true. An amazing future awaits us!"

Aquarius means well, although it assumes that all disharmonious conditions on a mass level can be corrected by implementing brilliant social reforms and by having progressive leadership. Once shown better models for creating new societies—ones based on greater equality and tolerance—the world is thus expected to radically improve. In theory, everyone will embrace diversity like never before, and prejudices based on fear and mistrust will be eradicated. Aquarius hopes that humanity will then turn its attention to unlocking the awesome gifts of expanded mind power, something that should help us all become further enlightened.

However, to have the Cosmos end the zodiac with Aquarius would imply that our collective future ultimately belongs to a super-race of geniuses—some who are perhaps telepathic, and all who are capable of astoundingly complex mental feats and the ability to operate with flawless, robotic precision. Think of people loaded with implanted computer chips, made to give them that extra intellectual boost—plus with replaceable body parts that help defy aging and death! Science fiction or inevitable reality? Aquarius is forever seeking ideal scenarios for all, and the thrill of enjoying advanced brainpower *and* extended life is certainly part of the Water Bearer's vision of an ideal future (of course, we'll all have to show a genius for social tolerance, as well).

However glorious will be the tomorrows that collectively await us, Aquarian-style, we still have a large and often painful chunk of human experience to undergo, one that is best symbolized by the last of the water signs, Pisces. As well as culminating the zodiac process, Pisces—coming before Aries—also symbolizes the less-observable, underground waters of spirit that feed new life potential ready to incarnate (think of our prenatal, Piscean water environment in the womb, just before we're born). We first emerge unformed from the oceanic, preconscious realm of Pisces, but eventually we return to its deepest waters in an impending state of fuller self-awareness, as we begin to dissolve all that has ever kept us feeling separate from others on our innermost level.

This hypnotic sign lures us into its powerful vortex to strip us of all the trappings of ego and selfish, worldly desire. Pisces guides us toward a vast sea of teeming, invisible energy that lovingly holds the content of all that exists in an unbroken, mystical state of Unity. Everything is One in this numinous, infinite Universe of the Fishes. Duality is only an illusion, perhaps a bad dream.

Full of Soul

As a mutable-water sign, Pisces is less able to establish fixed, rigid ways of viewing the world. It doesn't easily define reality in concrete terms. The Fishes are subject to much change in their perceptions, depending on the flow of life's continuous currents. Mutable water is very open and responsive to the hidden emotions of others, especially their unspoken sorrows. Pisces' sensitive feelers quietly reach out in all directions to detect subtle undertows in people. Indeed, receptivity is highly pronounced, yet Pisces doesn't suffer the petulant moodiness common to cardinal Cancer, nor the dark brooding of fixed Scorpio. If anything, it feels weighed down and deeply saddened by the inhumanity that occurs throughout the world. A soul-weary depression can result, as the Fishes naturally empathize with victims everywhere—and not always those of the human kind. However, Pisces also identifies with saints, mystics, gurus, and other cosmic light-bearers who try to redeem humanity's soul and lift our spirit to otherworldly dimensions.

The Fishes feel our joy and pain as their own, which is something Aquarius isn't able or willing to do. Pisces, not an emotionally detached sign, has a vast overview of existence that allows it to pull back and perceive the deeper purpose of humanity's highs and lows. It essentially perceives earthly living as a struggle—after all, integrating spirit with matter is tough work—but Pisces also senses that this task can be made easier once we recognize our true spiritual essence. Our destiny is to evolve our way back Home to the indefinable Oneness of All, that impossible-to-conceive state of pure being in existence before the Big Bang's awesome "Let there be light!" beginning of time and space. Most Piscean types certainly aren't consciously contemplating life as esoterically as this, but they do sense larger, even fated, life patterns at work to enrich each soul's path and give it multilevel meaning (yet not in the more intellectualized manner of Sagittarius). What Pisces senses about life stems from a deeper knowing.

This last sign has the most unguarded ego of all, and thus it is highly vulnerable to outer invasion—especially the energies of others, but also from all sorts of environmental pollutants. The Fishes are quite susceptible to the psychological ups and downs of human experience, but are at odds with themselves regarding such instabilities. One fish swims toward the light, and is always ready to help heal and unify all beings wounded by life's harsher, unjust realities. Social underdogs and disenfranchised people are warmly embraced by the redeemer side of the Fishes. None are turned away, as this facet of Pisces is filled with compassion and empathy.

The other fish descends into darker, shadowy depths and—sensitive to the horrors of living—is dragged down in spirit by a fragmented, confused world in turmoil. This part of Pisces is most susceptible to merging with life's seamier elements, as if unconsciously identifying with all that is most unredeemable and hopeless. This is the fish more troubled by clouded vision and feelings of emptiness. Perhaps it takes two fishes to symbolize Pisces because together they reflect the totality of life in its varying stages of integration and disintegration. Piscean types typically find themselves pulled in such contrasting directions (i.e., world-renowned humanitarian by day, chronic alcoholic by night). Perhaps no other sign, except Scorpio, is capable of such extreme, divergent expression.

Vanishing Pool

As Aries is the sign of the greatest self-interest—something it needs to properly develop—Pisces is the sign of the least self-preoccupation, although it is enthralled with and even addicted to the intoxicating outpourings of its own unconscious. This suggests it sometimes has difficulty escaping from its own inner world. However, Piscean subjectivity is powerful and boundless. What it vividly feels inside itself typically stems from outside sources (such as the strong emotional energy currents of other people). The Fishes keenly pick up on whatever is drifting in the atmosphere, yet they seem to lack the psychological filters needed to reject that which is unhealthy to body, mind, and spirit. Their door is always wide open, letting anything enter—including all that is undesirable and even sabotaging on a soul level.

One big temptation for Pisces involves the loss of a personal, ego-driven identity. Here's a case where the malleability of mutable water makes retaining a structured sense of self difficult. "Mold me into anything you want to," says Pisces, "I'm truly impressionable." Somebody should show Pisces a NASA close-up shot of the pockmarked Moon and ask, "Is *this* how you want to end up looking?" The Fishes are easily bombarded by all kinds of random energies, as if they lack the defense mechanisms that all the other eleven signs have learned to employ. Amazingly, this sign totally surrenders itself to life.

Unlike its opposite sign, Virgo, Pisces is not selective in the experiences it allows itself to undergo. This lack of discrimination is often what gets it in deep trouble, but it also makes Pisces the most tolerant and nonjudgmental sign of all. To discriminate would be to weed something out, and that goes against the Piscean longing for unity.

Nonetheless, Pisces needs to avoid letting its ego vanish into a black pool of nothingness, since it can otherwise tolerate living out its life as a cipher or an invisible being, one forever unnoticed by the world. Something in this sign makes it feel it's not supposed to stand out and grab for the world's attention. (Leo would make a wonderful publicity agent for the Fishes—"First," roars theatrical Leo, "we gotta change that name. How about the Fabulous Flaming Fishes?") Wisely and maturely serving some greater universal cause is exactly what the Cosmos has in mind for Pisces, but to just senselessly undergo an ego-disappearing act—and confusing it with true spirituality—is a major blind spot of this sign. Pisces types need to preserve a strong but resilient sense of self, in order to make their dreams come true.

Walking on Water?

Pisces is like Sagittarius in that it wholeheartedly believes in the impossible. Both signs, never wanting to give up on hope, place great faith in life's potential for last-minute miracles. Both believe in beautiful, grand finales, complete with unearthly rewards waiting at the end of the cosmic rainbow—although Sagittarius is more apt to head to Las Vegas first to see how luck can miraculously manifest! Pisces instead prays for a little more peace on earth to ease the plight of humans undergoing misery everywhere.

This is a sign that sometimes interprets the world too melodramatically, although famines and pestilence and ravaging, incurable diseases are all devastating reminders of how clearly hellish living on Earth can be for those less fortunate. They are not figments of an overactive imagination. Yet if Pisces would allow itself to say it actually hates one thing with a passion—not an easy thing to for the Fishes do—it would choose human cruelty. This is the most humane, "do-no-harm" sign the zodiac offers.

Do-gooders of the world typically have a strong dose of Pisces—and its associated planet, Neptune—in their charts, at least when they identify with the ideals of the fish moving toward the light. (Piscean "no-gooders" are the ones who blindly follow the other fish into darker, toxic waters.) Humanitarian service is an excellent way to channel Piscean energy, although it puts us in emotional contact with how precarious life can be—a sudden disaster can change everything in one's world overnight. Maybe Pisces doesn't allow itself to become too attached to the material world, knowing how life-altering fate can be, and how temporal everything is, security-wise. Profound Pisces teaches us to be in the world, but not of it—to have one foot in the door of the material realm, but to have the other submerged in the transcendental waters of more eternal matters. Its understanding of life's greater meaning can be comprehensive.

All this sounds like a temperament that seeks purity on the physical realm and perfection on the spiritual plane, one that smacks of a somewhat unreal yearning for sainthood. Actually, here's a chance for the ego to come out of hiding and (unfortunately) swell out of proportion, as some otherworldly Piscean types perceive themselves to be cosmic ambassadors from higher dimensions—perhaps even aliens, from other galaxies, who are using their "special powers" to help step up the soul energies of all earthlings on this planet. Pisces feeds such fantasies.

Sadly, Pisces can con itself into believing its own grandiose, spiritual hype—who's to prove otherwise?—while using its charisma to mesmerize its starry-eyed followers. New-Age con artists come under this sign, as well as those who use imaginative ways to bamboozle the unsuspecting. It's a shame to see Piscean types who want to connect with Spirit so badly that they'll use any fraudulent or self-delusional means to do so.

Rather than attempt to conjure up supernatural powers and mystify others by adopting the ethereal persona of a wizard or sorceress, Pisces would be better off chucking the theatrics and instead going down to the soup kitchens in the inner cities to do some real magical work—or volunteering to help out at hospices, or even getting involved in fundraising charity events. Heck, Pisces may discover it does have supernatural power in these areas, the kind that gets others motivated to give of themselves to those seemingly less blessed in life. Pisces Liz Taylor found her true calling when she turned her attention to promoting AIDS awareness. Her ability to connect to the hearts of so many along these lines throughout the years has been phenomenal, and her efforts here are a perfect example of Piscean energy at its best.

Imagine

Saving the world is a mighty big task that could prove too much for any one sign to accomplish, although Pisces seems to be the only one interested in taking on that job. Yet in playing the role of savior, one could easily end up a martyr, fighting for a lost cause and perishing. But if inspired enough, the Fishes will risk becoming sacrificial lambs if that's the only way their dreams can instill wondrous, collective visions in others—such as those involving global harmony, universal love, and even a world without war, sickness, or hunger.

Pisces imagines a better life for everyone, one that is free of all such pain and discord. It is understandable, then, why this sign suffers disillusionment like no other. Is this world too cold-hearted and indifferent to appreciate the selfless objectives of the Fishes? Sometimes that's how Pisces feels, and this prompts it to escape into the depths of its own illusionary inner world and thus remain insulated from harsh, mundane realities.

The Fishes will have to be careful when retreating under these conditions, since their own form of virtual reality is much more awesomely appealing than anything the outer world can dish up. A better path to take is one that allows us to harness the incredible resources of Piscean imagination, and to use such abilities for the greater good of society (yes, Pisces still needs to realize that it's part of the social structure, and not some forsaken soul living on the outer fringes—even though this sign is comfortable playing the hermit, at times, and living a secluded life, far away from mainstream worldliness).

Pisces is blessed with the power to positively channel archetypal energy from the collective unconscious, meaning that it can tap into angelic realms and provide us with the rarest and loftiest of images. Beauty expressed on this level can be exquisite and is able to soothe our deepest selves. It is good for all Piscean types never to deprive themselves of the finest their culture has to offer in the realms of art, music, and drama. This safely allows them to have the transcendent experiences they secretly crave and need.

Closing Time

Being the last sign of the zodiac, Pisces symbolizes the poignant endings of conditions that have already peaked and are now preparing to break down and dissolve. The cycle that began with Aries—fresh and vigorous—is coming to a meaningful close here, implying it's now time to rest, reflect, and let go of our attachment to the material world. It's the assignment of the Fishes to further the disintegration of all that once gave us solid support and concrete meaning.

Life thus seems to be in a woozy state of collapse and uncertainty, almost as if the Cosmos is drunk and a bit disoriented (hmmm . . . and after being so disciplined and organized in Capricorn). Nothing is to hold its shape for long. Everything is fluid and constantly changing, yet not for the purpose of instigating new beginnings and getting our little ego all pumped up. Changes here lead to a cessation of self-willed activity, as Pisces instead teaches us to stop asserting ourselves in action just to satisfy earthy ambitions. Instead we are to descend to our depths to experience stillness and contemplation. Who could have imagined that the zodiac would finally lead to all of this? Yet, from water we came and to water we return, hopefully in a more illuminated state of self-awareness.

As a result, Pisces feels it can't trust permanent security for long, at least not in a worldly sense. It knows that everything eventually dissolves. Yet society still expects us to build reliable, tangible structures, as we accumulate things of material value. (In fact, Taurus got all this going quite a while back on the day it received its first paycheck and went to town!) But Pisces is not sure that such "stuff" is what it needs to be amassing. It knows material attachments won't last forever, and they really don't even feed us what we need on a soul level. "Everything is destined to break down or fall apart," realizes Pisces. And some things end in disturbing ways that play havoc with our emotions.

Thus, the Fishes—at least unconsciously—have determined not to exclusively possess anything, no matter how precious. Yet they *are* willing to share what they have freely and lovingly with the rest of the world. Sharing unconditionally like this is one way to prevent any sense of ultimate loss. As this slow process of dissolution takes over, Pisces is challenged to distill the deeper meaning—the underlying essence—from all experiences on Earth, and then to offer that essence back to the Universe, to later be recycled for the collective enrichment of all. It's not to be retained for self-seeking purposes, since Pisces is the most universally oriented sign of them all.

Neptune Heals

Neptune—Pisces' associated planet of inner illumination—helps us tap into the one eternal reality that underlies the conscious, material realm in which we humans become so engrossed. Neptune symbolizes an indescribable, cosmic stillness, where time and space do not exist—at least not in the normal manner. This is the least earthly of all the planets, which is fitting for a sign that is the least materialistic in orientation. Both Neptune and Pisces enjoy retreating to more quiet, inner places of the heart and soul. Worldly ambition is not strong, but big, beautiful dreams of universal love and harmony do appeal emotionally to both.

However, Neptune is more prone to be extreme in its release of irrational feelings that flood our consciousness and alter our senses. It enables us to plug directly into our unconscious yearnings. Pisces—being more subject to our cultural climate—instills an obligation to focus on often neglected societal concerns that affect the welfare of many. We feel driven to apply this sign's energies to humanitarian issues. Yet Neptune—temperamentally a mystic—is content at times just to have us enter its subjective, magical world to explore its wonders, typically while we're alone. It's less drawn to organized community involvement and doesn't feel the same sense of active duty to serve that Pisces does (although strongly Neptunian types do need altruistic social outlets to keep them balanced—too much seclusion and avoidance of human contact can get them in trouble psychologically). If anything, it's Pisces that needs to find quality time alone, away from others who can be energy drainers, since the Fishes are surrounded too often by dependent people in need.

Neptune, like Pisces, can be a marvelous healing force. Both planet and sign inspire us to dissolve all that impedes our growth and that destroys life, although we humans sometimes unwisely use these energies in distorted ways and end up destroying ourselves, rather than society's negative elements. Neptune and Pisces do not have a healthy sense of boundaries and can fail to shield themselves from unwanted external forces (even those coming from darker areas of the unconscious). This leads to great vulnerability, although it seems Neptunians suffer more here than Piscean types, who appear to apply greater detachment (a trick they picked up from both Aquarius and their opposite sign, Virgo). Perhaps the Fishes simply choose to ignore what otherwise could prove bothersome. Neptune is more prone to absorb its surroundings, and the people in them, than is Pisces, even if this is not all that obvious on the surface.

Pisces also seems to be better at visualizing life's larger schemes. Neptune may sense that a vast, underlying force is in operation, but Pisces is better able to understand how all the pieces of anything fit to comprise a whole. Pisces is more observational than Neptune, who gets its information from internal sources, not from the outer world. Unlike Neptune, a planet more apt to be blinded by its subjectivity, Pisces is less devoted to its beliefs. Still, both keenly sense that there is much more to life than meets the eye—a profound awareness that meditation and contemplation can reveal to us.

Closing Comments

Wherever Pisces is in our chart describes where we're guided to go within and discover how to make this often confusing area of our life work best for us. Outside advice won't always make sense, probably because it doesn't sensitively address our internal needs (plus, until we can better articulate such needs, nobody can really help us). Our Piscean parts require gentle treatment and tender concern. Here we have hidden wisdom that needs to be coaxed out of us, once we learn to value listening to our inner voice. Following the path of worldly success will not appease the hungers and insecurities we may feel inside. Tuning in to a more transcendent reality—which helps us feel more purposefully connected to something larger than ourselves—seems instead to give us greater peace of mind and a sense that we can visualize a better future for ourselves.

Pisces also helps us become more accepting of what we cannot change (compared to Neptunians, who are more prone to seek "miracle" cures and other quick, magical fixes for what ails them). Self-deception tied to misplaced faith may be stronger in Neptunians. Pisces, at least for the sake of balance, can draw from the strengths of its opposite sign, analytical Virgo (a sign less prone to place faith in things unproven). Still, Neptune tunes into the Piscean desire to take away the pain in people and to restore their souls with hope. We won't grow properly with our Piscean energies if we remain too narrow-minded to believe that there are positive, universal forces guiding us toward spiritual fulfillment. This part of our life needs our fluid imagination and our emotional receptivity. We need to keep our sensitivity heightened and ready to do some transformational good in the world.

FAMOUS PISCES TYPES (natal Pisces placements listed)

Michelangelo, artist: Sun, Moon, Mars

Elizabeth Taylor, actress: Sun, Mercury, Mars, North Node

Edgar Cayce, psychic: Sun, Mercury, Venus, Saturn

Billie Holiday, singer: Mercury, Venus, Mars, Jupiter

Glenn Close, actress: Sun, Mercury, Mars

Alexander Graham Bell, inventor: Sun, Mercury, Saturn, Ascendant

PART TWO

Sign Combinations

Chapter Five

Signs that Square & Oppose

SIGNS IN ASPECT

Now that the twelve signs have been individually introduced in chapters 3 and 4, let's look at how they interrelate when paired up. Here, in part 2, I analyze some of the themes and challenges that any two signs will typically deal with when combined. Each sign has its own specific set of traits, unmatched by any other sign. However, due to the aspect relationship formed—in other words, how many signs apart the two are—any sign can share its individual qualities with a degree of ease or difficulty, depending on the nature of the other sign in question.

Even when two signs seem to share much in common—as do signs of the same element, such as Aries/Leo—they still have a few differences in temperament that will need to be ironed out. Yet when two signs appear to have absolutely nothing in common, as in Aries/Pisces (seemingly at first to be a "Gee, why even bother getting involved?" relationship), the truth is that they actually do share a few complementary traits that will help them pull their energies together in a growth-producing manner.

If the zodiac's twelve signs symbolize essential parts of a greater whole, then these important facets of our being ideally will work together to serve a higher purpose—that of fostering our integrated self-awareness. We need to embrace the psychological processes represented by all these signs. Any dissimilarities shown are not intrinsically divisive (likewise, our eyes and our feet may not seem to have much in common, but it sure is good to be able to see what we're about to step on, at times, especially when barefoot). The friction that so-called "incompatible" signs often generate can spur our evolutionary development, which thus accelerates our spiritual progress.

I find it ludicrous to think, for example, that Taurus and Sagittarius can never, ever see eye to eye about anything, and that they'll always frustrate each other's needs and remain hopelessly incompatible. Often the astrological advice given—when trying to be constructive—is for us to do our Taurus parts in those areas where they seem the most appropriate, but then shift gears and display our Sagittarian qualities in those life activities that need and welcome such fiery energy.

While this is a nice and tidy way to look at things, it still hints that these two signs can never be in the same room together, cooking up a tasty meal for us to enjoy. I guess I'd rather that all twelve signs find some degree of common ground or even accept their differences, and then try to find creative ways to blend those differences.

Most of us have our Sun, Moon, and Ascendant in at least two signs (there are those rare people who have all three in one sign—perhaps in this case we'll need to consider the sign of the ruler of the Ascendant as well, since that should likely involve a different sign). When you read the many descriptions that follow, consider first your Sun/Moon combination—unless you're born under the New Moon phase (in which your Sun and Moon are usually in the same sign). Then check out your Sun/Ascendant and Moon/Ascendant combinations. All these are apt to reveal the more outstanding features of your personal nature.

When it comes to the remaining planets, it's best to first consider the signs of your natal Sun through Mars, since these are the more personal parts of your nature that show greater degrees of self-interest. They represent qualities with which you may more easily identify. However, many astrologers typically include all the planets—from Sun through Pluto—and even the lunar nodes in their analysis. Some also devise a rating system, based on points, to determine a chart's element and mode emphasis. We can also do this for the actual signs in which our natal planets fall.

For example, the Sun and Moon might be given two points apiece, while the Ascendant and Midheaven receive one point each. Mercury through Mars might be given one-and-a-half points apiece, plus one point each for Jupiter and Saturn. Every outer planet—whose signs are less intrinsic to our growth—could receive one-half point. I'd probably give the North and South Nodes each one point, since they seem to offer us valuable information regarding our personality dynamics. Also, add an extra one-half point to the planet that rules the Ascendant (which gives us additional clues about how we view ourselves and formulate a surface identity that we're willing to show to the world).

Tally up all these numbers to see which two signs dominate. If three or more signs are emphasized equally—at least according to their number count—pick the two that involve the Sun or Moon. (I actually prefer to just eyeball the chart and get a feel for what seems to be highlighted, without resorting to the numbers game. Still, it's fun to do the point system and see what you come up with.)

There's no way I can cover everything that could be said when comparing any two signs, and still keep this book from becoming too hefty in size. Perhaps what I do say about them will help you insightfully flash on other unmentioned issues, which is how astrology really works once you've studied it for a while. Things just pop out of your unconscious storehouse of collective wisdom. I have also included a list, at the end of each sign/sign interpretation, of famous people who have or had their natal Sun and Moon in these signs.

Sometimes such individuals seem to fit the nature of these signs impressively—almost as if they are living, breathing archetypes—and other times they don't seem at all to be sterling examples of the principles at work. Nonetheless, we need to keep in mind that we only know these famous folks according to their public personas (their career images are sometimes carefully crafted). We aren't privy to how they really are, or once were, in their more private moments. It could be that their professional situation does not or did not allow for the easy release of certain traits that are more comfortably activated once away from the glare of the spotlight. Famous people's real natures may not be anything like how they package themselves in a professional sense (it could be that the qualities symbolized by their Midheavens and Tenth-House planets override more personal parts of their charts, at least while the eyes of the world are on them).

Well, it's time to explore the sixty-six possible sign/sign combinations. In this chapter, I have chosen to begin with signs that square or oppose one another. In chapter 6, I will cover signs that sextile or trine each other, and in chapter 7, I will examine signs that semisextile or quincunx one another.

Signs that Square

Let's start this chapter with those sign combinations that have traditionally been considered to be stress-producing: signs that square. These are the pairs that often rub each other the wrong way, until they realize that they can also produce energy-releasing sparks. Any two signs that square each other are actually dynamic duos that help us powerfully grow, once we learn how to consolidate their energies better in a self-directed manner. After all, they represent two essential parts of our developmental process, and thus they each need to be validated and supported. We shouldn't let them pull us apart or make us feel split from within.

Squaring signs must find smart ways to get along. They need to help—not thwart—each other, even though they may start out assuming that they have absolutely nothing in common. In truth, they possess valuable resources that can be shared effectively. Yet to successfully do this will prove challenging. It seems the Cosmos loves to bring together such "odd couples" in our charts, perhaps just to see what transformative potential will be actualized by such frictional stimulation.

Each sign squares two other signs of the same mode in the zodiac. Squaring signs—like signs that oppose one another—are traditionally considered to be tensional. Unfortunately, traditional astrology believes in sidestepping conflict at all cost. However, twenty-first-century astrology acknowledges that a little creative friction can become the driving force that helps us bring out our best. Still, these signs are said to work at cross-purposes and are thus assumed to be incompatible and even combative.

Naturally, then, they are primarily the signs that mass-market astrology paperbacks eagerly tell us to avoid if we wish to stay happily married. The seemingly sensible advice here, for example, would be for Taurus to stick to its own kind—Virgo or Capricorn—but never to stray, let's say, into the stranger pastures of Aquarius. Yet what if we were born with a mix of Taurus and Aquarius in our own chart? Well, we'll just *have* to make this combo work for us, since these energies will be part of our makeup for a whole lifetime!

Any two signs share a few things in common—yes, even Taurus and Gemini—traits that materialize once these signs are pressured to interact. Even if they don't share many commonalities, each sign has qualities that could benefit the other. Any two signs also have dissimilar features that require a more tolerant, cooperative spirit on our part if they are to blend well. This applies even to signs of the *same* element, those that naturally trine each other. The standard line is that trining signs imply nothing but harmony and mutual understanding—let's even throw in good karma from past lives. Yet, since no two signs are exactly alike, attitude adjustments will be needed (for example, we shouldn't assume that time-efficient Virgo is always thrilled by the sometimes lethargic way Taurus can waste a whole day "relaxing").

Generally speaking, squaring signs don't easily understand why the other acts the way it does—feisty Aries is baffled by Cancer's moody behavior, showy Leo can't fathom secretive Scorpio, gung-ho Sagittarius finds wishy-washy Pisces too lacking in enthusiasm, and so on. Yet a wise and perhaps mischievous Cosmos seems to draw these signs to each other, again and again, to help them iron out their differences and instead capitalize on what they can effectively combine and make work. No sign is forever to avoid—or engage in battle with—another sign, since, as said before, all twelve signs comprise the essential parts of the ideal whole. Nonetheless, it will take effort and patience to learn the secrets of healthy integration. So let's start with the four cardinal signs, each of which squares two other signs of dissimilar elements.

Aries/Cancer

Will these two signs ever get along? At first glance, you'd think, "Not a chance!" Aries rides roughshod over most tender feelings, while the Crab is already quite touchy about the least little disturbance in its atmosphere, especially the noisy kind that the Ram easily creates. Cancer doesn't like direct, forceful approaches to conflict solving, yet Aries has no time or patience to gently wade through emotional waters, so as not to create too many ripples. It faults the Crab for taking everything too darn personally, and in ways that hinder effective action (and when Cancer gets its feelings hurt, things can come to a halt as it withdraws to brood). Yet Aries also takes things very personally—something they both have in common—although the Ram never slows its momentum, and it certainly doesn't retreat when it's upset. It instead comes on even stronger, impetuously pushing its way forward to knock down immediate obstacles.

Still, Aries and Cancer—both being headstrong cardinal signs—are impelled to attract or even create minicrises, if need be, since cardinality operates best when it can quickly clear the air and start over, once an issue has been resolved. Signs of this mode don't like feeling stuck in predicaments for too long. Things are not to drag on. Actually, Aries and Cancer are self-absorbed once problems arise, plus they certainly aren't the most objective of signs to deal with when things are going badly for them. When situations get too uncomfortable, they seek instant relief by letting off a little steam. At least they both are alert and responsive to what's happening around them (Cancer more deeply so, of course, being a water sign). They each also know a thing or two about getting defensive (the Ram is a notorious head-butter, while the Crab can threaten would-be intruders with its snapping claws).

Nonetheless, Aries is teaching us to pull away from others so that we can retain our independent identity, while Cancer is all about gathering people closer to us for long-term security and deep bonding. Perhaps this is precisely why they rub each other the wrong way at times. Aries barks at Cancer, "Stop with the hugs and kisses, you're suffocating me, and I'm gonna be late!" To this, Cancer weeps, "You're so selfish and ungrateful. I'll never cook dinner and clean the house for you again . . . oh, here's your lunch bag—eat everything, don't forget to bring back that spoon, and how about buying me another box of tissues on your way home?"

It would appear that life is never dull for these two signs, yet such a volatile mix of emotion and adrenaline could easily prove to be too much. If we have Aries and Cancer highlighted in our chart, we'll need to learn more about the benefits of composure and of thinking things through before letting our strong, impulsive feelings get the better of us. When Aries and Cancer don't work well together, it's panic time, when our overreaction to current situations keeps us from thinking straight and making wise moves.

In general, one problem that gets in the way of smoother interaction is that the element of fire (Aries) is pitted against the element of water (Cancer). Water is too sensitive to withstand the seemingly abusive treatment that Aries can dish out (the Ram's brusque ways, alone, can jar the Crab's more delicate sensibilities). However, cardinal-water Cancer implies emotions that quickly surface, which for Aries is good, since the Ram doesn't deal as well with signs that keep too much within for too long. It knows how to fire up the Crab and get it to respond openly—actually, "lashing out" is more what occurs. Aries thinks fights are healthy and honest ways to use up any overflow of passion—now, if it could only convince Cancer that this is true. This combo may appear stormy and discontent at times, but we get to learn the psychological value of getting things off our chest instead of letting issues fester.

ARIES/CANCER ASTRO-LEBRITIES

Aretha Franklin, singer: (Sun in Aries, Moon in Cancer)
Dennis Quaid, actor: (Sun in Aries, Moon in Cancer)
Emma Thompson, actress: (Sun in Aries, Moon in Cancer)

Arlo Guthrie, folk singer: (Sun in Cancer, Moon in Aries)
Barbara Cartland, romance novelist: (Sun in Cancer, Moon in Aries)
Bob Fosse, choreographer: (Sun in Cancer, Moon in Aries)

Cancer/Libra

Cancer loves how well Aries can handle things that need quick attention—the Ram never seems flustered—and also how this fire sign does it all with courage and confidence, qualities that the Crab can't often muster when the going gets tough and the sky is falling. Still, Cancer now looks toward Libra and anticipates a much more pleasant relationship (the frustrated Ram called it quits, anyway, and took off). After all, Libra—associated with peace-loving Venus—oozes obvious charm. The Crab also likes hearing that everyone else gets along with friendly, accommodating Libra.

Yet the hard truth is that air—a lover of clarity and verbal directness—doesn't understand the cloudy underworld of less-articulate water very well. Water's raw, instinctual feelings, in turn, don't want to be met with logical air's accustomed intellectual detachment, since this unsympathetically smacks of indifference. "Understand me deeply," pleads water, "Don't just observe me from a distance and take mental notes on my reactions. Feel my pain!"

Well, at least Libra is one air sign that likes to get more intimately involved. Still, the Crab can feel it when the Balancer is miles away in its head, even when it's smiling and acting as cordial as can be. Cancer has a knack for knowing when people are not "there" in the emotional moment. It hates cool responses, yet often misreads them.

Libra is willing to bend over backwards to meet the varying needs of each sign, up to a point. Remember, it expects others to reciprocate, and will use its cooperative nature to test people out: "Are they going to be fair with me, or are they users?" Libra, sensitive to being manipulated, is also learning how to do just that in its partnerships (and it could be argued that Libra taught Scorpio every trick it knows regarding how to handle relationships).

This sign thus doesn't much like it when Cancer uses its whiny emotionality—its cranky side—to get its way, plus the Crab can resort to pouting and to pulling little guilt trips on others when it's feeling insecure or hurt. Libra, being more detached, is able to pull back calmly and reflect, "You know, you did that very same thing to me last week. But did I make an issue of it? Did I try to attack you and make you feel bad? No, I handled it all rather maturely." When Libra tries to get back at Cancer—and here the Balancer is great at turning the tables—it uses much finesse in its counterattack and ends up coming off as smooth as butter!

Cancer, at times, seems as helpless as a baby—but that could be a ploy to get attention. However, Libra—although not parental in nature—does seem to enjoy being a helpmate. It can be an understanding companion, willing to listen to others and offer advice. If we have these two signs emphasized in our chart, we probably have a calm, maternal ability to help others clarify their needs and thereby gain a welcome perspective concerning their pressing life issues (both signs show concern for others undergoing stress—both act as tension relievers).

We apparently have counseling skills (or at least the temperament for being a sounding board for people). But, when put upon by chronically needy types, we may have a hard time saying, "No, I'm not interested in helping you. Find someone else, and leave me alone!" It would be quite a breakthrough in consciousness if Cancer/Libra types could actually say these words and mean them.

Kindness is a common denominator. Both signs show consideration for others. Still, Cancer does mother people a bit too much for Libra's taste, and Libra presents a polished, perfect image to others than Cancer knows in its gut is artificial at times. Still, this combo can work out fine if we learn when to give others the breathing space they need (Cancer's lesson), but also when to enjoy quiet, in-depth contact without always having to take sides in interpersonal matters (Libra's lesson), especially when such "discussions" become outright debates that only ruffle emotional feathers—ours or another's. Still, both signs try to maintain peace when possible.

CANCER/LIBRA ASTRO-LEBRITIES

Arthur Ashe, tennis pro: (Sun in Cancer, Moon in Libra)
Janet Leigh, actress: (Sun in Cancer, Moon in Libra)
Sylvester Stallone, actor: (Sun in Cancer, Moon in Libra)

Eleanor Roosevelt, humanitarian: (Sun in Libra, Moon in Cancer)
Paul Simon, musician: (Sun in Libra, Moon in Cancer)
Mira Sorvino, actress: (Sun in Libra, Moon in Cancer)

Libra/Capricorn

Sometimes Libra inwardly criticizes Cancer for being too spineless and intimidated to stand up for its rights, or too indirect or emotional to plead its case effectively. It's true that a whimpering Crab, low in self-esteem, can let itself be treated like a doormat, if that ensures it will at least never be abandoned. If emotionally messed up enough, Cancer types can cling to unhealthy attachments. Yet Libra despises that sort of insecurity and will assertively bolt out of any bad union, once it's had enough (although deciding *when* to leave can be tricky).

At least with Capricorn, Libra senses it's dealing with a more self-motivated, poised, and proficient sign who's ready to grab for some power in society. Although Libra is less ambitious about climbing to the top, it is as appearance-conscious as the Goat. Both signs want to make good first impressions, and that means abiding by certain social formalities. Look good and you will be treated well, is their philosophy. Obviously, they can make the mistake of thinking that a sophisticated air is most important to achieving worldly success.

Traditional astrology considered Saturn to be "exalted"—doing its best—in Libra (although Venus in Capricorn gets mixed reviews). Libra is as interested as Capricorn in laying down the law. The Balancer is not afraid to evaluate both sides of a dilemma objectively and impartially, and then pass judgment (as it attempts to balance the scales of justice). It does this with an almost eerie coolness that is devoid of emotional bias. Libra is very focused on the consequences for the actions of those who break the rules. Capricorn takes on the role of judge, the one who enforces the law and doles out the punishment. This is all done with a sense of solemn duty, not vengeance (after all, the Goat has a society to run and simply needs to impose regulations, now and then). Thus, together, these signs are all about doing the right thing in the eyes of the social system.

By behaving according to the expectations of others, Libra and Capricorn run the risk of being insincere at times (perhaps they seek approval too much and will only act in ways that are acceptable to others). They are more careful not to make waves unnecessarily by showing what they really feel deep inside. Here's a case where their fears of public judgment override any impulse to reveal their real selves, and this can be problematic (setting them up later for an "identity" crisis whereby, after a point, they hardly know what they are all about).

Actually, Libra tends to mirror others better than does Capricorn, and is less rigidly locked in by any limited persona. Still, if we have these signs emphasized in our chart, we'll have to make sure we don't show others only what they want to see. Although this may make us popular, and help us achieve great heights in a worldly sense, we risk losing touch with our true selves.

One benefit of learning the rules of society's game is the cultivation of a sophisticated demeanor. Both signs can be classy and urbane, although Libra perhaps is like this for more aesthetic reasons. They each recoil in distaste at coarse, boorish behavior (and note how Libran etiquette books are loaded with Capricornian do's and dont's). Both are obviously supporters of appropriate behavior. Civility means a lot to them and rudeness is seldom tolerated.

However, Libra is better at understanding why some people act as badly as they do, while Capricorn just thinks all inexcusable behavior needs to be curbed (here's where air has an advantage over earth when it comes to having a broader perspective on things). Libra at times will bend the rules to allow for other people's errors in judgment, much more so than the hard-nosed Goat. It's better at putting itself in another's shoes and figuring out human motives.

We who have this Libra/Capricorn combo are social creatures who are out to impress others with how decent and responsible we really are (not that there's anything wrong with that). We're willing to toe the line if doing so proves personally advantageous in the long run (although our critics would call us opportunistic). We can kiss up to authority when it benefits us. Yet, at all times, we'll need to make sure we continue to nurture those internal qualities that genuinely make us who we are—not the glossy package we carefully present to the world.

Libra/Capricorn Astro-lebrities
  Matt Damon, actor: (Sun in Libra, Moon in Capricorn)
  Susan Sarandon, actress: (Sun in Libra, Moon in Capricorn)
  Johnny Carson, television personality: (Sun in Libra, Moon in Capricorn)
  Dyan Cannon, actress: (Sun in Capricorn, Moon in Libra)
  Nicolas Cage, actor: (Sun in Capricorn, Moon in Libra)
  Joan of Arc, saint: (Sun in Capricorn, Moon in Libra)

Capricorn/Aries

Capricorn doesn't care much for open opposition, but at least Libra can be very cooperative and willing to follow the Goat's lead (*if* the plan of action sounds smart and is well designed—something that Libra's mentally adept input helps ensure will be the case). Yet Capricorn is not so certain if it's going to have such an agreeable partnership with the Ram. Aries doesn't like being bossed around, especially by a sign that assumes it's a natural-born authority figure ("Father knows best"). This independent fire sign does not want to be parented by anybody.

Aries favors hot, impetuous action and lives in the moment. Capricorn lives in the now as well, but its moves are based on cool-headed deliberation and the ability to plan its strategy. Aries cares little about planning its activities. It hates to feel bound by inflexible timetables and organized agendas. Yet Capricorn plays by the books and is a stickler for following proper procedure, and punctually so. Rules are not made to be ignored in the Goat's world of high-pressured responsibility, since too much is at risk, with so many depending on reliable results.

Still, although the Ram seems like some brash, young upstart to the more mature, seasoned Goat, these signs share a love of dynamic challenge and forward motion. Their headstrong ambition drives them to move out into life and overcome all obstacles, except that the scope of operation for Capricorn is much larger and more consequential—one wrong move and the Goat's out of the game, whereas the Cosmos almost always allows the Ram to start all over again.

Little seems insurmountable to these two, since their will to succeed is powerful. Determination keeps them from giving up, although Capricorn is blessed with greater staying power. Like Libra, Capricorn knows about the law of cause and effect, and the penalties that await those who are less sure-footed in life. The Goat thus acts cautiously and patiently. Aries instead throws all caution to the wind and embraces risk. It defies the Fates.

If these two signs are highlighted in our chart, our strength may lie in executing action in a direct, no-nonsense manner. We don't wait around for others to get things going, not when we can independently get in the driver's seat and take off on our own. Self-reliance is strong, as well as a driving need to prove to ourselves—and to convince others—that we are capable enough to handle anything tossed our way (although Capricorn is customarily more prepared than Aries, a bigger believer in spontaneity).

Perhaps the biggest hurdle to overcome here deals with self-discipline: Capricorn has it, while Aries hates it. If the Ram in us starts jumping into a project too soon, without a careful review of the details involved, failure may result. Capricorn teaches us to make more timely moves, based on sizing up a situation in pragmatic terms. It's then that we can succeed, slowly and steadily. A lack of patience can therefore be a major stumbling block for us.

Capricorn admires Aries' guts and its willingness to fight for what it wants. The Goat doesn't like feeling fearful, and while not a daring risk-taker, it's willing to face up to what it secretly dreads—potential rejection for not being qualified or good enough. Yet by dealing with such fears, it tests its true abilities and opens doors that lead to opportunity.

The Goat would love to use the Ram's self-assurance—and occasionally its bravado—for those times when this often-reserved earth sign needs a little fiery flair to get itself noticed. Aries doesn't perceive life as having the obstacles—those waiting to dash even the best-laid plans—that Capricorn sometimes sees everywhere. The Goat needs to infuse its life with a bit of the Ram's idealism, since pessimism and self-doubt are self-limiting ways to approach success.

In general, these two signs can be pushy when trying to attain what they want, although Capricorn can seemingly wait forever, while Aries wants it now! Self-centeredness can be strong, and emerges quickest when the Ram and the Goat feel thwarted in action enough to resort to defensive tactics. That's when they'll do whatever it takes to survive and get back on track. This combo can make us look tough on the outside—showing no vulnerabilities—but we're probably too driven to relax and enjoy life properly. Yet it can also be the signature of one whose grit and perseverance results in an uphill climb that culminates in high achievement.

CAPRICORN/ARIES ASTRO-LEBRITIES

Al Capone, gangster: (Sun in Capricorn, Moon in Aries)

Diane Von Furstenberg, designer: (Sun in Capricorn, Moon in Aries)

Albert Schweitzer, humanitarian: (Sun in Capricorn, Moon in Aries)

Sarah Jessica Parker, actress: (Sun in Aries, Moon in Capricorn)

Al Gore, politician: (Sun in Aries, Moon in Capricorn)

David Letterman, television personality: (Sun in Aries, Moon in Capricorn)

Taurus/Leo

While squaring cardinal signs tend to stir up action that pushes for dynamic change—and maybe head-on confrontation—squaring fixed signs resist altering themselves to accommodate one another. They don't like giving in to demands, and thus power struggles and impasses can ensue. Pressure can build. Yet the tremendous resources bottled up in these signs need purposeful release, so life brings on forceful, uncompromising conditions that make this fixed group finally bend and yield to one other. Once they willingly exchange their assets, they find it's not such a bad thing after all, and wonder why they hadn't conceded sooner. But until then, they refuse to budge, stubbornly adhering only to what they know about life, which can result in a narrow perspective based on rigid assumptions.

Taurus is a very possessive sign that enjoys holding on tightly to whatever it owns. Everything about the Bull's world is geared toward magnetizing substance of value, and then building a solid, material base of security from those resources it has attracted. This sign is very economical in how it uses its energies—it hates to see them wasted or even wrongly used.

On the other hand, optimistic Leo feels it has plenty of fiery energy to burn—and even squander—and it's not afraid to give that energy out to the world. It's interested in radiating itself to others in grand style. It won't hold itself back due to any fear of running out of fuel (Leo doesn't expect to suffer shortages in life). The Lion thus sees the Bull as a tightwad—on all levels—who's too content with living a safe but dull life. Yet Taurus faults Leo for always being willing to gamble with its future security, just to have fun expending itself colorfully in the here and now. (Remember, squaring signs can't easily figure each other out).

Still, the Bull and the Lion are very strong-willed and are not easily deterred from satisfying their desires. Like all fixed signs, they can be single-minded in their goals. They also expect to be treated well in life, and do not tolerate being deprived of whatever they want to have or wish to experience. Self-value is a Taurean issue; self-esteem is equally important to Leo. Both signs obviously want to feel good about themselves, with Leo showing a greater interest in receiving praise from others (Taurus is more self-contained and depends less on favorable reviews—if the Bull is pleased with its own efforts, that's good enough).

There is also a possible indulgent streak with this combo. Taurus likes to pamper itself with comfort and sensual pleasure, especially if it's not going to cost too much. It's an earthy sign wanting to appease its physical appetites. Leo doesn't care how much its pleasures will cost (in fact, it connotes a higher price tag with greater value). The Lion seeks the best in life that it can afford, since it thinks so highly of itself. A taste for luxury is common, something that the frugal Bull frowns on. We who have a Taurus/Leo emphasis may swing between periods of careful budgeting and wild splurging—we'll need to avoid going overboard with either tendency.

Loyalty based on enduring feelings can be evident. Both signs form strong attachments to those they trust and respect. They also wish to be seen as trustworthy and honorable in their intentions, although no sign beats Taurus for utter dependability (earth always delivers what it promises and is much more grounded than fire). Neither sign is devious or underhanded in its approach to getting what it wants.

This pairing thus implies honesty, strong integrity, and an inner strength that others can count on in times of need (although the Lion is more comfortable playing the hero role than is the Bull). A Taurus/Leo emphasis is found in the charts of those who take a very personal approach to living, one based on strong inner direction. There's an obstinate nature here that could perhaps use a few lessons in flexibility, as both signs won't take no for an answer. Nonetheless, there is an authentic self-expression that indicates a strong backbone and an ability to handle even arduous times with dignified self-composure.

TAURUS/LEO ASTRO-LEBRITIES

Queen Elizabeth II, monarch: (Sun in Taurus, Moon in Leo)
Willem de Koonig, artist: (Sun in Taurus, Moon in Leo)
Barbra Streisand, singer-actress: (Sun in Taurus, Moon in Leo)

Bill Clinton, U.S. president: (Sun in Leo, Moon in Taurus)
Mick Jagger, rock idol: (Sun in Leo, Moon in Taurus)
Carl Jung, psychoanalyst: (Sun in Leo, Moon in Taurus)

Leo/Scorpio

Leo teaches the sometimes-stingy Bull to develop a generous heart and even a taste for flair, as there's more on life's menu than just meat and potatoes. In turn, sensible Taurus tones down Leo's more extravagant traits, which helps channel the Lion's exuberant energy into practical and even lucrative avenues of self-expression. On the other hand, watery Scorpio—with its famous intensity—heats up the Lion's passion, but often in temperamental ways. Leo's already a dramatic sign, one that paints its life in vivid colors. Scorpio throws in extra-emotional fervor and a measure of inner turmoil, and the results of such a fire-water mix can be explosive at times.

It's probably no mystery why the Lion isn't all that cozy around the Scorpion. Leo prefers signs that are upfront and have nothing to hide —especially those signs that are entertaining, as well. Scorpio won't display its feelings easily and acts like it has plenty to conceal. It also won't go out of its way to please or amuse anyone. Leo is afraid that Scorpio makes life all too complicated, thus taking much of the spontaneous joy out of it. The Scorpion is not playful in the carefree manner that Leo can be.

Being fixed signs, expect stubborn feelings to linger, especially when both are upset. These two won't let things slide if they feel they've been offended—both have issues with pride to work out. Whatever bothers them is not something that they'll quickly shake off, probably because emotional detachment is not one of their stronger features. There's nothing cool-headed about them, although Scorpio can at times appear aloof and distant, while Leo can seem invulnerable and is not easily shaken. Both show strength and determination on the surface. Yet internally, it's a different story, as each is plagued by less-obvious insecurities. Leo and Scorpio also have a distaste for any weaknesses they find in themselves, failings that the outer world will rarely get to see.

Deep in Scorpio's psyche is the realization that the ego needs to transform itself periodically. Leo's ego pretty much hogs the stage when it can. Scorpio finds that troublesome and wants Leo to do a little honest, inner digging to uncover why it demands so much personal attention and adoration. Always upbeat about itself, the Lion doesn't feel it needs such psychoanalysis and doesn't like being investigated— "I've got nothing to hide. What you see is what you get." Leo then adds, "I'm not a twisted introvert who always tries to read into things."

The Lion does think that the suspicious Scorpion sees life too darkly. Of course, Scorpio is unconvinced that Leo's trusting, unguarded approach to the world is wise—it seems naive and too idealistic. "People are tricky and you gotta watch them like a hawk," warns Scorpio.

Those of us with these signs emphasized in our chart will need to ease up on any Scorpio paranoia we may have regarding what people can potentially do to hurt us, since Leo seems to bring out its best when it feels admired and loved, not despised or victimized. Noble-hearted Leo doesn't understand treachery at all, and therefore doesn't even think about betrayal. But Scorpio knows that everyone has a dark side, and thus this sign is wary about opening up fully to anybody. It needs to partake of the almost childlike hope Leo has about how glorious life's adventure can be: "Come out from underneath that rock, Scorpio, and feel the bright sun lovingly warm your body. Enjoy life to the fullest and anticipate its bounty." Perhaps Scorpio will ponder all this, but it still advises, "Learn to read people better than you do, Leo. You expect too much, yet not everyone wants to keep you happily on your throne, especially when you come on so strong and try to exclusively run the show!"

Actually, these signs—when working well together—often display a gusto for full-bodied living. There's nothing mild-mannered or lukewarm about them. They can be extremely focused in their creative pursuits, and very autonomous in how they operate—no interference from anyone, please! If not careful, they can abuse power and control in ways that others find quite heavy-handed. When joining forces, these two need to learn how to just let things flow.

LEO/SCORPIO ASTRO-LEBRITIES

Ben Affleck, actor: (Sun in Leo, Moon in Scorpio)

Kathie Lee Gifford, television celebrity: (Sun in Leo, Moon in Scorpio)

Alfred Hitchcock, director: (Sun in Leo, Moon in Scorpio)

Julia Roberts, actress: (Sun in Scorpio/Moon in Leo)

Larry Flynt, publisher: (Sun in Scorpio/Moon in Leo)

Whoopi Goldberg, actress: (Sun in Scorpio/Moon in Leo)

Scorpio/Aquarius

That Leo/Scorpio mix is passionate, all right, but a bit too hot to handle at times. And when things are not going so great, their Oscar-worthy emotional responses can be gut-wrenching. But when Scorpio "teams up" with Aquarius—and that's how the Water Bearer likes to put it—the temperature drops to much cooler degrees. Actually, Scorpio always carries its hidden stash of frozen fire, which it is able to instantly thaw when needed, in case things start to get really frigid. Ironically, Scorpio doesn't realize it has such a powerful ego (the same thing it usually accuses Leo of flaunting) until it has to deal with the Water Bearer. Unlike Scorpio, Aquarius is an altruistic sign that rarely covets what others possess, unless it's an awesome IQ—although not even that, since Aquarius knows it was already born wildly brilliant!

The contrast of temperaments found here is such that Scorpio actually starts to feel itself to be the greedy one who selfishly demands a lot from others. It's almost insatiable when it comes to feeding its emotional hunger. Yet hanging around transpersonal Aquarius makes the self-conscious Scorpion worry that it truly *is* more of a taker than a giver—more an energy-sucking black hole of obsessive need.

To makes matters worse, Aquarius doesn't appear to have a manipulative bone in its body, plus its unusual life is an open book, *and* it has tons of sparkling friends. Meanwhile, lonely, brooding Scorpio sometimes even scares the pigeons in the park—probably due to the menacing look of wearing dark glasses on cloudy days. In Scorpio's opinion, Aquarius doesn't seem to need a lot, because it already has it all—the result of living a life based on inner freedom and the courage to show one's true colors in public. (Scorpio often seems to be a little too concerned about who has whatever it secretly craves.)

Meanwhile, the Water Bearer intuits that the Scorpion is a bit of a malcontent and a little too mysterious to be appreciated intellectually. Scorpio also seems to get too caught up in a complex of details, and it accepts little at face value. The Scorpion could benefit from Aquarius' ability to quickly flash on the overview of any situation with dispassionate clarity. "Ditch the emotional intensity and those nasty responses that go with it, and plug in to pure, accelerated mind power," advocates Aquarius. "It's the only way to fly!" Scorpio does get too wound up about things and people it cannot control, and so a little mental detachment couldn't hurt. Of course, the Scorpion is suspicious that high-flying Aquarius is way out of touch with ordinary human feelings, and may need one day to get down to the bottom of why it's so darn impersonal in all its relationships.

If we have these two signs highlighted in our chart, we probably started off life feeling alienated, though on different levels. Both Scorpio and Aquarius could claim not to be easily understood by most folks, but then again, they are quite capable of having odd, unsettling reactions to simple social interchanges. Aquarius take the unpredictable path—as if it's fun to shock people or catch them off guard—while Scorpio is just plain silent and seemingly unresponsive in ways that others find cryptic and even a bit creepy. (Of course, this can be a fabulous combo for livening up Halloween.)

Still, going rapidly from smoldering intensity to cool emotional distance, and back, is not an easy pattern to which others can relate. We'll need to be less abrupt when our moods are ready to shift, plus become more sensitive to how our sudden chill factor perplexes others who thought we were getting intimate with them.

As these are two fixed signs associated with defiant planets—Pluto and Uranus—self-will is strong (even though Aquarius would rather call it something else, since it is uneasy identifying itself with words that begin with "self"). These two signs are also stubborn. Aquarian inflexibility applies more to its abstract principles of Truth and the ideals that it expects to work for all. Scorpio's obstinacy is rooted in its hatred of being forced to bend to the iron will of another (it would rather die first). So don't expect to find a temperament that easily accommodates people. Scorpio/Aquarius is quite capable of flatly saying "no" to others.

Also, with this combo, we can contain stormy feelings for a long time—hoping that by not releasing them, we deaden their power. Instead, we eventually blow like a volcano, usually at a most inappropriate occasion, and baffle everyone. At that point, even the Aquarius part of us doesn't care how many people witness our major eruption!

SCORPIO/AQUARIUS ASTRO-LEBRITIES

Dylan Thomas, poet: (Sun in Scorpio, Moon in Aquarius)

Calista Flockhart, actress: (Sun in Scorpio, Moon in Aquarius)

Neil Young, musician-songwriter: (Sun in Scorpio, Moon in Aquarius)

Jules Verne, writer: (Sun in Aquarius, Moon in Scorpio)

Helen Gurley Brown, writer-editor: (Sun in Aquarius, Moon in Scorpio)

James Dean, actor: (Sun in Aquarius, Moon in Scorpio)

Aquarius/Taurus

This combination, at first, seems like it would be difficult to blend. Aquarius is an air sign that seeks to elevate mind power to electrifying levels of brilliance. Its mental world involves inventive, innovative concepts that are not bound by practicality or common sense. Taurus is an earth sign whose consciousness is firmly planted on the ground and is less stimulated by abstract thought or theoretical reasoning; it is more aroused by what tangibly exists.

The Water Bearer is the coldest of the air signs and the Bull is the warmest of the earth signs. Aquarius requires emotional detachment in order for it to remain clear-sighted and unbiased, yet Taurus depends on its feelings and instincts to better understand the nature of physical reality. The Bull likes to touch, while Aquarius is a touch-me-not (although it will engage in impersonal group hugs, as long as they're quick). These signs thus appear to have little in common. However, both are fixed, meaning that they both are steady, determined, enduring, and able to concentrate on their goals until desired objectives are met. These two are unlikely to quit, once strongly motivated to tackle a project, so they reinforce each other's tendency to have committed interests.

Taurus may be warm and affectionate (earth can contain heat), but the Bull can be so placid that it appears expressionless. That makes it harder for others to register what this sign is feeling, although it comes in handy when playing poker! You cannot read Taurus like a book, unless it's feeling very comfortable and relaxed around you—but at least it's habitual enough to be predictable. Aquarius also doesn't show much emotion on the surface—except when outraged by some social injustice, but that's not the same as expressing feelings of a personal nature. Together, then, these signs may seem unresponsive to more sensitive, human conditions (at least compared to a more emotive Cancer/Leo mix). If the Aquarian side of this combo dominates, expect a degree of emotional aloofness combined with Taurus' calm exterior.

At the same time, if we have these signs emphasized in our chart, our feelings won't get in our way while we're attending to more practical or societal concerns. Level-headedness is commonly seen, as we're not the excitable type. Aquarius likes to think before plunging into action—it's really not all that impulsive—and Taurus cannot be rushed until it deems the timing to be right.

With less energy feeding our emotionality, we probably won't suffer the anguish and anxiety others do when personal problems arise. We'll probably have few sleepless nights, no matter what our predicament is (here's where being detached and even-tempered is a blessing). Still, we'll have to watch out about becoming too opinionated. The Bull feels secure in its perceptions and doesn't waver, while the Water Bearer "knows" when it's right about the "truths" it intuitively flashes on, even if the rest of the world thinks otherwise. Adaptability is not easily found.

When well managed, this combo provides suitable, durable outlets for fresh, experimental ideas. Taurus is good at finding the right material in which to clothe well-defined concepts (but it doesn't care to waste time on anything vague and ill-conceived). Thus, to get the Bull interested, the Water Bearer will need to "talk some sense" and plainly show how its innovative notions can be applied in useful ways. The pressure is on for Aquarius to come down from the clouds and ground its ideas better, which is good.

On the other hand, Taurus needs to become less earthbound in its evaluations of "reality" and instead allow Aquarius to bend the Bull's mind and convince it that alternative possibilities do exist. It'll just require a completely different perceptual framework to realize the wisdom in this. But is a somewhat rut-tolerant Taurus willing to budge? If so, its world can transform into a more exciting place. Both these signs only limit themselves—and us—when they resist exchanging their valuable resources. The blend of uncommon intuition with good, old-fashioned "horse sense" seems to reward us with the best of both worlds.

AQUARIUS/TAURUS ASTRO-LEBRITIES

Tony Blair, British prime minister: (Sun in Taurus, Moon in Aquarius)

Uma Thurman, actress: (Sun in Taurus, Moon in Aquarius)

Andre Agassi, tennis pro: (Sun in Taurus, Moon in Aquarius)

Ronald Reagan, U.S. president: (Sun in Aquarius, Moon in Taurus)

Germaine Greer, writer: (Sun in Aquarius, Moon in Taurus)

Jackson Pollock, painter: (Sun in Aquarius, Moon in Taurus)

Thus far, we've seen how cardinal signs that square one another do so in ways that evoke direct, decisive action. Sometimes open confrontation is needed to bring matters to a head. People born with many planets in these signs seem to live eventful lives filled with energetic activity. They seize the moment and move forward into experience.

Fixed signs that square each other are less apt to plunge into activity until an organized plan of action has been devised, and they are the ones who want to be in charge of operations. Until then, matters move slowly but deliberately. Once they get started, fixed signs have great staying power and see matters to their conclusion.

In contrast, mutable signs, like Gemini and Virgo, want several options before making a move. They are less consistent in their objectives, as they adapt to ever-changing situations. Their plans are seldom firm. The impulse to start things is not as strong, and it's harder to remain steady on any course of action initiated. Detours taken can lead to improvements, although they can also result in an ineffectual scattering of forces (where much nervous energy is expended for nothing). Also, due to their mercurial nature, these signs retain a youthful energy even into maturity.

Gemini/Virgo

Gemini seems to represent quintessential mutability, probably because it's also a breezy, changeable air sign. It never wants to get stuck going down only one path, not when alternative routes look more interesting. This is one reason why the Twins can seem noncommittal and easily distracted (it's not necessarily because they are "flaky" or unreliable). Variety is what life is all about for them. Virgo, certainly not as restless for change, may seem less mutable because it's also a steady, patient earth sign that excels at practical adaptability.

Making little adjustments that help improve conditions is something Virgo does easily, once it has carefully analyzed the situation. What may help integrate this combo better is the fact that each sign is associated with Mercury, the planet always on the lookout for bright ideas that make life easier. At issue, however, is how useable these ideas are in application. Virgo appears more adept at fleshing out the details that make any concept more workable.

The Twins' mentality shows a quick mind and a keen logic at work. Gemini is smart at figuring things out—even after just a quick scan of the situation at hand—and is able to devise shortcuts and clever solutions that trim the time and effort required to do something, thus simplifying certain procedures. Gemini is even good at passing along its tips and insights, and therefore has a facility for teaching others what it knows.

A problem, however, is that it gets bored with its own techniques and wants to change them, almost without warning. Variation is stimulating to Gemini, but the resultant inconsistencies can aggravate Virgo—to which Gemini is tempted to say, "Loosen up and chill out! Why should there only be one right way to do something?" Indeed, the Analyzer *is* a stickler for getting things done correctly, and on time.

Virgo is almost obsessed with order and function, whereas Gemini is more fascinated with the random nature of life, where matters of fleeting interest aren't required to serve any useful purpose other than to momentarily delight the mind and to relieve the predictable monotony of routine. Yet for the Analyzer, the mind must craft its ideas in a more concrete, coherent fashion, something that requires a meticulousness that Gemini finds unnecessary.

In fact, the Twins often think the Analyzer goes way overboard with tedious detail and ultraprecision, taking all the fun out of learning things firsthand by trial and error. "Better read that manual before you really mess things up," advises Virgo. Gemini instead likes to be free to monkey around on its own, pushing buttons left and right, to see what will happen next. It's experimental in a more carefree way. Still, sometimes Virgo is absolutely right—it pays to study how something works before tinkering with its many intricate parts—plus we need to make sure that we can later put back together what we've disassembled.

If these two signs are highlighted in our chart, we're probably highly alert and observant, spotting everything happening around us. Our Gemini side is content simply to observe and maybe casually ask a few questions. Our Virgo side, ready to give critical reviews, asks more relevant questions that sound like a cross-examination at times (similar to Scorpio). These two Mercury-ruled signs pay homage to the rational intellect, viewing it as our only source of accurate, pertinent information.

Intuition and imagination are valued less, if at all—although Gemini does appreciate witty forms of fantasy, perhaps seeing them as creative springboards for the mind. (Gemini would probably enjoy *Alice Through the Looking Glass* or *Gulliver's Travels*, or any such whimsical work that also includes clever and well-written social commentary. Virgo is uneasy with anything too fictional, and instead sticks to more technical, fact-based material.)

Gemini/Virgo types have minds that need a lot of mental stimulation and a variety of topics to explore. These are the eternal students of the zodiac (capable of being excellent teachers as well). Restlessness and an excess of nervous energy can keep them from focusing on something long enough to feel inwardly settled, unless the Virgo side dominates—Virgo can work long and hard to master whatever it finds worthy of study.

GEMINI/VIRGO ASTRO-LEBRITIES

Frank Lloyd Wright, architect: (Sun in Gemini, Moon in Virgo)
Courteney Cox Arquette, actress: (Sun in Gemini, Moon in Virgo)
John F. Kennedy, U.S. president: (Sun in Gemini, Moon in Virgo)

Claudia Schiffer, supermodel: (Sun in Virgo, Moon in Gemini)
Buddy Holly, musician: (Sun in Virgo, Moon in Gemini)
Grandma Moses, painter: (Sun in Virgo, Moon in Gemini)

Virgo/Sagittarius

Virgo appreciates Gemini's good mind, although it feels this air sign needs to harness its intellectual energy better instead of darting off in so many directions and diluting its mental strength. (Of course, the Twins beg to differ, but that's at least how Virgo sees it.) It also finds Gemini too indiscriminate and careless regarding what it feeds its mind (the Twins can clutter their heads with stuff that has a "heard today, forgotten tomorrow" quality). Virgo cannot understand how Gemini can find such trivial, irrelevant information so enjoyable. To the Analyzer, it's a big waste of precious time.

However, when dealing with Sagittarius, Virgo quickly becomes aware that trivia is not what captures this fire sign's interest. The Archer shoots its arrows of curiosity into skies of wider expanse. It's equipped to grapple with life's largest issues: God, Truth, Morality, and Ultimate Meaning. Skeptical Virgo wonders whether Sagittarius is guilty of overreach.

Sagittarius is a sign associated with our search for that which will explain existence in a unifying manner—theories and beliefs that point to life's higher purpose. The Archer is inclined to assume that there is one underlying, guiding principle governing all the laws of the Cosmos. This sign intuitively believes that a divine hand plays an all-knowing role, involving a universal master plan. Our task is to aspire toward a greater comprehension of this grand, cosmic design.

Virgo finds such thinking to be speculative, at best (delusional, at worst). The Analyzer is less at ease with conjecture and anything that is inherently unprovable. Of course, the Archer would love to shoot a few arrows of insight and inspiration into the heart of shortsighted, faith-challenged Virgo, as if to say, "Stop peering through the microscope to observe the small and inconsequential, and start looking instead through the telescope to witness vast, faraway worlds of infinite wonder."

Virgo is into specifics and particulars, not Sagittarian generalities and indefinites. It wants to define something well, with crystal clarity, yet the Archer is less willing to be limited by precise definitions. Virgo finds Sagittarius to be careless about its "facts" and unwilling to accept even a little criticism. The Archer's "logic" seems flawed or skewed to Virgo, who imposes more stringent standards of evidence.

In turn, Sagittarius hates how literal Virgo can be about everything in life (meaning you have to watch the words you use around the Analyzer, since it becomes so easy to say the right thing the wrong way). Sagittarius is more than outspoken—it's blunt in a manner that Virgo sometimes finds appalling. Honesty and sincerity aren't everything to Virgo, if it also means being an inconsiderate loudmouth who really doesn't know what he or she is talking about.

If we have these two signs emphasized in our chart, our Sagittarian side is probably less rash than usual in behavior. We are more apt to think our theories through before getting on our soapbox to broadcast our opinions. Of course, Virgo might induce us to think that we *do* know it all because we've done the rigorous study required. This can actually be a scholarly combination (where a Sagittarian thirst for knowledge blends with Virgo's sharp, critical mental faculties and its penchant for accuracy). Both signs think highly of their mental powers, yet Virgo/Sagittarius types—when mismanaging their energies—may come across as being intellectually arrogant and intolerant of stupidity. Sagittarius at least inflates the Analyzer's tendency not to want to be wrong about anything.

One pitfall here is that hyper-rational Virgo will trigger the orthodox and even dogmatic side of Sagittarius, resulting in the confident but narrow mindset of a skeptic, an expert debunker, a hard-nosed scientist resistant to all but a material view of the Universe, or someone who only puts "faith" in things that are able to be tested and measured in the material realm, not the spiritual. That's when the Archer's sky suddenly seems very small and starless.

VIRGO/SAGITTARIUS ASTRO-LEBRITIES

Alan Dershowitz, lawyer: (Sun in Virgo, Moon in Sagittarius)

Mary Shelley, writer: (Sun in Virgo, Moon in Sagittarius)

Elvis Costello, musician: (Sun in Virgo, Moon in Sagittarius)

Maria Callas, opera singer: (Sun in Sagittarius, Moon in Virgo)

Kenneth Branagh, actor-director: (Sun in Sagittarius, Moon in Virgo)

Sheila E., musician: (Sun in Sagittarius, Moon in Virgo)

Sagittarius/Pisces

Although Virgo is not as heavy in temperament as the other earth signs, Sagittarius feels the weight of the Analyzer's influence. Virgo helps the Archer expand more productively, as here its fiery idealism is more grounded in worldly reality and better tested by a sounder judgment. Still, the Analyzer's energy is too wrapped up in the pressing concerns of mundane living to keep Sagittarian spirits soaring. After all, it's hard to feel free as a bird when you've also got to mow the lawn and do three piles of laundry.

Nothing Virgo/Sagittarius does can be considered a complete leap of faith, since a cautious optimism is at work—and at times, so are exaggerated worries and doubts. But when Sagittarius hooks up with Pisces, such limitations seem to disappear, along with common sense. This is an impractical duo, yet one that has a marvelous way of communicating with the angels on high. Both signs hold strong beliefs based on unquestioned faith. Perhaps little miracles happen for them more than for any other combination of signs.

Pisces' old-fashioned ruler is Jupiter, the same planet that is associated with Sagittarius. This provides a few extra common denominators. These two signs are generous in spirit, big-hearted, expansive in scope, but can easily go overboard in their response to life, ignoring sensible boundaries. Although the water element is typically self-protective and able to create emotional "barrier reefs," the Jupiter side of Pisces is less guarded—watery Jupiter is more like Neptune—and thus it's as trusting of the world as is Sagittarius.

However, both signs can suffer from using poor judgment. They want to believe in the goodness of life in their attempts to uplift humanity (the Fishes are especially concerned with themes of redemption). But their visions are not always grounded in reality. Pisces also swims in darker pools of psychological disintegration, and is thus sensitive to the illnesses of the soul that plague people (something that is even more governed by Neptune). Sagittarius, avoiding the murky realms of the unconscious, seeks to move optimistically toward the light rather than dwell in the psyche's shadows.

Pisces vividly feels the hidden pains and deeper insecurities of the human condition, which are issues a more upbeat Sagittarius would rather dodge. The enthused Archer wants life to be an ever-broadening adventure that cheerfully raises our collective consciousness to greater heights of understanding. This sign acts as the natural pep coach of the zodiac; it's the Cosmos' spunky, enthused motivational speaker trying to pump us up with positive attitudes and high hopes.

In contrast, watery Pisces experiences troubling mood swings that sometimes make it feel low in spirit and even hopeless about where the world is going. There is a sadness in the Fishes that the Archer may never understand, but there are also Piscean depths of wisdom, as well, that Sagittarius may never reach, at least from an emotional perspective. Often setting its sights on what's happening on the surface of society, Sagittarius is commonly caught up in social and political crusades. The Archer is an activist at heart and one with the courage required to right the wrongs of the System. Yet all this keeps it from looking deeply within its soul for answers in the introspective way that meditative Pisces does.

We who have these two signs emphasized in our chart may burn with an idealism that has us feeling very out of sorts with the less noble, humane ways of the material world. We yearn for better outcomes for all, but are discouraged by how few actually share our enlightened vision of a more unified planet, one teeming with people of good will and charitable hearts. We may sometimes feel we really belong in another galaxy far away from the grime of earthly living.

Pisces is more otherworldly than is Sagittarius, but the Archer does have its moments of wanting to climb aboard a spaceship, rocket away, and live out its *Star Trek* fantasies. Since we do live in a sometimes user-unfriendly world that can be brutish and devoid of beautiful, inspirational dreams, we can find ourselves quite discouraged and filled with discontent.

We seek grand escapes, yet they'll need to be ones that don't damage our soul and render us out of touch with the emotional reality of others. Creating distance by overdeveloping our intellect, while numbing our feelings, won't lead to the satisfying sense of inner peace we seek. We need to stay active and remain on the cutting edge of social reform, never giving up on our universal dreams. Humanity hungers for Sagittarius/Pisces light bearers who can show the world better and more loving ways to live.

Sagittarius/Pisces Astro-lebrities

Joe DiMaggio, baseball player: (Sun in Sagittarius, Moon in Pisces)

Monica Seles, tennis pro: (Sun in Sagittarius, Moon in Pisces)

Gianni Versace, fashion designer: (Sun in Sagittarius, Moon in Pisces)

Victor Hugo, writer: (Sun in Pisces, Moon in Sagittarius)

Jennifer Love Hewitt, actress: (Sun in Pisces, Moon in Sagittarius)

Albert Einstein, physicist: (Sun in Pisces, Moon in Sagittarius)

Pisces/Gemini

The Pisces/Sagittarius combo is one that inspires us to rise above the ordinary concerns of daily survival, so that we can instead ponder life's ultimate meaning. These are philosophical, transpersonal signs, able to consider the totality of existence from vast but often logic-defying perspectives. Metaphysically speaking, why are we all here and where are we collectively going? What is our overall spiritual purpose?

Such big questions do not have simple, easy answers, yet they represent our ongoing quest for deeper soul meaning.

However, when Pisces joins forces with Gemini, the Fishes are pressured to come up with more useful, coherent insights about how the world really works—not how it ideally could or should work. Of course, Gemini is not all that earthbound—being an air sign—but it does want the human mind to work in a concrete, clarity-producing manner. Gemini is capable of rational, scientific assessments and wants hard proof that things are clearly what they appear to be, and are not the illusionary byproducts of an overactive imagination (or mental illness).

Pisces, however, is famous for its mental fog attacks and its excursions into surreal, inner worlds where logic is irrelevant. It's a psychic, dreamy sign that needs to work harder at concentrating on mundane matters at hand, without losing its focus due to its strange, internal wanderings. Yet the Fishes have uncanny feelings that help them detect and understand the less-sobvious factors involved in human affairs (something Gemini cannot do, no matter how many nosy questions it asks).

The combination of talents suggested here can heighten one's awareness of multilevel energies in operation regarding any human predicament. Gemini's job is to spot, observe, and articulate the obvious problems needing sensible, clear-headed solutions. Pisces instead seeps into a situation's hidden layers in order to uncover less visible facets that explain more about why things turn out the way they do.

Pisces is a much better listener than Gemini, but both signs are open to hearing what others have to say. However, Gemini is less at ease when people emotively pour their hearts out, while Pisces loses mental concentration quickly if what it's hearing is too dry, technical, or lacking in human interest. Both signs are easily distracted and cannot stand to be bored with either too many detailed facts (Pisces) or vaguely defined fictions (Gemini).

A strength and a weakness of this combo is its flexibility—this is probably the most elastic duo there is. On one hand, this means that they are very suggestible and are open to taking alternative paths. There's little here that's one-track-minded or stubborn. Yet, on the other hand, the mix of Pisces and Gemini needs a little self-discipline when it comes to following through on matters often begun with much hopeful enthusiasm. These signs are too easily detoured by all kinds of sidetracking events that interrupt any smooth flow already in operation. Once off track, they are less inclined to energetically get back into the swing of things.

Those of us with this combination highlighted in our chart should not try to tackle too much at once, since that only scatters our energies and leaves much up in the air, in a state of disorganization. We end up looking ditzy and ill-prepared to others. Hyperstimulation needs to be avoided—even though we crave it—because it only makes us feel fragmented.

Actually, our Pisces side will need quality time away from all mental activity. It is nurtured by silence and stillness—not the usual social busyness that Gemini always manages to drum up for itself. However, the Gemini in us doesn't want life to become too quiet; it requires a lively dose of situational variety and plenty of people who'll offer interesting feedback. We'll thus have to make time for that, too. To experience the best of both worlds, we need to communicate our deeper perceptions of life, all while having faith that others will find us lucid and loaded with insight. We can enchant people with our engaging tales about human observation, once we discover effective, imaginative outlets to help us express our ideas.

PISCES/GEMINI ASTRO-LEBRITIES

Françoise Sagan, writer: (Sun in Gemini, Moon in Pisces)

Rupert Everett, actor: (Sun in Gemini, Moon in Pisces)

Elizabeth Hurley, model-actress: (Sun in Gemini, Moon in Pisces)

Tony Randall, actor: (Sun in Pisces, Moon in Gemini)

Adelle Davis, nutritionist-writer: (Sun in Pisces, Moon in Gemini)

Anthony Armstrong Jones, photographer: (Sun in Pisces, Moon in Gemini)

SIGNS THAT OPPOSE

Signs that face each other across the zodiac—180 degrees apart—are called "polar opposites"—a term that, unfortunately, makes these signs sound as if they are as different as night and day. In some respects, they are. Yet, in other ways, they're on the same wavelength, which gives them a built-in readiness to cooperate. They both are members of the same mode, and—unlike signs that square—their elements are traditionally compatible. For example, fixed signs always oppose fixed signs, yet fixed earth only opposes fixed water, and fixed fire only opposes fixed air; the opposing elements are thus complementary. Apparently it's this blending of elements that interrelate so well that gives opposing signs their potential for constructive interplay, resulting in a state of creative balance.

Opposite signs have a clear view of one another, allowing them a perspective unmatched by any other sign-to-sign relationship. Each totally sees what the other's all about, although that doesn't always mean they like or understand what they see. After all, these signs are positioned as far apart from each other as any two signs can be. There's a good reason why they want to keep each other at a healthy distance. For one thing, such distance allows for both a greater perspective and a sense of being apart, and thus different, from that which is observed—something that could help develop objectivity. Opposing signs are not to merge and become more like each other, but are to retain their separate identities while working side by side in harmony. The best marriages in life are also said to function this way.

What can mess things up here is when one sign's energy is expressed excessively, at the expense of the other, who then suffers from underdevelopment. The imbalance that results brings out the worst side of both signs, who by then are feeling antagonistic toward each other. Such a lopsided relationship provokes extremism in behavior. As we underexpress a sign at one end—and feel frustrated—we probably overexpress the other sign in an exaggerated manner, much to our detriment. Moderation seems to be the key to effective usage of our opposing signs, and that becomes something we must consciously try to manifest. Therefore, before we can achieve a needed balance, opposing signs push for our greater awareness of the contrasting needs and issues that these signs represent.

Even if we weren't born with planets in opposite signs, our opposing houses have opposite signs on their cusps. The following information may help us figure out how to deal with those areas of our life. We also have a natal North Node–South Node axis in our chart that involves opposing signs. Thus, some of the themes addressed here may apply to the challenges of our nodal pattern. And, of course, sometimes we'll have a relationship with somebody whose Sun sign is opposite ours. We may need a few pointers regarding how we can better deal with that. Let's take a closer look at these polar opposites and see how we can wed their finest qualities within our psyche.

Aries/Libra

Aries is a sign that doesn't need close relationships in order to know itself—at least that's its perhaps naive assumption, since it seems to readily enjoy doing a lot of things alone and unsupervised. The concept of having a helpmate is alien to its psychology. The more Aries does for itself—on its own terms—the more capable it feels, and the less willing it is to have anyone else interfere and copilot the experience. Autonomy is a natural and desirable state of being for the Ram.

Libra is just the opposite in that it's less willing to wing it alone and tackle life without active assistance from others. Perhaps it's less a matter of Libra not wanting to be alone to do things independently, despite appearances suggesting otherwise, but rather that Libra knows two heads are often better than one, and that a creative, well-coordinated collaboration can enhance any project. Getting feedback and input from others is important, since it affords needed objectivity. This all sounds nice, yet perhaps Libra *is* indeed a bit too dependent on others, although not in a cloying Cancerian manner.

The Ram—a little raw around the edges and less skilled in the niceties required to facilitate smoother social interaction—could benefit from going to Libra's charm school to learn a few smart tips on how to put others at ease, in ways that get them to support bold, Arien enterprises. The Balancer is good at presenting itself and its objectives in a more polished manner, which is something Aries fails to do in its hurry to initiate its personal projects.

Libra knows the importance of first impressions and realizes that Aries comes off, in the beginning, as too brash and eager—and impatient—to learn how to wait for the right time to strike. Poise is not an Arien trait. Of course, Aries is quick to note that Libra can seemingly wait forever for the perfect moment to arrive. It sits on issues way too long to keep momentum going. The Ram is also irritated by the Libran habit of asking too many other people for advice, when just taking the big plunge and hustling to stay ahead of things seems to be the better way to go.

There's also the issue of handling conflict: Aries is not actively looking for trouble, but it does thrive on confrontation and competition—after all, the Cosmos gave the Ram those big horns and that hard head to butt its way into life and charge against any opponent. Aries gets to know its strengths when it has something to fight for or fight over.

But Libra, who ironically is more adept at winning wars by using strategy—not mere brute force—is nonetheless reluctant to do open battle. It needs to toughen up and realize that not everyone is willing to play by Libran rules of civility. Others who lack integrity and decency will unfairly seek the upper hand and try to take advantage of "nice" signs like Libra. Aries, itself, is one of those pushy types that the Balancer dreads upsetting. Yet the Ram is the perfect sign to teach Libra how to stick up for its rights and not be mistreated by any tyrant or bully.

We with a natal Aries/Libra emphasis are learning all about the pros and cons of self-assertion. Coming on too strong drives others away. Not coming on strong enough frustrates our intentions and only invites others to play hardball with us, which is not what we want. Life can become quite uncompromising when we fail to work out a needed balance between the Arien drive to thrust ourselves vigorously into situations versus the Libran tendency to let others run the show. However, Libra can sit on its resentment, as its identity becomes undermined by others in charge. Sometimes what is at issue is learning to curb excitable impulses and instead to value calm deliberation.

Being that two cardinal signs are involved, when friction reaches a boiling point, a crisis blows the lid off of any unspoken tension. The action needed to change things for the better is then swiftly taken, and the results—while disruptive for a while—help us restore a new balance. In the end, we must satisfy our own needs up front while also finding agreeable ways to engage in the give and take required to appease others. Otherwise, certain impossible relationships will need to come to a halt, as both parties are pressured to call it quits.

ARIES/LIBRA ASTRO-LEBRITIES

Rosie O'Donnell, comedian-actress: (Sun in Aries, Moon in Libra)
Johann Sebastian Bach, composer: (Sun in Aries, Moon in Libra)
Elle MacPherson, supermodel: (Sun in Aries, Moon in Libra)

Martina Navratilova, tennis pro: (Sun in Libra, Moon in Aries)
Luciano Pavarotti, opera tenor: (Sun in Libra, Moon in Aries)
Sarah Ferguson, former Duchess of York: (Sun in Libra, Moon in Aries)

Taurus/Scorpio

Taurus is a sign of amazing composure—that's no surprise, since it values serenity—and it is probably the only member of the zodiac able to feel true, lasting contentment. The problem is that nothing seems to endure forever without undergoing some measure of change, since without it, nothing really grows further. Interestingly, Taurus loves to watch things grow—flowers, that is, not taxes—yet it is reluctant to personally undergo changes of whose pace and duration it cannot control. The Bull prefers to takes its sweet time pondering what needs to be altered in its life, if anything. Cautious by nature, it is reluctant to eliminate that which it has worked so hard to build in its life.

Polar-opposite Scorpio has different plans. Being a fixed-water sign, it is quite capable of hanging on to its feelings for a very long time and is fiercely resistant to having them altered, at least by others.

Yet—and here's why the Scorpion is often in inner turmoil—there is something hard-wired in this sign's psyche that compels it to go on a secret mission to "search and destroy." Nothing is to remain permanent, as if frozen in time.

Scorpio has the strongly Plutonian instinct to revamp itself and its lifestyle, once a certain level of stagnation has been reached. It's at this critical point that extreme, dramatic, and utterly life-altering changes can be made. More self-aware, tuned-in Scorpio types pick up on any distress signals earlier on and willingly implement needed changes in less drastic ways.

It is likely that the Scorpion looks at the Bull with a mixture of envy ("How does that sign keep its energy steadily consolidated for so long without the bottom falling out?") and disgust ("How can it stand to have anything stay the same forever?"). Taurus does seem to have antitransformative qualities, and yet inertia is exactly what Scorpio must avoid to develop properly. How do these two signs form a healthy relationship without resorting to seemingly unresolvable power struggles?

Taurus sometimes too easily accepts people and things at face value and doesn't feel it should have to snoop around to uncover anything hidden, at least not in the investigatory ways of sometimes-sneaky Scorpio. Staying on the surface of life keeps the Bull's world relatively simple and free of conflict (remember, this sign wants gentle treatment in life, and that means never having its feathers ruffled). Who knows the trouble it'll find if it starts to go any deeper into life's murkier areas? Taurus likes solid dry land, not eerie-looking swamps.

Scorpio, however, knows that a vast, psychodynamic underworld teems with potent but unexamined energies that eventually need to surface and force self-confrontation. When we don't help facilitate this need, these pent-up energies erupt beyond our control. In some ways, Taurus is a perfect candidate to experience such eruption, since it tries hard to keep all this intensity under lock and key. But something eventually snaps, and this normally sweet and placid sign becomes a raging bull.

Those of us with this combo emphasized in our chart are power-houses who know how to hold our emotions in—even in grueling situations in which others would crack up—but then we reach a not-too-obvious critical point, where suddenly all that self-control goes out the window. A ferocious release of repressed tension has us instead spewing lava-hot feelings like an exploding volcano. Our inclination is to swing back and forth between these two extreme behaviors, making us potentially ticking time bombs. Of course, this is no sane way to live. It is better to accept the best that both signs have to offer, and to stop trying to obstruct the inevitability of deep change (and that goes for our often stubborn and willful Scorpio side, too).

We need to surrender to a greater vision of what we can be, realizing that this won't come about without a struggle. These signs share a gritty sense of realism when they join forces, and so it's doubtful that idealism will ever pose a problem. Still, surges of self-destructive behavior can take their toll (when fixed signs go down the wrong path, bad habits can become entrenched).

On a more positive note, these signs have a tremendous sense of resourcefulness and an indomitable will that can help them overcome just about anything. Yet why wait until it's crisis time—when life hands over a few do-or-die ultimatums—before we finally change from the inside out and renew ourselves? If we remain conscious and cooperative, nothing involving this growth process has to be radically forced on us.

Taurus/Scorpio Astro-lebrities

Bono, singer: (Sun in Taurus, Moon in Scorpio)
Joseph Heller, writer: (Sun in Taurus, Moon in Scorpio)
Harry Truman, U.S. president: (Sun in Taurus, Moon in Scorpio)

Prince Charles, British royalty: (Sun in Scorpio, Moon in Taurus)
Demi Moore, actress: (Sun in Scorpio, Moon in Taurus)
Dan Rather, news anchor: (Sun in Scorpio, Moon in Taurus)

Gemini/Sagittarius

Just as fixed Taurus/Scorpio can be emotionally wound up tighter than a drum, mutable Gemini/Sagittarius energy can be as loose as a goose. Getting stuck in rigid attitudes is not a problem for these two at all. If anything, both signs are too easily thrown off course by tempting distractions that allow their minds to wander and explore. These are the travel signs of the zodiac, and they're always ready to hit the road and place themselves in unfamiliar surroundings at a moment's notice (more so Sagittarius, who's a natural globetrotter and a citizen of the world). If physical travel is not an option, then invigorating mental excursions are sought.

Gemini loves Sagittarius' sense of adventure, since it practically guarantees that the Twins will seldom be bored, all cooped up at home, with nothing but yesterday's newspaper to reread. Even if Gemini does have more relevant, mundane things to do, the Archer invites it to drop everything and take a sudden, out-of-town vacation. These signs need mobility.

Gemini and Sagittarius are arguably the two most casual and talkative signs of the zodiac, always eager to keep the communication ball rolling (this is a far cry from the often tense and tight-lipped Taurus/Scorpio relationship). When it comes to skimming life's surface, and enjoying the heck out of it, these two signs can't be beat. Who needs to delve into the psyche's gloomy depths? Why be so poker-faced and serious, when a little childlike silliness is just a joke and a prank or two away? Clever wit and social satire belong to these two signs, who do take time to smile at life and become amused by its comings and goings. Perhaps because we're dealing here with mutability of a peppy air and fire nature, adaptability comes easily as does a willingness to embrace change, seeing it as a needed breath of fresh air.

However, being opposite signs, there are some major differences in temperament. Gemini is often too satisfied with its surface understanding of life to go any further with its curiosity. It also doesn't put a lot of trust in unprovable articles of faith that require mindless or unquestioned devotion. Nonetheless, studying religion, philosophy, and metaphysics can be of momentary interest, offering the Twins a somewhat fascinating glimpse into major systems of thought that have had a powerful influence on humankind.

Frankly, Gemini is up to studying just about anything for short periods of time, simply for mental stimulation and the joy of learning. Still, unlike the Archer, Gemini doesn't easily believe in what it hears and reads along these lines, and is afraid that many well-meaning people are being duped by false hope and unrealistic expectations. Science, a more reliable discipline that worships the rational mind, feeds the Gemini intellect what it wants. The Twins don't wish to be ignorant of any true facts pertaining to the "real" world.

What Gemini thus does is play the devil's advocate, the one who tries to poke a few holes in the wild theories and holy proclamations that Sagittarius loves to distribute, far and wide, to anyone who'll listen with their heart and soul—not just their ego-driven intellect. Sagittarius finds Gemini superficial in this regard and guilty of undue skepticism. It feels that the Twins become hyperlogical and are quick to doubt things, just to engage in a little mental gymnastics.

If Gemini would stop using its brain so much and instead listen to its inner voice, then maybe it would really expand its mind. That's how Sagittarius see it. Actually, when it comes to faith and belief, Sagittarius can be very single-minded in a devotional way. It is able to target its fiery energy on issues that trigger its burning zeal and endless enthusiasm. It's not detached about such matters, as is Gemini.

Those of us with a Gemini/Sagittarius natal emphasis are high-spirited and lively in our communication ability. We'd probably make good teachers and are ever-curious about the world around us and beyond. Yet we can also be quite changeable regarding what inspires us (maybe we're sold on feng shui one minute, selling its philosophy to everyone we know, but the next we're not too sure if it isn't all just an elaborate mind game meant to enthrall the gullible and the superstitious). Having our doubts, while also yearning for absolute truths, can nonetheless urge us to become eternal students, never wanting to stop gathering knowledge that might lead to greater wisdom.

Gemini/Sagittarius Astro-lebrities

Donald Trump, tycoon: (Sun in Gemini, Moon in Sagittarius)

Joan Rivers, comedian: (Sun in Gemini, Moon in Sagittarius)

Liam Neeson, actor: (Sun in Gemini, Moon in Sagittarius)

Noel Coward, writer-actor: (Sun in Sagittarius, Moon in Gemini)

Anna Freud, psychoanalyst: (Sun in Sagittarius/Moon in Gemini)

Jonathan Swift, writer: (Sun in Sagittarius/Moon in Gemini)

Cancer/Capricorn

After traveling all over the map and seeing the sights with restless Gemini/Sagittarius—and having the liveliest of debates about science versus God—we'll find this next duo to be decidedly more staid and conservative. The Crab and the Goat prefer to stick to what's familiar, since their goal is to ensure safety and security. For them, the unknown is less appealing, although the entrepreneurial side of practical, ambitious Capricorn impels it to take a few calculated risks when courting success. It's watery Cancer—often hampered by subjective fears—that's more guarded and unwilling to deal with the unpredictabilities and dangers that await us "out there" in life.

Still, both have a respect for the tried-and-true ways of living and will do what they can to keep certain time-honored social rituals alive. As both have a respect for tradition, they seek to build solid structure from comforting, reliable elements of the past, whether regarding family matters (Cancer) or business endeavors (Capricorn).

The Cancerian facet of this opposition represents the more sentimental, teary-eyed side that wants to cling to the fondest memories of its idealized past (such recollections are undoubtedly selective in ways that foster nostalgia). The Crab is immensely sentimental and often feels oddly out of sync with today's ultramodern world (it loves what is old and somewhat faded, not what is modernistic and lacking an emotional history). The Goat, while not as misty-eyed about the past, admires antiquity and anything dignified that has stood the test of time.

However, Capricorn is also a hard-nosed realist who's firmly planted in the here-and-now world of commerce and social enterprise.

The Goat is looking to get ahead in the world and to become influential. It has an opportunistic nature and will capitalize on anything that offers it the winning advantage it seeks. Capricorn thinks the Crab needs to get tough and develop a thicker skin. It must stop always blaming the past for why things aren't "coming up roses" in the present. The Goat, although prone to dark moods fed by pessimism and secret self-doubt, is no whiner and has little respect for those who are.

In contrast, the Crab feels nurtured when it can periodically retreat to its private inner home, where it can reestablish its natural emotional rhythms so they flow more smoothly. Attaining glory in a worldly sense is less desired, yet bonding with loved ones on a deep level is highly cherished. Capricorn, less comfortable with an overload of powerful feelings, certainly does not wish to see itself as needy. It comes from the stiff-upper-lip school of hard knocks, and doesn't dare show the world anything resembling helplessness or vulnerability. But because of that, it's considered cold, distant, aloof, or worse— and all because it has opted to work on developing an adultlike maturity, even during its more tender years, that is misinterpreted as being a little too stiff-jointed on the feeling level.

The Crab can teach the Goat how to get better in touch with its often-neglected gut realities. "Let those tears flow," advises Cancer. "Stop acting like you don't have a tender, softer side. More than respect, you need a good hug and some home-cooked meals." This kind of talk unnerves Capricorn, although deep down inside the Goat does crave such closeness and caring. Yet sometimes it is so seamlessly identified with its outer role in society that it just doesn't know how to let its hair down and be itself. Both signs have a shyness about them, although Capricorn would rather call it being reserved, not timid.

With a Cancer/Capricorn emphasis in our chart, we're probably cautious—being on the orthodox side—about how we venture forth into life. We are concerned about how others judge us, and thus we'll exert just enough self-restraint in public to keep people from forming negative opinions of who we really are. We also tend to hide behind sturdy, social-support systems—large or tightly connected families for

Cancer, and huge business conglomerates for Capricorn. If an active, committed family life is not for us, then we'll find that our career—which we'll nourish with care—becomes our safe haven and our emotional harbor.

However, being ever on the defense, we'll need to watch out about appearing hard and crusty (Cancer has that hard-shelled, crabby potential, while Capricorn has its gruff, prune-faced, "bah-humbug" side). The reality is that we are more uncertain of ourselves than perhaps the world will ever know.

Cancer/Capricorn Astro-lebrities

Ernest Hemingway, writer: (Sun in Cancer, Moon in Capricorn)

Liv Tyler, actress: (Sun in Cancer, Moon in Capricorn)

John Glenn, astronaut-politician: (Sun in Cancer, Moon in Capricorn)

Janis Joplin, singer: (Sun in Capricorn, Moon in Cancer)

Sir Isaac Newton, scientist-physicist: (Sun in Capricorn, Moon in Cancer)

Mary Tyler Moore, actress: (Sun in Capricorn, Moon in Cancer)

Leo/Aquarius

The Cancer/Capricorn pair is not one to make waves in society unnecessarily. These signs toe the line in hopes of gaining long-lasting rewards for their exemplary social behavior, both in public and private sectors. They won't do anything foolish to jeopardize their future security or to damage their reputation. Yet, with this next opposition, our urge is to throw all caution to the wind and have a blast living our lives authentically, free of inhibition—and who cares if the neighbors don't like it! It's time to get a little bohemian and brighten up our life with color by embracing anything that's different.

Leo is certainly a sign that seems sure of itself, enough to stand out in all social situations as someone special; it's no wallflower. Aquarius doesn't have to try as hard as Leo sometimes does to draw attention for being one of a kind. It's typically odd by nature, but in a fascinating, appealing way. Together, these signs can team up to present a sparkling, personality package to the world that shakes up the status quo, while also dazzling and delighting audiences everywhere. "How do these two get away with it?" is what more uptight, conservative signs want to know.

The secret is having guts. Timidity never gets a person anywhere worth going, and so Leo and Aquarius each sense that, to live a life of individuality, you've got to take the world by storm and let them know that you *must* be allowed to be your ever-loving, creative self. Yet none of this will work if self-assurance and self-honesty aren't part of the deal. Leo is an unabashed exhibitionist, and Aquarius apparently likes that part of the Lion's makeup. It has a high regard for free souls everywhere who dare to come alive and release their special potential.

However, the Water Bearer is uneasy with all the ego baggage that often comes with such self-extension. While it loves the idea of personal freedom of expression, it doesn't want people to selfishly revolve around themselves and thus fail to contribute to the greater good in society.

Leo looks at Aquarius as being too group-oriented, and the Lion wonders how well will it be able to stand out in any crowd in which everybody seems equally interesting. There is also the issue of who's going to run the show. Leo favors being the sole leader, in charge of many, while Aquarius demands a more democratic setup, where no one individual is to rule over the rest like a monarch.

Leo will thus be learning about how to comanage projects with others who are equally qualified, but Aquarius must learn to recognize and value the contributions of each member of any group endeavor, rather than to simply focus on the team as a whole. Aquarius needs to show more heart in these matters, while Leo needs more detachment, so that it doesn't take everything too personally. The Water Bearer is not all that understanding of Leo's dramatic need to be the main, center-stage attraction.

Both these willful signs are determined to follow their own self-chosen paths without outer interference. Battles with authority may result, as each tries to sidestep the rules of the System in favor of doing its own thing, even if that means going against established rules of social conduct. However, Leo does seek approval and acceptance, and won't upset others too much and risk alienation. Still, it does believe that some rules are made for others to follow—but not the Lion. Aquarius is less addicted to being loved and adored by the public, since its focus is on applying more abstract ideals and principles on collective levels. If it breaks the rules of society, it's doing so for a more progressive purpose: the freedom of all individuals to determine how they want to live.

Those of us with a Leo/Aquarius emphasis in our chart will need to find expressive ways to exercise our individuality, while we also network with those whose individual rights we'll need to observe and honor. Life will probably allow us to show off how unusual and offbeat we are, compared to those who follow more conventional lifestyles. We are learning to sustain the courage to be ourselves, even if that means we'll make a few waves in society and maybe be labeled as controversial.

Leo keeps the Aquarius in us from acting like a social misfit or a malcontent, because the Lion knows how to be crowd-pleasing and entertaining in whatever it does. It puts on a great show that thus allows it to enjoy special social privileges—something Aquarius alone can't easily accomplish. Our charismatic nature seems to have wide appeal, as long as our commitment to our individualism doesn't become overpowering to others.

Leo/Aquarius Astro-lebrities

Jacqueline Susann, writer: (Sun in Leo, Moon in Aquarius)
Henry Ford, auto maker: (Sun in Leo, Moon in Aquarius)
Melanie Griffith, actress: (Sun in Leo, Moon in Aquarius)

James Joyce, writer: (Sun in Aquarius/Moon in Leo)
Gypsy Rose Lee, stripteaser: (Sun in Aquarius, Moon in Leo)
Sonny Bono, singer-politician: (Sun in Aquarius, Moon in Leo)

Virgo/Pisces

From the colorfully individualized style of Leo/Aquarius, we come to this final pair of opposing signs—both of whom are low-key and even humble in their demeanor. They may not share the sparkle and pizzazz of a sometimes outlandish Leo/Aquarius, yet Virgo/Pisces is learning to value a more quiet, reflective life while responsibly attending to the many details of day-to-day living. These signs are introspective and are certainly not showy. They're often more the observers of life than the participators, as they shun the spotlight and seek less attention.

You'll know when Leo/Aquarius walks into a room, but you may not notice the unassuming presence of the Analyzer and the Fishes. They seem to blend in a crowd without much fanfare (no grand entrances for them). What they are here to do is serve the needs of others—yet not in a lowly, servile manner. They instead exemplify the importance of rendering social service as a way to prevent collective disorganization from resulting in a total breakdown of society. These two thus want to fix things that are damaged. Their goal is to make everything well.

However, their styles of healing differ. Virgo is the pragmatist, the one to first look for more obvious causes of any illness or malfunction. It's less quick to investigate hidden factors until it has scrutinized likely probabilities (no matter what's being analyzed). It also believes in practical remedies with proven track records, as its main objective is to support what is most workable.

Pisces looks beyond the surface for deeper clues that can explain external unrest and even *dis*ease. The Fishes look to the soul for answers, but Virgo seeks "more sensible" solutions. This opposition apparently pits faith against reason, but not in such a cut-and-dried manner, since adaptable mutable signs are involved. Stubborn opinion is not a problem here, although Virgo is not easily moved by anything that appears illogical. Indeed, Pisces can seem quite delusional at times.

Pisces is also the side of this combo that feels the suffering of others and is not detached along these lines as is emotionally restrained Virgo. The Analyst never merges its energies with anything outside of itself—it keeps its essential being intact while it renders service. Cool and efficient, it dutifully does its job expertly, yet without much passion or feeling. Pisces is trying to teach Virgo to release emotion in ways that will enable it to feel more intimately united with the rest of life. The Analyzer doesn't identify with the masses as easily, but instead stands apart. The Fishes sense that Virgo is afraid to lose its identity (and its mind) by getting too deeply involved with the messier energies of others, and yet Pisces will attempt to break down barriers that prevent soul connection. Doing so helps further humanize Virgo.

On the other hand, Pisces is very much fed by its active imagination. It needs to sort out reality from illusion, since the boundary line between the two can be rather thin. Virgo can teach the Fishes about the value of being discriminate, about how to better distinguish what is helpful versus what is harmful to us. Also, honoring the needs of the body is very much on Virgo's mind (Pisces believes that soul development should be its sole concern, and that our attachment to things of the physical world is a main source of our pain and sorrow). Still, Virgo knows that without good health, we can't even accomplish our spiritual work very well. Bodies need to be maintained properly, not ignored or neglected. Pisces needs Virgo's expertise in this area, since body, mind, and soul all must coexist as one integrated unit of consciousness, for optimal results.

If we have Virgo/Pisces highlighted in our natal chart, we'll need to be careful not to become meek in a manner that allows the world to take advantage of us, since we often do not appear very assertive in getting our needs met. Sometimes we put others first, too much, and then wonder why we always end up holding the short end of the stick. Rather than feel like second-class citizens, we'll need to conduct ourselves in ways that solicit good treatment and respect from others.

Being less self-critical, and thus less willing to sabotage our dreams of a better life, will help in this regard. We shouldn't so easily accept leftovers, not when others of lesser character and ability are partaking in life's abundance. We, too, have a right to enjoy every opportunity that comes along, without feeling unprepared or undeserving.

Virgo/Pisces Astro-lebrities

Michael Jackson, singer: (Sun in Virgo, Moon in Pisces)

Macaulay Culkin, child actor: (Sun in Virgo, Moon in Pisces)

Johann von Goethe, writer: (Sun in Virgo, Moon in Pisces)

Edward Kennedy, politician: (Sun in Pisces, Moon in Virgo)

Alexander Graham Bell, inventor: (Sun in Pisces, Moon in Virgo)

Luther Burbank, geneticist: (Sun in Pisces, Moon in Virgo)

Chapter Six

Signs that Sextile & Trine

SIGNS THAT SEXTILE

Sextiling signs, although different in temperament, complement one another very well. They blend traditionally compatible elements—air-fire, earth-water—while also combining mixed modes (thus, here we don't have cardinal battling cardinal, fixed resisting fixed, or mutable trying to sidetrack mutable). Perhaps because these signs share less similar dispositions, compared to signs that trine one another, they are more stimulating in that they offer a variety of behavioral options—more choices of self-expression.

For example, Aries is certainly not the same as Gemini, yet many qualities of this air sign allow the Ram the stimulating avenues of direct self-expression it needs (for one thing, Gemini doesn't like to stay still, and neither does ever-active Aries, and so both signs will move on to something else rather than remain bored).

Still, there is a little bit of friction to be experienced, but usually that's when we refuse to cooperate and yield to the needs of both signs, not just the one we seem to favor. We could take turns trying to use these signs' energies when the occasion permits, but it would also be good to find smart ways to bridge their energies so that both are actively engaged at the same time.

Since we don't take any talents shown here for granted—as they feel less innate to us—there's less a tendency to become too self-satisfied regarding these special abilities (they don't come as easy to us as do the gifts shown by our trines). Instead, we feel encouraged to continually improve any skills suggested by the signs—and planets—in question. The more we practice, the better we get. Our sextiles don't involve the internal struggles that our squares do.

Sextiles, when well managed, keep us on our toes, alert to opportunity and ready to put our developing abilities into action. While we may not feel impelled to make anything big out of these energies—unlike the way we feel driven when squares or even oppositions are involved—it's nice to know that these resources are there, waiting to help us grow when we're ready to put them to conscious, lively use.

Aries/Gemini

Aries is a sign built for action, movement, and vigorously fresh starts in life. The Ram is brimming with youthful vitality; it seeks suitable outlets for its irrepressible energy. Gemini is also a sign that needs to move out into life and explore its surroundings (it'll even bring its binoculars in order to view any interesting action from a distance, which thus cuts down on needless physical exertion). The Twins, like Aries, symbolize a youthful energy fed by curiosity. In addition, they need to know how ordinary things in life interrelate.

Both signs are alert, wakeful, and ready to go out and eagerly meet the world head-on (of course, Aries pushes its way through, while Gemini is more apt to shake hands first and open lines of communication). Aries/Gemini energies can be impatient when life is not able to support the quick pace that these two signs must have to enjoy being in the moment. They hate it when matters drag on, and will look for diversions to break up any monotony (their combined actions can become rather mischievous).

However, Gemini—realizing it takes two to tango—is interested in the experiences of others, much more so than self-absorbed Aries, who's only focused on its own affairs. Too much involvement with others simply gets in the way of whatever the Ram wants, since people seem to have different opinions (surprise!) about how to do just about anything. Aries doesn't really enjoy listening to what others think, although Gemini does. The Twins like the Ram's boldness, since that guarantees its willingness to go after whatever grabs its attention. Both signs hate to feel held back from doing something. They instead seek firsthand experience (although Gemini is equally capable of experiencing life vicariously—it'll probably talk Aries into taking big chances, while it stands back to takes notes on what results). Aries is not all that sociable a creature, but Gemini knows how to introduce the Ram to peppy people who allow this sign to demonstrate its fiery abilities—and hopefully receive positive feedback for its efforts.

Both signs like things that are new, and they hate repetition. These two are quick-change artists who'll resist going down the same dull paths in life. They're only stimulated by variety. They know little about applying the brakes in life, and tend to go at whatever interests them at a rapid pace. Of course, they keep the same speed going when they switch gears and travel down a new road. Rest is needed, but remaining still for long is no easy feat—this sounds like a real fidgety pair, always thinking, "What can I do next besides sit around and drum my fingers?"

If we favor our Gemini side, we'll want our mental development to get the most out of Aries' dynamic energy. We can have pioneering instincts in the area of communication, with an eye toward what will speed up the process of getting our ideas to circulate quickly. But Gemini tends to be a little scattered when it's going too fast to concentrate properly, which is only aggravated by the short attention span of the Ram. We could seem hyperactive in our early years in ways that might worry educators, since our ability to be distracted is enormous.

Hopefully, as we mature, we'll find a wide range of things to interest us and to use up all our vigorous mental energy. If we favor our Aries side, then being on the go is more important, as well as tackling many things alone—without help—and thereby finding that we are blessed with versatility. We are certainly not dependent on others to do things for us, and even loathe supervision (we don't want authorities telling us exactly how to do something, especially when we already know a smarter and speedier way to do it).

With an Aries/Gemini emphasis in our chart, we are probably vivacious and easily animated when enthused. People may like to be around our energies when we're feeling confident about ourselves and are thinking we have everything figured out. Sometimes Gemini unrealistically has too many things it wants to do at once, and doesn't know what to begin first. But Aries is quick to drop anything that develops a snag, and instead move on to what's most accessible and hassle-free. It doesn't want to be juggling too many things at the same time.

We may want to connect with many people in our lives, but very few of them seem to remain permanent fixtures, since both signs have a dread of being trapped in oppressive, highly dependent relationships. We'd rather keep things light and noncommittal, yet that could make us seem more superficial than we really are (remember, we also have other signs in our chart that describe less restless parts of us that need to be further developed). Altogether, Aries/Gemini is a peppy combo showing a zest for any arousing activity that engages us mentally and physically.

ARIES/GEMINI ASTRO-LEBRITIES

Reba McEntire, singer: (Sun in Aries, Moon in Gemini)
Ewan McGregor, actor: (Sun in Aries, Moon in Gemini)
Bette Davis, actress: (Sun in Aries, Moon in Gemini)

Isadora Duncan, dancer: (Sun in Gemini, Moon in Aries)
Jackie Stewart, racecar driver: (Sun in Gemini, Moon in Aries)
Helen Hunt, actress: (Sun in Gemini, Moon in Aries)

Taurus/Cancer

This next combo is certainly less filled with the excitable, nervous energy that keeps Aries/Gemini on the move. Taurus/Cancer is more like what Aries/Gemini would become if given a strong enough sedative. The Bull and the Crab seek security, although for different reasons. For Taurus, the issue is less emotional, since this earth sign simply seeks to protect what it owns (its material goods are valued and thus deserve to be kept in a safe place). Security for Taurus also helps ensure stability, meaning that things stay put—nothing changes suddenly.

Yet, for the Crab, "security" has other layers of meaning, since this sign feels not only anchored by certain material attachments—especially its home—but also by the people it cherishes. Although collected physical objects tend to remain in place—usually in the Crab's closets—people may leave and never come back when intimate connections break down. This is a major Cancerian fear, since its psychological security is very important.

Taurus realizes that Cancer is cautious in its actions, always making sure that nothing unexpected happens to disrupt its life. This is something the Bull appreciates, since it is sure it can count on the Crab during times of need (although Taurus is so self-sufficient that such "times of need" are few and far between). Still, it's good to know that the Bull has back-up support when necessary, and from a sign that is famous for its nurturing strengths.

Cancer loves Taurean reliability—it's easy to feel more secure when you're dealing with someone who's dependable. Although the Crab is more emotionally complex than Taurus—and thus, a bit of a pain to be around when it's in "panic" mode—the patient Bull is very glad to receive the benefits of warm Cancerian feelings and loving concerns. Working together, these signs can make anyone feel wanted and loved. There's nothing aloof or distant about them.

Yet sometimes what is most needed in some relationships is proper breathing space and a little elbow room. Unfortunately, these two can suffocate others by demanding too much closeness and familiarity, even though Taurus is less dependent on having someone around all the time. Much of the Bull's energy is wrapped up in supporting itself materially, not sustaining others emotionally. (Imagine somebody with heavy Taurus/Cancer energies married to another person with a prominent Sagittarius/Aquarius emphasis—that's certainly not a match made in heaven!) Both these signs need consistency in their lives. They want a steady, predictable interaction lacking in dramatic fireworks. They also have strong nesting instincts and like settling down and not always being on the go. Rest and relaxation are important to both; a less-hectic pace is appreciated (although there is a possibility that if life slows down too much, things start to get on the lazy side). Both signs are good at putting off what they don't wish to do.

We who have Taurus/Cancer emphasized are likely to want to build solid, enduring foundations in our lives that will never collapse. We're willing to do what it takes to surround ourselves with material comforts (nothing too extravagant) and caring relationships that clearly show deep bonding. Regardless of our gender, we give off strong "Earth mother" vibrations, and others in need find us soothing (including plants and animals). Ours is a tender, nourishing, sustaining energy that supports growth. Perhaps living in a rural or rustic environment (or at least visiting such places) will help show us how powerful our instincts are when relating to Nature.

Trying to find security through external situations is a hit-and-miss proposition, even though we will need outer stability to help us feel more at home with ourselves. But if anything, we'll need to learn how important it is to feel internally secure, especially since that is something more under our control. Being anchored from within, perhaps as a result of deeply valuing who we are and trusting our power to build security for ourselves, is vital to our long-term happiness.

TAURUS/CANCER ASTRO-LEBRITIES:
Steve Winwood, musician: (Sun in Taurus, Moon in Cancer)
Leonardo da Vinci, artist-inventor: (Sun in Taurus, Moon in Cancer)
Dr. Benjamin Spock, pediatrician: (Sun in Taurus, Moon in Cancer)

Meryl Streep, actress: (Sun in Cancer, Moon in Taurus)
Marcel Proust, writer: (Sun in Cancer, Moon in Taurus)
Ann Landers, advice columnist: (Sun in Cancer, Moon in Taurus)

Gemini/Leo

Here's Gemini again, pairing up with another fire sign in a manner that keeps mental energies burning brightly, except that Leo is better able to sustain its fiery output than cardinal Aries. The Twins are thus less easily distracted by short-lived bursts of enthusiasm. Constant change—something that the Ram tries to enforce—is less desirable here. Leo also has a solid sense of self, and this helps give the Gemini side of us the focus needed to apply its versatility better, and in ways with which we can truly identify.

Our creativity becomes a more personal statement of who we are, not just of what we can impulsively and quickly produce at will. In fact, fixed Leo may deliberately slow down the action so that it can attain greater control over the manner in which Gemini unfolds its many talents. While the Twins don't always take their skills seriously—since they're developed so easily—Leo does put its heart into whatever it produces, and wants nothing but first-class results.

Perhaps a problem for these sextiling signs is that there may be an abundance of talent that cannot all be put to use at the same time, due to how varied that talent is. Confident Leo, looking at Gemini's stimulating options, knows it would enjoy doing several things, but is there enough time? (Energy is less a concern.) Gemini doesn't mind being labeled a dilettante—it's not ashamed to dabble here and there, since variety is what keeps it going. Yet such a term, implying amateur status, is insulting to the Lion. Leo instead has big dreams of being a major influence in its field of interest, not someone with a little luck and talent who produces less-memorable creations, now and then. The self-assured Lion tends to overestimate its abilities and is further egged on by optimistic Gemini, who's ready to try anything new. Luckily, the sextile's energy allows us ample opportunity to discover how best to take advantage of our talents.

Gemini/Leo is another one of those youthful combinations. Very much kids at heart, both signs have a fun-filled, playful side to them. They don't care for stuffy behavior and love to do things spontaneously, although perhaps not in the spur-of-the-moment manner of impulsive Aries/Gemini. (Leo doesn't like to be that caught off guard —it tries to orchestrate its splashy productions for maximum effect, usually leaving little to chance).

Leo provides friendly but typically cool-headed Gemini with a little extra warmth. The Twins, encouraged to be more affectionate than usual, are less detached. However, Gemini—normally an impartial observer—may find itself more swayed by emotion than reason, since Leo is not as rational about things once its passions have been stirred (Leo's heavy drama seldom makes logical sense, but it does make for good theater).

Those of us with Gemini/Leo highlighted in our chart are usually happy and outgoing. We will welcome the world into our lives and will put on entertaining performances for those we love and trust the most. Leo can let its hair down even more with Gemini. Arrogance is less a problem for the Lion, since the Twins aren't hung up on feeling superior to others. In fact, Gemini tries to communicate to a wide range of people on their own terms—only a flexible mind can do that.

It would be good to narrow down the list of wonderful things we feel we can do in this world, and then concentrate on those that are the most fun. Leo needs to learn to be less performance-sensitive (as it only expects rave reviews), but Gemini teaches us to just enjoy our experiences, first and foremost. Let's not be as concerned with what the entire front row thinks of our opening act. Our spontaneous impulses are usually worth following.

Gemini/Leo Astro-lebrities

Paul McCartney, musician: (Sun in Gemini, Moon in Leo)
Helena Bonham Carter, actress: (Sun in Gemini, Moon in Leo)
Walt Whitman, poet: (Sun in Gemini, Moon in Leo)

Mae West, actress: (Sun in Leo, Moon in Gemini)
Tony Bennett, singer: (Sun in Leo, Moon in Gemini)
Shelley Winters, actress: (Sun in Leo, Moon in Gemini)

Cancer/Virgo

Combined with Taurus, Cancer is almost a bit too concerned about establishing everlasting security, since both signs are heavily into their attachments and don't handle risk very well. Still, Taurus' stabilizing influence helps reduce the Crab's emotional anxiety, as the Bull is less easily unnerved about such matters and doesn't have a pessimistic streak. The risk factor is still bothersome to Cancer/Virgo, maybe even more so, since this combination stimulates a worrywart potential.

Virgo is certainly not as calm as the Bull, probably because the Analyzer is the nervous type who thinks too much about things that could go wrong. This makes this sign feel a little jumpy when Cancer, sounding a bit fearful about its future, paints a picture of anxiety for Virgo. Because this is a sextile relationship, nerves and emotions never really get the best of us, since we are urged to find smart ways to appease the needs of both signs. However, for this to happen, we'll have to exert sensible self-control regarding our thoughts and feelings about the security and safety issues of our lives.

The Analyzer isn't very comfortable with emotionality, but it seeks to understand precisely what triggers Cancer to react in certain ways, which is not an easy task (since there's never just one clear-cut factor at work). Nonetheless, the Crab needs to sort out its own feelings better in order to track down the general source of its periodic unrest, and here's where Virgo can help. The Analyzer seeks to provide excellent service, with meticulous attention paid to details, but Cancer knows that the addition of a warm sense of caring seems to make all the difference when attending to very human situations. This can be a great combo for those of us in fields where knowledge and instinct join forces to help others with pressing needs. Virgo supplies sharp analysis and the ability to weed out less-relevant factors, while clarifying the more essential issues, while Cancer provides its often accurate gut feelings about people, especially those undergoing tough times.

When handled well, this sextile means Virgo's not as cool and collected as it normally likes to be, since now its ability to sympathize with others is heightened. Cancer lets the Analyzer know that it's okay to feel for others and that it's alright for such feelings to defy logic. We're not to avoid emotions or downgrade their importance to our growth, since they are a meaningful part of the order of life.

Virgo, in turn, lets the Crab know that security issues can often be resolved in more pragmatic ways, but reasonable self-discipline regarding our emotions will be needed. (Don't jump the gun and panic, Cancer, until you've gathered all the pertinent facts that can shed light on your situation; take time to do your homework before getting all worked up.) Virgo also needs the influence of the Crab to keep it from becoming too dry and colorless in temperament. Cancer's active imagination can be put to practical use, plus the Crab's hunches about people and situations help Virgo pinpoint problems needing correction.

Cancer holds on tightly to its material possessions, partly due to its fear of loss and deprivation. Virgo believes in being well stocked with essential goods—that means Band-Aids and batteries more than it does ice cream and cookies (the last two are typically found on Cancer's list, since this sign craves its comfort foods). Still, Cancerian anxiety can get to Virgo's fretful side, and we may end up having an oversupply of all kinds of items (this is also a Taurus/Cancer issue). Hopefully, by applying Virgoan common sense, we'll be more careful and discriminating about what we collect and save.

Those of us with Cancer/Virgo emphasized in our chart are usually out to make things better in our immediate world, and that means attending to those smaller issues of life that can interfere with efficiency when neglected. We're keenly attentive to details. Both signs like to tidy up their surroundings—Cancer knows the importance of keeping its nest clean, while Virgo feels it must give anything dirty a good scrubbing. If not careful, too much time can be eaten up by keeping everything well maintained.

Virgo's not a pack rat, yet it hates to discard something that is still—barely—operable. It needs to stop trying to keep certain things running forever. Cancer has more sentimental reasons for hanging on to its junk. Both signs need to adopt an "out with the old, in with the new" policy more often. Altogether, this combo reflects a quiet, modest temperament that receives much emotional satisfaction from being useful to others. We just need to be careful not to become slaves to our routines and habits, both at home and on the job.

CANCER/VIRGO ASTRO-LEBRITIES

Bill Cosby, comedian-actor: (Sun in Cancer, Moon in Virgo)
Angelica Huston, actress: (Sun in Cancer, Moon in Virgo)
Neil Simon, playwright: (Sun in Cancer, Moon in Virgo)

Queen Wilhelmina, Dutch royalty: (Sun in Virgo, Moon in
   Cancer)
Richard Gere, actor: (Sun in Virgo, Moon in Cancer)
Tuesday Weld, actress: (Sun in Virgo, Moon in Cancer)

Leo/Libra

Leo loves to shine for its audience and it knows how to evoke emotion in others. Libra, while less dramatic, also has a talent for captivat-
ing people. Together, these signs suggest an above-average degree of
charisma and charm, plus a knack for always putting one's best foot
forward. Both signs seek approval—they *really* want to be liked, even
loved by others, and will do whatever it takes to please. Actually, Leo
has its limits, since its dignity prevents it from begging for attention
(wearing a clown suit is as far as it'll go).

Libra is also poised enough not to go too far when soliciting attention, since it hates feeling pushy (but being a cardinal sign, it is more
assertive than it cares to admit). The blend of these sociable signs suggests an upbeat ability to make others look and feel good. Since both
are appearance-conscious, there is a need to enhance and beautify the
outer world. These signs have a great sense of style and realize its importance in getting others to notice them (it's not just a matter of exercising personal taste, but of using flair to create an eye-catching
image that others find attractive and desirable).

It's important for those of us with this combo to cultivate a more
refined way of living, since both signs detest anything coarse and unsophisticated (actually, Leo saves its slapstick comedy routine for others signs, but tries to impress Libra with its best behavior). It is
important, however, that we don't wind up cultivating mannerisms
that may look polished, but feel artificial and shallow.

We may also have an air about us that tells others we expect to be
pampered and given the best treatment from life all the time. We can
look like spoiled types who refuse to struggle to obtain what we
want. We may expect easy access to the finer things that the world
has to offer, yet this attitude of privilege can rub others the wrong
way. Luckily, the sextile keeps Leo/Libra energies from becoming too

obnoxious, although both signs can get hung up on living a luxurious lifestyle, and they tend to show off a bit too much.

Libra helps tone down Leo a bit, since the Lion can engage in brassy behavior from time to time (usually when feeling insecure). The Balancer knows that much can be gained by turning on its power to persuade, more so than by acting bossy and demanding. Libra loathes making a big scene about anything, even when upset. Yet a dissatisfied Lion often thinks "The louder, the better!" when it wants to draw attention to its problems—this is not a very subtle sign.

Perhaps Libra keeps Leo more mindful of good manners and of showing others proper courtesies. The Balancer is trying to convince the Lion that treating people well is the best way to always get what you want out of them, rather than getting on one's high horse and acting like arrogant royalty.

If we have a Leo/Libra emphasis in our chart, we are probably very likeable and popular with many people. We seek out dynamic relationships that are based on both mutual respect and creative energy. The people to whom we get the closest need to be fun and entertaining, with as much vitality to offer us as we offer them. Leo's influence can allow Libra to feel less dependent on others and more able to enjoy its own quality time alone, perhaps working to improve its talents.

Leo also provides the Balancer with enough backbone to allow this air sign to feel better about saying "no!" to those who try to suck Libra into their hectic life predicaments (otherwise, the Balancer is too easily thrown off-track by the pressing affairs of others and can resent such intrusion). Libra is working to establish better boundaries in its relationships, yet Leo easily insists that it will not be taken advantage of by anyone. Its sense of self is such that it will not tolerate personal abuses of any sort. This is something that the Libra in us needs to hear. It is better to be alone than to endure unhealthy, ego-sabotaging partnerships with folks who turn out to be rigid and controlling. Leo forces Libra to stand up and defend its own rights, not just those of others.

Leo/Libra Astro-lebrities

Julia Child, chef-writer: (Sun in Leo, Moon in Libra)

Wilt Chamberlain, athlete: (Sun in Leo, Moon in Libra)

Iman, supermodel: (Sun in Leo, Moon in Libra)

Oscar Wilde, writer: (Sun in Libra, Moon in Leo)

Catherine Deneuve, actress: (Sun in Libra, Moon in Leo)

John Dewey, educator: (Sun in Libra, Moon in Leo)

Virgo/Scorpio

Here is a combination of two signs known for their ability to analyze even the smallest things in life. Little escapes their attention. Their capacity to handle details is enormous, but so is their inclination to keenly observe the world with a critical eye. Virgo's urge to correct something that's not working well is less intense than Scorpio's, who'd rather either force a complete overhaul or demand the total elimination of whatever is defective. This water sign's measures are often too drastic and emotionally driven to suit Virgo, who'd rather first try out various techniques to see what can be fixed. Is anything of use still salvageable?

Virgo's approach is calm, reasonable, and wisely patient. Scorpio seems more compelled to destroy and start all over again, even when doing so would plainly be a case of overkill (the Scorpion seems to get irrationally angry inside when simple things don't work right, while Virgo is merely annoyed and inconvenienced). Hopefully, Virgo will convince Scorpio how becoming enraged by any problem—major or minor—just makes matters worse. A cooler head is needed if a sensible, workable solution is to be found. Flexibility is the key.

Scorpio contains hidden, pent-up fury in its depths, but it does appreciate the way Virgo carefully and rationally thinks things through. Thoroughness always appeals to the Scorpion. Virgo leaves practically no stone unturned when it's reviewing a problem at hand. Actually, both signs can be a bit obsessive-compulsive when they join forces, since they can't seem to rest until a disturbing issue is resolved.

Emotional intensity is mixed with nervous energy here, resulting in behavior that at times borders on the neurotic. Still, Virgo/Scorpio must uncover the bottom-line reasons for why something or someone is malfunctioning. The difference is that Virgo depends on its logical mind to help it backtrack and trace any problem to its root cause, while Scorpio uses its psychic sensitivity to feel out the hidden factors of any complex situation. Together, this combo is unbeatable at detective work, whether in trying to solve a crime, uncover a mystery of science, or probe deeply into a troubled psyche.

While it is hoped that the sextile will bring out the attributes of both signs, Virgo/Scorpio energies are still tough to live with (ask any Gemini/Sagittarius type). These signs can be very picky about everything, as they notice too much at times, plus everything to them is a serious issue or a potential crisis-in-the-making. When is there time to enjoy living, for two signs who are so preoccupied with what can go wrong in the world? They want to prevent damage in life, yet they are too hung up on things breaking down and causing trouble.

Careers that call for expert repair and renovation are right up Virgo/Scorpio's alley. Once committed to a task, it's a total commitment. Their ability to stay focused is awesome, but at times their stick-to-it-tiveness can lead to exhaustion. If we favor the Virgo side of this combo, then perhaps we can better appreciate moderation. Otherwise, Scorpio can goad us to go to extremes in our endeavors.

Those of us with Virgo/Scorpio highlighted in our chart will only put out enduring energy when we are fascinated by what we're doing. We can feel almost hypnotically fixated when working hard on a project, so much so that we won't tolerate any interruptions. It is thus important to have demanding tasks that use up a lot of our mental and emotional energies. We'll need to learn the art of true relaxation. Otherwise, we may feel tense all the time, especially during those rare moments when we're idle or underemployed.

There's little about this mix of signs that is light and playful, which are qualities we need in order to prevent too much heavy responsibility from piling up on our shoulders. It would be wise in this lifetime to examine our psychological motives for doing anything (perhaps by reading a wide range of self-help material). We need to figure out what really makes us tick (and why we demand that people in our lives be so perfect). Still, it's great if we are drawn to deep and complex studies, since we'll always have ourselves to research for a lifetime.

VIRGO/SCORPIO ASTRO-LEBRITIES

Richard Burton, actor: (Sun in Scorpio, Moon in Virgo)

Jodie Foster, actress: (Sun in Scorpio, Moon in Virgo)

Jonathan Winters, comedian: (Sun in Scorpio, Moon in Virgo)

Maria Montessori, educator: (Sun in Virgo, Moon in Scorpio)

William Saroyan, writer: (Sun in Virgo, Moon in Scorpio)

Kate Millet, writer: (Sun in Virgo, Moon in Scorpio)

Libra/Sagittarius

Leo/Libra has fun packaging itself in suave, appealing ways that open doors of social opportunity. Although able to interact amiably with others in an upbeat manner, this combo is still about self-enhancement—looking good in the eyes of those it wishes to impress. But now with Sagittarius entering the picture, Libra is able to center its energies on more high-minded ideals. This is a gregarious influence, even more so than Leo/Libra. Perhaps due to the potential snob factor in Leo, Leo/Libra is choosier about whom it wishes to socialize with—the right crowd of "beautiful" people. Sagittarius is less concerned with status and prestige, and is more interested in the social conscience of others: Do people ever think about human needs on a global scale? Do they feel like universal citizens? What hopes do they have for humanity's future?

The big and lofty issues of life spark an activist spirit in the Archer. The lifestyles of the rich and famous are less relevant to this sign, although it does like to see life becoming more rewarding for all. Libra, concerned about social injustice and inhumane treatment, is more interested in defending human rights and protecting civil liberties, when joined with crusading Sagittarius—a sign of "the people's" advocate (similar to Aquarius).

Sometimes being very idealistic about society can pose problems, since the reality of how people actually treat one another can be very disheartening. Libra believes in fair play, while Sagittarius supports diversity. These signs thus feel individuals should be able to enjoy a wide range of constructive, social freedoms. Libra/Sagittarius has a legalistic mindset and is as concerned about the rights of individuals as it is the rights of the community. The basic outlook of this combo leans toward liberal thinking (but not always, since sometimes its adherence to the law—even from a religious stance—can result in zealous, orthodox views; however, it is typical for justice here to be tempered with mercy).

Libra idealistically envisions a perfect world where everyone is happily in a state of harmony and peace. Sagittarius tries its best to bring a little heaven to Earth. It seeks to break down social barriers that keep people feeling like strangers to one another. It may be that these signs are too hopeful in their expectations of what society is capable of becoming, and yet Libra/Sagittarius types need to keep their standards high to remain inspired. They may have difficulty coping with human conflict. Sagittarius likes to take up sweeping, global causes and do battle against the biased policies of the powers-that-be, while Libra will defend the weaker and those unjustly treated by others.

Yet on a personal level, they can't handle disharmony as well. Getting openly mad or becoming the target of another's anger is something Libra/Sagittarius tries to avoid (outspoken Sagittarius can surely let its blunt opinions fly like sharpened arrows, wounding others unintentionally, but when blended with Libra, it's more interested in developing wisdom and understanding).

If these signs are emphasized in our chart, we probably have an intellectually refined nature and are in search of life's greater meaning. We seek sound moral guidelines to live by. Philosophically optimistic, we may yearn for a future of social improvement based on spiritual principles (or at least ethical, humane treatment).

We are very people-oriented in a somewhat impersonal way, but we're more restless with the social game-playing typically required to make it in the world (Libra doesn't mind playing such games, to some extent, since many perks are involved—yet not Sagittarius, a sign with an untamed, defiant side that urges it to break away from the herd once it feels it's being false to its real self). Some of us sense that our mission in life involves broadcasting our beliefs to others, although with a measure of charm that can win over nearly any audience. Our sincerity and honesty shine through, which only adds to our public appeal.

LIBRA/SAGITTARIUS ASTRO-LEBRITIES

Christopher Reeve, actor: (Sun in Libra, Moon in Sagittarius)

Brian Boitano, figure skater: (Sun in Libra, Moon in Sagittarius)

Friedrich Nietzsche, philosopher: (Sun in Libra, Moon in Sagittarius)

Jane Austen, writer: (Sun in Sagittarius, Moon in Libra)

Henri de Toulouse-Lautrec, artist: (Sun in Sagittarius, Moon in Libra)

Emily Dickinson, poet: (Sun in Sagittarius, Moon in Libra)

Scorpio/Capricorn

It's hard to think of two signs more serious than these. Scorpio/Capricorn energies can feel heavy, sometimes in a dark, brooding sense. The emphasis is typically on self-control, which—if not careful—can become repression, especially on emotional levels. These two tight-lipped signs closely guard their private affairs. Both are also responsible, no-nonsense types who tend to be all business and no play. Whatever they set out to do, they do with a great sense of commitment and stamina. Activity has to be purposeful, not leisurely, for them to justify their involvement.

However, Scorpio does have an emotionally fed intensity that scares the Goat, who is reluctant to expose its feelings for fear of the world's harsh judgment. Showing weakness of any sort is what Capricorn avoids (it thus internalizes all its insecurities while presenting to others its more capable, self-reliant persona). Scorpio is also guarded about what it reveals emotionally, yet is famous for its memorable eruptions when provoked beyond its ability to conceal its feelings.

These signs find each other's strength and determination appealing. There are both single-minded enough to succeed in their goals, being more driven to press on with their ambitions than are most other signs. They can cut through obstacles in their path with a ruthlessness that can be alienating. Scorpio/Capricorn types can appear very chilly and distant in demeanor when they want others to back off and not pry into personal matters.

Both signs do not take well to being teased or poked fun at, especially in a public setting; they can get defensive. They'll need to work on developing more trust in others. Cultivating a sense of humor—although not biting humor—surely would help them lighten up and become more socially accessible. Otherwise, expect to find icy walls built to ward off close but unwanted human contact. These signs don't like being approached by the "wrong" people.

Scorpio is trying to teach the Goat to be more sensitive to things of a less-material nature, such as the underworld of the human psyche and the possibilities that invisible realms coexist within the physical dimension of waking consciousness. Uncanny hunches are not typically what Capricorn feels (it's too mentally calculating to receive such flashes of insight). Instead, the Goat thinks long and hard about its strategies, yet worries that its plans are not foolproof—and this can be an anxious way to live.

Although an excellent analyst, Scorpio goes by its less-rational gut feelings when its trying to mastermind a plan of action. It looks deeper for needed clues about what to do to make sure it succeeds with the fewest problems. Of course, Capricorn is blessed with excellent organizational ability, which also helps further any project. Together, these signs can concentrate deeply on what they're trying to accomplish—as if immune to distractions—and they'll seemingly take anything to its completion.

Capricorn yens to be a respected authority who wields social power (it's those Goats who don't abuse such power who receive public honor). This sign feels impelled to rise to top positions of influence. Scorpio also feels drawn to roles of power—including the psychological power to internally transform people—but it senses that seeking total control over others comes at a price. The Scorpion has a weird ability to step back and scrutinize its behavior, even as it fully engages in intense activity. It knows when it is being cruel and abusive, although it may choose to persist in this manner. It also feels deeply that it will be annihilated should it continue pursuing paths that are destructive to others.

Capricorn doesn't realize when it's on that same path, since it evaluates its motives in more pragmatic ways. Yet, its sense of the workings of fate makes the Goat wonder about the inevitable consequences of its self-seeking social transgressions—when will the ax fall? Thus, these two ambitious signs can get uptight about what could happen if they try to grab for power for all the wrong reasons.

Those of us with a Scorpio/Capricorn natal emphasis are dependable in rock-solid ways, but we probably don't make promises easily, knowing how obligated we can later feel. We also believe we need to be solely in charge of our affairs, rather than share our duties (partly because we secretly feel others are incompetent, and also because we are self-reliant). However, life will teach us the value of yielding to the expertise of others, as well as the importance of cooperating with those who have a good sense of their own power. Our instinct is to stand apart—we can appear aloof—in order to structure our private world without interference. We can also feel lonely when pursuing our single-minded desires. Yet our sense of thrift and discipline help us survive hard times when financial resources are lean—our ascetic tendencies come to the fore.

SCORPIO/CAPRICORN ASTRO-LEBRITIES

George Patton, military general: (Sun in Scorpio, Moon in Capricorn)

Lee Grant, actress-director: (Sun in Scorpio, Moon in Capricorn)

Robert Kennedy, politician: (Sun in Scorpio, Moon in Capricorn)

Henry Miller, writer: (Sun in Capricorn, Moon in Scorpio)

Ralph Fiennes, actor: (Sun in Capricorn, Moon in Scorpio)

Kate Moss, supermodel: (Sun in Capricorn, Moon in Scorpio)

Sagittarius/Aquarius

With Sagittarius and Aquarius, we are truly in the realm of collective experience, where sweeping ideals and futuristic visions are to take shape. Life here is viewed from a very wide angle, with concern placed on the universal welfare of humanity. Both signs are also highly supportive of individual freedom and one's right to go against the majority rule. These two squirm when feeling boxed in by society's traditional rules of conduct and will openly rebel when necessary. They can't be pigeonholed or possessed. Their urge is to tear down walls of conformity that have kept people from living out their fullest potential. Actually, Sagittarius seeks to participate in the best of all possible worlds. Prosperity is accepted and enjoyed, as long as attaining it doesn't violate the Archer's moral beliefs or spiritual principles. It acknowledges material abundance and elevated social status as opportune ways to help spearhead worthwhile humanitarian projects. Ever-generous in spirit, Sagittarius is the sign of the philanthropist concerned with society's advancement and with serving the greater good.

Aquarius is the more defiant side of this combo, since it doesn't fit into mainstream society as smoothly (being fixed, Aquarius resists). Yet it does realize that group power is one way to initiate major change in society—people, creating mass movements, must come together and advocate progressive reform, even if that upsets the status quo and threatens to eliminate leaders currently in control. Aquarius is better able to organize its revolts than is fiery Sagittarius, who makes a lot of noise and can be a temporarily disruptive force, but then may have little follow-through (mutability reduces perseverance, while fixity strengthens it).

Sometimes the changes that Sagittarius envisions are too theoretically unsound to actually work (the critical details needed to implement major reforms are left out), but the Archer is basically here to inspire and promote lofty goals. Other signs—like Capricorn—are better equipped to work out the organizational nuts and bolts of whatever it takes to make significant social dreams come true. Sagittarius acts as society's moral conscience.

The Water Bearer also has wondrous visions about the world of tomorrow. This is a highly intuitive sign also blessed with a scientific objectivity that enables it to be inventive in useful ways, and in a manner from which all people can benefit. It's also a sign that is less religious in tone than Sagittarius, meaning it doesn't automatically perceive the

Universe to have a greater cosmic plan at work that will lead people to the spiritual realization of One Truth.

Experimental Aquarius is simply out to discover the workings of many lesser "truths" along a diversity of paths. It's more humanistic in attitude and doesn't get as emotionally wrapped up in its beliefs as does the Archer (although it will get excited when it has that "eureka" experience of knowing). Together, these signs are less caught up in the past and are reasonably involved in the developments of the here and now, but they really come alive when dealing with what could possibly happen in the future. They are farsighted and willing to endorse positive thinking.

Those of us with Sagittarius/Aquarius highlighted in our chart may feel out of touch with the norms of mainstream society, but we're usually glad that's the case (both signs feel that being individualistic is a good and natural thing). We can be tremendously idealistic, yet in a manner that has us feeling discontent with much of life as it is—unless we can pitch in and help improve the human condition. We don't expect to do this alone and are thankful to have a broad range of colorful friends and inspirational acquaintances with which to network. We'll need to learn the importance, however, of being alone and of appreciating our own space.

Faulted for often being on the emotionally impersonal side, we need to make sure we're not so mentally overloaded and physically hyperactive that we fail to take the time required to sort through our feelings, which may be underdeveloped due to our neglect. The world we gravitate toward is exciting and filled with the adventure of discovery, but it's good to know when to slow down and honor our vulnerable human parts, those that emerge best within more intimate relationships.

SAGITTARIUS/AQUARIUS ASTRO-LEBRITIES

Andrew Carnegie, philanthropist: (Sun in Sagittarius, Moon in Aquarius)

Margaret Mead, anthropologist: (Sun in Sagittarius, Moon in Aquarius)

Richard Leakey, anthropologist: (Sun in Sagittarius, Moon in Aquarius)

Yoko Ono, artist: (Sun in Aquarius, Moon in Sagittarius)
Charles Dickens, writer: (Sun in Aquarius, Moon in Sagittarius)
Jennifer Aniston, actress: (Sun in Aquarius/Moon in Sagittarius)

Capricorn/Pisces

This next sextile involves two transpersonal signs who feel obligated to contribute something of importance to society—something that can ensure economic and cultural stability (Capricorn) while also helping humanity feel unified on deeper, spiritually bonded levels (Pisces). Capricorn works hard to slowly build a sturdy, enduring framework of civilization. Its main concern is the organization of a society governed by duty-driven authorities who enforce law and order.

Capricorn also instills in us (sometimes by using guilt and shame) the need to be responsible citizens who will obey the rules and promise to do our part to keep our community sound and sane (that means no crazy, reckless, lawless behavior). If we stray too far from the established, sanctioned ways of doing things, we run the risk of being harshly judged and penalized. Violating social standards will not be permitted in Capricorn's potentially authoritarian world; we are to behave as expected—or else! (Capricorn assures us that well-earned material rewards and titles only go to those who "get with the program.")

Pisces—indeed, a different fish—ignores society's rules and regulations and instead taps into the hidden, emotional wellspring of any culture's development—the soul of a people. Pisces is more sensitive to society's dreams, fantasies, ideal visions, creative yearnings, escapist needs, and even its potential for decay and disillusionment. The outer trappings of power and authoritative control mean little to this sign, who instead directs its attention to the underlying oneness of the human race. The Fishes symbolize a realm of otherworldly reality that Capricorn can hardly imagine, much less comprehend.

Still, what unites these two signs is their need to shield society from elements that would otherwise tear it to pieces, resulting in a total breakdown of order and civility. The Goat supports legal processes that protect society's standards regarding right and wrong, while the Fishes put their trust in the impartial but unerring laws of karma. Capricorn wants justice now, but Pisces believes in eventual, divine retribution.

Still, Pisces influences Capricorn to show compassion when laying down its set, social rules and when punishing those who dare to defy them. The Goat can be too hard-hearted at times, and needs to take a softer, more lenient stance on human behavior (after all, it's tough being perfect while also being human at the same time—something Capricorn should know by heart). Of course, the Goat is often too critical of the Fishes' "bleeding liberal" policies, seeing them as sorry excuses allowing people to ignore their social responsibilities—and in ways that lead to all sorts of societal difficulties.

Thus, Capricorn demands that Pisces quit dreaming and instead wake up and get real. Yet who's right here? Maybe they both are. Their sextile relationship coaxes them to find creative channels to integrate these two ways of looking at society and how it can best develop. Both signs are shy and even reserved—although Pisces does have its whimsical moments of magical self-expression. Capricorn and Pisces are wise beyond their years, humble, and able to make personal sacrifices for the sake of the greater good.

With a Capricorn/Pisces emphasis in our chart, we can quietly endure in our ambition, and are less worldly than we may appear. We often feel driven to do something that eases the lives of those less fortunate, yet we may have to climb to a powerful position in society before we can help humanity on broader levels. Our demeanor may be unassuming, giving us the appearance of being laid-back (which hard-working Capricorn never really is), but we may actually idealize the struggle required to reach our highest goals.

Fame and acclaim become meaningless if we lose our soul in the process, explaining why we may be reluctant to go down certain paths that otherwise could guarantee our success (Pisces ignores the standard rules of the game when it comes to "making it" in society). Still, when we handle this combo well, we are blessed with vision, sensitivity, empathy, and strong spiritual values that all help us remain clear about who we really are—deep down inside—no matter how high up the social ladder we climb.

Capricorn/Pisces Astro-lebrities

Martin Luther King, Jr., civil rights leader: (Sun in Capricorn, Moon in Pisces)

Simone de Beauvoir, writer: (Sun in Capricorn, Moon in Pisces)

John Denver, musician: (Sun in Capricorn, Moon in Pisces)

Juliette Binoche, actress: (Sun in Pisces, Moon in Capricorn)

Sybil Leek, witch: (Sun in Pisces, Moon in Capricorn)

Dinah Shore, singer: (Sun in Pisces, Moon in Capricorn)

Aquarius/Aries

The combination of these two headstrong signs makes for a powerful individualism, for better or worse. Aquarius may be airy (open-minded), but it's fixed as well (stubborn) when it comes to following its own inner guidelines regarding action and behavior. Aries can identify with that policy. The Ram seeks autonomy in action and will fight against the constraints of external authority, much the way the Water Bearer does when defending humanity's civil rights. However, Aquarius is also fighting for the freedom of all people, whereas Aries is more self-serving. It's more interested in an experience when it can personally gain from the actions it takes.

The Ram shows little awareness or interest in the future growth of the collective. What it wants instead is immediate self-satisfaction, without the complication of having to adjust or yield to others. Aquarius believes in teamwork, where everyone joins in harmony to support a common cause that benefits all. No one individual is to stand apart and function independently from the group's need, even if contradictory Aquarius unexpectedly does. Yet it is this part of the Aquarian experience that Aries finds scary. After all, the Ram belongs to no one!

Arien boldness appeals to Aquarius, who realizes that social revolution cannot be carried out by timid, vacillating, or image-conscious people. Aries doesn't care what others think and thus feels uninhibited.

The Water Bearer wants to enlighten the Ram about the value of social cooperation, since those who live in a vacuum unwisely cut off all lines of friendly support. Aries thus needs to become less self-absorbed and more sensitive to important social issues.

However, Aquarius also needs to know when to break away from too much peer focus and instead allow for greater self-involvement (we can't always lose ourselves in the group dynamic). Also, the Ram thinks all these lofty social objectives that preoccupy cool-headed Aquarius are unreal at times. How about showing a little passion and even some real personal anger?

"Why detach so much from your gut feelings, just because they don't neatly fit your mental ideal of who you think you are?" asks Aries. In the Ram's eyes, Aquarius needs constant reality checks, since it seems divorced from the rawer elements of its humanness. How free can a sign really be when it routinely represses its more needy or selfish side?

Working together, these two signs spark a talent for innovative, trail-blazing activity—they're quite willing to stick their necks out for the sake of experimental progress. Luckily, they can be so sold on the rightness of their objectives that even rejection—while disappointing—is not devastating to them. In fact, it just makes for a stronger resolve and a heightened sense of defiance. Sometimes it's the Aries side of this combo that acts prematurely and without any sense of the broader issues involved, and this can lead to stunning failures. Yet when the Aquarius side gets the upper hand, spontaneity may go out the window, as the Water Bearer tries to craft brilliant ideas that address the needs of many, and in a manner that often requires more deliberation than Aries can tolerate (not to mention the need for a final group vote).

Frankly, Aquarius is a bit too democratic to suit Aries (whose slogan is "My way, now!"). The Ram can't figure out how anything can ever get off the ground when so many individualistic people are polled for their opinions on what needs to be done. Aquarius is a bit too forum-oriented or committee-addicted, while Aries likes to operate alone without interference.

If these two signs are highlighted in our chart, we are torn between wanting to become part of a group whose ideals we find socially advanced, versus wanting no part of any team that tries to tell us how we must behave if we wish to remain as members. It's thus hard to know where we fit in society—who really are our peers? We want to participate, and yet we also need to be left alone to pursue our personal goals our way, without social rhetoric breathing down our necks and pressuring us to become unrealistically impersonal in our ambitions.

We do feel surges of humanitarian energy, but we also realize that we don't like to take orders, even from the most enlightened of leaders. There is a degree of interpersonal disruption evident in even our close partnerships. Both signs have difficulty remaining loyal to anyone who attaches too many conditions to a relationship (plus these signs are not all that intimate to begin with). We are free souls at heart who are learning, maybe the hard way, how liberating emotional honesty can be in our one-on-one partnerships.

AQUARIUS/ARIES ASTRO-LEBRITIES

Ellen DeGeneres, comedian-actress: (Sun in Aquarius/Moon in Aries)

Thomas Moore, philosopher: (Sun in Aquarius/Moon in Aries)

Virginia Woolf, writer: (Sun in Aquarius/Moon in Aries)

Tennessee Williams, playwright: (Sun in Aries, Moon in Aquarius)

Sandra Day O'Connor, Supreme Court justice: (Sun in Aries, Moon in Aquarius)

Steve McQueen, actor: (Sun in Aries, Moon in Aquarius)

Pisces/Taurus

Pisces is the least worldly, materialistic sign of the zodiac, while Taurus is the most heavily invested in earthbound living. Yet, together, they can find common ground (as suggested by their sextile relationship alone). Both are very gentle signs that believe in letting life unfold at a slow and natural pace. They don't rush things nor do they like to be pushed into action until they are inwardly ready (even though, unlike the Bull, Pisces won't resist being forced into doing something against its will). Passivity can be a problem for this combo, since both signs are prone to attacks of inertia. They don't enjoy having their energies stirred up unnecessarily by outer (aggressive) forces.

Their capacity to feel is strong, but Taurus adds a stability that the impressionable Pisces temperament needs. The Bull has powerful, earthy instincts that guide its direction in a practical and timely manner (also explaining why is doesn't like to be rushed). It has a good sense of when to do something and when instead to rest, and it doesn't appreciate others altering its tempo. Its inner promptings are sound (as if based on knowing when action taken will lead to fertile results). To this, Pisces adds its uncanny intuition, since it has an almost psychic sense of when to surrender to activity and when to retreat. Both signs cannot explain how they know what they know along these lines, yet they obediently follow the wisdom of their deeper rhythms.

Pisces dwells in a private world of beautiful, self-created fantasies and dreams. Taurus is better grounded in material reality and needs to experience life in more tangible ways. For the Fishes, the flow of imagination is strong and vitalizing. Pisces somehow knows that all that exists in the world first came from the invisible dimension of Spirit; thus, it chooses to remain close to the Source of all that magically emerges into being. Taurus is less content to deal with anything that lacks true physical form. It has a harder time visualizing what doesn't already exist, or perhaps it doesn't value such intangibles as much. The inner realm of Pisces seems devoid of reliable structures that make the Bull feel safe and secure, plus Piscean images continually change like the patterns in a kaleidoscope.

Those of us with a Pisces/Taurus emphasis will need to learn how to creatively blend the Piscean capacity to tap the depths of our unconscious with Taurus' ability to turn energy into solid form (and even market it for a profit). The creation of art, music, or physical beauty is one way to merge the resources of these signs. It seems that Taurus can help Pisces establish sane boundaries in ways that keep it from feeling vulnerable, since Taurus is very good at putting up walls and defining its personal territory. Ultrareceptive Pisces can otherwise be easily invaded by all sorts of random forces in undermining ways.

The Fishes act like martyrs at times, sacrificing themselves for some greater universal cause. However, the Bull never wants to feel like a victim or a loser. It sets limits on how much it will give of itself to others. This is a valuable lesson that Pisces needs to learn. Still, the Fishes can teach Taurus to become more malleable in its attitudes. Stubbornness can thwart the flow of success that Taurus seeks, since outside influences—those that enhance the unfoldment of opportunities—are thus blocked from contributing any helpful input.

Although the Bull typically wants everyone to butt out and allow it to stay on its fixed course of action, this is not always the best way to proceed (especially when Taurus is feeling a bit too defensive about all this). Pisces is simply trying to get Taurus to surrender to unseen, guiding forces that wondrously allow all things to creatively fall into place, once the Bull stops being so determined not to use alternative measures.

If we have these signs natally highlighted, it will be good for us to immerse ourselves in surroundings where Nature is at its most exquisite. Pisces needs inspiration, and so, breathtaking landscapes can uplift its soul, while also helping Taurus' physical senses come alive. Sensuality and spirituality go hand in hand; this is not a combo that can endure asceticism or sensory deprivation for long. Our inner and outer worlds must be ripe and overflowing with color and sound.

Pisces/Taurus Astro-lebrities

Fats Domino, musician: (Sun in Pisces/Moon in Taurus)

Henrik Ibsen, writer: (Sun in Pisces, Moon in Taurus)

Jerry Lewis, comedian-actor: (Sun in Pisces, Moon in Taurus)

Audrey Hepburn, actress: (Sun in Taurus, Moon in Pisces)

Jerry Seinfeld, comedian: (Sun in Taurus, Moon in Pisces)

Nora Ephron, writer-director: (Sun in Taurus, Moon in Pisces)

SIGNS THAT TRINE

Trining signs have long been given the best reviews of any sign/sign relationship. Their strongest selling point is that they induce harmony, supposedly because their approaches to life are so similar that there is hardly a trace of friction to be found between them—or so traditional astrology claims. Seeing eye to eye as they do, these signs—sharing the same element—don't block the flow of each other's energies; they don't threaten one another, and their interplay is thus nondefensive.

Signs that trine use their individual qualities in peaceful but sometimes passive ways. They often lack that special "oomph" that well-managed squares can provide. Trining signs don't live in a world of crisis and pressure. This may be relaxing, but it's not what motivates us to bring out our best. Stress has a creative way of testing our abilities and spurring us to achieve more than we ever suspected we could. Yet such motivational stress is lacking here.

In some astrological circles these days, it's chic to find fault with anything that trines anything, since this aspect has gotten an "all dressed up and nowhere to go" kind of reputation. Trining signs are like luxury sedans that lack spark plugs: they look great but can't get started. However, we wouldn't enjoy having every feature of our chart caught up in a high state of dynamic conflict (i.e., nothing but signs that square and oppose one another).

Our trining signs are to be enjoyed, and even indulged in, as long as they don't render us lazy and too satisfied with the status quo of our lives. When we feel this good, we're usually not thinking about making big changes. We'd rather continue along the smooth, tension-free path we're already on. Yet when we need to use the finest assets of these combos, such resources are always available and are ready to be put into action, with a little extra effort.

These "gifts" are not to be wasted, although often that's exactly what happens. But if our chart shows a sufficient amount of tension elsewhere, then any planets in trining signs help us "make it through the night," whenever our soul needs to feel uplifted and filled with optimism. Plus here is where we can tap into rich veins of creativity that

won't require tremendous effort. Although such signs, when combined, have their minor differences to work out, it's usually nothing
that's truly bothersome or too difficult to handle.

Aries/Leo

Having these two signs emphasized in a chart is often the best news a
growing ego can receive. The Ram and the Lion are very self-oriented
and are happy to be alive, as long as they can remain free to follow
their own self-chosen paths in life. A double dose of fire suggests a lot
of vitality at one's beck and call. It also indicates a need for an upbeat
lifestyle where vigorous action is guaranteed. These signs hate to be
still for long. They instead love to generate a little excitement in their
lives. They have plenty of creative energy to burn and simply need
more adventurous outlets.

What is underscored by this fiery association is courage—having
the guts to be true to our real self rather than feeling we must accommodate others by becoming, in essence, somebody that we are not.
Aries is particularly keen on doing whatever it desires, without restriction, whether this meets with another's approval or not. It's less interested in pleasing people, if that means it can't act the way it wants to,
when it wants to. Leo, sensitive to the threat of social rejection, is more
careful about the manner in which it lets its hair down. After all, the
Lion seeks an appreciative audience and won't risk getting needlessly
booed off the stage.

Leo is willing to take charge of its own publicity campaign in order
to persuade others to give it a "thumbs-up" review, and so it does care
about its approval ratings. Aries is more bluntly a "what you see is
what you get" sign; it's not one to cater to popular demand. When
combined, these two signs give off very strong, self-assured energies.
They act with confidence and believe that little will block their path to
achievement (even if inwardly they know they are taking risky chances
in life). With this combo, not only is there enough motivational fuel to
fill our tank (Aries), but our ego's engine is in superb shape (Leo).

Both signs, even when in a position of command, still have an ado-
lescent quality about them, as if they're not yet fully matured. They

burn with youthful idealism, and can be innocent and even naive in many ways. Temperamentally, they are less prepared to accept a cut-throat, cynical world. At their best, these two are honorable in intention and forthright in action. They won't plot or scheme to get what they want, but will instead bravely do battle in an upfront manner (sneak attack or underhandedness is not their game). Yet not everyone else is as straightforward, a realization that may dishearten these fire signs. Aries is really not all that noble or high-minded in its affairs, but it is plainly honest in how it presents itself. Leo's the one that tries to be magnanimous, probably because it views itself as a hero, not a villain.

What Leo may not like about Aries is that this cardinal sign is a little rough-and-ready in action, behaving in ways not dignified enough to suit sometimes stately Lion, who's more class-conscious. Of course, the Ram is no snob and doesn't put on airs, but sometimes its impulsive actions may prove an embarrassment to Leo, a sign that takes everything too personally (in fact, so does Aries). Leo likes to control its affairs, even orchestrating the way things unfold, yet in a manner that appears to be unrehearsed—but it's Aries who'll spontaneously live in the now.

If Aries/Leo energies are highlighted in our chart, any regal bearing (Leo) on our part can be offset by our more off-the-cuff Arien ways of asserting ourselves. However, this could keep us from becoming pompous and acting as if we are superior to others. The Ram won't support Leo's bloated sense of self-importance, but it will reinforce the Lion's potential self-centeredness. These signs have an unabashed "me first" orientation, yet because a trine relationship is involved, such self-absorption spurs us to make easy use of our talents, since we have something to prove to ourselves regarding our potential greatness. We want to see how brightly we can shine and how far we can propel our dynamic energies.

Both these signs are geared toward leadership, with Leo seeking to direct others, while Aries is happy simply to lead itself in any direction that allows for freedom of self-expression. We probably won't tolerate being supervised by others for long, but will develop our strengths and skills so that we can remain in charge of ourselves, independent of outside authority. Being fiery in disposition, we like to strike out on our own and willfully thrust ourselves into exciting experiences that show off our assets (Leo's pride and its need for first-class treatment help keep our sometimes combative Aries nature in check, meaning we can assert ourselves in ways that don't create as much head-to-head conflict with others).

Still, we may give the world the impression that we're here to create our own life, free from the influence of others, and thus we won't bow down to social rules and regulations that are obviously made for somebody else to obey, not us! Flare-ups of temper may overheat an already dramatic personality that refuses to endure a humdrum existence. We'll fight for our right to remain as individualized as we are, knowing we were born to be exceptional in some way. Our challenge is to get others to notice and applaud just how special we really are.

Aries/Leo Astro-lebrities

Peter Ustinov, actor-writer: (Sun in Aries, Moon in Leo)

Gloria Steinem, writer-editor: (Sun in Aries, Moon in Leo)

Andrew Lloyd Webber, composer: (Sun in Aries, Moon in Leo)

Whitney Houston, singer: (Sun in Leo, Moon in Aries)

Antonio Banderas, actor: (Sun in Leo, Moon in Aries)

Peggy Fleming, figure skater: (Sun in Leo, Moon in Aries)

Taurus/Virgo

When these two signs combine, the focus is typically on hard work and productive output. Taurus has endurance and likes to stay clear-headed about the tasks it must perform. Virgo, too, is very appreciative of clarity, and tries to simplify projects by adhering to intelligent ways of organizing all materials at hand. Both signs, when working well together, emphasize proficiency and order. Taurus provides the steady focus needed to keep Virgo from getting off-track due to too many unnecessary details (the Bull also likes to keep things simple).

This combo is associated with competency, but we'll need to be careful not to end up functioning like a reliable piece of machinery instead of the sometimes imperfect human beings we really are. Both signs hate to make mistakes—Taurus especially hates the costly ones, while Virgo loathes the careless ones. A degree of anxiety may be felt whenever oversights and slip-ups occur, or anything else that hints at disorder.

However, since these signs trine each other, they are more apt to spot errors than make them. While not quite as sharp-sighted as Virgo/Scorpio, these two notice even tiny flaws because they are patient and painstaking in their observations. Detail work may be appealing (as long as it's not too tedious for Taurus, a sign that otherwise quietly endures once fully engaged in its work).

Virgo is very sensitive to the Bull's tendency to go at too slow a pace. The Analyzer has a talent for being both quick and thorough on the job—once it has established a systematic method for doing things—and it can be superefficient, as a result. Mutable Virgo is quite adaptable, but fixed Taurus—once it's hung up on something—can remain stuck due to a lack of flexibility. Its instinct is not to look for a workaround, something Virgo otherwise would do after many attempts to get itself unstuck. Taurus also is less punctual than Virgo, unless time is money. Actually, the Bull's sense of timing is very good in most practical matters. It just sees no need to borrow Virgo's stopwatch, since running like an ultraprecise clock is less appealing to the Bull.

If anything, those of us with Taurus/Virgo emphasized in our chart will have to be aware of our tendency to become too caught up in dull routines. We are very good at handling repetitive activities, and really do enjoy going down the same track again and again—doing so helps us feel secure. The problem, however, it that we can get thrown for a loop when something unscheduled comes along to shake up our predictable patterns (like when Sagittarius/Aquarius energies knock on our door). These are very conservative, earthy signs that cannot handle too many surprises in life, especially those that are destabilizing.

The trouble with trining signs is that they seldom challenge each other to change for the better. They happily retain the status quo of their relationship. In this case, Taurus and Virgo reinforce a tendency to always play it safe in life by avoiding risks. Perhaps this keeps things humming as usual, but it also prevents fresh, stimulating circumstances from energizing us. If we feel our personal life is all work and no play, there's a reason: We hate taking chances with the unknown, and we thus get mired in ruts of our own choosing.

Yet when it comes to dependability, few other sign combinations come as close. We are very conscientious and duty-bound, but only once we value the services we are providing. Virgo is quite humble and Taurus is low-key in its operations. Others could take us for granted, since we don't appear to need a lot of praise for our efforts. Still, the Taurus side of us must be appreciated or else it'll go on strike and quit working. The Bull can even build up much resentment when it feels it had been taken advantage of by ingrates who use people in thankless ways.

If our Virgo side is well developed, then we probably are too discriminating in our relationships to allow such abuse to happen to us. It's only when our Virgo parts function in "slave mentality" mode that people tend to treat us in demeaning ways, noting how little we complain or resist. Taurus/Virgo energies can turn us into workaholics—especially if attaining material comfort is our main objective—although Taurus will eventually need to relax and enjoy the fruits of its labor. Virgo will just have to rationalize such relaxation as being therapeutic, since it otherwise feels it has no right to "goof off" and do little but waste precious time.

These signs are very realistic about their expectations in life. They work well within their limits (often the same ones that fire signs rebel against). In fact, such set boundaries help the Bull and the Analyzer feel shielded from life's potential disruptions, especially those that are apt to happen when we veer off course and alter our habits. A stubborn nature can be mixed here with a critical temperament in ways that can make us feel uptight about living in a flawed world that seldom behaves in the orderly ways we expect it to. With all this earth, we'll need to learn how to lighten up and go with the flow more often.

Taurus/Virgo Astro-lebrities
  Michelle Pfeiffer, actress: (Sun in Taurus, Moon in Virgo)
  Daniel Day-Lewis, actor: (Sun in Taurus, Moon in Virgo)
  Candice Bergen, actress: (Sun in Taurus, Moon in Virgo)

  Hugh Grant, actor: (Sun in Virgo, Moon in Taurus)
  Greta Garbo, actress: (Sun in Virgo, Moon in Taurus)
  Tommy Lee Jones, actor: (Sun in Virgo, Moon in Taurus)

Gemini/Libra

This is obviously a combo that can be counted on to be sociable and very curious about people. These two signs are fans of pop culture. Gemini's lightness combines well with Libra's positive approach to forming healthy alliances. The flexibility of the Twins blends nicely with the Balancer's sense of give and take, resulting in an easygoing style of relating to others. The double emphasis of air also suggests an ability to look at life without emotionally coloring one's perceptions. Ideally, this means being able to remain objective when evaluating whatever or whomever is being observed. Opinions thus rendered are based more on reason, as well as a clearer comprehension of "the facts" at hand. Looking at things without bias is important to these signs.

Libra not only appreciates factual information, it also knows how to put things in proper perceptive; like Gemini, it's able to see the many sides of an issue. If these signs are highlighted in our chart, there is a part of our nature that believes in analyzing situations fairly, even when the results don't support or confirm our assumptions or expectations. It takes a good deal of emotional detachment to do this. When working together, these signs can truly be impartial.

Actually, there is a side to Gemini that can play loose with the facts, probably because it wants to tell the most interesting stories possible, and thus a little embellishment is sometimes needed to enliven an otherwise duller reality. Even Libra knows what to say to sound persuasive, and this may mean omitting certain details just to slant things in an intended way. Together, these signs can excel in public relations work (Libran diplomacy mixed with Gemini's way with words can make anything look more attractive, sometimes more than it really is). As this trine relationship urges these signs to bring out their best, intellectual honesty is encouraged (with Libra adding a degree of ethical uprightness).

Gemini/Libra energies are great for getting people enthused about participating in social projects, especially those of a fun nature that require coordinated action. These signs have a knack for bringing folks together in the spirit of friendly cooperation. However, in more personal relationships, Libra is less willing to associate with just anybody, since its sensibilities are more refined than Gemini's. The Twins do not always use discretion in their social affairs and can even show poor judgment—perhaps one result of not knowing how to read people emotionally.

Still, Gemini seems to know how to quickly bail out of any momentary commitment that is not to its liking. Libra is better at initially sizing others up before inviting further involvement. It tries to screen people better than Gemini does, and in such a personable way that nobody realizes they're being evaluated, even while being kept at an arm's-length distance. Sometimes it's hard to know what's going on behind that famous Libran smile.

A problem here is that these signs can encourage superficiality. They focus so much on the social niceties people share, that a relationship's worth tends to be judged by how cordially people treat one another—meaning, let's not get ugly and lose our temper! Being air signs, Gemini and Libra believe the best way to handle our problems is to talk rationally about them (politely taking turns to make our point without resorting to harsh words—hmmm . . . it's no wonder this antiseptic approach leaves Aries/Scorpio types cold). Both air signs have a tough time handling unpleasantness in close partnerships, so they try to avoid people who are too passionate in their feelings (although the Cosmos has a way of bringing volatile people into their lives to help them get better in touch with their neglected emotions).

Those of us with these signs emphasized natally will need to work at seeking more depth in our intimate unions. We need to take time to share our feelings instead of just further feeding our intellect. Perhaps having fewer people in our lives will allow for better emotional focus —besides, too much socializing can leave us scattered. However, it will be important for us to pursue a good education so that we can make the best use of our brainpower and deploy our communication skills more fully.

This is an excellent combination for public speaking, unless we also have a few counterproductive patterns—if any—in our chart that might indicate mental inhibitions or intellectual insecurity (like a square or opposition between Mercury and Saturn). Is there a shyness symbolized that keeps us from expressing our thoughts about relevant social issues? Once we find the courage to speak out and voice our opinions, we may discover that others are charmed by how we think and what we say. It is important that we don't compulsively become social butterflies who are afraid to be alone too much, since it's in such moments of solitude that we may be able to have perceptive inner dialogues that help shed needed light on our relationship issues.

GEMINI/LIBRA ASTRO-LEBRITIES

George H. Bush, U.S. president: (Sun in Gemini, Moon in Libra)
Josephine Baker, dancer: (Sun in Gemini, Moon in Libra)
Norman Vincent Peale, writer: (Sun in Gemini, Moon in Libra)

Phil Hartman, comedian: (Sun in Libra, Moon in Gemini)
Gwyneth Paltrow, actress: (Sun in Libra, Moon in Gemini)
Groucho Marx, comedian-actor: (Sun in Libra, Moon in Gemini)

Cancer/Scorpio

When two water signs join forces, their relationship is one that involves many unconscious exchanges that are often too subtle to observe at first glance. The depths of our inner world belong to Cancer, Scorpio, and Pisces. These internal realms of darkness can be restful and protective, but are also forbidding at times. Don't expect Cancer to urge us to explore the scarier parts of our psyche's underground. Of all the water signs, the Crab is the most eager to operate through instincts that readily surface. It likes to foster emotional interactions that visibly nurture our human relationships, and it also shows a protective concern for preserving those things that we actively possess for our security.

Cancer tries to shield itself from acknowledging its more complex emotional realities. It's most afraid of those inner conflicts that could trigger psychological upheaval, the kind that threatens to permanently sever this sign's closest attachments. Thus, the cautious Crab hides in its shell rather than risk exposing itself to such potential trauma—it's attitude is, what we don't know won't hurt us. Naturally, that does not mean our internal conflicts then disappear.

In contrast, Scorpio seems to want to dwell deep down below, where it can probe our interior recesses and look for untapped sources of hidden power. Scorpio is quite able to fearlessly plumb our depths, but it can be ruthless about routing out anything it finds to be in a state of weakness or deterioration. It can penetrate Cancer's tough shell by using its special X-ray equipment, which easily reveals all of the Crab's secret vulnerabilities.

These signs, however, do share heightened emotional sensitivity as a common denominator. Both can be very touchy and defensive when they feel they're under attack. Still, the trine relationship suggests that Cancer/Scorpio types are adept at figuring out people's ulterior motives. Such depth of understanding—when mixed with water's innate compassion—keeps them from taking everything too personally (although water signs are certainly not detached or objective, they are empathetic in ways that help them dissolve feelings that otherwise keep them forever on guard). Water signs try to erase lines of division that create emotional barriers between people. They urge us to merge more fully with others.

Any double dose of water, however, is a warning that we may not have enough of a protective layer of psychological skin needed to keep us from being invaded by the more harmful energies of others. We can absorb people's negativities in ways that jeopardize our emotional well-being. This is one reason why people with a water emphasis need to be alone a lot. This helps them clear out any otherwise depleting energies accumulated from those with whom they have especially difficult relationships. Solitude is necessary for Cancer/Scorpio types to replenish their souls. They can only take so much shallow socializing and worldly busyness before they reach their bursting point and must then retreat to their own quiet sanctuary.

It's no wonder that others consider Cancer/Scorpio folks to be mysterious and hard to read. The Cancer side of us can seem very accommodating, able to mother others in need and offer strong emotional support. But when our Scorpio side surfaces, it's like a chill in the air—suddenly, we demand our privacy and perceive people as intruding on us, particularly those who become too needy in ways that we detest.

It is hoped that, with the trine, people with this combo are sensitive enough to know when they need to be totally by themselves, before they become cranky and icy in disposition. Both signs are good at clamming up or becoming impossible to reach once they shut down emotionally. If allowed the seclusion they crave, they will eventually emerge feeling refreshed and, once again, able to offer others their strong, nourishing energies.

Those of us with these signs highlighted in our chart tend to read into other people's behavior, looking for clues as to what's really going on below the surface. It's hard to relax around others when we're always playing the detective (plus our highly receptive nature makes people feel uncomfortable, almost as if they're in imminent danger of being sucked in by a black hole).

If our feelings get hurt (as they easily do for Cancer), our Scorpio side can slyly divert attention elsewhere so that nobody gets a glimpse of our pain. The Scorpion thinks it's demonstrating inner strength by doing this, when actually it's only driving away those who could facilitate a needed healing process. It's important that we don't become too inaccessible to those who freely offer us their warmth and love (especially considering Cancer's hunger for such open displays of affection and Scorpio's need to feel less emotionally isolated in the world).

CANCER/SCORPIO ASTRO-LEBRITIES
Patrick Stewart, actor: (Sun in Cancer, Moon in Scorpio)
Lena Horne, singer: (Sun in Cancer, Moon in Scorpio)
Fred Hoyle, astronomer: (Sun in Cancer, Moon in Scorpio)

Bo Derek, actress: (Sun in Scorpio, Moon in Cancer)
Theodore Roosevelt, U.S. president: (Sun in Scorpio, Moon in Cancer)
Jane Pauley, television journalist: (Sun in Scorpio, Moon in Cancer)

Leo/Sagittarius

Leo is able to revolve around its own needs quite well when it links up with equally self-involved Aries. This dynamic duo fearlessly face the world on their own terms and insist that they be allowed self-expression in any manner they see fit. Leo and Sagittarius also share this philosophy—perhaps even more so, since the Archer is very demanding of its freedom to explore life without short-sighted authorities breathing down its neck, or throwing a book of regulatory codes its way. Leo feels quite at home with any sign that's unafraid to tell the world to back off and give it plenty of room to spread out and discover its greater potential (since that's typically how the Lion feels, as well).

Adventure beckons these signs, as both are eager to live a robust life free of the restrictive social structures that less hearty souls abide by without complaint. These signs think big and expect a lot out of life. There are quite ready to take great risks that offer great rewards to those unwilling to give up on their dreams. Actually, Sagittarius is at times even too daring for Leo. The Archer shows less interest than the Lion does in controlling its environment. With an innocent sense of abandon, it will instead take chances that defy common sense.

Leo is more concerned with taking charge over the direction toward which it is heading, rather than depending on dumb luck to point the way. While Sagittarius plans little regarding its future, and instead lets inspiration be its guide, Leo is better organized (which is why it excels in positions of central management). Still, this trine relationship suggests a wonderfully creative blend of faith in self and trust in the Universe. This often results in being in the right place at the right time when it comes to receiving life's bounty. Leo/Sagittarius types seem blessed with the ability to demonstrate that their glass is always more than half full—it's overflowing. They are nothing if not supremely optimistic.

Sometimes extravagance becomes a problem for Leo, especially when it goes shopping with Sagittarius, a sign that also lacks restraint when seeking abundance. When combined, these two show an appetite for impressive worldly rewards, plus they feel quite deserving of good treatment. These are not the signs astrologers associate with problems regarding self-esteem. Their handling of the material side of life (especially money) tends to be impractical—saving for a rainy day is not easy. Yet they have faith that the Cosmos is generous and forever supportive of their needs, and so it's unlikely that they'll worry about future financial security. Leo/Sagittarius energies help us realize that we create our prosperity by sustaining an unshakable belief in ourselves and in our personal vision of a better tomorrow.

These signs will take a chance on anything that looks promising, even gambling on winning lotteries or whatever else they prize. Sagittarius can convince Leo that self-discipline and hard work aren't really what make somebody a winner (no matter what Capricorn says). The Archer instead is certain that winning is a direct result of believing deeply that one deserves to enjoy the best that life can provide (of course, Leo already thinks this way, yet it still feels driven to assertively prove its worth to the world).

Sagittarius is certain that worldly enrichment is our reward for being tuned in to our innate goodness, rather than striving to be somebody special in the eyes of the world. It could be said that Sagittarius offers Leo a more spiritual way to look at life, and that includes the need to go beyond purely egocentric desires for personal attainment. Sagittarius also wants other members of society to feel important and deserving, and thus urges Leo to expand its interests to include broader social concerns where the Lion can radiate its ego power for the good of all.

The larger-than-life outlook of these signs allows them the courage to do big things in dramatic, attention-grabbing ways. If Leo/Sagittarius energies are highlighted in our chart, we exhibit a mix of color and daring that makes us stand out in a crowd as charismatic individualists. We also can be darn lucky throughout life, as if angelic forces guide our path. We are learning to trust that miracles can happen for us once we let go of our (Leo) need to control our future.

It is good to not remain too homebound, since there is a fascinating world of diversity out there that needs exploring. It's likely that people of all social backgrounds will gravitate toward us, since our appeal can be universal (as long as we don't let any Leo snobbery get in the way). We do well in life when we are in a position to inspire others to do their best and never give up on their highest goals. These signs are strong morale-boosters.

LEO/SAGITTARIUS ASTRO-LEBRITIES

T. E. Lawrence, adventurer: (Sun in Leo, Moon in Sagittarius)

Martha Stewart, entrepreneur: (Sun in Leo, Moon in Sagittarius)

Herman Melville, writer: (Sun in Leo, Moon in Sagittarius)

Jane Fonda, actress-activist: (Sun in Sagittarius, Moon in Leo)

Winston Churchill, British prime minister: (Sun in Sagittarius, Moon in Leo)

Christopher Plummer, actor: (Sun in Sagittarius, Moon in Leo)

Virgo/Capricorn

Taurus/Virgo is an industrious, hard-working pair that believes in sustained effort and self-discipline as the keys to success. However, Taurus also has a side to its nature that needs to relax in comfort and slowly enjoy the fruits of its labor. Self-gratification and sensual pleasure are as important to the Bull as material security. Although Virgo/Capricorn also values the work ethic, this combo is less apt to take time to rest and indulge in the rewards of success. These signs are almost manic about staying busy and keeping themselves productive—every minute must count for something useful. Idleness is to be avoided, unless these two wish to be nagged by feelings of guilt.

It's easy to see how all this can lead to a pattern of overwork and an inability to relieve built-up stress—too much focus is put on being forever preoccupied with heavy duties and responsibilities at hand. Of course, since this is a trine relationship, these earth signs can work out highly organized ways to conduct business, so that day-to-day matters flow easily in a sensible and timely fashion (this can make work seem less laborious). Nonetheless, actions taken are purposeful and usually well thought out. Although Capricorn can handle details, it would rather leave the tedious and less essential ones to Virgo, who doesn't relish being in the limelight as much as the Goat does.

Humility is a common denominator, although Capricorn also feels itself to be very important when taking on roles of authority (the Goat is actually a Leo in disguise when it comes to seeking celebrity and honor). Still, Virgo/Capricorn types try not to draw too much attention to how competent they are, since others find such expertise intimidating. They'd rather put the focus on doing a job well, and in ways that earn them respect. (Maybe Virgo involved in other sign combinations might feel itself unworthy of open praise, yet not as much here when teaming up with Capricorn. The Goat expects all signs with which it interacts to aspire to the heights of achievement—it doesn't want to associate with losers who think less of themselves.)

If these signs are emphasized in our chart, we probably show a level-headed maturity, even when young, regarding how we deal realistically with the world on its terms. We carefully observe how society is structured—noting which behaviors lead to surefooted accomplishment—and are selective concerning the social contributions we'll make to the world. Actually, we can be too self-critical about our performance in ways that hinder our self-confidence. We can become frustrated when we can't do things perfectly, which is something we surely don't want others to observe in us. Mistakes are taken too much to heart, even though on the outside we typically appear cool and collected, no matter what predicament we find ourselves in. Inside, there can be a lot of stomach-churning tension. Life is teaching us to be easier on ourselves—in reality, only certain diamonds are flawless, but not us humans!

Highly pragmatic, we are less likely to be in the grip of turbulent emotions that would have us unravel at the seams. We're not easy to read on the surface, since here we like to show a strength and calmness that suggest we're always in control of situations (actually, Virgo can get a bit twitchy when overloaded with tension or fear, yet Capricorn can look as solid as granite, even under the most trying conditions). Any fears and doubts are kept hidden from public exposure.

While capable of handling worldly tasks that require planning and perseverance, strongly Virgo/Capricorn types will need to interpret life in a less-literal manner. Imagination may be lacking (although it may be indicated by other factors in our chart). Instead, things are usually only conceived of in rational, concrete terms. These signs need substantial proof before they will accept the reality of metaphysical principles at work. Yet once convinced, they typically become firm believers. Still, spiritual matters for them must have practical application.

Always accountable for their actions, dependable Virgo and Capricorn are not likely to make promises they cannot keep. Their energies are valuable to any undertaking that requires utter reliability and intelligent organization. These are sobering influences. At times, Virgo/Capricorn types can be too serious about the duties they handle. Life will teach them to lighten up and not turn everything into demanding tasks that require heavy management and high maintenance.

Virgo/Capricorn Astro-lebrities

Terry Bradshaw, football pro: (Sun in Virgo, Moon in Capricorn)
Salma Hayek, actress: (Sun in Virgo, Moon in Capricorn)
Brian De Palma, director: (Sun in Virgo, Moon in Capricorn)

Betty White, actress: (Sun in Capricorn, Moon in Virgo)
Stephen Hawkins, physicist: (Sun in Capricorn, Moon in Virgo)
Gwen Verdon, dancer: (Sun in Capricorn, Moon in Virgo)

Libra/Aquarius

The Libra/Aquarius combo is gregarious and interested in what goes on in society, as these two signs love to observe people's behavior.

Both support the civil rights of individuals and thus denounce any governmental control that infringes on freedom of thought. Libra and Aquarius do not want to be told by authority figures what they can and cannot expose themselves to intellectually. Nobody owns their minds.

Actually, Aquarius is more apt to defy conventional thought, including those traditional ways of thinking to which Libra conforms without qualms. The Water Bearer risks being labeled an "outsider" for not fitting seamlessly into the Establishment. The more adaptable Libra agreeably blends into the existing patterns of a culture, and even attempts to enhance such social customs.

There is less attention placed on satisfying exclusively self-focused needs. The cultivation of collective understanding and tolerance is sought. Libra/Aquarius types can be very liberal in their attitudes about society, although the Libra side wants everyone to abide by those laws it deems to be fair. It's the Aquarius side that doesn't always cooperate, rebelling unpredictably when it realizes that certain rules or traditions of society have become stifling or obsolete. The Water Bearer is much more futuristic than Libra, yet the Balancer is willing to consider any progressive social vision that is well presented and supportive of equality.

Together, these signs lean toward idealism and abstract thought, especially those concepts geared toward improving society on its broader levels. Libra tries to keep Aquarius from becoming too impersonal and detached in its mental evaluations of the human condition. It also encourages this sign to show more consideration for others rather than insensitively jolt their sensibilities in the name of Truth (Libra tries to build bridges between people, using friendly diplomacy). At the same time, Aquarius keeps Libra honest about how it presents itself to the world, since the Balancer is sometimes too image-conscious to take a firm stand on social issues that are deemed to be controversial. Libra doesn't want to offend people, but Aquarius says that sometimes social progress involves revolutionary thinking and the courage to disrupt the status quo.

Libra/Aquarius types are probably always doing a mental juggling act, trying to gauge whether and when to boldly defend their lofty principles and support unpopular causes—those that might alienate others—versus lying low, toning down the fiery rhetoric, and finding more reasonable ways to influence society's thinking on hotly contested issues that divide the public. Aquarius wants to be a catalyst for change, stirring things up on the social scene, whereas Libra seeks less rabble-rousing ways to get its message across. Yet sometimes Aquarian protest of the unsettling variety is often the only way to get society's full attention. Abiding by accepted social protocol gets us nowhere, or so the Water Bearer believes.

With these two signs emphasized in our chart, we'll need a lot of room in our partnerships to mentally grow. Suffering another's emotional insecurities—the kind that lead to jealousy and possessiveness—becomes too burdensome to endure. It can make us feel suffocated and oppressed. Commitment to any long-term partnership needs to be well thought out, since we can be quite restless and can feel trapped when we realize we're in the wrong relationship. It's obvious that developing a strong friendship with someone we may even marry is critical to the success of that relationship. We also can feel freer when we're not exclusively caught up in traditional marital roles.

As amiable as we are—both signs can be superfriendly—we still have a cool side to our nature that rationally observes rather than passionately reacts to life (Libra does have its moments of passion, but it can be expressed in ways that leave this sign feeling unbalanced). Perhaps we need to work more on establishing true intimacy in our closest unions, especially if we find ourselves attracting watery individuals for our primary relationships. Our mind needs to be educated about the value of expressing ourselves from our heart. It could be that we may get our feelings aroused by learning new things that expand our awareness of life. Our big life passion could involve continuous intellectual exploration.

Unlike Gemini/Libra, this combination is less content to live in its head in a self-satisfied world of ideas and thoughts. It instead seeks to network with other stimulating minds who are willing to pool their intellectual energies together to serve a progressive social cause. We have a talent for working with large groups in ways that galvanize the spirit of community activism and volunteerism. With Libra involved, perhaps our social revolution unfolds along aesthetic lines.

LIBRA/AQUARIUS ASTRO-LEBRITIES

Annie Leibovitz, photographer: (Sun in Libra, Moon in Aquarius)

Arthur Miller, playwright: (Sun in Libra, Moon in Aquarius)

Cheryl Tiegs, supermodel: (Sun in Libra, Moon in Aquarius)

Burt Reynolds, actor: (Sun in Aquarius, Moon in Libra)

Geena Davis, actress: (Sun in Aquarius, Moon in Libra)

Buzz Aldrin, astronaut: (Sun in Aquarius/Moon in Libra)

Scorpio/Pisces

Cancer/Scorpio energies blend very personal, self-absorbed emotions with darker and more complex feelings that are typically provoked in intense one-on-one relationships. The Scorpion seeks to remain in control of these potent energies, but sometimes in ways that create further underground tension in its partnerships. Meanwhile, the easily injured Crab tends to retreat into itself in order to nurse wounds that it has held on to ever since childhood (the kind of chronic, energy-draining stuff that Scorpio tries to eliminate, once and for all).

Yet with a Scorpio/Pisces emphasis, we emotionally show less self-interest. Scorpio can certainly demand satisfaction of its own private needs, but it also feels a compulsion to overcome its selfish streak and use its powerful emotional insights to transform others who struggle with their inner selves. Pisces, being even less self-centered, feels a strong social obligation to heal humanity rather than dwell on its own human needs. Of all the water signs, it sees the bigger picture of life and thus tries to use its energies in universally redeeming ways. The Fishes try to inspire Scorpio to rise above any feelings of hostility and revenge, and instead to put more focus on developing compassion for others.

Scorpio already leans in this direction (being a Pluto-associated sign, it knows firsthand how difficult it is to let go of self-destructive feelings). The mutable Piscean way of nonjudgmentally embracing life can lead to inner peace and spiritual empowerment. Yet there is something unfathomable in fixed Scorpio that fights its own soul transformation, tooth and nail. Pisces idealism can encourage Scorpio to let go of its own guarded wounds and instead learn to trust the world more that it normally does. Scorpio here must be willing to surrender to outside sources of power that, in turn, offer protective and wise guidance. The trine relationship encourages these signs to freely exchange assets that are well received and put to creative use.

Piscean imagination combined with Scorpio's talent to tap into the depths of any experience permits Scorpio/Pisces types to dig into the psychological mysteries of human nature. They have the ability to unveil the contents of people's inner worlds in poignant terms, perhaps through art, music, or drama (for those blessed with such talents). All the intensity compressed inside Scorpio needs to find Piscean outlets that permit creative release, especially in expression that moves people on emotional levels. Scorpio can dam up its energies when it tries to overcontrol its feelings, but Pisces helps dissolve blockages that then allow emotions to flow.

The Scorpion eventually discovers the importance of honest self-examination regarding its less apparent motives. A deeper awareness of what makes us tick, and where our untapped strengths and resources may lie, can help us avoid being victimized by life—or by any unrecognized, conflictive parts of ourselves. Pisces needs the influence of this fixed sign to keep it from dissolving its ego structure and thus losing its needed sense of volitional will. The Fishes, by nature, don't easily fortify their sense of being separate and individualized from others. However, Scorpio will fiercely guard itself against any outside forces that threaten annihilation. The Scorpion won't allow itself to be subjugated to the will of another—it strongly holds on to its center of power.

This combination suggests an otherworldly ability to navigate the invisible seas that connect people on almost psychic levels. Scorpio excels at staying afloat amid turbulent waters, although there is something about its psychology that often attracts the choppiest of waves (such Pluto-oriented folks are intrigued by and drawn to the fiercest storms of life). Yet Pisces symbolizes calm, tranquil pools of waters that cleanse and heal the soul. Those of us with these signs emphasized in our chart are learning to swim, not sink, in an oceanic realm of emotions that are sometimes less than soothing and secure, particularly those that we absorb from others. We'll need to learn how to filter all incoming energies that otherwise could prove overwhelming and devitalizing. Blame it on Piscean vulnerability, yet even Scorpio can become fixated on negative forces that manage to invade its usually well-defended interior.

Also, we'll need to know when we're becoming too psychologically waterlogged, due to taking in the energies of problematic people in our life who know how to bring us down to their chaotic level. We instead need to have time alone to draw in spiritual inspiration of a soul-renewing kind. Let's allow Nature's miracles and wonders to give us the full support we need to help restore our vitality, even when unsatisfying relationships have nearly sucked us dry.

Scorpio/Pisces Astro-lebrities

Hillary Rodham Clinton, lawyer-politician: (Sun in Scorpio, Moon in Pisces)

Martin Scorsese, director: (Sun in Scorpio, Moon in Pisces)

Joni Mitchell, musician-artist: (Sun in Scorpio, Moon in Pisces)

George Harrison, musician: (Sun in Pisces, Moon in Scorpio)

Elizabeth Taylor, actress: (Sun in Pisces, Moon in Scorpio)

John Steinbeck, writer: (Sun in Pisces, Moon in Scorpio)

Sagittarius/Aries

What both Sagittarius and Aries have in common is a burning drive to go out and meet life head-on, with a measure of daring and innocence. Both signs have a strong faith in themselves and in the actions they take. Although Sagittarius senses it's being inspired and guided by benevolent forces, as if on a special mission, Aries instinctively feels it can direct any outcome by its own assertive power—it thus plunges fearlessly into new experiences. The Ram puts much stock in the strength of its self-will; it's confident that it can plow through any obstacle in life. Sagittarius/Aries energies enable us to believe that we'll assuredly be on the winning side of any circumstance, and that our success is well deserved.

The big difference lies in the nature of those goals. Aries is ready to take advantage of all immediate opportunities that allow it to go forward in life quickly, regardless of what's happening in the affairs of others (those who often are seen as competitors, the ones that Aries must somehow beat to the finish line). The Ram likes to tackle things alone, without people crowding in and trying to take charge of operations. Sagittarius, though also a very independent sign, is flexible enough to work with others in its campaign to improve society (in fact, this is crucial, since the Archer doesn't care to attend to the many details involved in enacting social reform; it depends on others to cheerfully handle those necessary tasks).

With Aries involved here, any urge to do good works in society is motivated more by personal ambition than by true altruism. (Remember, here we have a personal sign joining forces with a transpersonal one.) Still, Aries does have pioneering aspirations, which Sagittarius can use to expand its vision of what would constitute a more enlightened society. Fresh solutions are sought, and thus the addition of Arien fire helps accelerate the Archer's collective ideals. The Ram, in turn, can get far ahead in the world when applying Sagittarian optimism, plus the Archer's mutable influence helps Aries succeed in less militant and aggressive ways. It tries to introduce a philosophical framework, one that helps convince Aries that, to have doors of opportunity open wide, it need not be so pushy. But the Ram does need to become more sociable and generous in spirit if others are to cooperate with what it wants to achieve.

If Sagittarius/Aries energies are highlighted in our chart, we are high-spirited, spunky, but probably opinionated and outspoken. We typically show a youthful, energetic approach to everyday living, and don't like to be slowed down by others—thus, we'll venture off alone to discover what our environment has to offer. If Sagittarius is a decidedly intellectual energy at work in us, then we are courageous in our search for Truth and in the way we expose social hypocrisy. We express our thoughts in frank and candid ways, even if not verbally (we are probably capable of at least some very lively e-mail messages and chat room responses).

Still, there is a naiveté—perhaps egged on by our upfront, honest approach to living—that can leave us disheartened and disillusioned when our high expectations are met by crushing defeats, due to those who don't play by ethical standards. We can't understand why some people will lie and cheat to get their way to the top, since that's not what we'd do. Aries may not be as noble as Leo, but is doesn't intentionally try to defraud others. All fires signs believe in putting their cards on the table and taking their chances—perhaps most so Sagittarius.

Together, these signs reflect a rebellious streak that allows them to ignore the standard codes of social conduct that others obediently follow. They are instead certain that rules are made to be broken. Even though this is a trine relationship, Sagittarius/Aries can ruffle feathers when it refuses to give in to authority and "settle down" (this can be a rambunctious combination). Society traditionally disapproves of rowdy behavior, especially when inappropriately displayed (these two signs don't care much about following protocol). They are direct and bold in action, which at best can be described as buoyantly enthusiastic. Still, the tendency is to go overboard when excited and to stir up more activity than is warranted for an occasion, and in noisy ways. Subtlety is not an attribute to be found here.

There is also an inclination to rush into things too quickly, without first doing the careful planning necessary to make sure nothing goes awry. Those of us with a Sagittarius/Aries emphasis typically are highly principled people of strong conviction who will forcefully promote any activity that we fully believe in. When we trust that we are on the right track in life, our energies get even stronger, as we dedicate ourselves to whatever captures our attention. However, we'll need to work at developing more staying power. Both signs are better at starting big projects than completing them.

Sagittarius/Aries Astro-lebrities

Mark Twain, writer: (Sun in Sagittarius, Moon in Aries)

Ellen Burstyn, actress: (Sun in Sagittarius, Moon in Aries)

Little Richard, singer: (Sun in Sagittarius, Moon in Aries)

Thomas Jefferson, U.S. president: (Sun in Aries, Moon in Sagittarius)

Joan Crawford, actress: (Sun in Aries, Moon in Sagittarius)

Pete Rose, baseball pro: (Sun in Aries, Moon in Sagittarius)

Capricorn/Taurus

Here we have two heavyweight earth signs joining forces and consolidating their power to manifest stability in very tangible, material terms. Capricorn/Taurus energies offer strength and endurance. Both signs won't readily give up on their objectives and are not easily sidetracked in their ambitions. Capricornian enterprise shows a determination to succeed in big ways that attract public attention and honor. The Goat wants to make its mark in society through some sort of solid, relevant contribution. Being a transpersonal sign, Capricorn feels its responsibility is to shepherd social development on a large scale.

Taurean ambitions are more personalized and private, and achievements made are quietly self-gratifying. The Bull is less interested in publicity or in being an authority figure, and so its definition of success is limited in scope. This suggests that, while perhaps bent on fame and name recognition, there is another side to Capricorn/Taurus types that likes to live a simpler life, far away from the glare of the limelight. Taurus finds some facets of the Goat's lifestyle to be too high-pressured, plus it hates always being on the move (fixed signs tend to think that cardinal signs are too jumpy and unable to stay still long enough to enjoy what they've accomplished).

Still, there is an ability to tackle projects with a tenacity that eventually brings about concrete results, since patience and levelheadedness are assets here that help us attain our goals. When these signs are emphasized in our chart, we are probably careful not to start something that we may not wish to finish—we'll slowly think about what's required of us before initiating action. Yet sometimes Taurus deliberates too much and misses out on opportunities requiring a snappier response (of course, the Bull then assumes the so-called opportunity wasn't meant to be). Remember, Taurus can be very passive at times, sometimes failing to strike while the iron is hot.

In contrast, cardinal Capricorn is quicker to jump on something that could lead to its social advancement. After mulling things over within a reasonable amount of time, Capricorn is thus able to make the commitment to forge ahead with plans. It has an entrepreneurial spirit that Taurus lacks, and will take moderate risks to get what it wants. Perhaps the Goat can provide the right level of motivation to get the Bull to capitalize further on its assets and skills (Capricorn will not tolerate laziness or the underuse of marketable talent).

It is likely that materialism is strong with this practical combo. Even if other parts of our chart suggest an active spiritual bent, we will probably also make sure that we are secure and comfortable in a worldly sense. Carefully handling money and resources helps us achieve the stability we seek. However, these signs don't want to pay more than they have to for luxuries; they tend to be bargain hunters. They may be tight with finances—and commonly can be cheapskates if insecurity takes over—but they will do what it takes to make sure they get their money's worth. Taurus is somewhat proud of this ability (being frugal and price-conscious), while Capricorn may try to hide the fact that—due to being image-conscious and wanting to appear successful and well-off—it refuses to pay premium prices.

Hard work is indicated by this duo. Earth signs know that steady effort in life makes worthy things materialize. Capricorn/Taurus energies allow us to slowly accumulate whatever it is that we want (whether it be material goods or professional titles). We'll have the pleasure of knowing that we've earned the valued assets that come to us the old-fashioned way: through self-discipline and patience. Both signs can be savvy about timing, and thus are not likely to do things until they feel the moment is utterly right. Again, Capricorn needs to give the Bull a nudge and let it know when the moment is reasonably ripe for success, or even totally opportune; but once Taurus gets moving, it can be almost unstoppable.

Capricorn/Taurus types are perhaps the most dependable of all combinations (blame some of that on Capricornian guilt). These folks believe in keeping promises they've made, even when doing so proves burdensome—and this is perhaps why they don't make many promises to others in the first place. They first need to assess the matter in question and weigh the pros and cons before getting involved. It may be that what is needed to help round out their personalities is more color, flair, and a liberal use of imagination. This keeps things from getting dull. They'll also need to be careful not to become slaves to routines and fixed schedules. It is wise to allow for periodic unpredictability.

We Capricorn/Taurus types are capable organizers and managers, yet Taurus enables us to run the show in a manner that puts others at ease. Our style is less regimented here than it would be with just Capricorn alone (although the crusty Goat is more affectionate than people would imagine, but perhaps only when it lets its guard down during private moments). Both signs, however, do seem to be very business-minded when pursuing their careers, and therefore won't take too many risks that could jeopardize their reputation.

Capricorn/Taurus Astro-lebrities

Isaac Asimov, writer: (Sun in Capricorn, Moon in Taurus)
Naomi Judd, singer: (Sun in Capricorn, Moon in Taurus)
Robert E. Lee, general: (Sun in Capricorn, Moon in Taurus)

Tammy Wynette, singer: (Sun in Taurus, Moon in Capricorn)
Jimmy Stewart, actor: (Sun in Taurus, Moon in Capricorn)
Cher, singer-actress: (Sun in Taurus, Moon in Capricorn)

Aquarius/Gemini

The Aquarius/Gemini combo is enamored of whatever the mind can produce, and most so if such output is novel or innovative. Intellectual stimulation is a must—anything to keep the brain busy and forever exploring something new. Actually, that's the Gemini side talking, since this mutable air sign finds nearly everything interesting, even if only briefly.

Gemini has a talent for gathering fascinating bits and pieces of information, and it doesn't care if such data is temporal in value. The Twins happily live in the moment and enjoy getting their hands on whatever arouses their short-lived curiosity. Yet Gemini is flexible enough to go on to new sources of knowledge that could further elucidate what it has previously studied or observed—or perhaps even contradict such data entirely. Although Gemini has an impulsive mind that lacks staying power and a steady sense of direction, it will try to take in as much as it can about the world around it.

Regardless of its somewhat breezy "here today, gone tomorrow" approach to learning, Gemini ends up scoring high on IQ tests and is nearly the brightest sign of the zodiac. However, there's another sign that typically hovers near the genius level, if not beyond, and that's Aquarius. Of course, not all Aquarian types are superwhizzes, intellectually, but the Water Bearer does seem to be able to sustain its mental interests, due to its fixity. It enduringly pursues and accumulates knowledge of a more complex nature. Aquarius is highly abstract in thought and is blessed with an intuitive kind of reasoning power. There is more than standard logic at work, since the Aquarian mind is apt to take sudden leaps that can result in totally new levels of insight and understanding, and typically does so with lightning speed.

In fact, Gemini is thrilled when Aquarius unpredictably catapults itself into unfamiliar territory in order to experiment with ideas—for one thing, this prevents boredom. The Twins like to go at a rapid pace and will take quick detours rather than get bogged down in thought. Being quiet and still is unappealing to them. Thus, the mental world of these two signs—when working in harmony—is very alive and exciting, although not necessarily practical and grounded. While Gemini's versatility mixes well with Aquarian originality, common sense may be lacking.

Folks with Aquarius/Gemini highlighted in their charts can be positively brilliant in certain sectors of their lives, but then they can seem clueless about how to deal with other areas—specifically those more mundane ones that most people would consider to be "no-brainers." What a paradox—to seem so smart and yet act so dumb at times!

Aquarius, however, is inventive enough to figure out how to accomplish a lot of things, even if not in the simpler ways that work best. However, we must give the Water Bearer credit for coming up with unusual solutions, since its mind is geared toward technological progress (the kind of stuff that looks odd to ordinary observers at first, but later helps revolutionize the way we live). Gemini can be quite clever in devising time-saving ways to do everyday things; it, too, is a sign that seeks smart solutions—although they end up being less elaborate than what "mad scientist" Aquarius concocts (sometimes you *do* need to be a rocket scientist to understand what the Water Bearer is talking about).

It would seem that a broad, liberal education is critical to the expanded development of the intellect for those of us born with these signs prominent in our chart. We don't do well with close-minded people or with groups and societies that heavily censor information (such as media controlled by "the State"). All air signs support democratic systems of social structure. Open intellectual discourse is vital to them. They suffer when trapped in confining environments that suppress free speech. Air obviously likes to circulate, without restriction, and explore various avenues of thought. Aquarius/Gemini types need a lot of room to move about intellectually. They need relationships that won't cramp their minds or their styles of communication.

If Aquarius/Gemini is emphasized in our chart, we'll need to be careful to avoid glorifying sheer brainpower at the expense of our emotional development (our feeling nature may seem less wondrous to us than our mind's phenomenal abilities). Even if we're of average intelligence, we still may avoid emotional experiences by retreating into our voracious intellect, whereby we feed our head more than our heart. (Hopefully, we have other parts of our chart that help put us in closer contact with our emotions.) Aquarius and Gemini can certainly be friendly signs, but they can also be unsympathetic to people riddled with psychological weaknesses—even if not cold and unemotional, these signs can simply be detached and indifferent.

AQUARIUS/GEMINI ASTRO-LEBRITIES

Wayne Gretzky, hockey pro: (Sun in Aquarius, Moon in Gemini)

Ann Gillian, actress: (Sun in Aquarius, Moon in Gemini)

Jack Benny, comedian: (Sun in Aquarius, Moon in Gemini)

Marilyn Monroe, actress: (Sun in Gemini, Moon in Aquarius)

Pat Boone, singer: (Sun in Gemini, Moon in Aquarius)

Kathleen Turner, actress: (Sun in Gemini, Moon in Aquarius)

Pisces/Cancer

Pisces and Cancer are emotionally vulnerable signs that underscore the spongelike quality of water. They each readily soak up their surroundings, for better or worse. Being highly sympathetic, these two are moved by the plight of people undergoing difficult times. They are more empathetic than judgmental. There is a depth of feeling that allows Pisces/Cancer types to intuit, almost psychically, things going on inside others that seem anything but obvious to the outside world. Such a high level of sensitivity can be put to good use in fields that deal with healing the body, mind, and soul. Yet it is important that people with this sign emphasis delve into their own psychological complexities, especially during times when they are feeling victimized or persecuted by others on some level.

It's usually the Cancer side of this combo that feels ever on the defense, although since this is a trine relationship, the Crab doesn't anticipate rejection from others as readily as it does when it squares other signs. Still, it has delicate feelings that are subject to changing moods, depending on the shifting energies of its environment. However, it's often the Pisces side of this duo that can distort reality in a manner that blows emotional misunderstandings way out of proportion. Pisces has a hard time accepting that human relationships are not perfect, and whenever conflicts occur, Pisces feels crushed and even confused. It easy to see how a mix of Cancer and Pisces energy can make us too thin-skinned to deal with the often harsh realities of living on Earth, especially when antagonistic human conditions arise.

Nonetheless, the Crab has a hard shell that protects it from letting certain conditions upset its security, although this shell can periodically crack. Cancer does manage to block out whatever it must to ensure psychological survival. It puts up a big wall to hide its feelings behind, while keeping others at bay. Similarly, Pisces turns to escapism to numb itself from feeling pain and disappointment. It protects itself by ignoring what's going on deep inside, even though this often backfires (as Pisces cannot afford to be unaware of the many levels of its emotional reality). When combined, these signs can tune out anything they find to be unpleasant or threatening to their safety needs. This can result in a lack of clear perception regarding people and situations, due to self-delusion.

Yet because this is a trine at work, it seems that certain emotions flow very well and can be a source of comfort (plus the realizations they provide help explain the otherwise perplexing behaviors of others). This combination suggests a vivid imagination, but one that—to keep from becoming problematic—needs to be plugged in to creative projects (otherwise it's easy to get lost in our own hard-to-articulate inner world and thus feel cut off from those who are not on our wavelength, which seems to be nearly everyone). Luckily, creative talents can pour out of us if we are willing to nurture them with loving attention.

Those of us who have Pisces/Cancer energies natally highlighted need to find healthy ways to merge with others and bond on intimate levels. We don't grow as well when we remain isolated from people or when we keep our emotions too well insulated. Yet because we are ultrareceptive, it's best not to have too many folks around us, especially those whose lives are continuous melodramas. We innocently but insidiously can get sucked into the chaotic whirlpools that such troubled people can create. Still, it's hard not to fall for the sob stories and hard-luck tales that we hear. Our knee-jerk reaction is to offer help to those down-and-out. That's fine, except that we'll need to do this in sensible ways that keep us from becoming too entangled.

Pisces/Cancer energies can be used to support universal causes that demand heightened public awareness, usually involving whatever it takes to eradicate the suffering of all living things. We may have a talent for inspiring people to compassionately offer meaningful assistance in any way they can—we skillfully know how to tug at people's heartstrings. This ability comes through loud and clear when we involve ourselves in charitable events or projects of a humanitarian nature. People may gravitate toward us (regardless of our gender) as if we are "Cosmic Mamas" who know how to make everyone feel included in the world and at peace with themselves. Our maternal warmth is offered unconditionally.

It will be important, however, to make sure that we emerge into the bigger world to use our emotional power to do good works, rather than to withdraw into a dream world of fantasy that nobody can share with us. Some Pisces/Cancer types are even suspectible to sinking into a darker realm of despair and anguish that ends up making them feel that their lives are worthless and devoid of meaning. With so much "water, water everywhere," we can either float, swim, or drown, depending on how successfully we navigate the swirling currents of our internal life.

PISCES/CANCER ASTRO-LEBRITIES

Drew Barrymore, actress: (Sun in Pisces, Moon in Cancer)

Kurt Cobain, singer: (Sun in Pisces, Moon in Cancer)

Liza Minnelli, singer-dancer: (Sun in Pisces, Moon in Cancer)

Duke of Windsor, British royalty: (Sun in Cancer, Moon in Pisces)

Kathy Bates, actress: (Sun in Cancer, Moon in Pisces)

Hermann Hesse, writer: (Sun in Cancer, Moon in Pisces)

Chapter Seven

Signs that Semisextile & Quincunx

SIGNS THAT SEMISEXTILE

Astrologers are quick to point out that signs that semisextile—just like signs that quincunx—are difficult to synthesize. In both instances, the signs involved share dissimilar elements *and* modes. They appear to have nothing in common, which can seem awkward at first, like throwing two people together who don't speak each other's language. However, I do believe that a few common denominators can be found between any two factors in our chart (whether sign, planet, or house). Thus, in this chapter I'll try to point out any similarities shared by signs that either semisextile or quincunx one another.

Initially it may seem strange that semisextiling signs would have a hard time joining forces. After all, they are next-door neighbors—just one sign apart—whose borderlines even touch; no other pair of signs makes such direct contact. Yet, because zodiac signs are arranged in a meaningful sequence, adjacent signs represent purposeful phases of life's twelvefold pattern of unfolding consciousness. Each sign precedes or follows another for specific reasons. There is a series of intelligent life stages at work here.

Constructively, the growth-producing experiences of a sign help set the stage for the emergence of the sign that follows it (i.e., Scorpio helps create the psychological atmosphere needed for Sagittarius to develop). Any sign can benefit by valuing its preceding sign, since it can draw vital, supportive strength from that sign's expertise. A sign can also enhance its awareness by realizing that it is unconsciously moving toward the following sign, so it's best not to resist this trend. Signs that semisextile can use their mutual resources to build inner stability, even if only on elementary levels. Instinct seems to play a key role here, as the subjective impulses generated by this mix of signs help us give form to something new, based on reliable traits and assets we already possess.

Unlike opposing signs, our perspective may be narrow, as here we feel less inclined to venture far from what is familiar to us. Semisextiles allow us to take small but steady steps in life, not big, daring leaps—as least not until we have sufficient experience in those life matters represented by the signs in question. Until then, we may be conservative in how we live out these energies and thus limit our options.

Nonetheless, single-mindedness may prevent us from being distracted or sidetracked in reaching our personal goals. What we need to grow is literally at hand. But because signs of different elements and modes are involved, we cannot afford to have rigid expectations or become stubborn and unwilling to change our habits. These signs need each other, even though each one's approach to life seems markedly in contrast.

Our job is to make any blending of semisextiling energies productive and valuable to our development. When we don't manage these energies well, we can be accused of inconsistent behavior, whereby we abruptly switch from one sign's traits to the other's. This makes us hard to figure out at times. Actually, a lot depends on the planets involved in these signs—any lack of continuity becomes more evident if personal planets are predominantly involved—for example, the Sun and Mercury in Capricorn with the Moon and Mars in Aquarius.

Since signs are symbolic of the human processes we undergo, those of us with semisextiling signs have the ability to use the qualities of one sign to enhance or refine the traits of the other sign that preceded it (i.e., Leo can help Cancer work on resolving its issues better).

Aries/Taurus

These first two signs of the zodiac are geared toward self-preservation. In order to grow best, Aries and Taurus focus less on others and more on what they want for themselves. They have a "go out there and get it" approach to living. They have strong desires, and there is a lot of animal instinct in them (this can make them seem less refined, since their energies are driven by powerful biological impulses—it's their hormones, not logic and reason, that often dictate their temperament). The Ram and the Bull are motivated to satisfy their immediate needs, first and foremost. This may seem selfish, but it's an orientation that these signs are learning to develop in a healthy, unapologetic manner.

Aries/Taurus types are comfortable when presenting themselves in natural ways. They don't like playing social games that require pretentious, phony behavior ("Unless I'm getting paid well for it," adds Taurus). These are the "what you see is what you get" signs who'll try to make whatever they like and dislike—or want and don't want—obvious to others. They believe in keeping their identities intact rather than letting the world mold them into what they know they are not. Yet if pushed in this direction, Aries and Taurus can become quite resistant, since being headstrong is another shared trait.

These signs will insist on establishing their own direction in life, and they refuse to allow others to interfere with their ways of starting (Aries) and finishing (Taurus) things. Naturally, they are still very different in disposition. Aries feels the urge to fight back whenever it's being opposed by the outer world. It resists by assertively moving out into life to butt heads. The Ram never takes the passive approach, not when a good fight can quickly clear the air. Yet Taurus resists outside pressure by either ignoring it—which may be difficult—or by remaining firmly unyielding to change. It can refuse to budge, and this alone can wear down the opposition.

When combined, such signs can be quite stubborn when determined *not* to go with the flow, if doing so means giving in to the demands of others. Aries/Taurus types function much better when they don't feel they're being forced to take action. They instead want to make their moves only when they are ready, and at a pace that is not to be determined by somebody else. They don't do well taking orders from others, although gentle persuasion can influence Taurus. These signs don't enjoy anything that is too complex and detailed. They find things that are simple and straightforward to be appealing—the less multileveled or multilayered, the better.

Taurus can teach Aries that slowing down helps turn fiery energy into consolidated power. Aries needs to learn how to contain its forces and build a stronger foundation from which to operate. Action must be followed by rest, which proves refreshing. Pushing nonstop leads to an early energy burnout. Taurus, when feeling stagnant, can draw from Aries' get-up-and-go spirit. The Ram shows the Bull that it never has to stay stuck in any situation, and that the courage to let go and try something new is a must if anything is to change for the better.

If Aries/Taurus energies are emphasized in our chart, we strive to keep our lives from becoming too complicated. We can be very physical people (not necessarily athletic) who like to engage in activities that stimulate our body and indulge our carnal senses. Aries provides the fuel that ignites Taurean sensuality, sometimes in aggressive ways that are not typically associated with the usually placid Bull. Taurus allows Aries to contain its hot temper and to endure frustrations longer than the Ram normally would. We can channel any anger into projects that required sustained energy to complete.

However, at some point, if we cannot constructively relieve our tensions, we're apt to discharge pent-up feelings in explosive ways, as even the Bull within us begins to rage. Arien anger is usually short-lived, but Taurus can keep it going for days (this sign doesn't let go of anything quickly, not even hostility). Still, at issue here is learning to be real with ourselves. Our sometimes raw, earthy, gut-driven responses to life should never be inhibited just to appease others. Keeping negative emotions inside makes Taurus feel anything but relaxed, so the Aries side of us pushes for immediate release.

We'll just have to realize that we are strong enough internally to handle whatever results from our honest self-expression. We don't care to please everyone, but we do need to feel content with both ourselves and the actions we take in life. Nonetheless, being quite subjective about who we are, feedback from those we trust can provide a few insights regarding how others see us. Let's learn to hear such observations without getting instantly defensive.

ARIES/TAURUS ASTRO-LEBRITIES

Elton John, singer: (Sun in Aries, Moon in Taurus)

Diana Ross, singer: (Sun in Aries, Moon in Taurus)

Bob Mackie, fashion designer: (Sun in Aries, Moon in Taurus)

Janet Jackson, singer: (Sun in Taurus, Moon in Aries)

Immanuel Kant, philosopher: (Sun in Taurus, Moon in Aries)

Grace Jones, singer: (Sun in Taurus, Moon in Aries)

Taurus/Gemini

Taurus doesn't seem to have much in common with Gemini, although it provides the sensible grounding that this sometimes flighty air sign needs in order to capitalize on its versatility. Besides benefiting from having its energies harnessed and given practical direction, the Twins also profit from the Bull's common sense and its ability to market any product of worth. In fact, this earth sign can't stand to see any talent go to waste. It knows how to package Gemini's assets in appetizing ways that can pay off.

As smart as Gemini is, it can scatter its attention at times and thus may not make intelligent decisions based on a careful assessment of the issues at hand. It sometimes skims over key points that deserve more thoughtful analysis and feedback. The Twins are therefore likely to leap before they look. Actually, life allows Gemini more leeway in this area, since this sign's growth often depends on switching gears in midstream and heading off in different directions that can turn out to be advantageous. Not much preplanning is required. This is something that Taurus also needs to try doing, now and then. Gemini—a sign of detours—can teach the Bull the value of not always choosing the safe, familiar path. The Twins also have an eye for spotting opportunities in the here and now that could later prove profitable—and Taurus likes hearing that!

Still, Gemini doesn't depend on using basic instinct to navigate its way around life, as do Aries and Taurus. Cerebral in orientation, this air sign instead relies on its mental prowess to steer it in interesting directions. It listens more to messages coming from its brain than from its gut. As a result, the objective, rational mind becomes overvalued (Gemini relies on logic to try to figure people out). However, the Bull knows that its own methods of perception help it accurately size up others. Such potent instincts are reliable tools that help Taurus deal effectively with its current reality.

The Twins try to avoid anything that will weigh them down, such as heavy emotions. Luckily, Taurean emotionality—being less complex than that of the water signs—doesn't make Gemini feel trapped in murky depths (the Twins are ill at ease with the melodramas and psychological instabilities that often plague water). Still, Taurus firmly latches on to whatever it finds to offer security, yet this is something that Gemini cannot afford to do. Being so overly attached can mean becoming stuck and even immobile, especially when attachments and dependencies become too energy-demanding (leaving Gemini feeling congested and confined).

Both signs appreciate coherency. Taurus especially wants consistency, while Gemini wants things to be intelligible. Both also dislike anything that is vague; they don't do as well with otherworldly matters, but lean more toward realistic evaluations of the physical world. The abstract and the theoretical are less appealing. Working together, this pair describes a mentality that won't permit imagination to distort factual information; even emotions are analyzed, especially since Gemini wants to understand Taurus' strong feeling response to life. Taurus, however, will need to learn how to articulate its feelings better so that Gemini can understand what motivates the Bull.

Gemini urges Taurus to become less single-minded and more willing to approach matters flexibly, especially since the Bull tries to control life too much. Adaptability introduces new people and experiences that enhance Taurus' security needs in the long run. Meanwhile, drawing on the Bull's steadiness of purpose helps the Twins stay on course, so that they complete their projects, rather than leave things up in the air while irresponsibly darting off to tackle something new. Gemini learns, maybe the hard way, that patience and dedication lead to ultimate success (without which the Twins are just spinning their wheels and getting nowhere in life).

Those of us with Taurus/Gemini emphasized in our chart are learning how to develop our Taurean talents along Geminian channels of self-expression—Gemini tries to disperse the goods that Taurus produces. We are very self-involved in our education about life (what we get out of any experience is more important to us that what others may receive). Perhaps Taurus introduces a conservative element that puts the brakes on Gemini's roving nature, suggesting that our mind does not embrace the wide range of interests that typically engage the Twins. The malleability of this air sign must also contend with the potential stubbornness of the Bull.

Gemini is usually faulted for not finishing what it starts (similar to Aries), yet Taurus has staying power. This helps reduce Gemini's natural distractibility, which thereby sharpens our focus and keeps us on track. We also are less apt to juggle too many things at once, since the Bull doesn't care to take on more in life than it has to. Our Gemini side may get a better chance to shine once it slows down and exerts more self-discipline, thanks to the endurance of Taurus. The Bull has a knack for materializing whatever is of true, enduring value.

Gemini has many assets that need to be better structured, and thus Taurus' ability to create solid, enduring form is essential (i.e., Gemini loves to think and talk, but it is Taurus who'll then encourage the writing of an actual book, as a concrete manifestation of what the mind can create). Taurus' stamina and practical know-how help us further appreciate and develop our Geminian skills.

Taurus/Gemini Astro-lebrities

Sigmund Freud, psychoanalyst: (Sun in Taurus, Moon in Gemini)
Catherine the Great, empress: (Sun in Taurus, Moon in Gemini)
Fred Astaire, dancer-actor: (Sun in Taurus, Moon in Gemini)

Isabella Rossellini, model-actress: (Sun in Gemini, Moon in
  Taurus)
Bjorn Borg, tennis pro: (Sun in Gemini, Moon in Taurus)
Joan Collins, actress: (Sun in Gemini, Moon in Taurus)

Gemini/Cancer

Gemini has an easier time relating to Cancer because of this water
sign's responsive nature. The Twins find Taurus' lack of animation to
be dull, plus the Bull's calm surface communicates little, which unnerves Gemini. However, rubber-faced Cancer shows its feelings, perhaps more visibly than it realizes (Gemini even gets cues from Cancer's
all-too-obvious body language). At least the Crab openly reacts to its
environment when its feelings are stirred, thanks to its cardinal energy.
Gemini enjoys expressive signs that are willing to reveal something
about themselves. Such peppy signs are alive and kicking, and perhaps
have something refreshing to say.

Highly alert to a variety of human experiences, Gemini and Cancer are curious about people's normal, day-to-day lives (even their
more trivial activities). To find out what's going on in the here and
now, Gemini has no qualms about exploring the mundane world of
others. No less nosy than Gemini, Cancer satisfies its curiosity in a
less-direct manner. Shy and often inhibited, the Crab tries to "feel out"
situations by picking up on the "vibes" in the air, without ever having
to encounter others as straightforwardly as does Gemini. Cancer quietly absorbs its environment, often without asking a question or saying a word.

However, once situations become emotionally complicated, Gemini quickly backs off and turns its attention elsewhere, while Cancer is
drawn even closer. The Crab feels compelled to offer emotional nurturance to those in need. Cancer is willing to get more involved,
whereas the Twins look for the nearest exit when things get too sticky
(as if they suddenly realize they have a plane to catch or lots of other
people to see). Obviously, Gemini does not share Cancer's maternal
urges, nor does it bond deeply with others. It feels less committed in
its relationships.

Actually, Gemini *will* listen to people's problems, but more so as a detached analyst who'll try to put the many pieces of any human puzzle together, just for the mental challenge of it all. Still, the Twins can often clarify issues for those who are confused, although mental clarity doesn't imply sympathy. It's Cancer that can put itself in another's place so that it can feel even the distress that an individual may be going through (all water signs are good at doing this).

The Twins and the Crab are also changeable in disposition. Cancer can be moody, although often its impressionable temperament is manipulated by external conditions of which it is often unaware. From the Crab's perspective, moods instead seem to come from somewhere deep inside. Cancer's temperament also reflects the less-obvious elements of its surroundings. It is tied to its environment in invisible ways that defy logic.

Gemini, in its eagerness to take in a variety of life conditions, doesn't wish to keep its focus fixed. It momentarily diverts its attention elsewhere, just to observe what's new and stimulating—it never lingers long enough to really soak up the atmosphere. The Twins are more apt to regard the scenery, rather than themselves, as changeable. They simply adapt in order to understand their immediate circumstances better. As a rational but detached observer, Gemini is careful not to color outer situations with its subjective reflections, unlike Cancer. However, both signs show a talent for mimicking others.

Cancer can teach Gemini to communicate by showing more feeling, since that's a great way to get others to listen intently (air alone can otherwise be a bit dry or impersonal when dispensing knowledge—it needs a more human touch). The Crab also encourages Gemini to apply its keen powers of observation to help decode the emotions of others. Meanwhile, the Crab can benefit from Gemini's ability to pull back far enough to gain a wider perspective on life. The Twins teach Cancer to get beyond raw emotionality and instead to look at people in a clear, objective light—free of subjective bias and hidden perceptual blind spots. The Crab needs to realize how suffocating its neediness can be, and thus how others rightfully require proper breathing space (Gemini), even in intimate relationships.

Those of us with Gemini/Cancer energies emphasized in our chart are learning how fluidly communicative we can be, once we overcome any self-consciousness resulting from our shyer Cancerian side. Many things interest us on both intellectual and emotional levels, but we'll need to avoid giving in to incidental distractions that can pull us in too many directions (a problem even for Cancer, not just Gemini). We love to learn all about life, but may shortchange ourselves if this is approached in too conservative a manner, since the Crab cautiously sticks to its traditional interests. Due to fears of the unknown, Cancer doesn't embrace what's new as easily as does Gemini, who instead dreads boredom.

If the Gemini side of us is dominant, we'll need to use our Cancerian sensitivity more often to explore life below its more common levels of everyday interaction. Our way of relating to people can then become less superficial, as long as we take time to listen not just to what folks are saying, but how they are saying it. Cancer tunes in to the tone that people use in conversation; it picks up on a range of subtleties and non-verbal clues that Gemini typically overlooks—after all, although the Twins may not be mind readers, water signs can easily penetrate the surface of others in order to get to the heart of how they really feel.

Gemini/Cancer Astro-lebrities

Bob Hope, comedian: (Sun in Gemini, Moon in Cancer)
Maureen Stapleton, actress: (Sun in Gemini, Moon in Cancer)
Thomas Hardy, writer: (Sun in Gemini, Moon in Cancer)

Calvin Coolidge, U.S. president: (Sun in Cancer, Moon in Gemini)
Gilda Radner, comedian: (Sun in Cancer, Moon in Gemini)
Henry David Thoreau, writer: (Sun in Cancer, Moon in Gemini)

Cancer/Leo

The Gemini/Cancer combo is a little tricky to integrate because, unlike the Twins, the Crab's instinct is not to detach its emotions when relating to others, one-on-one. Rather than seeking space—it prefers enclosures—Cancer wants intimacy once assured it can safely open up and not worry about exposing its vulnerable side. Meanwhile, the Twins don't see why any sign should be all that hypersensitive about itself. Yet it's Gemini's lack of understanding in this matter that upsets touchy Cancer, a sign that doesn't appreciate being told to "toughen up."

However, Cancer happily realizes that Leo is emotional, not cool and cerebral; the Crab can relate to the passionate outpourings of the Lion. Both are capable of warmly giving of themselves to others. Yet both tend to overfeel and are led more by their hearts than by their heads—more by sentiment than by reason. For better or worse, these signs can be visibly moved by people and circumstances, and once thus aroused, their response is anything but low-key. Strong feelings can surface in honest, self-revealing ways.

As Cancer/Leo types have an emotive disposition, often resulting in a theatrical streak, their life situations are felt in vivid terms. When joining forces, it's hard for these two signs *not* to be demonstrative. When such folks are provoked, their feelings are sometimes expressed in an overstated manner. It's not easy to stay calm and rational when caught up in the moment of powerful emotion. When combined, these signs interpret things so personally that they can readily take offense at real or imagined slights. They can feel humiliation, more than they care to admit, especially if receiving disrespectful treatment in a public setting.

Yet both can also—if they wish to—cover up any sense of injury, rather than indulge in heavy scenes that'll only makes matters worse. (Although fiery Leo is less inhibited than Cancer, the Lion won't react as blindly and uncontrollably as does a disturbed Crab whose dam has burst; Cancer's gushing waters can be a furious force—all water signs can react to life with a primal intensity.) Leo's innate sense of dignity keeps it from appearing too defeated or wounded, unless playing up hurt and pain works to its advantage (although normally, the Lion certainly doesn't want to appear weak and pathetic).

Leo can teach Cancer to value self-assurance. Although the Crab has uncanny instincts that should serve it well, it can also be plagued by inner doubts that damage its self-esteem. It needs to have more faith in its strengths, as does the confident Lion. In turn, Leo benefits by drawing from Cancer's ability to make others feel nourished and secure. Adopting a more empathetic, caring disposition helps the Lion seem less egotistical and self-serving. While "fans" may be in awe of Leo's larger-than-life qualities, they can more personally relate to the ordinary human vulnerabilities of Cancer. The Crab also offers Leo the wisdom of knowing when to be silent, less conspicuous, and even humble (since nobody enjoys anyone who's onstage all the time, forever grabbing the spotlight away from others).

If Cancer/Leo energies are emphasized in our chart, we will need a lot of attention from others in this lifetime. Our Leo side clearly knows this to be true, but should our Cancer parts deny this reality, we could typically end up the victim of dark moods that can result in psychosomatic symptoms. Both signs crave love and affection, and enjoy lavish treatment in this regard. We can give as good as we get in these matters. Yet, it is likely that we have very particular needs that we expect others in our lives to be sensitive to, and thus we can hardly cope with being met with rejection or indifference. We must have people who will react to us, for better or worse, and not go into a deep-freeze emotional state.

Cancer sometimes acts like a hungry and needy infant. As dramatic Leo can magnify even Cancer's shortcomings in attention-demanding ways, we could suffer bouts of immaturity should we can fail to incorporate the Lion's sense of independence and self-reliance. To make the best of Leo's energies, we'll need to find creative ways to develop security from within—we could find ourselves disappointed if we instead expect such security to come from others. By giving in to our ego drives, somewhat innocently, we may find that they help us discover how we can best anchor ourselves by establishing a strong identity. We can learn to create our own inner support system, no matter how harshly the outer world treats us.

When the social atmosphere is right, expect a colorful, vibrant personality to shine here. With Cancer/Leo types, the introvert and the showoff combine to make for an interesting but sometimes unsteady temperament. When Leo is feeling good about itself, it radiates a warm glow that energizes others; but when Cancer is feeling bad, it can turn cold and look for a place to hide (or, while wearing its suit of emotional armor, it can lash out and defend itself from potential attack). Any steamy mix of fire and water won't be able to keep pent-up pressures internalized for long.

CANCER/LEO ASTRO-LEBRITIES

Ken Russell, director: (Sun in Cancer, Moon in Leo)
Phoebe Snow, singer: (Sun in Cancer, Moon in Leo)
Tom Hanks, actor: (Sun in Cancer, Moon in Leo)

Mae West, actress: (Sun in Leo, Moon in Cancer)
Sean Penn, actor: (Sun in Leo, Moon in Cancer)
Emily Brontë, writer: (Sun in Leo, Moon in Cancer)

Leo/Virgo

Leo/Virgo energies help us become discriminating in our tastes and more selective in our needs. Following Cancer, Leo no longer identifies itself as just another member of the tribe, but as one who stands out as being special, privileged, and immune to the social or familial pressure to conform. Everything in its life is to define and support what Leo exclusively is at heart, not what others try to condition it to become instead. The Lion realizes that it has the power to create itself freely, at will, in bold and colorful ways that often go against early parental programming. For Leo, even traditional authority is not to be blindly or obediently followed. The Lion is ready to make up its own personal rules of conduct, and have fun letting its hair down while doing so.

Virgo is even more particular about how it views itself. Its sense of inner purity compels it to guard against "contamination" by outside influences. The Analyzer is ever on the alert when it comes to detecting and repelling anything undesirable that may invade its carefully constructed boundaries. It fears having close contact with anybody or anything that could tarnish or corrupt its high standards. This is one reason why Virgo is reluctant to simply "go with the flow" in life and join the crowd. It's very choosy about the kinds of experiences it wants to have, realizing how out of order it can typically feel whenever it goes against its better judgment by disregarding its inner principles and submitting to unhealthy situations.

Leo/Virgo types are thus picky about the lives they live. Leo demands first-class treatment. It won't associate itself with whatever's in a shoddy or shabby state, and wants to have the finest that life can offer, since it feels it deserves as much. Virgo, while not as demanding of having the best—especially if "the best" is costly and not absolutely necessary—still likes to keep things in excellent shape. It's willing to conscientiously maintain whatever it values, so that such items continue to function without problems, as if they're good-as-new. Leo's not quite that fastidious, but it does appreciate Virgo's efforts to keep everything in tip-top condition (since this enhances outer appearances, something that is important to the Lion).

Actually, both signs are sensitive about being seen in a lesser light and thereby criticized. They fear showing to the world their mistakes, their "dirty laundry," or anything else that could subject them to ridicule and shame. What people think of them does matter a lot. Perhaps much of their energy understandably is used to develop impressive levels of competency—they want to be experts in their fields of interest (Virgo makes Leo work much harder to polish its act and brightly shine, while Leo gives Virgo the big ego push it needs to confidently show off its proficiency—and the heck with low self-esteem disguised as so-called "humility").

However, Leo insists on drawing attention to itself—sometimes the showier, the better—whereas discrete Virgo shuns the spotlight in favor of working unassumingly in low-visibility environments. The Analyzer is satisfied to quietly toil away and do any demanding job at hand as efficiently as it can. It doesn't need heaps of praise or splashy public notice—but it does need a moderate display of sincere appreciation from those it respects. Virgo teaches Leo how to share the glory with others who are equally deserving. Big projects that capture society's attention are seldom single-handedly orchestrated, since they involve essential details that are managed best by many dedicated workers. Virgo advises Leo to trust the creative power of others, as well.

However, even Virgo has difficulty trusting the expertise of signs (and people) other than itself. Its "know-it-all" disposition (although not displayed in an arrogant manner) is coupled with self-sufficiency, urging Virgo to act alone without interference. The Analyzer doesn't wish to risk having others come in and botch things up (it sees only itself as being capable of doing things correctly). Leo, of course, must be the head director of any enterprise, and therefore doesn't easily delegate power roles to others. Thus, Leo/Virgo energies suggest that we can become sticklers for taking charge of our personal matters, rather than risk having somebody else run the show, only to make a mess of things.

Those of us with a Leo/Virgo emphasis in our chart have both charismatic flair and managerial ability (our Leo side), plus a head for details and organization (our Virgo assets). We probably have a talent for marketing ourselves in smart, well-thought-out ways (Virgo instills in Leo a sense of realistic self-appraisal that this fire sign needs, so that it learns to work effectively within its limits). Leo may brag about its magnificent capabilities, but at least Virgo can back up such blatant self-promotion with skills that are truly outstanding. Leo helps Virgo apply the willpower and endurance needed to best exploit its talents, and all without a discouraging self-criticism creeping into the picture.

Leo/Virgo Astro-lebrities

Dustin Hoffman, actor: (Sun in Leo, Moon in Virgo)

Princess Anne, British royalty: (Sun in Leo, Moon in Virgo)

Robert Redford, actor: (Sun in Leo, Moon in Virgo)

Twiggy, model: (Sun in Virgo, Moon in Leo)

King Louis XIV, French royalty: (Sun in Virgo, Moon in Leo)

Martha Raye, actress: (Sun in Virgo, Moon in Leo)

Virgo/Libra

The Virgo/Libra combo helps us refine our nature even further, more so than Virgo/Leo. We are not just discriminating about how we present our individuality to the world, but are also selective about the partnerships in which we'll invest our time and energy. Virgo involved with any sign prompts us to evaluate the pros and cons of that sign's behavior more thoughtfully. The Analyzer's discerning eye and Libra's sense of clear perspective are now to be applied toward workable relationships—both those on the job and in marriage (or its equivalent).

Idealistic Libra can be a romantic at heart who longs for harmony and happiness in close unions, but who also has a talent for noticing faulty behavior that keeps people in a frictional state of imbalance. Being airy, Libra can emotionally detach when assessing situations that involve a clash of interests and values. It nonetheless pushes for a restoration of equilibrium whenever possible, rather than endure a lack of peace and understanding. Still, it has hope for the best in its relationships and will do whatever it takes to make a partnership turn out to be a smashing success.

Virgo is more the realist who spots even the minor flaws of any relationship, sometimes much too easily. It senses that getting intimately involved with others requires a willingness to work hard to keep things functioning smoothly. The Analyzer harbors no illusions about how tough harmony can be to achieve. It thus doesn't enter unions with high expectations, an attitude that Libra finds to be unfortunate and self-defeating. "If we expect little of worth in our partnerships," says Libra, "that's pretty much what we'll get." Virgo, of course, says it just calls it like it sees it—the unvarnished truth, not some unrealistic ideal.

The Balancer makes an excellent people watcher who loves to study the rituals of relating. The art of social interplay is born in this sign, as are the formalities that make sociable interaction pleasant and based on fair play. Libra needs its partnerships in order to grow, even if those unions turn out to be stormy. However, Virgo is a self-contained sign that doesn't look to others for its balance and support.

Being an earth sign, it learns early on to supply itself with what it needs without ever imposing on others.

With such a sometimes standoffish disposition, Virgo's well-being does not depend on having close relationships. The Analyzer will thus need a lot encouragement before submitting to long-term partnerships, since it knows that its routine ways of handling its life will undergo modifications that it won't necessarily enjoy. (Human partners are more demanding than are pets and plants, learns Virgo; at least dogs and cats won't tease the Analyzer for being such a neatfreak and a worrywart.)

Virgo/Libra types are probably cool-headed in their social affairs. They are apt to have impeccable manners and like to appear well groomed. If other parts of their chart suggest that physical appearance is less important an issue, then these folks at least like to be mentally well organized and crystal clear in their thinking. Both of these signs are capable of analyzing things without letting emotional biases get in the way. Virgo is unlikely to yield to persuasion, if doing so goes against its better judgement (plus the Analyzer will never fudge with the facts). Although not rigid, Virgo applies common sense when evaluating a situation. It is unfazed by sentimental considerations or the pressure to look the other way and ignore certain inconvenient realities.

However, Libra is prone to let its need to be liked sometimes cloud its decision-making process. It tries to please too many people at once, which is a losing battle. It seems to have the social graces that an often more awkward and insecure Virgo lacks, yet Libra can behave in artificial ways if it lets its need for social acceptance at any cost take over. Virgo would never bend over backwards that much if doing so felt phony or unnatural. It would rather be alone and left undisturbed in its own solitary world than try to become attractive to others in such a contrived manner.

The Virgo/Libra combo implies an eye for aesthetic composition (Libra) and intelligent arrangement (Virgo). The urge here is to put order into life in ways that make things more comfortable and beautiful. Designs created are of the "form follows function" variety, serving practical purposes (Virgo likes to craft things that are usable, not just lovely or abstract). Any sign linked up with Virgo has assets that can be used in a vocational manner. The Libran beauty that appeals to Virgo is not necessarily physical (visual); it can just as easily be of an intellectual nature (as even physicists, mathematicians, and cosmologists can create intricate theories that reflect the elegance of symmetrical structure at work).

Those of us with Virgo/Libra energies highlighted in our chart are probably helpful and courteous to others. We are considerate of the minor details of life that make matters run smoothly in relationships. In return, we want others to be reasonable with us and civil in behavior—no heated arguments or rough stuff, please! Libra especially fosters pleasant, agreeable relationships, while Virgo simply wants to deal with folks who are level-headed and sane. Both signs are easily embarrassed in public by the rudeness of others, so we'll want people to be as composed as we are—in other words, we will appreciate those who think before they speak or act.

VIRGO/LIBRA ASTRO-LEBRITIES
Shania Twain, singer: (Sun in Virgo, Moon in Libra)
D. H. Lawrence, writer: (Sun in Virgo, Moon in Libra)
Agatha Christie, writer: (Sun in Virgo, Moon in Libra)

William Faulkner, writer: (Sun in Libra, Moon in Virgo)
Deborah Kerr, actress: (Sun in Libra, Moon in Virgo)
Niels Bohr, physicist: (Sun in Libra, Moon in Virgo)

Libra/Scorpio

Virgo/Libra is a very rational, less-emotionally driven combo concerned with appropriate social behavior (these signs want others to interact with them in decent, mannerly ways). However, Scorpio brings out the passionate side of Libra that cautious Virgo does not. Both signs show a keen interest in how others behave; they observe and study human interaction very well. One-on-one relating becomes particularly important to Libra and Scorpio, with special emphasis put on the "significant other" theme.

Learning about give and take in intimate relationships is vital for the proper development of these signs. As the sharing process is highlighted here, an awareness of what is of mutual benefit in personal unions is fostered. This requires a sincere interest in learning about another person's world—something that intrigues both signs. These two share a talent for strategy and skillful social maneuvering. Each is able to manipulate people and situations, although in different ways.

Libra has long been known for its suave ability to charm others to act on *Libra's* behalf, all while convincing them that it was initially their idea or desire to do so. The Balancer can be quite tricky in how it indirectly asserts its will, typically through the actions of others. (Libra has been known to pit two adversaries against each other while it "plays the middle" with finesse, a result of this sign's ability to see and understand all sides of an issue.) The Balancer keenly observes and evaluates the outer packaging that people use to present themselves to society. Appearances and open demonstrations of intent mean a lot to this sign (who doesn't want to play guessing games, but seeks forthrightness in others—as long as it doesn't lead to ugly confrontations).

Scorpio focuses more on tapping into the hidden facets that people seldom show the world. The Scorpion knows that appearances are not always to be trusted, and that open demonstrations sometimes prove nothing about one's underlying intent. This water sign readily picks up on subtleties in human interaction. Of course, even Libra is an astute observer of the understated in relationships (although unlike Scorpio, the Balancer is less eager to rush to judgment regarding the "ulterior motives" of others).

Libra tries to play fair, based on its conscious, intellectual assessment of the facts at hand; it weighs all sides with thoughtful deliberation. Scorpio struggles with its suspicious nature, and at times is tempted to treat people in underhanded ways rather than risk openly revealing its vulnerable feelings and true needs. Yet, periodic cover-ups aside, Scorpio is ultimately as interested in the clear, unvarnished truth of any matter as is Libra. Both signs dislike fooling themselves, especially regarding others (this slant on disclosing truth in relationships begins with Virgo/Libra, a combo more comfortable with facts than fantasies regarding the human condition).

Libra/Scorpio types are typically drawn to human investigation in some fashion. They are driven to explore the heights and depths of intimacy in close partnerships. It is imperative that they choose a life mate whom they can trust explicitly, since these signs are quite commitment-oriented at heart. Both can also do well at fighting for relevant social causes that allow them to persuade other to enlist their talents and skills in a worthwhile manner. Scorpio often comes on too strong, once its intensity has been unleashed, yet Libra teaches the Scorpion to turn on the diplomacy, when doing so helps motivate others to cooperate, without the threat of power struggles erupting. Naturally, Scorpio shows Libra the disadvantages of being too nice—pitfalls can be created by not making waves when needed.

Those of us with Libra/Scorpio energies highlighted in our chart show a zest for relating to others, but we are willing to uphold our principles fiercely when need be. Nobody can really expect to get away with stepping all over us without a fight (here's where our Scorpio side can play dirty if that's the only way to win). We will negotiate first before we resort to hardball tactics in order to crush our opposition, assuming we value our Libra parts enough to negotiate and restore peace to any social situation that has otherwise gotten out of control.

However, others better not take advantage of our kindness and patience—which have their limits—since after bending over backwards enough times, we'll simply explode and do a lot of damage to those who have provoked us. Underneath the carefully cultivated, polished way we handle ourselves in the world is a more volatile temperament that really won't take "no" for an answer. Nobody had better underestimate our determination to have things turn out our way in the long run. There is much emotional power lurking beneath our surface charm.

Libra/Scorpio Astro-lebrities

Julie Andrews, actress-singer: (Sun in Libra, Moon in Scorpio)
Truman Capote, writer: (Sun in Libra, Moon in Scorpio)
Nancy Kerrigan, skating pro: (Sun in Libra, Moon in Scorpio)

Leonardo DiCaprio, actor: (Sun in Scorpio, Moon in Libra)
Sylvia Plath, poet: (Sun in Scorpio, Moon in Libra)
Ted Turner, business mogul: (Sun in Scorpio, Moon in Libra)

Scorpio/Sagittarius

Scorpio is a paradox in that it is highly secretive and unwilling to re-veal much about itself, yet it also has a profound need to plumb the depths in order to uncover the underlying truth of anything that is typically hidden from view. At some point, the Scorpion feels pres-sured to expose what has long been concealed, even that regarding its own private self. Mystery gives way to revelation. The themes of expo-sure and "truth revealed" are also very much connected to Sagittarius, a sign of expanded vision regarding the workings of Truth on a uni-versal scale. After undergoing its transformative process, Scorpio finds that its inner renewal involves an acceptance of the Archer's philoso-phy of open, candid social expression. This water sign begins to realize the value and benefit of being less cryptic and indirect with others. It learns to trust.

Sagittarius draws from the penetrating awareness of being that Scorpio has developed through its deep investigation of life. The Archer uses such profundity to convince itself of one thing: If life has its depths, it also must have its heights. The Scorpion unrelentlessly stalks the psyche's less-accessible regions, but Sagittarius seeks to ad-venturously experience the breadth of life, even in elevated realms be-yond the human dimension—in other words, cosmic reality or the Mind of God. Scorpio soon realizes that moving into Sagittarian con-sciousness is like being released from a dark prison into a spacious, mind-expanding world filled with a warm, shadow-dissolving light.

What both these signs have in common is a burning zeal for ideas and ideals that they believe in, which results in a powerful sense of conviction. Yet such unwavering certainty, when not balanced by com-mon sense or objectivity, can lead to fanaticism. Scorpio adds unlim-ited fuel to the fires of Sagittarian idealism. Mere beliefs turn into articles of absolute faith, the kind that are immune to reason or to the opinions of others—they are simply not to be questioned or opposed.

Obviously, when the blend of these signs is mismanaged, a degree of pigheadedness (fixed Scorpio) renders Sagittarius heavy-handed in its theories, and more opinionated in its concepts that usual. An unattractive dogmatism, which seems to have no limits, puts others on the defensive. Scorpio/Sagittarius types have a touch of the crusader with militant undertones in them. They'll need to be careful not to aggressively push their ideologies on to others.

What Sagittarius offers Scorpio is a much needed sense of innocence (a quality that all fire signs have, enabling them to trust that life will be a positive experience with little to fear). The Scorpion is too aware of the undermining way that fate (and karma) operates to ever approach life in a state of naiveté. This water sign is always on guard, whereas Sagittarius—who feels it has nothing to hide—is ever-ready to invite the unfamiliar into its world. Perhaps in the back of the Archer's mind is an awareness that if it were to confront mortal danger, it would be able to marshal the powers needed to do battle and survive. This includes the Scorpionic strength of will that allows Sagittarius to confidently espouse its "mind over matter" philosophy.

Noting the actual glyphs of these signs, it's interesting that Scorpio and Sagittarius share a similar motif: the ominous stinger of the Scorpion, able to barb its prey, seems to transform into the arrow of inspiration that directs Sagittarius' rapt attention heavenward. Arrow symbols imply an implicit direction, pointing the way to a specific destination. Scorpio/Sagittarius types need to have something vast and all-consuming at which to aim their forces, in order to keep energies from becoming destructive or nonproductive. They need to focus on goals that they feel passionate about. Actually, Scorpio provides the drive and endurance needed to succeed against all odds, while Sagittarius keeps vision and optimism alive, even during the most grueling of times. The aimlessness that comes from straightjacketing the potential of both signs can lead to trouble and to a great amount of inner discontent.

Those of us with Scorpio/Sagittarius energies emphasized in our chart are born with lots of guts and a willingness to fearlessly explore life. Searching for something that has enormous personal meaning and vast social impact can motivate us to equate the accumulation of both knowledge and wisdom with temporal and spiritual powers. Our secret desire is to be aware of all that is, which is no small feat. Whatever we believe in, we do to the nth degree. It's obvious that this blend can result in extremism, especially if we favor the Scorpio side of our nature (with its control hang-ups). Of course, Sagittarius adds a little charm to Scorpio's otherwise unapproachable demeanor.

Our curiosity is powerful, as we forever wonder how life really works on all levels (especially those harder-to-fathom ones). Our orientation moves us beyond mere one-on-one involvement. Scorpio realizes that focusing on the ills of society helps provide the emotional balance this sign needs; otherwise, internally obsessing about its selfish desires can be hellish. Sagittarius, the last of the fire signs, it gearing us toward a new start involving our robust, idealistic participation in collective experience. However, being more tolerant of people in the world around us enhances our deeper self-understanding.

SCORPIO/SAGITTARIUS ASTRO-LEBRITIES

Carl Sagan, astronomer: (Sun in Scorpio, Moon in Sagittarius)
k.d. lang, singer: (Sun in Scorpio, Moon in Sagittarius)
Billy Graham, evangelist: (Sun in Scorpio, Moon in Sagittarius)

Bette Midler, singer-actress: (Sun in Sagittarius, Moon in Scorpio)
Steven Spielberg, director: (Sun in Sagittarius, Moon in Scorpio)
Lesley Stahl, journalist: (Sun in Sagittarius, Moon in Scorpio)

Sagittarius/Capricorn

For Sagittarius, morality is a hot issue, at least in principle if not in practice. The Archer is less concerned with those who do wrong, and is more interested in folks who do right—how much inner goodness can decent citizens evoke in the name of civic participation and social betterment? Scorpio/Sagittarius types, while tuned in to social values, are often only charged up about morals and ethics once they feel a sense of righteous indignation. Stormy, less-forgiving Scorpio usually insists on punishing those who break society's laws. (Meanwhile, the Scorpion demands to live by its own private code of behavior, willfully ignoring certain cultural dictates—this is something it shares in common with Aquarius. Scorpio has a problem bowing down to any supreme authority and surrendering its will.)

Sagittarius may seem rebellious and is always the one to question mindless, mainstream conformity. Yet is does have a soft spot in its heart for cultural traditions, especially those that go way back (here's a broad-minded sign that may wish to climb aboard the starship *Enterprise* and voyage into the future, yet it still wants to preserve and even endorse ancient Native American rituals). In this manner, the Archer is as respectful of certain customs as is Capricorn, a sign that honors the past and all the solid, social groundwork laid down by civilizations of long ago. What both share is an emphasis on principles that help structure the collective mind, while giving people clear, legal guidelines by which to live.

Capricorn, of course, is more interested in law and *order*, and can thus attempt to limit the degree of social freedom that Sagittarius champions (as long as we all play by certain agreed-upon rules—mainly those that keep mass chaos from breaking out—we should enjoy much flexibility regarding our personal social conduct, thinks the Archer). Sagittarius is a lenient sign that will temper justice with mercy. Although fiery in its rhetoric, it's not always willing to crack the whip and demand that people conform to established regulations (it's probably even the first sign to ever take advantage of legal loopholes). Being a fire sign, Sagittarius is apt to believe, at times, that it is above the law (just like Scorpio feels under certain conditions). Yet the Goat sternly reminds us that the rules of the game apply to everyone, unconditionally.

Sagittarius/Capricorn types are typically law-abiding and conventional in their attitudes toward society. However, if our Sagittarian side is stronger, then a little rule-bending is in order. The Archer will marginally do whatever it takes to please the powers that be, but then it'll daringly let its hair down and mischievously push the envelope wherever it can in society (it's a bit of a defiant thumbnoser, like the planet Uranus). If our Capricorn side dominates, then we may glorify productivity and turn our earthly ambitions into a nearly religious experience (anything connected to Sagittarius can be glorified, even the Goat's burning drive to scale the heights of worldly success).

Those of us with Sagittarius/Capricorn emphasized in our chart are oriented in life in ways that are decidedly less personal and instead more collective in awareness. Delving into our private inner world doesn't appeal to us as much as relating to larger public venues, where we seem to have a talent for inspiring people to become involved in their communities. Taking on the responsibility of relevant social participation is an important message that we may feel obligated to broadcast on some level. Being a "do-gooder" in the eyes of the world is an image we may wish to cultivate. Both signs place a high value on integrity. However, Sagittarius, while meaning well, promises big things it often cannot deliver. It doesn't plan its actions as well as the Goat does, and doesn't recognize its limits as realistically.

However, Capricorn needs to draw from Sagittarius' optimistic vision during those times when the Goat feel too downtrodden by the harsh ways of an exacting world that seemingly lacks a heart. The Goat must keep hope alive to prevent it from being crushed by depression or damaged by cynicism. Earthbound living cannot satisfy all human aspirations. In turn, Sagittarian dreams will seldom fly if they are not grounded by Capricorn's pragmatism; such high-minded goals need an organized, workable structure to help them survive in the world.

Perhaps the main objective here is to learn to retain our Sagittarian spiritedness and our faith in the promising future that awaits us, while also realizing that we're here to contribute something of social worth that may take time to unfold properly (Sagittarius hates things that seemingly drag on, yet Capricorn doesn't trust "overnight" success, knowing that certain pertinent steps along the way may have been ignored in a rush to "go public"—the foundation on which such quickie enterprises rest may thus be shaky).

We will do well if we can be philosophical about any unforeseen circumstantial delays that are beyond our control (Capricorn often experiences life as unfolding too slowly). Yet we'll also need to remain steadfastly on target regarding our wordly ambitions, and less willing to abandon ship the moment the waves of life start to get choppy. Let's learn to persevere with a smile on our face and a song in our heart!

SAGITTARIUS/CAPRICORN ASTRO-LEBRITIES

Richard Pryor, comedian: (Sun in Sagittarius, Moon in Capricorn)

Judi Dench, actress: (Sun in Sagittarius, Moon in Capricorn)

Brad Pitt, actor: (Sun in Sagittarius, Moon in Capricorn)

Tiger Woods, tennis pro: (Sun in Capricorn, Moon in Sagittarius)

Mary Tyler Moore, actress: (Sun in Capricorn, Moon in Sagittarius)

Henri Matisse, artist: (Sun in Capricorn, Moon in Sagittarius)

Capricorn/Aquarius

Sagittarius encourages Capricorn to be peppy and cheerful in disposition, just as it helps put a big smile on Scorpio's face from time to time—the Scorpion can otherwise seem grim and intense in ways that spook others. Somewhat like Scorpio, the Goat can also appear too solemnly single-minded as it ambitiously strives to achieve its well-structured goals. The addition of a little playful Jupiterian fire thus helps relax and lighten the temperaments of these two otherwise weighty, no-nonsense signs.

However, although Aquarius is known for being friendly in its customarily detached manner, it doesn't get aroused by ordinary emotions. It can be as cool and collected as Capricorn, although the Water Bearer seldom suffers the repressions commonly experienced by an uptight, self-restrained Goat. That's because, unlike Capricorn, Aquarius' feeling nature is less rigidly controlled. It's an air sign that is merely too impersonal in its social contacts to ever let emotionality cloud its perceptions of people and of life itself (of course, the Goat doesn't want its feelings to spill out and distort reality, either). Nonetheless, this combo doesn't sound warm and cuddly. Open displays of affection don't come easily, plus there's little here that is innocently childlike in nature.

Both signs are geared toward taking on collective projects needed to keep society in good shape. Capricorn, as we know, sets up the laws by which all citizens are to abide. Such structures are to provide social cohesion, which protects against disorganization on a large scale. Aquarius, however, knows that as a society's structure becomes restrictive, it also becomes more oppressive to the members of any culture, especially those who have awakened to their individualism. The Water Bearer thus rebels against stale traditions. It seeks more liberating ways for people to collectively interact. Still, what both signs share is a social conscience that keeps them ever-interested in what goes on in the world. These signs find it unsatisfying to revolve exclusively around themselves, as if oblivious to what's happening on the mass level.

Capricorn/Aquarius types, although enthused by timely collective progress, can seem less demonstrative in more private, one-on-one situations. They may appear gregarious (Aquarius) in a down-to-earth manner (Capricorn), but there can also be an aloofness that keeps others from getting close to them. They can seem a little chilly on the emotional side and are not easily touched by sentiment or moved by tears. In fact, the emotionality of others may make them feel uneasy and quick to create a safe distance. If anything is to get them in touch with their feelings, it'll more likely involve campaigning for social causes that are to awaken society and shake it out of its complacency (especially if the Aquarian side dominates). This pair finds getting involved in important issues in society—especially as a key player—to be very tempting.

There is a scientific bent to these signs, suggesting that their ability to reason is strong. Capricorn/Aquarius types are unlikely to gravitate toward mystical realms or indulge in a world of fantasy. A more hard-nosed approach to the search for truth is suggested. Although Aquarius may be inventive, it likes to feel it's on solid ground regarding its assumptions, and is willing to put its experimental concepts to the test. This sounds like pragmatic Capricorn, as well. However, if the power of the rational mind is overemphasized, the ability to embrace imagination or to understand things of a spiritual nature can be diminished.

The capacity to appreciate the more subtle truths of life is also weakened, probably because the reality of the soul is denied.

Those of us with Capricorn/Aquarius energies highlighted in our chart are very much activists at heart, even if on the conservative side. We're willing to become involved in community affairs by supporting groups and organizations that bravely advocate fresh ideals that challenge mainstream thinking and social conformity. Our sense of civic duty is usually strong, and we're farsighted enough to promote progressive causes whose timeliness help them succeed. Our Capricorn side urges us to take on supervisory roles in these matters, or else to function on some other important level of responsibility for the welfare of others.

We may also tend to be a paradox, someone who is filled with contradictions. The Goat can be old-fashioned in many ways, while the Water Bearer can easily break ties with past traditions and experiment with matters of a futuristic nature—upholding traditions is thus of less interest to Aquarius. It is important that we find humanitarian outlets whereby we can pragmatically network with others and help organize major projects that can awaken social consciousness on some level.

Capricorn/Aquarius Astro-lebrities
Denzel Washington, actor: (Sun in Capricorn, Moon in Aquarius)
Diane Keaton, actress: (Sun in Capricorn, Moon in Aquarius)
Muhammad Ali, boxer: (Sun in Capricorn, Moon in Aquarius)

Sarah McLachlan, singer: (Sun in Aquarius, Moon in Capricorn)
Peter Gabriel, singer: (Sun in Aquarius, Moon in Capricorn)
Betty Friedan, writer: (Sun in Aquarius, Moon in Capricorn)

Aquarius/Pisces
Capricorn/Aquarius types are very concerned with shaping society in progressive ways, yet they are sometimes too cautious about enacting needed reform. Capricorn doesn't trust "overnight" changes that try to revolutionize culture by shaking up honored traditions, yet Aquarius feels hampered when forced to cooperate with bureaucratic systems that make headway at a snail's pace. The Water Bearer has a special

distaste for those ruling bodies that cling to political power while fighting real social advancement tooth and nail. Yet Capricorn won't flirt with anarchism by allowing a permissive, "anything goes" policy—not when it's in charge of governing the potential unruly masses (Capricorn has a powerful paternalistic streak that can border on dictatorship). Thus, these signs must grapple with fundamental tensions due to a conflict of interest.

However, the Aquarius/Pisces duo reinforces the humane, altruistic side of each sign. Pisces is very concerned about those whom society tends to neglect or treat poorly. No matter how people are classified according to social rank, the Fishes feel that all souls are bonded on an inner level and operate as one mass unit of consciousness. Aquarius won't go that far in its thinking, but it does believe that a respect for human diversity helps support social unity. Like Sagittarius, Aquarius believes that it takes all types of individuals to make the world interesting. Still, Pisces knows there are underlying truths about life that go beyond anything that even an ideal society can formulate.

What Aquarius unconsciously leans toward for its further development is the Piscean ability to feel things clearly on emotional levels (where we normally don't expect "genius" to operate). The Fishes can be quite precocious in their ability to feel out the hidden factors of a situation, even on a large-scale manner; this gives their hunches and feelings a prophetic quality, more than just Aquarius' flashes of insight. Plus, for Pisces, Aquarian tolerance is not enough if it doesn't also evoke empathy. Of course, Pisces can benefit at times from the Water Bearer's ability to emotionally detach when observing the overview of any situation. Sometimes, the Fishes' feelings are so overwhelming that they can become paralyzing, especially when illogical fears take over. Airy Aquarius provides a degree of needed rationality, even though some would find its brand of logic to be uncommon.

Aquarius/Pisces types can seem like "bleeding-heart liberals" to more reactionary folks who would rather have all members of society abide by set rules of conduct. (Perhaps those with an Aquarius/Capricorn emphasis feel torn along these lines, since the Capricorn side of them believes in a continued support of established social standards; it wants all citizens to shape up and contribute to the System.) Aquarius/Pisces folks seem to have an extraordinary amount of compassion and understanding of the human dilemma (perhaps we are gods-in-the-making, but we are nonetheless earthbound and ignorant of the power of our eternal beings).

The need to do good works in society, without receiving any glory for one's efforts, seems to be a strong theme of these altruistic signs. They identify with the unconventional elements of society, as they clearly reject status-quo values regarding prestige and prosperity. Aquarius is less spiritually focused than Pisces, but it will fight for those human freedoms that can eventually allow us to connect with our soul's reality (although it's harder to get to our Pisces hidden treasures when we live in a world that denies the importance of nurturing an inner life). Aquarius helps us shake off the social pressure to conform, so that we are in a better state of mind to explore what we are really all about inside, on our own terms.

Those of us with Aquarius/Pisces energies highlighted in our chart may not be easily understood by others, since we seem to operate on a different wavelength than most people. It's as if we are not completely of this Earth. We seem to ignore the rules and regulations set up by our society, in favor of designing our own creative pattern of living (which may appear to be no pattern at all, since consistency may not be a strong trait within us). We'll need unusual stimulation in life to keep us engaged; otherwise we'll detach from most mundane affairs that seem too worldly to relate to. We'd rather go where inspiration and intuition lead us.

Our ability to feel for those in desperate need urges us to become involved in charitable causes that may not always be popular. Our ecological concerns can even seem "far-out" to others (think of those first Aquarius/Pisces types who were frantically trying to get nations to address the ominous ozone-layer problem—many were probably viewed as crazy). These folks can seem like prophets "crying out in the wilderness" in their attempt to appeal to an ignorant, indifferent world to come to its senses—only to be labeled instead as "wackos" or "outer-fringe alarmists." This is a tough combo to have, if we're living in highly industrialized societies that show little regard for Nature and the planet as a whole.

AQUARIUS/PISCES ASTRO-LEBRITIES

Paul Newman, actor: (Sun in Aquarius, Moon in Pisces)

Toni Morrison, writer: (Sun in Aquarius, Moon in Pisces)

Garth Brooks, singer: (Sun in Aquarius, Moon in Pisces)

Glenn Close, actress: (Sun in Pisces, Moon in Aquarius)

Prince Edward, British royalty: (Sun in Pisces, Moon in Aquarius)

Joanne Woodward, actress: (Sun in Pisces, Moon in Aquarius)

Pisces/Aries

Pisces, at first, seems to have little in common with Aries. It is the least self-seeking of all signs, whereas Aries is the least willing to put itself in other people's shoes long enough to feel what life must be like for them—something that empathetic Pisces has little trouble doing. The Ram doesn't understand selflessness, yet the Fishes are reluctant to take a "me-first" approach to life. Still, Pisces is learning to listen to and trust its inner voice, rather than be swayed by external influences that pull it emotionally in different directions (to best develop its strengths, Pisces needs to feel unified from within). Aries is a sign that typically only listens to itself, while blocking out all unwanted "noise" coming from its environment, especially critical feedback.

When well managed, this combo can tune out distracting facets of the world that divert our attention from our subjective awareness of self. While Aries doesn't contemplate life with any sense of true depth, it nonetheless is keenly in touch with itself whenever it spontaneously acts on its instincts; impulse quickly ignites self-styled action. Uncertain Pisces is usually slow to move its energies out into the world and to act assertively on its desires and needs. Yet doing so is often the only way for the Fishes' magic to manifest. The Universe cannot and will not do all the work, no matter how devotedly Pisces may chant or meditate.

With Aries involved, Pisces needs to better materialize the gifts of Spirit by applying physical effort, backed by a little courage and daring. This water sign can learn a lot from watching Aries generate the heat and vitality required to manifest something new in the world. The Ram never asks for permission before acting on whatever it finds stimulating—it just takes the big leap in the hope and with the faith that it will succeed. Ironically, Pisces is loaded with hope and faith, except when dealing with the material world in practical terms, where it often feels inadequate and riddled with self-doubt.

Although sometimes content merely to contemplate abstractions and intangibles, Pisces must discover how to manifest its power as structured form, and in inspiring, imaginative ways. Pisces also learns from Aries how even the most beautiful, collective dreams are best realized by first activating personal will and determination.

Both signs do best when adopting a "To thine own self be true" policy. They do poorly when others try to lead them by the nose and dictate their lives. Aries and Pisces often have to be by themselves, without social interaction, to recharge their batteries. Fiery Aries—while not a sign that can really appreciate long stretches of solitude—adopts a positive, self-encouraging attitude toward acting independently; it needs to feel free to do what it wants, without others getting in the way. Thus, flying solo comes natural to the Ram. Pisces, in order to renew its soul, must periodically go into seclusion. Tranquility is important to all water signs, but Pisces—who psychologically takes on the burdens of the world—is most in need of periodic internal rest, and that means shutting off excess outer stimulation and turning within for a little peace.

Thus, this combo supports lifestyles that remove us from crowds. A lone-wolf streak is evident, even if this is only inwardly perceived. Pisces/Aries types are not at home with many of the social rituals expected of them; they tend to withdraw from situations that require gregarious behavior (although Pisces can sacrifice its needs, now and then, and play the chameleon who blends in to any social environment, something uncooperative Aries has less success in doing). It is important to make sure that being alone doesn't turn into loneliness (the Fishes are susceptible to feelings of social rejection and suffer a sense of isolation when unable to merge with others; Aries is less prone to need people's company).

Those of us with Pisces/Aries energies emphasized in our chart seem to be full of paradoxes. On one hand, we appear to be head-strong, self-assured, and full of dynamic energy (Aries). People see us as quite willing to tackle immediate challenges with a sense of self-as-surance. Yet our Pisces side can harbor irrational fears, even those that allow us to underestimate our strengths. We tend to retreat from situations that we feel we cannot emotionally handle, due to our acute sensitivity to conflict. Withdrawing into ourselves becomes our de-fense, whereby we shut out all outside influences, in favor of a some-times unhealthy self-preoccupation.

Actually, because Pisces is highly adaptable, the Aries part of us—even if somewhat innocently—will spur us to take chances in life by going down new paths in imaginative ways (with Pisces, we may even feel guided by protective, unseen forces). Still, there will be times when a strange passivity takes over and we fail to grab for opportuni-ties in the here and now that could launch us in a fresh direction. It's best not to mull over matters too much, but instead to take action when the inspiration hits—and it will!

PISCES/ARIES ASTRO-LEBRITIES

Jean Harlow, actress: (Sun in Pisces, Moon in Aries)

James Taylor, musician: (Sun in Pisces, Moon in Aries)

Lynn Redgrave, actress: (Sun in Pisces, Moon in Aries)

Hugh Hefner, publisher: (Sun in Aries, Moon in Pisces)

Victoria Addams, singer: (Sun in Aries, Moon in Pisces)

Kareem Abdul-Jabbar, basketball pro: (Sun in Aries, Moon in Pisces)

SIGNS THAT QUINCUNX

Like signs that semisextile, signs that quincunx share dissimilar elements *and* modes, and thus appear different in many ways. Their oddball relationships are stimulating but often frictional—they can act as irritants to each other—even though these signs are less openly confrontational than are signs that oppose. They are also less sharply at odds with one another than are signs that square. Our sense of what both signs can offer each other is not all that clear, at least not at first.

Still, quincunxing signs nag us to find sensible, well-considered ways to adjust any faulty attitudes—as some internal corrections are needed—in order to improve our understanding of how to better apply the strengths they represent. Until then, such signs do not work well together because their temperaments and objectives are too dissimilar (also, they are not next-door neighbors, as are signs that semisextile).

Something here may seem out of focus, and this can result in an unproductive exchange of energies—at least until we consciously work to integrate these contrasting forces better. Until then, frustrations can occur that leave us feeling ineffectual and at loose ends, especially regarding how to satisfy the needs of these signs.

The tensions produced by quincunxing signs pressure us, at some time, to take analytical measures to resolve our inner differences. Something inside us here is not working well and needs to be fixed. We are motivated to thoughtfully make essential modifications that can enhance the way we function, yet this requires that we first dissect the parts of us that are problematic. Once we reassemble the energies of these signs, we are able to utilize them more effectively. From this perspective, quincunxing signs help us undergo personal alterations that are therapeutic.

We may also need to learn to handle these energies in a more organized and discriminating manner, since we otherwise can drain ourselves if we become careless in our expression of these signs. Remember, we are pressured to improve the interaction of our quincunxing signs, and thus we must learn to spot and eliminate traits and habits that are unproductive or self-defeating. Greater self-discipline can help us better regulate these forces. Whatever impedes our inner growth must be routed out. A spirit of cooperation on our part is helpful, since without it, things can remain dysfunctional, and in ways that adversely affect our physical or mental health (and even how we socially adjust to the world).

Quincunxing signs feel as if they are in a strained but curious relationship, one that requires constant adaptability. They don't seem to read each other easily—as if they have personal biases or blind spots —therefore, smooth interaction becomes a challenge. Yet unlike signs that square, signs that quincunx don't discomfort one another in ways that demand that they dynamically act on resolving their tensions; or sometimes they act in indirect ways that fail to address the crux of the matter. Such energies are not always efficiently utilized, as we are often in the dark about why certain traits of these signs seem to be out of alignment within us. However, because a degree of disorganization is present, we may need to adapt to the fact that life will have its flaws and that any mistakes we make are actually steppingstones to self-improvement.

Therefore, we'll need to make a conscious effort to restructure these signs' energies so that we can achieve success, even if only in small ways. Perhaps we can even function well in situations that are otherwise chaotic or unstructured; we are less often thrown off course by things that are disorderly, since somehow such "not so picture-perfect" conditions seem familiar to us on an inner level. If nothing else, quincunxing signs help create interesting personalities!

Aries/Virgo

The thought of trying to find something in Aries that is similar to Virgo may seem far-fetched. It's clear that the Ram is weak on staying power. It lacks the motivation to finish whatever it starts, should matters drag on or lose their initial momentum. This is quite unlike Virgo, who can be painstakingly patient and attentive, quietly persevering until its work is completed. Virgo outlines its task with care, thoughtfully fleshing out details before even beginning projects. Aries instead feels impelled to daringly take the big plunge, perhaps only later to discover the unanticipated complexities involved.

This eagerness often renders Aries insufficiently equipped at the start, whereas Virgo is typically well prepared. Aries thrives on impulse, capitalizing on spontaneity. Virgo is more secure when it can intelligently evaluate matters; it prefers thoroughly planned activity. Aries relishes the thrill of welcoming the unknown, since this provides the levels of challenge, excitement, and tension on which the Ram thrives. Yet Virgo is unnerved by the unpredictable elements of life and finds such "excitement" to be nerve-racking and sometimes foolhardy.

So what might Aries and Virgo have in common? Well-managed Virgo energy has a talent for unclogging whatever could slow down the workings of any system. Valuing efficiency, the Analyzer aims to unclutter and streamline whenever possible. Although observant of life's many pieces, Virgo seeks to reduce experience to only that which supports the most useful basics. Similarly, Aries also wants to trim the fat and focus solely on what it regards as the prime focus of its immediate interest. It, too, hates clutter, and seeks to remove any barriers in its way, although its methods of removal are sometimes hasty and careless.

Thus, both Aries and Virgo want quick and easy access to things. Aries simply *wants* it, refusing to be bogged down by obstacles (red tape) or too much detail (small print). Virgo realizes that all this takes more than an Arien act of sheer will. Virgo first organizes, categorizes, and compartmentalizes so that—later on—it is assured ready availability. While their tempos differ, both signs desire similar end results. They certainly dislike to search for things they need at the moment (of course, Virgo is better at keeping track of where it last placed or saw something than Aries, who can instead toss various things here and there without paying adequate attention).

Aries/Virgo types can be very impatient with people who don't get to the point; these signs dislike long-windedness in others and are not impressed by those who brag a lot (actually, Aries itself is guilty of boasting about its exploits, being an irrepressible fire sign, while Virgo is truly humble and even self-effacing at times). Also, self-conscious

Virgo can evoke Aries' less-secure nature (even though inner self-doubt often goads the Ram to push personal limits aside, as it thrusts its way into life; it has something to prove to itself about overcoming any weaknesses). Folks with this combo thus can work hard improving themselves rather than knuckle under when confronting challenges.

There is also a testy side to the nature of these two signs. The Analyzer can be irritable when things don't work as they should, whereas the Ram gets downright angry when something malfunctions. Both signs loathe wasting time and needlessly waiting around, since there's always so much to do (these signs love staying busy). Yet peevishness can result when Aries/Virgo types have to deal with slow-witted people who don't have their act together. Aries/Virgo folks demand speedy efficiency. They'd obviously like to do things without the annoying interference of those who are less alert and competent.

Those of us with Aries/Virgo energies emphasized in our chart, especially when the Aries side of us is stronger, are apt to energetically accomplish a lot in a day, as long as we stay organized and focused. Outside distractions need to be eliminated for us to work at our best. This may be tricky, since Aries unconsciously invites new stimulation to keep things from becoming tedious, and so its focus is less steady. But maybe this is good for our Virgo side as well, since concentrating too much mental energy on just one thing can be draining and even unhealthy. Aries has to do something physical to be satisfied, which helps Virgo get its proper exercise (otherwise, the Analyzer ends up only exercising its mind too much, while failing to look after its bodily needs).

We also can be hard-working once we feel we are in a competitive situation. When a clear, realistic goal is in sight, we are determined to succeed, once left alone to devise our strategy. However, we'll need to brush up on our "people" skills. Neither sign is all that sociable; they prefer more time alone, with no one to cater to. We may have a no-nonsense way of handling people that can seem to lack emotional sensitivity (we're more functional and exacting than warm and sympathetic). We also may not relax around others easily and may fidget when we have little to do. Since we detest being idle, it is best for us to stay productive and active.

ARIES/VIRGO ASTRO-LEBRITIES
Emmylou Harris, singer: (Sun in Aries, Moon in Virgo)
J. P. Morgan, financier: (Sun in Aries, Moon in Virgo)
Camille Paglia, writer: (Sun in Aries, Moon in Virgo)

Jeremy Irons, actor: (Sun in Virgo, Moon in Aries)
Lily Tomlin, comedian-actress: (Sun in Virgo, Moon in Aries)
Leonard Bernstein, composer: (Sun in Virgo, Moon in Aries)

Taurus/Libra

Immediately, we see that these two signs are associated with Venus. This combo suggests a disposition that is usually pleasant, agreeable, and—emotionally—not easily ruffled. Poise and composure are emphasized. Being rushed, pressured, or treated roughly creates internal disharmony for these two peacemakers, while gentle persuasion and kindness work wonders. Taurus especially seeks to operate at a slower pace, since it enjoys savoring the moment, but also because it needs a quiet, unhurried environment in which to feel secure and grounded.

Libra enjoys a quicker and more dynamic tempo than does Taurus. The Balancer, after all, is cardinal in orientation and is thus more movement-oriented. Still, this duo describes a temperament that seeks to avoid tension and conflict in life. These signs appreciate cooperation and support harmonious outcomes. Pleasurable activities that are relaxing and stress-reducing are actively pursued.

Both signs, being affectionate, need open demonstrations of love and gentleness from others. However, Libra—as an air sign—seeks more than hugs and kisses; it also needs to hear sincere words of love said out loud. Such tender, verbal communication is less forthcoming from Taurus, but reassuring physical touch—less important to Libra—is essential for the Bull. Taurus and Libra are each keenly attentive to beauty in all its expressions; symmetry and color coordination are quite appealing. Artistic Taurus loves the beauty of physical form, and even melody in music, and so does aesthetic Libra. In addition, this Venusian air sign also enjoys the refinement of well-crafted thoughts (literature) and theories (elegant scientific hypotheses). Not limited only to that which appeals to the physical senses, Libra enjoys beauty's more abstract qualities.

Being appreciated seems to be important to Taurus/Libra types. These typically calm and easygoing personalities tend to be genuinely sweet and nice to others, yet they want to be shown equal consideration in return. Actually, Taurus is less ingratiating than is potentially crafty Libra, who'll sometimes flatter others just to ensure the success of its personal objectives. The socially unsophisticated Bull is less manipulative in its human interactions (probably because it's less psychologically savvy about people and doesn't really want to expend energy trying to figure them out). Yet Libra will use subtle strategies to put itself in desirable social situations, and sometimes at the expense of others (although the Balancer rarely sees it that way).

The Bull is very much attached to what it sees and feels—there is little about its nature that can be called aloof or impersonal (however, Taurus can show an indifference to that which arouses little or no initial emotional response). On the other hand, Libra can express an interest in someone or something, while it still manages to keep an arm's-length distance, emotionally. It can observe things with dispassionate objectivity, once it has established sufficient space. In contrast, Taurus operates on a more instinctive and even hormonal level. It almost cannot help having strong, sensory reactions to whatever it finds itself magnetically drawn to—responses that are clearly more a product of instinct than intellect.

Folks with this combo emphasized can immerse themselves in the material world in order to gratify their appetites (Taurus), while they also learn to pull back and intelligently evaluate such experiences (Libra). They need to determine here if and when they are unwittingly creating unwanted, personal imbalances. Are their indulgences going too far? (For example, both signs have a "sweet tooth," which can lead to becoming unappealingly overweight.) Libran-style vacillation is less a problem for Taurus, although inner hesitancy can lead to immobilization when both signs are unsure about making final decisions. Libra dreads facing unwanted consequences, while Taurus instinctively senses when it's moving in a dubious direction that could make its life complicated (and that's when the Bull slams on the brakes and instead firmly holds its ground).

Those of us with Taurus/Libra energies highlighted in our chart have an easy charm that helps put others in a more relaxed frame of mind. Our magnetism readily attracts people, which is perhaps something that Libra enjoys more so than Taurus (being a less sociable sign). We are challenged to discern, through trial and error, when it pays for us to become less fixed in our ways or rooted in our impressions. Our Libra side is teaching us to be more yielding to those who, in the long run, can help us attain the valued Taurean security we need. We mustn't be so quick to reject their assistance and good advice, for fear that we'll end up obligated to them at a later date (which is one reason why the Bull would rather remain totally self-sufficient).

If we can overcome the tendency to stall—especially when taking some sort of action is actually better than taking none at all—we will find that Libra's sharp perspective combined with Taurus' sound instincts can become invaluable assets that help us weigh all our available options in life. We may excel in careers requiring that we carefully listen to others and determine how to clarify and best implement their needs in sensible ways (of course, we hopefully will do the same for ourselves). If potential bouts of laziness can be overcome through conscious self-discipline, then Taurus/Libra can be a productive mix of energies that will teach us how to find practical ways to please ourselves and others at the same time.

Taurus/Libra Astro-lebrities

Henry Fonda, actor: (Sun in Taurus, Moon in Libra)
Judy Collins, singer: (Sun in Taurus, Moon in Libra)
Billy Joel, singer: (Sun in Taurus, Moon in Libra)

Angie Dickinson, actress: (Sun in Libra, Moon in Taurus)
F. Scott Fitzgerald, writer: (Sun in Libra, Moon in Taurus)
Carrie Fisher, actress-writer: (Sun in Libra, Moon in Taurus)

Gemini/Scorpio

Here are two signs that seem to be in stark contrast: Gemini is unwilling to stick to one topic long enough to develop a penetrating understanding of it, while Scorpio is committed to delve deeply into any complex subject it finds enthralling. Unlike the Twins, the Scorpion will thoroughly investigate matters of interest, and often silently so; however, it's not one to quickly communicate whatever it knows or has uncovered from its careful study of life. It would rather quietly mull over what it has secretly unearthed. Actually, to accept the often unsettling findings of Scorpio's inner probings requires a keen mind, like Gemini's—one that is highly flexible and free of emotional defensiveness. Deep psycho-exploration here thus combines with a helpful and necessary degree of cool-headed detachment.

In contrast, airy Gemini likes to quickly get its thoughts off its chest, and has little trouble verbalizing what it knows, and in an animated way that others find lucid (even if too chatty at times). The Twins hate to unnecessarily keep listeners in the dark regarding here-and-now information. They will also casually scan the immediate environment just long enough to get the gist of what's happening. Gemini doesn't need to dwell intensely on something or somebody to satisfy its momentary interests; its restless spirit renders it mentally ever on the go.

However, what these two signs have in common is curiosity. They each want to know the "hows and whys" behind a wide range of conditions in life. Both could be accused of being nosy in their search for clear answers, with Gemini being more obvious and to-the-point about wanting information than Scorpio. Actually, the Scorpion has a burning need to know facts that are mostly hidden, yet it won't initially take Gemini's straightforward approach to get at the information it desires. It will instead penetrate issues in more indirect ways.

Still, these signs, when skillfully combined, suggest an astute awareness regarding what's happening in the moment. Eagle-eyed Scorpio can effectively joins forces with wide-awake Gemini in a manner that suggests a high state of alertness and mental acuity. They are good at sizing up people and situations quickly.

However, Scorpio—with its capacity to fixate on whatever stirs its emotions—looks at Gemini as a sign quite lacking in an ability to concentrate powerfully. (One thing that the Scorpion cannot be accused of is being easily distracted.) However, the Twins can never be faulted for being so darn focused on an issue that they become dangerously obsessed. Gemini would hate to feel that it is being consumed by its interests, unlike single-minded Scorpio, who'll opt to get even deeper into its subject matter (the Scorpion comes even more alive when it is totally absorbed in something it feels it must possess, and that includes worldly knowledge and spiritual awareness).

This quincunx relationship requires constant mental adjustments regarding when to give intriguing matters our full and undivided attention versus when instead to take brief, interesting mental notes on life, and then willingly move on to something new. Gemini never wants to feel it's getting too fixated in its observations, whereas Scorpio loathes the superficiality that results when the Geminian mind is content to casually skim the surface. Plus Scorpio knows that what we say and what we really feel inside are often two different things.

If Gemini/Scorpio is highlighted in our chart, we are probably learning to exert self-control when it comes to communication, since we realize that our ill-chosen words can sting others at times. Actually, if our Scorpio side dominates, we often can be too upset to even talk when angered. Our wounded feelings are thus left unexplained, which can lead to needless misunderstandings. Yet if our Gemini side is more accessible, we are apt to run away from our hidden darkness or from those heavy relationships that could force us to confront our inner, painful parts. Gemini is not particularly eager to be psychoanalyzed— and when is that ever a fun thing to do? ask the Twins.

Gemini/Scorpio types like to inspect their surroundings a bit to see what can be revealed (although the Twins sense when it's best to stop poking around before something overwhelming blows up in their faces). As Scorpio is aroused by that which is less forthcoming (it becomes more persistent in its probings), it needs to learn when curiosity becomes downright intrusive. (At least Gemini knows the value of "changing the subject" when things start to get a little tense—plus it'll do anything to keep from getting bored, and to the Twins, Scorpio's passions can sound tediously one-track-minded.) Obviously, any field of interest that requires a sharp and adaptable intellect can capture the attention of this combo.

We'll need to know when to lighten up by working on developing a healthy sense of humor (brooding Scorpio is often not a barrel of laughs). Gemini helps effectively de-intensify Scorpionic energy whenever it's appropriate to do so, such as during those more carefree, social moments when an easygoing style boosts the communication process (Scorpio needs to learn to appreciate the art of mingling, something at which Gemini is an expert). On the other hand, there are occasions when focusing on things for long periods of time is essential, and that often will involve being alone, Scorpio-style. Gemini must be willing to adapt to such moments of solitude without feeling that it's undergoing some sort of unfair punishment. The Twins need quietness and stillness to keep from overcharging their already energized nervous systems, and Scorpio is thus an excellent sign to teach Gemini how best to do this.

GEMINI/SCORPIO ASTRO-LEBRITIES

John Wayne, actor: (Sun in Gemini, Moon in Scorpio)
Alanis Morrisette, singer: (Sun in Gemini, Moon in Scorpio)
Isadora Duncan, dancer: (Sun in Gemini, Moon in Scorpio)

Bonnie Raitt, singer: (Sun in Scorpio, Moon in Gemini)
Art Garfunkel, singer: (Sun in Scorpio, Moon in Gemini)
Goldie Hawn, actress: (Sun in Scorpio, Moon in Gemini)

Cancer/Sagittarius

What both Cancer and Sagittarius share in common is restlessness, thanks to the "I gotta move" cardinality of Cancer and the "I get around" mutability of fired-up Sagittarius. Cancer actively moves about within its subjective, inner realms in an attempt to discern what might best help it feel safe and settled. Its nature is to be forever responsive to its private, security needs. Yet the Crab has a harder time finding similar emotional contentment in the outer world, where it instead makes its moves indirectly, cautiously, and according to its ever-changing moods.

Sagittarius' restlessness is based more on an impulse to venture forth far beyond its place of origin; longing for external adventure, it's not a sign to go within and easily internalize its energies. Unlike Cancer, the Archer is certainly not the sheltered, homebody type, and the urge to mother others is nearly nonexistent. However, as a born social crusader, Sagittarius is protective of its upright, moral principles and broad-based ideologies. It will fight to preserve what it perceives to be time-honored, universal truths, and will also defend the rights and liberties of the oppressed, along with all other mistreated underdogs of society.

A sense of "family" and a need for human connection are shared by both signs. The Crab and the Archer must feel they are essential members of some larger social system. These signs don't do as well when isolated from others—they must have people in their day-to-day world. Cancer interprets a "real" family as mostly involving those who are related by blood ties, whereas Sagittarius will wander the globe in search of all possible kinds of kinship—the Archer belongs more to the diverse family of humankind.

Nonetheless, each sign seeks to experience meaningful social contact. Whether clannish and tribal (Cancer) or universal and impersonal (Sagittarius), these signs place importance on relating to others with genuine warmth and honesty. Fiery Sagittarius is much more open and gregarious than is the guarded Crab, who'll only blossom when the social atmosphere is right (watery Cancer must feel safe before it'll expose its often lively, expressive personality to others).

Sagittarius' ruling planet, Jupiter, has traditionally been regarded as being exalted in Cancer—meaning that here it can supposedly function at an optimum level. Jupiter and Cancer do seem to share a common desire to offer a comforting home to those who are helpless (stray cats, stray dogs, stray people) or to folks who are simply "on the road." Perhaps such an urge to shelter is mostly a Cancerian theme (explaining this sign's association with hotels, motels, hostels, and "bed-and-breakfast" inns). Still, Sagittarius is willing to freely share its pup tent, and just about whatever camping gear it owns, with any weary traveler in need. Both signs are blessed with a sense of hospitality, making others feel truly welcome.

Expect those with Cancer/Sagittarius highlighted in their chart to have a supportive, kindly, impressionable nature that allows them to open themselves sensitively to a wide range of human experiences. Their approach is based on strong feelings and intuitions (although the Archer is more at home with complete strangers than is the Crab). Cancer can be a real "softie," while Sagittarius is generously big-hearted. Together, they can unselfishly give of themselves to those in need. Both can also become passionately involved in issues that stir their souls, although they may have a hard time being objective or unbiased regarding such matters. They'll stick to their gut instincts and inspired hunches, rather than be swayed by cool logic or social pressure from others. They are not the detached, indifferent type.

Of course, Cancer is often too emotionally vulnerable and touchy for Sagittarius' taste; the Archer would rather not get as readily caught up in the stickiness of intimacy, or subject itself to the possible restrictions that binding attachments place on one's personal freedom. The Crab wants to get close and cozy, while the Archer demands plenty of uncluttered space in which to stretch. Cancer tends to stay put, happily at home, while Sagittarius has a yen to wander afar. The Crab is comforted by its familiar territory, while the Archer craves environments that are foreign, exotic, or even wild (as can be found in unspoiled Nature).

Those of us with these signs natally emphasized may try to downplay our tender and sentimental nature, should our Sagittarian side reflect our outer disposition (that's when others have little idea of how easily our feelings can get hurt, or of how insecure we are in our close relationships). Any sense of feeling emotionally wounded can often be masqueraded by Sagittarius' hearty sense of humor (being comical serves as a buffer against feeling pain). Some of us may even use abstract thinking or excessive spirituality as a way to avoid our feelings.

If our Cancerian side is more evident, needed internal adjustments will involve our development of a more encompassing intellectual perspective, one that allows us to pull back emotionally and envision the grander scheme of things. Along with any depth of human understanding, we'll need greater breadth of awareness. Even cultivating a philosophical sense of acceptance—not resignation—will help us feel less vulnerable to the ups and downs of life.

Cancer/Sagittarius Astro-lebrities

Milton Berle, comedian: (Sun in Cancer, Moon in Sagittarius)

Pierre Cardin, fashion designer: (Sun in Cancer, Moon in Sagittarius)

Jesse Ventura, wrestler-politician: (Sun in Cancer, Moon in Sagittarius)

Jimi Hendrix, musician: (Sun in Sagittarius, Moon in Cancer)

Julie Harris, actress: (Sun in Sagittarius, Moon in Cancer)

William Blake, poet-visionary: (Sun in Sagittarius, Moon in Cancer)

Leo/Capricorn

Leo and Capricorn seem almost glaringly opposite, at first. Leo, ignoring or defying its personal limits, boldly pours itself out into the world. Capricorn, fearful of judgment and reproach, conducts itself with a self-imposed reserve in order to secure the approval of both key authorities and society at large. The Goat, keen on following social protocol, sets up appropriate behavioral guidelines, while the Lion's "inner child" daringly sidesteps the rules of the game to instead openly embrace spontaneity and the will-to-be.

Leo is joyously extroverted and vividly self-expressive. Yet Capricorn, for all its social strivings, is an introvert at heart who's seldom comfortable with exposing its guarded inner nature. Although Leo burns brightly, with much heat and flame, Capricorn is cooler to the touch and can willingly subdue any momentary surge of passion in order to control its outer environment. Unlike Leo, Capricorn contemplates the consequences of its actions before taking the first step.

So, what could these signs possibly share in common? For one thing, Leo and Capricorn both want to operate in the driver's seat, where they can take charge of situations. Each shows an interest in managerial positions, and is often eager to act as a project's head supervisor. Leo will easily take command over any enterprise in which it is vitally interested. Capricorn also wants to run the show, although with a degree of cautiousness and unresolved insecurity. Capricorn seems to work harder to prove itself through its achievements, while Leo confidently approaches its goals fully expecting to ultimately receive approval and recognition. The Goat seems to unconsciously seek permission to do what otherwise comes naturally to the Lion.

Leadership roles and the ambition to reach greater social heights are interests that Leo and Capricorn share. The fixity (focus and concentration) of the Lion works well with the earthiness (the need to achieve tangible, solid results) of the Goat. Leo admires Capricorn's steadfast approach to attaining ultimate success via integrity and deservedness, rather than due to scheming power ploys or ruthless strategy. Capricorn has a high regard for Leo's undaunted feelings of self-assurance and its ability to centralize its power base in a seemingly well-orchestrated manner (the Lion is not scattered or fickle). Together, these signs can move mountains if need be in order to reach the pinnacle of achievement. Perseverance becomes a valued common trait.

Those folks with Leo/Capricorn emphasized in their chart have an important need to be honored and respected. They can be vulnerable in this regard, although they typically refuse to reveal this about themselves. Due to their contrasting psychological slants on life, Capricorn believes it must *earn* the world's respect and praise, while Leo assumes such recognition to be its birthright—Leo asks, "Why *wouldn't* anyone hold me in high regard?" Being held in such high esteem and appraised in a positive light are objectives that drive Leo/Capricorn types to make much happen for themselves in the world.

Capricorn is notorious for its ability to turn stony and chilly if approached or handled the wrong way—typically by someone to whom it feels superior, status-wise—yet, so can a miffed Leo, when on the receiving end of shoddy treatment or rudeness. However, due to its immensely forgiving nature and big-heartedness, Leo doesn't stay as cold, detached, or aloof as long as the Goat does. Still, both signs can be unduly class-conscious—social snobs of the worst kind. Leo/Capricorn types unfortunately are capable of judging and evaluating the worth of others based strictly on external appearances (although should this attitude be delicately pointed out to them, they will likely feel bad about this shallow, materialistic outlook of theirs).

Those of us with Leo/Capricorn highlighted in our chart can show an ability to operate outwardly with a great sense of self-command, which easily impresses those who admire such shows of inner strength and self-direction. We try to develop a sturdy "backbone" and will not knuckle under when the chips are down and the going gets tough. We probably won't function well if under the yoke of authority figures (even though Capricorn, with its fascination for paternalism, can accept being taken under the wing of a parental mentor—at least until it can finally take charge of itself and strike out on its own). Leo, however, will not enjoy being parented in such a manner and will pull away from this setup much more quickly and defiantly. In general, being a boss—rather than having a boss—is more appealing to the Lion and the Goat.

Leo and Capricorn want to identify themselves as winners, yet when defeated, their outer show of dignity and composure covers up any feelings of bitter disappointment very effectively. There can also be a certain level of classiness to be found with this combination, a certain polish in their self-presentation. Both signs are very performance-sensitive when under the spotlight and rarely permit their weaknesses to show.

Expect Capricorn to seldom get swept away by its emotions. Leo energy is often too theatrical and showy for Capricorn's taste. The Goat hates wasting time and precious resources, even if Leo figures there's always more where *that* came from, so why worry? The Lion's motto could well be "Live life well, love life fully." However, when managing both signs effectively, we handle ourselves in a no-nonsense manner once well-defined goals and objectives are at stake. Harnessing an enduring, purposeful energy is a must for any long-lasting rewards to be achieved here. We have what is needed to move upward in life socially and stay on top of our game.

Leo/Capricorn Astro-lebrities

Arnold Schwarzennegger, actor: (Sun in Leo/Moon in Capricorn)

Lucille Ball, actress-comedian: (Sun in Leo/Moon in Capricorn)

Napoleon, French emperor: (Sun in Leo/Moon in Capricorn)

Diane Sawyer, journalist: (Sun in Capricorn/Moon in Leo)

Faye Dunaway, actress: (Sun in Capricorn/Moon in Leo)

Jeane Dixon, psychic: (Sun in Capricorn/Moon in Leo)

Virgo/Aquarius

When Virgo and Aquarius join forces, it is quite unlikely that emotion will get in the way of clear-headed thinking. A cool, detached, highly cerebral quality results from this combination of signs, as well as a powerful reasoning ability that supports unbiased, scientific analysis. Both the Analyzer and the Water Bearer are intellectually eager to take things apart in order to reveal the fundamental factors in operation. Both signs, blessed with a healthy curiosity and a thirst for ongoing knowledge, seek to deal with the unadulterated facts, even when such realities defy normal expectations (especially so with Aquarius). Virgo/Aquarius types are typically intolerant of stupidity, willful ignorance, or muddled thinking.

Cautiously observant Virgo seeks to apply its ideas in sensible, workable ways, while Aquarius is content to adventurously explore those more offbeat, abstract realms that reflect the beauty and elegance of pure thought—Aquarius doesn't always invent useful theories, but it is capable of creating futuristic concepts that boggle the mind and challenge conventional thinking. However, practical Virgo isn't satisfied until it can put all wild-sounding theories to the acid test. "Show me the irrefutable proof," says Virgo.

Virgo and Aquarius each have an ongoing interest in finding smarter ways to improve the world. Both signs have a humane streak and a strong interest in civilizing culture. Unselfish Aquarius has a powerful social conscience; the Water Bearer senses that widespread human cooperation is vital to the otherwise elusive dream of world peace. Virgo knows the value of social service; it works hard to organize life in sensible, intelligent ways that keep society's engine running smoothly. The Analyzer will take effective measures to avoid collective chaos (although sometimes its compulsive need for order can seem repressive to futuristic Aquarian goals).

Together, Virgo and Aquarius foster an enlightened mindset that helps elevate community standards through educational and technological means, rather than purely by economic development. Neither sign enjoys slow, time-wasting procedures; each instead seeks to create better social systems of efficiency. A big difference, however, is that conservative Virgo tends to think small, while visionary Aquarius is likely to innovate on a universal scale. Somewhat restless with Virgo's limited focus, Aquarius finds the uninteresting minor details of any social project to be less essential than the broader, illuminating principles at work. Nevertheless, the Analyzer is gifted with a wonderfully pragmatic sensibility that most Aquarian enterprises need to succeed.

Those with Virgo/Aquarius emphasized in their chart are on the impersonal side; they are certainly not the sentimental type, easily moved to tears. Instead, they will likely adopt a more rational approach to life that suggests a practical idealism at work. Actually, Virgo will roll up its sleeves and work hard to support any reasonable, reality-based cause—one that will not disrupt society in a radical manner. Yet Aquarius has a revolutionary spirit that sometimes suggests a theoretical and impractical slant on controversial social issues. The Water Bearer can talk about needed improvement, all without knowing how to implement down-to-earth ways to make lasting reforms. Aquarius will need to draw on Virgo's patience and level-headed outlook on life, and not expect major progress to occur overnight.

On the other hand, Virgo will need to allow Aquarius to brainstorm unconventional solutions to life's common problems, since the Water Bearer "knows" a lot, intuitively, without first having to do painstaking research (unlike the Analyzer). Aquarius regards Virgo's method of fact-finding to be tedious and uninspiring. The Water

Bearer will instead take unexpected detours or use unorthodox short-cuts to get the data it needs.

Those of us with this combination will want to explore much of what life has to offer, especially that which is less understood or is in need of clarification. We are not afraid to be exposed to knowledge of all sorts, and thus will not tolerate censorship. Our intellect demands the freedom to explore whatever captures our attention. Although we may be blessed with a greater degree of objectivity than usual, we'll need to be careful that we don't lose touch with the feelings of others or even distance ourselves from our own emotional needs.

It would be good for us to work on being less dispassionate, since our demeanor may seem a tad too remote and lacking in drama (although others may find us to be interesting individualists). Our more personal, private feelings are certainly not easy to read on the surface. Still, as we must make do with what the Cosmos has given us, the combo of Virgo and Aquarius allows us to find progressive and practical outlets in which to use our brainpower, and hopefully in brilliant ways that will benefit timely humanitarian enterprises.

VIRGO/AQUARIUS ASTRO-LEBRITIES

H. G. Wells, scientist-writer: (Sun in Virgo/Moon in Aquarius)

Sophia Loren, actress: (Sun in Virgo/Moon in Aquarius)

Scott Hamilton, pro skater: (Sun in Virgo/Moon in Aquarius)

Vanessa Redgrave, actress: (Sun in Aquarius/Moon in Virgo)

Boris Spassky, chess pro: (Sun in Aquarius/Moon in Virgo)

Gertrude Stein, writer: (Sun in Aquarius/Moon in Virgo)

Libra/Pisces

Libra and Pisces are known to have a soft spot in their hearts for those in need of sympathy and encouragement. These signs can put themselves in other people's shoes long enough to induce deeper understanding and even compassion, especially for the unfairly treated underdogs of society. Being gentle spirits at heart, Libra/Pisces types know how to be calming and soothingly supportive to those in need.

The Balancer and the Fishes would never regard themselves as cold, selfish egotists. They are more givers than takers in relationships—

they'll bend over backwards to please others and keep the peace. Yet, if anything, they often feel much too affected and sometimes even over-powered by the energies of others—especially in ways that make these signs feel at odds with themselves. No wonder those with a Libra/Pisces emphasis can seem weak-willed, prone toward vacillation, and ham-pered by self-doubt. They have a problem acting directly on their de-sires, as if they must first seek permission from others.

Although they have trouble standing up for themselves, they iron-ically have little fear of fighting for the civil rights of others. However, unlike the Balancer, Pisces is not emotionally detached enough to ob-jectively view the many sides of an issue with a cool, logical head. It doesn't share Libra's mental composure. The highly emotional Fishes feel for the needs of all parties involved, with equal intensity, yet in ways that prevent this sign from taking a firm, final stand on various matters in question.

Perhaps both signs suffer from indecisiveness when too many choices are present; these are the more deliberate types who'll need plenty of time to carefully mull things over, rather than give in to sud-den, ill-considered impulses or rush to judgment. Yet sometimes this actually becomes a stalling technique used to postpone or avoid taking committed action. Libra especially dreads the consequences of faulty decision making, while Pisces remains indecisive in order to escape from confronting certain realities, especially unpleasant ones.

There is also a problem with learning how to say "no" to those who'd otherwise try to pressure Libra/Pisces types to go against their feelings, or to surrender unwisely to the iron will of another in a self-sabotaging manner. These folks can easily be taken advantage of by more domineering types who don't play fair. They can even be bullied should their passivity and potential cowardice be taken to the extreme. (Libra and Pisces will try to placate their enemies rather than engage in head-on combat; these signs are anything but bloodthirsty.)

However, being of the cardinal mode, Libra does have an assertive, fighting spirit—yet frustratingly, it often fails to defend itself ade-quately when necessary (that is, without relying on its allies to pitch in). Self-sacrificing Pisces can feel used in relationships, so much so that it can end up feeling like a victim or martyr. It needs to have a healthier sense of boundaries and self-imposed limits regarding how much of itself it will give to another. Even peacemaking Libra tends to yield too much, just to please people in an attempt to avoid conflict. Both signs need to get tougher by becoming less accommodating in their dealings with others.

This combo suggests a well-developed aesthetic sense, with actual artistic talents that need to be put to use and enjoyed. Repelled by that which is coarse or ugly, both signs—when adjusting well to one another—are drawn to beauty, refinement, and all that produces harmony. These signs are sensitive to the ambience of their surroundings. They have a hard time tolerating squalor (although, when very much out-of-tune, disorganized Pisces can create a visually chaotic environment that does little to uplift the soul).

Those with Libra/Pisces highlighted in their chart may have a temperament that can prove useful in the counseling fields. They make good listeners and are patient with others who are caught up in various life dilemmas, although airy Libra cannot handle too much emotional melodrama, unlike watery Pisces. In fact, Libra sees Pisces as being too readily able to identify with people's instabilities, while Pisces sees Libra as sympathetic but still too cool and detached to feel what others are really going through. Still, these signs will lend an ear to those undergoing tough times, and even offer a fresh perspective or an inspiring vision. If anything, they'll need to make sure their kindly, considerate natures are not being unfairly taken advantage of by devious, chronic users.

Those of us with a Libra/Pisces emphasis have delicate sensibilities that cannot easily tolerate the coarseness of life or the rudeness and even cruelty of people. These diplomatic signs support humane treatment, and together they instill a need to reach out and make society a better place to live. Idealism is strong. However, we'll need to toughen up psychologically so that we can stand up to the onslaught of worldly reality—with its heart-sinking disappointments and its blatant social injustices—rather than develop an ivory-tower intellect, where we remain numb to the emotional hurts and pains of ordinary living. We can help others tremendously once we learn to value our needed peace-making skills and our effective powers of persuasion.

Libra/Pisces Astro-lebrities

Rita Hayworth, actress: (Sun in Libra/Moon in Pisces)
Eugene O'Neill, playwright: (Sun in Libra/Moon in Pisces)
Marie Osmond, singer: (Sun in Libra/Moon in Pisces)

Michael Caine, actor: (Sun in Pisces/Moon in Libra)
Patricia Hearst, kidnapped heiress: (Sun in Pisces/Moon in Libra)
Frederic Chopin, composer: (Sun in Pisces/Moon in Libra)

Scorpio/Aries

Both Scorpio and Aries are associated with Mars, which suggests a double-dose of self-will and steely determination. These signs take nothing lightly, plus their fighting spirit is alive and well. This combo is made for combat and confrontation on all levels. Scorpio prefers to do battle in very shrewd and sly ways, since it's a master of subtle and somewhat sneaky maneuvers. The main "weapon" it employs is its psychological astuteness, which includes the ability to sniff out another's hidden vulnerabilities.

However—when in attack mode—Aries is more upfront about its intentions while also less complex in action. Aries doesn't want to struggle too hard to seize what it wants, while Scorpio will wait patiently for the pivotal moment to make its move. When provoked to anger, both signs can go for the jugular (and Scorpio will even hit "below the belt"). The Ram and the Scorpion won't readily allow themselves to be pressured by others or pushed around. Scorpio/Aries types are quite skilled in the art of self-defense and have a near-hatred of cowardly behavior (in themselves and in others). Together, they give off an air of strength and utter self-sufficiency (although deep emotional dependencies plague Scorpio, unlike Aries).

Nonetheless, Aries won't lay low and secretly plot its moves the way the Scorpion does. It feels unnatural for the Ram to conceal its actions or to prowl about in total darkness. Typical of the fire element, Aries strives to come clean and be direct about its intentions, and it certainly will not act underhandedly. Yet Scorpio finds this Aries' "out in the open, got nothing to hide" approach clearly lacking in a potent, self-protective strategy that is most needed for living in a world that cannot always be trusted. Before taking action, scheming Scorpio first sizes up any potential threats to its security or to its ability to control its surroundings. Yet Aries doesn't understand such Pluto-inspired guardedness, since the Ram is one of the zodiac's least-paranoid signs—it never expects to be ambushed or undermined by anybody.

Actually, Scorpio does admire Arien bravery, at least when it's not merely an example of foolhardiness in action. Living too much in the "now" can lead Aries to innocently do some pretty careless things, thinks Scorpio, and all because it didn't properly estimate the risks or hazards involved. But Aries sees the lack of true spontaneity in otherwise passionate Scorpio as an unfortunate deficiency (plus the Scorpion is tempted to prey upon the weak, whereas the Ram will boldly engage in warfare and such with an equal adversary—and even with someone mightier, David-and-Goliath style).

Those with Scorpio/Aries highlighted in their chart are fiercely independent, yet they need to be careful not to become too much the lone-wolf type who can't get close to anybody (actually, it is Scorpio—ironically, the needier of the two—who comes off, at first, as less approachable). These signs are natural challenge-seekers who love to test their power in the world. They can also be subject to temperamental outbursts when their actions are blocked by others. Scorpio/ Aries types are anything but mild-mannered and easygoing (and an all-too-quiet Scorpio can be a time bomb waiting to explode). They'll drive themselves (and others) hard, as they capitalize on vital opportunities in the moment.

If anything, Scorpio is trying to slow down Aries' tempo so that any action taken is not premature and thus less effective. The Scorpion believes in a gradual buildup of tension and desire to ensure a level of focus and concentration needed to overcome any obstacle. Any opponent is to be worn down psychologically by this sign's dogged persistence. Of course, sometimes Arien impulse—leading to sudden and decisive moves—works wonders to resolve issues before they become full-blown Scorpionic crises. The Ram can teach the Scorpion when to just take the plunge and dare to see what becomes stirred into motion as a result (Aries relishes rapid changes more so than cautious Scorpio).

In any event, we're dealing here with two very intense signs that hate to lose in the game of life, although their styles of winning differ. There is a militant quality with this combination that smacks of heavy-handedness. Scorpio/Aries types can be uncompromising and willful to the extreme. They can also have a powerful magnetism that some find quite sexy, but perhaps in a darkly dangerous way that arouses deeply buried responses in all parties involved.

Those of us with a Scorpio/Aries emphasis have to be careful not to turn our life into one big battle after another. If we have a problem with Arien impulse control, learning more about our psychological depths (Scorpio) may help us better understand what triggers us along these lines, thus preventing an endless clash of wills in our relationships. Since we take things so very personally—both signs can lash out when feeling criticized—we'll need to work on developing greater objectivity about ourselves. We're a mix of the pioneer and the revolutionary, each in need of demanding but rewarding avenues of creative release. Finding such outlets becomes an all-consuming task worth dedicating ourselves to.

Scorpio/Aries Astro-lebrities

Bill Gates, computer software pioneer: (Sun in Scorpio/Moon in Aries)

Jamie Lee Curtis, actress: (Sun in Scorpio/Moon in Aries)

Martin Luther, religious reformer: (Sun in Scorpio/Moon in Aries)

Eric Clapton, musician: (Sun in Aries/Moon in Scorpio)

Harry Houdini, magician: (Sun in Aries/Moon in Scorpio)

Francis Ford Coppola, director: (Sun in Aries/Moon in Scorpio)

Sagittarius/Taurus

Restless Sagittarius enthusiastically soars to stratospheric heights—even when only on abstract mental journeys—while tranquil Taurus stays firmly planted on stable ground and is content to graze in familiar pastures that promise nothing out of the ordinary. How much more different could these two signs be? Actually, one thing they share is an easy acceptance of prosperity. Both enjoy feeling rewarded by life in generous amounts. Neither believes in undue material self-denial and each thus expects to enjoy the finer things that good fortune can provide (although, for the more philosophical Archer, "good fortune" is not limited to monetary gains or worldly goods).

Taurus will work hard and steadily to earn and preserve its valued assets, while Sagittarius, perhaps on a sudden hunch, will buy fistfuls of lottery tickets in hopes of winning massive sums of money—instant wealth—thanks to its belief in sheer luck and good karma. Yet Sagittarius also gets bored and becomes antsy with too much material abundance, especially should it lead to fire-squelching inertia (that earthbound feeling of being fat, lazy, and uninspired). Feeling too pampered by earthly luxuries eventually becomes unappealing to the Archer, who'd rather use the blessings of wealth and privilege as a means to explore the world or to promote a universal appreciation of cross-cultural diversity. This sign has a philanthropic heart and believes that everyone needs a broad education in global awareness.

Taurus finds its inner peace by staying closer to home, where it can savor security in solid, basic ways. For the Bull, venturing abroad entails too many needless risks and unknowns—and even cultural adjustments—for it to be an attractive proposition. Luxury is not quite a Taurean obsession, since this sign favors frugality. The Bull is fixated on getting its money's worth on tangible purchases rather than gambling it all away in a bid to win the jackpot overnight, Sagittarian-style.

Being surrounded by possessions of quality and beauty is certainly important to the Bull, who's an excellent appraiser of that which is truly valuable in material terms (Taurus is famous for its discerning material instincts). Both signs love Nature, but in different ways. The Bull is happy to inhale the sights and sounds of the natural world from the comforting security of its well-tended backyard. A quiet walk down a nature trail or along the beach at dawn is the kind of serene, outdoor exposure Taurus enjoys.

Yet the Bull is less apt to "rough it" in the wilderness without at least a few creature comforts—unlike Sagittarius, the zodiac's natural backpacker who's willing to hitch a ride to wherever adventure leads. Sagittarius loves the game of challenging nature in daredevil ways (like climbing Mount Everest or getting precariously close to the rim of an active volcano's crater). The Archer also doesn't want to remain still when in natural settings, but is constantly on the move, exploring new territory. It has a great time feeling it's on exotic expeditions, preferably thrilling and mind-expanding ones.

Those with Sagittarius/Taurus emphasized in their chart may have to watch out about becoming too dogmatic in their beliefs. Taurus is famously stubborn, while Sagittarius is openly opinionated. Together, folks with this combo may not care to be intellectually challenged once their minds are made up about something (actually, Sagittarius invites theoretical debates, but Taurus remains unmoved by differing views). Still, their faith and trust in something can be solid as a rock. The Bull helps the Archer ground its lofty assumptions about the Cosmos in ways that make them more practical and workable (Sagittarius tends to overgeneralize matters, while Taurus prefers to define things in more specific terms).

However, Taurus will need to adjust to Sagittarius' ability to leap into experience without first having set expectations, aside from the overall sense of stimulation that new situations provide. The Bull usually likes to know what to anticipate ahead of time, but in this case, it will periodically need to trust how the future unfolds. Sagittarius often creates its own problems due to poor judgment—it overestimates positive outcomes while ignoring pertinent details along the way. Taurus thus provides a needed dose of reality which, although somewhat deflating, protects Sagittarius from overextending itself in unwise ways.

Those of us with Sagittarius/Taurus highlighted natally are probably very honest—even if a bit too direct—and are honorable in our

intentions; typically, our integrity is strong. Our sincerity is also evident to others, who sense we don't care much for phoniness in people.
What you see is what you get. Yet sensual Taurus combined with
"more is better" Sagittarius can also suggest an indulgent streak. We'll
need to know when to stop gorging ourselves (not only on food, but
on whatever else makes us feel good—including all the consciousness-
raising delights of the spiritual realm). We tend to overdo, since our
appetite to enjoy ourselves is powerful. Still, the Bull and the Archer—
working in harmony—will make sure that we treat ourselves to a little
heaven on Earth, especially if we've been generous in spirit to others
in need.

Sagittarius/Taurus Astro-lebrities

Dionne Warwick, singer: (Sun in Sagittarius/Moon in Taurus)

Jim Morrison, singer: (Sun in Sagittarius/Moon in Taurus)

Lucy Lui, actress: (Sun in Sagittarius/Moon in Taurus)

Liberace, pianist-entertainer: (Sun in Taurus/Moon in Sagittarius)

Glenda Jackson, actress: (Sun in Taurus/Moon in Sagittarius)

Johannes Brahms, composer: (Sun in Taurus/Moon in Sagittarius)

Capricorn/Gemini

At first, Capricorn seems too focused and heavy-handed for a sign as
casual and light-hearted as Gemini to handle. Of course, the Twins are
nonetheless curious about all the other signs—the Goat included—
and are mentally adaptable enough to find clever ways to communicate with each of them. Usually, Gemini will try to meet any sign on
its own mental turf (it's good at temporarily trying on another sign to
see how well it fits). The Twins learn to mimic those signs it has had
time to study (it's skillful at mirroring back the traits such signs display). For Gemini, imitating others is a fun game, although Capricorn
would hate to discover that its behaviorisms are the source of another
sign's fleeting amusement.

Gemini is quite playful, but Capricorn can almost be too serious-
minded for its own good. The Goat doesn't see life as loaded with the
surplus of lively options that Gemini perceives, and thus Capricorn

feels pressed by time to make the most of the few solid opportunities that do present themselves, as much as the limits of its circumstances allow. For this go-getter earth sign, there is a driving need to stay on track in life early on and to make every move count.

Yet Gemini loves its momentary distractions and diversions—anything that briefly veers off the main path to allow for a refreshing change of pace and scenery. So what could these signs possibly have in common? Gemini applies cool-headed logic when observing life. Emotions or sentiment seldom interfere with its evaluations. Capricorn, too, is less apt to let feelings get in the way of its rational analysis and practical decision making. In fact, the Goat's controlled demeanor gives the false impression that it's devoid of warm feelings. Thus, when combined with Gemini, Capricorn is mostly concerned about being clearly understood; it communicates with consummate precision and an air of authority. It wants its ideas to be recognized as important.

The Twins are somewhat impressed that Capricorn at least has its facts straight and can even verify much of the information it succinctly presents (it's obviously a careful thinker and a planner). Gemini has little trouble following Capricorn's steady train of thought. However, the Twins note that while accurate with its data, the Goat is not especially articulate or even relaxed or casual in its communications. But it is highly organized, which is something that can benefit the less-focused, less-orderly Gemini mind. Capricorn seems to hold back from getting things off its chest, for fear of critical judgment from others. Part of its adjustment to Gemini involves developing detachment, regarding the opinions of others. The Twins teach the Goat not to worry so much about what people think or say. Perhaps Capricorn projects its own rigid thinking onto others too much.

Capricorn/Gemini types are learning to appreciate mental self-discipline. The ability to concentrate helps keep them from otherwise scattering their attention in nonproductive ways. Patience is also to be learned (resulting in the power to say the right thing effectively at the right time). Often, Capricorn is too insecure to spontaneously speak its mind, for fear of offending others or sounding ignorant, or even unprepared. Gemini tries to let the Goat know that it's okay to shoot off one's mouth and make mistakes now and then; after all, the Twins laugh off their own silly errors, so they advise Capricorn to quit being so hard on itself.

The Goat likes to put real potential to use, and certainly feels that a mind like Gemini's is a terrible thing to waste. Such a sharp mentality needs proper harnessing in order to work as efficiently as it can. For Capricorn, that means dedication to an ongoing education. Gemini might end up with a Ph.D. or two, thanks to Capricorn's ambition, but it doesn't want to turn out to be brainy but dryly intellectual (which can happen when earth combines with air). Such a Capricorn/Gemini temperament could reflect the way society envisions professional mathematicians: great with numbers and abstractions, but a little awkward at cocktail parties. These types are uncomfortable with small talk and friendly chitchat (Capricorn even hates to waste speech).

While those of us with Capricorn/Gemini emphasized in our chart may appreciate a wide range of intellectual interests, we also realize that to get anywhere in life, we must stick to what we know best. The Goat in us is a realist who understands the consequences of spreading oneself too thin (something of which Gemini is often guilty). When we blend these signs well, after sufficient trial and error, we end up with a polished intellectual that has excellent faculties of discrimination. A discerning mind results that seldom gets sidetracked by nonessentials. Also, Capricorn thinks big and in societal terms. It keeps Gemini from getting too caught up in the trivial and the frivolous (frankly, the Twins could use a dose of seriousness).

In some fashion, Capricorn seems to get younger as it gets older (it loosens up, after starting out in life too psychologically weighed down by a sense of duty and responsibility). Gemini never quite loses its Peter Pan–like qualities, no matter its actual age. This combo of signs can thus be a delight as we advance into our elder years. We exhibit a mix of childlike sparkle and a mature wisdom earned through those life experiences that test our mettle most.

Capricorn/Gemini Astro-lebrities

Johannes Kepler, astronomer: (Sun in Capricorn/Moon in Gemini)

Joan Baez, singer-activist: (Sun in Capricorn/Moon in Gemini)

Louis Pasteur, scientist: (Sun in Capricorn/Moon in Gemini)

Stevie Nicks, singer: (Sun in Gemini/Moon in Capricorn)

F. Lee Bailey, lawyer: (Sun in Gemini/Moon in Capricorn)

Wynonna Judd, singer: (Sun in Gemini/Moon in Capricorn)

Aquarius/Cancer

Cancer is notorious for hating to take risks. A homebody by choice, it seems fearful of the big outer world's potential to randomly provoke security threats. What could the often timid Crab possibly have in common with a daring sign like Aquarius, who'll instead openly explore this crazy, collective experiment called life in an unusually robust manner? Surprisingly, a few similar themes can be established.

The Water Bearer can be unpredictable—especially when bored and restless—and will erratically refocus its attention on fresh mental stimuli as a sure-fire way to keep itself intellectually revved up. Such shifts can be radical. Cancer—especially when feeling insecure and crabby—will rapidly swing from one agitated mood to another (being cardinal, it is capable of quick and vigorous reactions). Cancerian changeability comes strictly from the gut and is at times irrational, whereas Aquarian instability (its Uranian side) operates mostly on dispassionately cerebral levels and is distinctly unemotional in tone. Nonetheless, both signs are prone to display sudden changes in behavior, the kind that catch others by surprise. Both show an unsettled, inconsistent side to their nature.

Aquarius is famous for its humanitarian concern for the plight of the downtrodden, the socially alienated, and all misunderstood rebels and rejects of society. It seeks to socially validate the worth and uphold the freedoms of all such underdogs, protecting them from further abuse. Cancer dreads social rejection and being misunderstood by others. The Crab is also sympathetic toward the helpless or whatever is in need of special protection from harm. It'll go on the defensive to shield the weak and the vulnerable from attack. Thus, Aquarius/Cancer folks feel the urge to assist and support those in dire need, and do so while exhibiting an odd mix of sensitivity and impersonality.

Cancer and Aquarius also share an interest in the concept of "family," yet from widely divergent perspectives. Aquarius is more the sociologist/anthropologist who thinks in idealistic terms of humanity at large, which involves themes of universal brotherhood and sisterhood. This broad definition of family involves strangers who share common ideological bonds. But for the Crab, bonding is a more intimate experience, requiring a smaller "tribe" of familiar faces on a steady, day-to-day basis—especially those who share a common ancestry.

While Aquarius tolerates—and even enjoys—communal setups where diverse groups, unrelated by blood, share futuristic ideals, the Crab's need for close emotional attachment does not resonate as well with the Water Bearer's intellectually abstract sense of social connection. Any group dynamic, for the Crab, has to seem personal and close-knit in order to work. Still, both signs appreciate friendly cooperation within any group structure.

Aquarius/Cancer types are often torn between wanting to forge ahead into the exciting world of tomorrow (Aquarius) versus attempting to retreat into the past by adhering to old-fashioned or outmoded conventions that provide a reliable sense of inner security (Cancer). If Cancerian consciousness dominates, then Aquarius' energy can display itself in a wayward, eccentric manner, whereby we rebel against advanced, innovative technology. Stubborn resistance to modernize one's life can have deep, emotional roots here. (Actually, Aquarius alone can willfully march in the opposite direction from any prevailing social trend, just to underscore its need for freedom from social indoctrination.)

Those of us with Aquarius/Cancer emphasized in our chart may respond to people in baffling ways. We can be walking contradictions—open and accessible one minute (Aquarius), but reserved and even withdrawn the next (Cancer). Actually, Cancer—due to the strong value it places on people's feelings—helps humanize detached Aquarius, who otherwise aloofly distances itself from certain emotional realities. This introduces an element of warmth that is often missing from the Water Bearer's temperament. Aquarius also offers Cancer a much-needed, wide-angled perspective on life, which helps the Crab become less caught up in petty grievances (we are less apt to get our feelings hurt over minor issues, since we are better at pulling back and allowing for a little objectivity). It's good to psychologically review our past to find out what we need to let go of, so that we can embrace a future that is less encumbered by burdensome emotional baggage. The skillful handling of this combo allows us to do so.

We have a genuine interest in helping people and in improving community relationships. We'll just need to know when we must have quality time alone to refresh our souls before we go out into the world once again to help reform society in humane, enlightened ways.

AQUARIUS/CANCER ASTRO-LEBRITIES

Clark Gable, actor: (Sun in Aquarius, Moon in Cancer)

Farrah Fawcett, actress: (Sun in Aquarius, Moon in Cancer)

Kenneth Branagh, actor-director: (Sun in Aquarius, Moon in Cancer)

Linda Ronstadt, singer: (Sun in Cancer/Moon in Aquarius)

Jerry Rubin, 60s activist: (Sun in Cancer/Moon in Aquarius)

Diana Spencer, Princess of Wales: (Sun in Cancer/Moon in Aquarius)

Pisces/Leo

What could Pisces, a sign of ego renunciation and selflessness, possibly have in common with Leo, a sign of self-approving ego? Leo oozes confidence and steady self-assurance; it knows it *will* have its way with life and be granted special privileges in all its personal endeavors. That's at least its assumption. Meanwhile, Pisces struggles with the concept of "I" and fears the consequences of undue self-preoccupation.

While "ego" can be a dirty word for Pisces, Leo finds that living a life as a complete nobody or just another nameless face—at the mercy of the collective will—is a dirty crime. This fire sign wonders why anyone would want to deliberately sacrifice anything as personal and vital as one's selfhood, just to fulfill some idealistic but impersonal group need. Actually, the Lion can be quite noble, high-minded, and filled with soaring and shining ideals. Meanwhile, Pisces endures suffering and pain while still believing in better tomorrows of humane love and social unification—the Fishes want a little paradise on Earth for everyone.

Both signs, when combined, push for optimistic outcomes based on a shared belief in luck and miracles. They each dream big dreams, have high hopes, and wish for all the best possible outcomes in life. Having faith and keeping the faith become central issues. Leo and Pisces are also big-hearted and generous in spirit. Leo likes to bestow gifts and rewards to those less blessed. It can be philanthropic and magnanimous to a fault. Pisces seldom thinks it has many worldly gifts to offer, but nevertheless pours out the inner wealth of its soul to those in special need. Folks with notable Pisces/Leo energies are certainly not tightwads or cheapskates. Stinginess is not in their nature. If anything, overdoing the kind-hearted "good will to all" bit may prove problematic when not tempered with a measure of common sense.

While polar-opposite Virgo can bring out Pisces' worrisome side —and Capricorn can evoke Pisces' fear of consequences plus its sense of social obligation or just plain ol' guilt—Leo stimulates Pisces' deep reservoir of emotionality and imagination. Expect Pisces/Leo types to have a dramatic streak and even a flair for the melodramatic. This colorful combo is excellent for acting and all forms of theatrics. Glamour-struck Leo loves to perform in glitzy ways, while Pisces yearns to lose its sense of self by playing the chameleon who masquerades in an outlandish, otherworldly manner. All avenues of creative escape are to be encouraged.

However, when storms clouds gather and our inner skies turn ominously threatening, some of us with a Pisces/Leo emphasis adopt darker moods that allow a more negative imagination to have full rein.

Emotionalism then manifests as hypersensitivity, undue touchiness, and even a weepy hopelessness. Reactions to perceived internal and external pressures can be exaggerated.

Practicality for both signs is an acquired taste. Leo believes in rewarding itself and sees no reason to be thrifty just for the sake of saving money and other resources. If the Lion really wants something, the cost factor becomes irrelevant. Pisces doesn't need a lot of material things for its happiness, nor do such physical possessions provide Pisces with the inner contentment it longs for. Still, it needs to curb a tendency to squander its worldly assets, like Leo.

Those of us with Pisces/Leo energies emphasized in our chart can also be extravagant in matters of love and romance. Here our heart definitely rules our head, making for sometimes gushing displays of passionate desire and intense yearning. Such romantic longings are typically less demonstrative for shy Pisces, a sign that possesses an enormous range of emotional subtleties and nuances. Still, the Fishes will accept no limits or boundaries when caught in the grip of a powerful love affair. Leo also throws all caution to the wind in its single-minded (fixed) attempt to woo all desirable suitors.

Each sign can luxuriate in love with the right "significant other." We may seldom be reasonable in our attempt to fulfill our needs and desires, yet we don't wish to be brought down from any emotional/sensual high we're on. Those of us with a Pisces/Leo emphasis can give and give some more, almost to a fault, even draining ourselves in the process. And should the love we offer be rejected or no longer appreciated, we can set ourselves up for a hard crash landing. We are not very good at emotional detachment when our heart and soul are aroused by another.

Astrologers should never underestimate the power of Pisces to put up a strong protective "barrier reef" by turning numb and unresponsive to feelings, when threatened or wounded. It defends itself by retreating to a hard-to-reach emotional space that can be nearly impenetrable. Such a similar shut-down state normally doesn't last as long for a pouting Leo, who feels more truly itself when radiating its innate sunniness and being upbeat about life. Yet for Pisces, a state of emotional with-drawal can hang around like a dark cloud for quite some time.

Both signs share an interest in protecting the innocent—whether they be children, animals, plants, and so on. Leo plays the hero who protects the weak from harm. Pisces—the savior—protects the social underdog, putting those it deems to be helpless under its fin to provide needed shelter and comfort. This combo can be quite soft-hearted. We Pisces/Leo folks share a capacity to smooth away life's rough and dis-tressing features and instead provide a warm sense of relief and com-fort. However, expect us to periodically indulge in sentimentalism.

PISCES/LEO ASTRO-LEBRITIES

Coco Chanel, fashion designer: (Sun in Leo/Moon in Pisces)
Percy Bysshe Shelley, poet: (Sun in Leo/Moon in Pisces)
Mata Hari, spy: (Sun in Leo/Moon in Pisces)

Lawrence Welk, bandleader: (Sun in Pisces/Moon in Leo)
Karen Carpenter, singer: (Sun in Pisces/Moon in Leo)
Jon Bon Jovi, singer: (Sun in Pisces/Moon in Leo)

PART THREE

Combining Signs
with Planets
& Houses

Chapter Eight

Planets in Signs

The zodiac personally comes alive for us once we link its energies to the planets and houses of our birth chart. This chapter offers some thoughts regarding natal planets found in each of the twelve signs. However, providing a more detailed, in-depth explanation of every planet/sign combination (i.e., Moon in Virgo, Mars in Pisces, Saturn in Libra, etc.) would encompass an entire book in itself. Even then, it's not possible to provide precise, astrological descriptions of how these planets and signs personally manifest for each of us. Nonetheless, helpful interpretive guidelines can be established. I'll touch on a few of the many planet/sign issues that exist.

Signs Influence Planets

How our natal planets—in their signs and houses—actually operate in our lives is something that might be better determined by an open, honest dialogue with a qualified astrologer during a professional session (or with ourselves, if we're long-time students of astrology and can look at our chart objectively). Although custom-tailored information cannot come from any astrology book, personal insights can be gleaned from in-depth, well-written texts. (Still, even trained astrologers are not all-knowing wizards who can instantly tell everything about a client's nature by just glancing at his or her chart. But experienced astrologers do make intelligent and often accurate assumptions regarding one's character traits, based on the symbolic details the chart provides.)

It is customary to consider a planet to be the one most altered by the characteristics of its natal sign, rather than to regard a sign as being primarily modified by the qualities of a natal planet. Although a sign's influence over a planet's expression typically predominates, both planet and sign actively blend their energies, for better or worse; a planet's nature is bound to determine which qualities of a sign will readily surface.

Still, don't expect Venus, while in Aries, to soften the disposition of this impetuous, aggressive fire sign. If anything, Aries hardens Venus by fostering a fondness for self-interest—especially in matters of love—and by encouraging assertive and impatient behavior in close relationships. Venus itself won't endow the Ram with charm, grace, or an appreciation for intimate sharing. Instead, it is headstrong Aries that conditions Venus to value more Martian traits, such as independence, self-reliance, and even a competitive, fighting spirit.

Mars Will Be Mars

As signs give us clues about the behavioral patterns that our natal planets adopt, they also best determine how these planets in action typically respond to various life situations, while even explaining the motives behind the action taken. Nevertheless, a sign does not change the fundamental nature of any planet. Mars will always be Mars, in whatever sign it is in, although that sign will color much of this fiery planet's expression. (It's like this: Bette Midler will always be Bette Midler, except that she'd give off completely different vibes if donning a nun's habit and wearing no makeup, versus dazzling a Las Vegas audience in her more glitzy, on-stage garb—it's the same Bette, but with a notably different look and demeanor.)

Grouping the Planets

The following descriptions are most relevant when the natal planets involved belong to the "personal" group: the Sun, the Moon, Mercury, Venus, and Mars. We can also sense, to a lesser degree, the workings of the natal signs of planets that make up the "social" group—Jupiter and Saturn. Yet we usually do not personally identify with natal signs associated with planets of the "transpersonal" group: Uranus, Neptune, and Pluto. (Our awareness of the traits associated with the signs of our North and South Nodes are also usually less conscious, perhaps until we further age and mature, and learn to more reflectively review our life from a soul perspective).

PLANETS IN ARIES

On Our Own

Having a planet in Aries is a sure indicator that there is a willful side to our nature—specified by the planet in question—that drives us to be clear and honest about ourselves, both in how we act and in what we desire. We are not to be hampered by those who unwisely attempt to thwart or deny our ever-emerging identity. We are learning here to fight against that possibility, directly and courageously. Nobody is to own us or dictate our moves. Our inner Arien fire energizes us to take charge of ourselves, without any need to first placate others or seek their permission and approval in matters most personal to our well-being.

Our Aries planets symbolize the budding development of a strong ego, especially along those lines that we personally deem to be well suited to our true nature, not someone else's limited view of who we are. The Cosmos permits us—without undue penalty—to engage in more "trial-and-error" or "hit-and-miss" situations than most signs are allowed. Our attempts to try something new—requiring guts and self-assurance—benefit our psychological growth, even if we don't actually succeed in our endeavors. It's making the effort and pushing hard that counts.

Since we can innocently take pioneering action once we feel the surge to move forward—and fearlessly ignore potential roadblocks—we openly dare ourselves to try our hand at many things that more self-analytical types would find too challenging and risky. Firsthand experience means a lot to Aries, as does the thrill of sheer spontaneity.

If there is a downside to having several Aries planets, it's partly due to a less-developed ability to understand what makes others tick, and what they need. We are less inclined to delve into the world of people, with any depth of perception. We probably won't see facets of ourselves reflected in those we attract—as if we're immune to projection—and we dislike folks who try to become too involved in structuring the details of our lives (we certainly don't want parental types breathing down our neck and setting up the daily rules by which we are to live).

Our Aries Planets

The **Moon** and **Venus**—two soft-hearted influences—don't feel quite at home in Aries, since this sign is not into "touchy-feely" interpretations of life. As the assertive Ram takes over, the passive-receptive Moon and Venus are less able to express their gentler ways. Yet, there is little about an Aries Moon or Venus that people misinterpret as a "pushover" mentality. Unwilling to submit to the domination of others, these two—while wearing fighting gear—are ready to clash, if need be, to protect their Arien autonomy. This Moon feels itself to be full of vitality, and will push forcefully to get its singular needs met—it's a bold-hearted Moon. Venus in this sign is not as polite, since Aries doesn't usually have patience for social niceties, nor does it take a tender approach to relating to others. Still, it won't act coy or play guessing games when it thinks it's in love—it wastes little time in pursuing another.

The **Sun** and **Jupiter**—being fire planets—feel emboldened in Aries and are loaded with a positive, can-do attitude—full speed ahead! They each admire the Ram's ability to give itself full permission to tackle whatever it desires in life, without feeling plagued by self-doubt. A go-getter's attitude is evident, backed by a daringness to try new approaches that prove vitalizing. Our ego is ablaze and feels potent when our Sun is in Aries; the will to take the lead is also strong, but an Aries Sun wants things to go according to its expectations, not someone else's. Jupiter here is quite a trailblazer, as Aries adds an entrepreneurial spirit to match this planet's adventurous streak. Perhaps impulsiveness is the main reason for poor judgment, as we can jump the gun and act too soon, when waiting would have yielded far better results.

Mercury and **Mars** get caught up easily in Arien momentum—they relish the fast and exciting pace of this quickly triggered sign. However, they also tend to be too headstrong in disposition, in ways that invite open confrontation. Still, they briskly take advantage of opportunities without much deliberation. Yet Mercury is a bit smart-mouthed in Aries; it fails to curb its tongue when riled. Aries thus turns argumentative, using Mercury to toss verbal ammo at any walking target. But this Mercury also suggests a pioneering mind that effortlessly

comes up with new ideas. Mars in Aries is a double dose of self-assertion in motion. This fired-up Mars moves swiftly, but sometimes lacks
a proper strategy—it plunges without looking, and refuses to use a
safety net. It also acts as if it were born without brakes, just an acceler-
ator. Still, Aries provides a fearlessness that allows Mars to forge
ahead, and not buckle at the knees, no matter how overwhelming the
task at hand appears—this Mars is a brave and ready warrior.

Saturn may initially feel at odds with much of what Aries stands
for, yet this quietly ambitious planet is determined to add strength
and endurance to whatever sign it is in. Here, Saturn helps weed out
Aries' more immature qualities, those that definitely hinder true accomplishment. Having little time for impatient signs that thoughtlessly leap before they look, Saturn instead implements restrictions
and delays in order to instill proper self-discipline. Aries in this regard
obviously needs a lot of work, according to Saturn. This planet's task
is made easier by the fact that the Ram has enough pluck to meet up
against all of life's obstacles and not be so quick to turn down a rousing challenge. Saturn likes knowing that about headstrong Aries.[1]

Healthy Anger?

Planets in Aries symbolize parts of us that need to acknowledge the
healthy side of anger, since we're likely to feel quite steamed up inside,
from time to time, and must find satisfying but appropriate ways to
vent our frustration. Life will also test the mettle of our Aries planets
when we face up to situational challenges and confrontational people.
It's never a good omen when folks with many planets in Aries timidly
respond to life or seek to withdraw from it. The Ram's dynamic energy is not to be stifled by undue fear or insecurity, since doing so robs
our body of energy—not to mention how inwardly frustrating behaving like a coward can feel.

We are also allowed to be more self-preoccupied without having to
be apologetic about it. We are freer to revolve around our own interests, to a degree. Life even permits us to quickly absorb our failures—
as long as we've enthusiastically tried to succeed—but then, we're to

pick ourselves up and continue to venture forth down fresher paths of Arien potential.

Brimming with Energy

Aries planets mean we are to discover what we need to feel vitalized by life. Our emerging strengths are to be activated and put to immediate use. Procrastination is best avoided. At times, we can rush things and thereby fail to do a decent job organizing our projects (one of the pitfalls of living too much in the Arien moment is not sufficiently planning ahead). Still, the Ram lets us know how great it is to be alive and brimming with vitality. Why stay still and be bored when there is so much to do that'll invigorate our abilities? We are also finding out how much better it is to be frank with others and not hold back what is bothering us inside. Getting all our tensions out in the open is a positive thing, as long as we don't overwhelm or antagonize people with more aggressive forms of self-release.

Our Future Prospects

Even if we don't have any planets in Aries at birth, the day will come when a planet by secondary progression or solar arc—such as the Moon—moves into this vigorous, self-motivated sign. That's when we get to see what it's like to take charge of our life in dynamic ways. We feel an inner power come alive, as greater self-will in action becomes apparent. The planet in question is allowed new starts regarding energized self-expression.

Planets in Taurus

No Big Rush

Having a planet or two in Taurus doesn't automatically mean we are destined to become "fat and lazy," even though complacency can be a problem with a strong Taurean emphasis—we get too comfy with the ways in which we habitually satisfy ourselves (although we're seldom the one who's complaining about that). Still, we may lack the heightened Arien drive to stay physically in motion, doing things all the time, rather than sitting or sleeping. Actually, planets in Taurus are learning to value sensible eating habits and proper rest. Always being on the go or eating in a hurry is not what the placid Bull desires.

Taurus also teaches us how to develop magnetism, whereby we draw to us those things that sustain us and provide desired stability. Constantly thrusting our energy out into the world, sometimes too forcefully, is counterproductive to what the Bull-related parts of us want and need. Composure and contentment are more what our Taurus planets desire. We are learning to inhale life leisurely in its most organic form—through sense-pleasing Nature itself.

Natal planets in Taurus imply that we are to value practical things as our life unfolds. Here is where we can nourish our talents and support self-worth in useful ways. Yet we won't appreciate being pushed or prodded, since we have our own reliable, natural timing to guide us, as well as an internal comfort level to consider. A slow and steady pace is typically a workable one for us—we'll only act on something once we feel good and ready.

Our Taurus Planets

The **Moon** and **Venus** feel at home in Taurus, even though they are also less challenged to grow beyond their accustomed responses to life. They have little trouble soaking up the Bull's energies in physical or emotional terms. The Moon is comforted to know that Taurus takes its security seriously, and that it carefully builds protective structures based on realistic needs. However, Taurus reinforces the Moon's possessive instincts, thus accentuating its difficulty in letting go of people and things. Venus, while less clingy in Taurus, also desires close physical contact. It enjoys fulfilling earthy, sensual appetites that provide lasting comfort. In love, the Bull is straightforward about its basic desires, and is content with loved ones who barely change in temperament—who remain predictable. Possessiveness, again, is an issue to resolve.

The **Sun** and **Jupiter** confidently make use of Taurus' determination to succeed in the material realm. Jupiter is especially receptive to prosperity, although here it's less careless about spending money—the Bull's conservative streak means it's not a risk taker. Jupiter is thus to expand in more pragmatic ways. It prefers here to stay closer to home rather than journey to parts unknown to seek its fortune. The Sun shows a determination to be materially grounded; money and possessions are related to self-esteem and power. We'll need to learn to enjoy the fruits of our labor, instead of just working hard to make a living. These two planets have an optimistic streak that favors Taurus' need to feel good about its life and secure about its future.

Mercury and **Mars**, two speedy planets, are made to go at a slower pace that'll seems less natural to them, when in this earth sign. Yet, this gives them opportunities to get more work done, without needless distraction or restlessness becoming a problem. Mercury is adaptable in whatever sign it's in, and will find stimulating things to do. Mercury here needs time to think things through, since it wants solid results. This Mercury plans its projects more carefully and hates wasting time, energy, and—of course—money! It's Mars that may balk at Taurus' unadventurous approach to living and its inclination to refrain from taking assertive and even impulsive action. (Luckily for Mars, the Bull likes sex and doesn't mind getting hot and sweaty.) Headstrong Mars can be most obstinate in Taurus, yet it is not so quick to be confrontational.

Saturn is an earthy planet and thus has more in common with Taurean values, such as thrift and self-discipline. The hard-working Bull gets Saturn's approval. This planet doesn't have to worry about a lack of structure in Taurus' life, since this sign likes to build a firm base of operations for itself. If anything, it's the sense-gratifying, indulgent side of Taurus that Saturn frowns upon. Also, the Bull's attacks of inertia concern Saturn, who'd rather make every minute a productive one. Together, these two can build well-organized material frameworks that last the test of time.

Penny Pincher?

Our Taurus planets represent parts of our makeup that allow us to live comfortably in our own skin. Here we can feel at ease with who we are, rather than strive and struggle to become something more. This is a sign that enhances our quiet enjoyment of the simpler things in life. Most planets in this sign will rarely rebel against routine (the one exception, perhaps, is Uranus); Taurus planets typically symbolize habit-prone facets of ourselves that do not welcome sudden or radical change. Life alterations that are gradually introduced are more easily accepted.

What about money? Planets in Taurus suggest that, while there may be an above-average interest in financial matters, extravagance is usually not a problem. This is a frugal sign. If anything, learning to enjoy spending our money is more a challenge. Taurus will indeed spend, but seldom foolishly. If our self-esteem is in good shape, we'll most likely buy those things that please us, without feeling pangs of guilt or anxiety. If self-worth is shaky, we can be tightwads who regret every penny we spend—money for us never provides contentment.

Bullheaded

As affectionate as we can be—even if not particularly demonstrative—those of us with several planets in Taurus need quality time alone. We're really not all that people-oriented, and probably feel uncomfortable in crowds (especially among strangers). Like Aries, Taurus planets promote self-sufficiency. We are unlikely to lean on others, but instead will conduct our lives so that we're able to handle our responsibilities without assistance.

There is a purpose for the famous fixity associated with planets in Taurus. We are not to let others divert our attention from pursuing our long-range goals. Like people with Aries planets, we are to remain single-minded in our intent, as long as it's clear that we're not staying stuck in ruts of our own making. Persistence is fine, as long as it doesn't degrade into sheer bullheadedness. Our instinct to stay put and to resist what's new in life is not always a smart way to operate. Yet if we are ever going to try fresh approaches to living, we do better when we are gently coaxed into the new conditions at hand—*never* pushed or forced!

Our planets in Taurus indicate we're very grounded, solid, and reliable. Yet we may attract others who aren't as sturdy inside or as dependable. Our inclination is to shoulder the responsibilities of those who are less organized or practical. But the one thing that gets Taurus in a state of rage is feeling deliberately used by ingrates who show little appreciation for the Bull's time-consuming efforts. That's when we refuse to be rock solid for others any longer (let them swim or sink). In a scenario such as this, expect our Taurus planets to explode!

Our Future Prospects

Even if we don't have any planets in Taurus at birth, someday a planet by secondary progression or solar arc—like the Moon—will move into this enduring, self-preserving sign. We can become more resourceful with our talents, in sensible ways that enhance our self-worth. It's time to enjoy the physical pleasures of earthly living, as we develop our artistic talents or aesthetic tastes. Also, current material and monetary concerns now require our practical assessment.

PLANETS IN GEMINI

In All Directions

Here's a case where having even one planet in Gemini feels like we're juggling two or three. Planets in this lively air sign act as if they are on an exploratory mission to eagerly observe the endless variety of life's ever-changing bits and pieces. These planets symbolize various parts of us that behave like eternal students, always looking for clear-cut answers to life's many questions. With several planets in this youthful sign, we may not appear to be fully grown up—we lack that trademark stiffness often associated with the humorless side of conventional adulthood. There is a bit of Peter Pan in us that keeps us effervescent.

Planets are perhaps more fidgety in this sign than they normally are in others. It's not in their nature to sit still while in toe-tapping Gemini. Mobility is important. We're likely to need a continuous change of scenery—and company—to keep us well stimulated. Our mind gets dull with too much of the same thing, and we thus get restless and eager to shoot off in different directions—any temporary diversion will do.

Our Gemini Planets

The **Moon** and **Venus** usually have a delightful time in this sign (especially Venus), although emotional depth is not what the Twins are all about—but neither is gloom and doom, deep insecurity, or fears of isolation (Gemini has little trouble socializing because it can easily drum up conversations with strangers). Thus, our lunar urge to connect to others is highly encouraged by this friendly and outgoing sign. Security for us is tied with keeping channels of communication open and active. Venus, while in Gemini, may forego its typical desire for intimacy in favor of establishing a wide range of fun, breezy alliances (unsentimental Gemini prefers less emotionally demanding contacts). This Venus has a knack for socializing and can interact with a variety of people, which keeps it from feeling bored. This sounds nice, but a Gemini Venus has to be careful not to relate to others in glib, shallow ways.

The fiery **Sun** and **Jupiter** enjoy the endless curiosity of Gemini. The Twins are always ready for something new, and these fire planets are dynamic enough to keep this sign busy and excited. These can be highly alert planet/sign combinations, always happy to learn more about everything, at least for the moment. The Sun likes to center its energies, even though it will take an act of solar will to keep Gemini well focused. Yet roving Jupiter is too undisciplined at times to prevent Gemini from unwisely scattering its forces. We can end up with a degree of attention deficit disorder, even though our optimism remains strong. We may try to do too many things at once, leading to disorganization. Still, the results seldom seem problematic. We thrive on change and will gamble with our future, especially wherever our enthusiastic mental energy takes us.

Mercury and **Mars** get intellectually revved up by Gemini and are ready for action. These are not tranquil planets, able to relax easily—so Gemini further accelerates their pace and increases a state of restlessness and even overactivity at times. We may find it difficult to sit around when there are so many things to do and people to bump into out there in the busy world. Gemini behaves in ways that Mercury seldom finds tedious. However, we could be accused of "spinning our wheels" mentally. We'll need to learn to concentrate on our interests more consistently. Mars is also apt to have too many irons in the fire, and intellectual energy can be squandered on short-lived, nonessential activities. Yet, when we are at our best, our versatility enables us to get a lot done quickly. When angry, this Mars uses sharp words—verbal barbs—to assault its intended target.

Saturn sees a potential for mind power in Gemini. It likes knowing that this sign is logical. The Twins refuse to cloud their critical faculties by resorting to subjective emotions. That may not always be a good thing to do, as we can overrationalize our real feelings, rather than dare recognize any existing vulnerabilities. Still, Gemini and Saturn support solid, intellectual frameworks that showcase exceptional mental ability (as long as Gemini helps Saturn avoid having anxiety attacks). Unduly worrying about things that could turn out badly is not what the Twins like to waste their time doing. Let's hope that Gemini will bring a cheerful disposition to a the sometimes too-serious Saturn (the planet associated with frowning).

Too Detached?

Gemini planets are usually happy planets. There is a childlike joy found in this sign that is only surpassed by Leo (fire is more exuberant than air). Gemini, actually not all that innocent about life, is more open to having random experiences than are most other signs. It's not one to prejudge situations it has never personally experienced (although it may be too susceptible to persuasive secondhand opinions). We can learn about life vicariously, but we'll need to be discriminating regarding information (sometimes the impatient Twins don't do the homework required to verify facts—they seek immediate answers but fail to double-check their sources).

Folks with many Gemini planets live a lot inside their heads, meaning that they may dwell in an almost exclusively cerebral world that is not always in touch with the more down-to-earth realities of living. Sometimes, such an overdeveloped mind can make for a personality that is too detached or lacking in empathy. Let's hope other factors in our chart point to a more active feeling nature. Otherwise, as smart as we may be, we're also probably a little too cool and unsympathetic in our responses to others (our relationships may suffer from being much too intellectualized, which can be a problem unless we're dealing with other strongly air types).

Willing to Bend

What makes our Gemini planets work best for us is when we apply their assets in a flexible, sensible manner. We need to stay elastic and willing to bend, as our circumstances change. Life seems to offer us lots of options, sometimes too many to coordinate at once. It pays for us to stay wide-awake when opportunity knocks, but to also learn when to commit ourselves to advantageous projects, rather than get nervous and talk ourselves out of them (for fear of being trapped). Sometimes great successes in life only come after tremendous efforts have been made, and that means our degree of stick-to-it-tiveness is often the key to our ultimate fulfillment. (This is easier to achieve if we also have planets in nearby Taurus.)

Communication is vital to us, and we usually excel in getting our messages across, since we can be vivacious in ways that encourage people to listen. Yet, if we are too quiet and even shy, our Gemini planets may internalize in ways that stress out our nervous system, leaving us jittery and cranky instead of peppy and expressive. That's not the way the Twins like to go through life—feeling all high-strung and tongue-tied. It is imperative that we do our best to continue educating ourselves, beyond our school years. We need to take advantage of all intellectual outlets that come our way—and, with lots of planets in Gemini, they usually do.

Our Future Prospects

Even if we don't have any planets in Gemini at birth, a planet—if only the Moon—will someday move into this intellectually energizing sign by secondary progression or solar arc. That's when a few of our bright ideas can shine and capture attention in sparkling ways. We can take advantage of options that now make themselves available to refresh our life. It's time to be less security-conscious and to make changes that allow us to enjoy new adventures of the mind.

PLANETS IN CANCER

Subjective Soul

Having planets in Cancer can mean we're sharply tuned in when it comes to picking up on people's changeable emotional atmospheres. We use our special internal radar to detect subtle psychological shifts in our environment that others may not perceive. This ability helps us develop a more reflective temperament, whereby we gain perceptive information about people in ways that bypass standard methods of intellectual fact-finding (such as Gemini's more straightforward verbal approach). However, being very subjective in our interpretation of information we receive can be problematic—emotional biases may prevent a fair and objective analysis.

With a planetary emphasis in Cancer, we can be troubled or frustrated by the nature of our own unsettled and sometimes unfathomable moods. We may become too easily ruffled by any unexamined uncertainties within us that we've unwittingly allowed to take root. Yet, planets in Cancer also challenge us to emerge from the trappings of a sometimes painful past, and to enlist our keen sensitivity to help us create healthier forms of security in the here and now. One way to encourage this is by keeping our feelings strong and reactive, rather than numb and buried. Our emotions cannot afford to stay bottled up; they must be free to surface and ventilate.

Our Cancer Planets

The **Moon** and **Venus** are very receptive to the Crab's warm, mothering energies. These planets' dispositions are even more tender and sympathetic when placed in this sentimental sign. Yet, they can also feel heavily put upon, since they cannot readily say "no" to the emotional demands of others (not without guilt or a fear of being abandoned). The "need to be needed" that comes with such planetary positions must find appropriate outlets. The Crab is less snappish when filtering its energies through planets that are as kind and considerate as these. The Moon's reflective and nostalgic sides may be more evident here. Still, when feelings have been hurt, this Moon's automatic defense tactic is to wall people off and become emotionally inaccessible. Venus in Cancer is also touchy in rocky relationships, yet is more willing to comfort upset loved ones in conciliatory terms. Its need to keep the peace in its partnerships is strong. If anything, it almost too easily accommodates others.

The **Sun** and **Jupiter** feel somewhat restrained by the timid and often overly cautious Crab. Yet, this cardinal sign may have enough push and drive to appeal to such energetic fire planets. However, the Sun can dramatize a sign's faults, while Jupiter magnifies them. Emotionality here can turn gushy, or perhaps it is simply displayed in warm and generous terms. Our strength may come from helping others feel comfortable and secure—but, as fire planets can be pushy, we need to make sure we don't force ourselves onto those who don't want or need our mothering (this is usually more of an issue for the control-seeking Sun to resolve, not carefree Jupiter). With these planets, Cancer tends to feel in big ways, but is less prone to overreact to petty insults (especially Jupiter). The Sun encourages us to uphold our sense of dignity and self-respect, so there's less "wallowing in our tears"; yet, when we do lose emotional control, we're dramatic about it. Jupiter would rather evoke the best qualities of Cancer, and share them with others in a less-emotionally charged atmosphere; it is generous in its emotional support, but less intimate in how it shares itself.

Mercury and **Mars** can turn edgy when in Cancer. The Crab, although not as calm or still around the nervous energy of Mercury, helps us better articulate our private feelings. When instinct and intellect successfully join forces, a smooth style of communication results. Perceptive listeners and poignant speakers enjoy such a Mercury. However, Mars in Cancer can prove troublesome; its assertive ways are too direct and selfish for the Crab's liking. Mars doesn't find quiet, gentle action to be stimulating enough. Suppressed hostilities and resentments pressure us to explode at awkward or inappropriate times. Although Cancer can nourish our Martian need to act on our behalf in the world, we can be as crabby and cranky as they come!

Saturn respects the security needs of Cancer, but doesn't care much for the Crab's ongoing state of vulnerability. Expect Cancer's shell to harden here to the point of utter impenetrability. This sign doesn't find Saturn to be sufficiently sympathetic to the human condition, as this is a planet that's fairly thick-skinned. Cancer is therefore frustrated by how fearful Saturn conditions it to feel about life—emotional trust earned the hard way. Developing inner security takes a lot of work. But reliable Saturn helps Cancer realize that a solid sense of safety can eventually be had, once maturity is fully established. It simply takes time.

Coming Home

At some point we'll feel a need to turn within for solace, instead of always looking for others to comfort and protect us. We're often disappointed and hurt when we realize that people typically fail to supply us with what we psychologically hunger for. Going inside ourselves to develop a deeper sense of shelter and invulnerability is a main Cancerian challenge. True security will be felt once we establish a sturdier foundation from within. We can even become agitated and stormy, should we ignore or dishonor our inner self. It seems that the more out of touch we are here, the more defensively we'll snap at the world, and the further we'll harden our protective outer shell.

Learning to find nurturing ways to "come home" to ourselves—in a state of peaceful self-acceptance—is critical to our happiness. Becoming chronically dependent on others in order to feel safe and wanted is unfortunately a way to perpetuate a constant state of insecurity. By developing internal strength, we begin to trust our experiences of closeness with others (the Crab is otherwise wary about being wounded in relationships, so all planets in this sign are on guard in this respect). Our temperament is decidedly on the maternal side, according to the natures of the actual planets in question.

Bonding, Not Binding

Cancer is an emotionally vibrant sign when its energy is flowing at its best. Others sense when we're inwardly secure, since our empowered feelings are then clearly expressed with confidence. We become a magnetic source of strength for people in need, yet we also know better than to let others latch on to us too tightly. We'll instead sensitively point them in those directions where they can better nourish themselves. It's not our job to put everyone with whom we bond under our wing, since being overly protective of others can keep them floundering in a weakened psychological state (perhaps that's something *we* also learned the hard way).

Planets in Cancer invite us to develop emotional ties that are deep and enduring. We shouldn't be afraid to feel strongly about others. We'll just need to recognize when certain binding attachments are the result of unresolved dependency hang-ups. If we smother others with our attention, or even receive such treatment in return, we have a problem that must be squarely addressed. Sadly, our neediness can drive loved ones away, making our greatest fear come true.

Our Future Prospects

Even if we don't have any planets in Cancer at birth, a planet—at least the Moon—will eventually move into this emotionally rich sign by secondary progression or solar arc. That's when we can learn to feed our soul better in nurturing and highly satisfying ways. We'll allow our feelings to reach out and touch somebody, as we learn to communicate in caring, intuitive ways. We're also learning to draw from our inner strength for support.

PLANETS IN LEO

Trusting Our Heart

If born with a few planets in Leo, we are here to have a love affair with ourselves. We're to find out how great we are. We just have to go about doing this in ways that others won't criticize as being smugly self-satisfying. Leo planets feel they are a cut above the rest, and thus act like they deserve special treatment. Actually, we are learning to trust our heart when it tells us that our life can be a wonderful adventure of our own making, *if* we just have the courage to be ourselves and to let our spiritedness shine. People will then find us to be warm-hearted and bubbling with self-confidence. Hopefully, we will truly learn to visualize ourselves in that same glowing light, as well.

Planets in Leo also have a reputation for being spoiled and acting snooty. These are sure signs of the defensive side of Leo at work—the Lion doesn't always act very nobly when it is overcompensating for its ego insecurities. It's true that, with Leo planets, we can easily be self-preoccupied; yet how else is this fiery sign to develop properly? We are here to grow a big, sturdy ego, one that is gutsy and self-assured enough to make its way grandly in the world—and honorably so, for the most part. Let's not get the impression that our Leo parts need to be toned down, so as not to overwhelm others. Perhaps this is sometimes good advice, but it also keeps the myth alive that having a strong ego is a "bad" thing. It's not. (For Leo, having a "bad hair day" is much worse!)

Our Leo Planets

The **Moon** and **Venus** in Leo are fairly comfortable here, since the Lion provides just the right amount of self-reliance needed to keep these planets from caving in to the neediness of others, those who'd otherwise suck our vitality dry if we let them. Leo does love to help give strength to the weaker, but it is not into long-term dependency scenarios. Although these planets like to feel involved in intimate relationships, they're in a sign that doesn't enjoy bending over backwards to cater to others all that much. Still, this Moon and Venus come across as vivacious and winsome when in the right social settings. They crave attention from their many admirers. Leo knows how to attract a crowd of admirers. If the Moon needs a boost of confidence, the Lion is quite able to project an air of self-assurance in a most convincing manner. This is a dramatic Moon of vividly expressed feelings that are sometimes too fiery in their delivery to satisfy purely lunar sensibilities. Venus in Leo is able to sparkle, due to its entertaining style and its playful energy. It's an upbeat Venus who can make others feel good, too. But our pride keeps us from acting like doormats in relationships. We want—and give—only first-class treatment.

The **Sun** and **Jupiter** agree that being in Leo is better than two lucky, fun-filled weeks in Las Vegas, with all expenses paid! Leo likes dealing with planets that aren't afraid to go for the gusto, and these two fireballs fit the bill. Actually, Jupiter is more likely to have a bigger appetite for entertainment in this sign, since it worships having a good time here. There is also a fearless disposition that enables Jupiter in Leo to take huge chances in life and often win. The Sun is more apt to accentuate the proud and dignified side of the Lion, plus both planet and sign have a natural interest in taking on desirable, top-dog positions. Acting as an authority figure comes easily. Still, our temperament can be overbearing and even obnoxious when we appear too sold on ourselves and unwilling to listen to constructive criticism.

Mercury and **Mars** are always ready for stimulation, and Leo doesn't disappoint where an endless outpouring of energy is concerned. Mercury doesn't feel mentally inhibited in this highly self-promotional sign; Leo uses language with flair, so people listen when this Mercury speaks. A colorful conversationalist can result from this blend. Still, it may be hard to appreciate someone else's viewpoint, since Leo does believe that its own ideas are superlative. Mars in Leo, being a double dose of headstrong fire, has no trouble taking action in bold and splashy ways. Perhaps it's a bit too willful at times, even bossy and demanding. Yet Leo loves the fact that Mars will act on impulse, and thus spontaneity thrives. We will vigorously follow our heart (assuming we have a wholesome attitude about being self-assertive, which is usually the case).

Saturn in Leo, like the Sun, wants respect. Leo doesn't clown around as much when it's working with this not-so-frivolous planet. The Lion takes itself very seriously; it realizes it has a shining image to uphold, one that centers around performing flawlessly. Yet that can result in a few larger-than-life anxieties, since Saturn is much too worried about being judged regarding any glaring inadequacies. Mistakes will not be made—in public—if both planet and sign can help it! The whole situation here could improve a lot if Saturn would just be willing to lighten up and enjoy the ongoing party that Leo's life can become.

Young at Heart

There is a childlike joyousness to be found, once our planets in Leo realize how sparkling their world can be with the addition of a little creativity, a sense of awe, and a lot of imagination. With these planets, we should always think twice about the consequences of growing up too soon; we need to capitalize on our talent for staying young at heart. The child energy within Leo is adventurous, but not security-conscious. Risks are part of the game to be played. Leo doesn't anticipate that things will ever go wrong, so why not take big chances in good faith?

The Royal Treatment?

However, there is perhaps at least one problem with having too many planets in Leo. We have a hard time bowing down to others, whose authority we don't even recognize. They may be squarely in the control seat, having charge over our destiny, yet we have a hard time letting people supervise us. We instead wish to run our own show. Thus, a battle of wills can erupt from time to time, and we can be accused of having an ego too big for its britches. Leo planets are more temperamentally suited for roles involving executive power. It's probably a better idea not to have a boss or an inflexible corporate structure to deal with—except that Big Business is often where the power roles that Leo craves can be had. Still, being under someone's thumb all the time can be a suffocating situation for us. We need to be treated with respect at all times, which is hard to feel when we're instead being dominated.

Planets in Leo encourage us to take on an optimistic, sunny approach to living. We may beam with pride about our achievements, while we view our upcoming future in rosy terms (less so if Saturn and Pluto are holding any other Leo planets hostage). We expect only the best, and due to sheer determination, we often get the marvelous results we wish for. But it's more than just exercising our will that does the trick—life is better able to give us the "royal treatment" because we hold ourselves in high self-esteem; plus, we effectively stay in touch with our heartfelt desires. Leo planets prompt us to create the kind of special person we want to be, without the interference of others. Obviously, we'll have control issues to work out, since we may want and expect everything to turn out our way, which isn't always likely to happen.

Our Future Prospects

Even if we don't have any planets in Leo at birth, someday a planet— the Moon alone—will move into this robust, self-celebratory sign by secondary progression or solar arc. That's when we have the guts to show the world the creative fire burning within us. We'll learn to direct own our life with a greater sense of pride and purpose. We're ready to have more fun living, as well.

PLANETS IN VIRGO

The Finer Details

Virgo, a sign often accused of an almost neurotic form of nagging, is actually more helpful to the daily discipline of living than astrologers usually emphasize. Virgo even feels that chronic complaining only compounds any predicament, but does little to implement a real, workable solution. This sign's fretfulness only increases when it feels its sensible suggestions for preventing confusion and disorder are ignored, thereby allowing aggravating mistakes to unnecessarily repeat. Planets in Virgo suggest our sharply focused mind can come up with simple, effective methods to improve the quality of everyday living for all. They indicate a talent for effective problem solving.

Born with Virgo planets, we can be sticklers for following procedures that not only make more sense, but that shave the time we expend in half (time and energy are precious commodities to Virgo, and are not to be needlessly wasted). We usually first work out the finer details of any project in our head—or on paper—before we actually begin to take action. Virgo planets are less enthused by any "learn as you go and hope you get lucky" approach. They prefer to carefully outline the steps required to ensure that a job is well done (it's the nerdy scientist in Virgo who demands that precise measures be taken).

Our Virgo Planets

The **Moon** and **Venus** are less apt to indulge in sentimentality when in this sign. Their feelings are subdued, thanks to Virgo's natural inclination to be discreet and cool-headed in matters of the heart. That doesn't mean the Analyzer takes a bloodless approach to life's more sensitive issues, but it does refuse to go overboard in its emotional expression. A Virgo Moon can certainly feel for others—especially concerning their health problems—yet it won't resort to hysterics or dramatic outbursts, no matter how frustrating are its own life circumstances (although should it stifle its emotions too often, it can develop physical symptoms). This Moon is choosy about expressing its typically well-contained feelings. Venus in Virgo thinks long and hard about another's suitability before committing itself to any long-term relationship (it's seldom swept off it's feet when in love). It is capable of a loyal, enduring love that puts a special emphasis on fidelity. Still, Virgo can underestimate Venus' natural need for displays of affection. It appears too cool and collected to suit some.

Although the **Sun** and **Jupiter** wish Virgo was a bit more lively and expressive, these planets know this sign will make every minute count when courting success. Virgo is not full of fiery ambition, but it hates to make thoughtless mistakes along the way that can damage one's reputation. For Jupiter, that means no opportunity is wasted, if based on real potential and not on momentary hype. Virgo is not self-promotional, meaning that this Jupiter won't be tooting its horn too loudly, especially if it's not really well prepared to embrace fame and fortune. First it's got to work hard to get there (Virgo also introduces Jupiter to the virtues of humility). The Sun will make the best out of whatever sign it's in, since appearing competent is important (this planet represents how we want to shine and impress the world). The Sun in Virgo excels at painstaking work that shows a masterful understanding of all elements involved. This planet can't afford to show off too much when in this modest sign, but it will present itself as an expert whose educated opinions people can trust—and this helps us feel good about ourselves. Self-pride is associated here with being knowledgeable, useful, and well prepared.

Mercury and **Mars** can do much with Virgo's energy, as long as this sign doesn't insist on getting bogged down in useless details. This Mercury, sometimes indiscriminate about taking in information, tends to over-research its material—a typical Virgo pitfall. It ends up with too much data, some of it unnecessary to achieve the best results. A little mental discipline is needed, and a lot less thoroughness (but don't expect meticulous Virgo to agree on this). Mars likes the fact that Virgo is intelligent, alert, and ready to tackle problems in a clear-headed manner. This planet needs to engage in challenging, stimulating activity to keep it from getting temperamental. Virgo will provide Mars with lots to do, and efficiently so. Mars in Virgo is highly industrious and well suited to getting tedious or demanding jobs done.

Saturn is an earth planet and Virgo is an earth sign. Saturn will make painstaking corrections where needed, which the Analyzer also deems to be critical for achieving optimal results. Yet these two can become fixated on obtaining perfect results. Virgo likes the fact that Saturn is hardworking and humble, as well. It's a task-oriented planet, just as Virgo is a sign with a strong work ethic. We can be highly dependable, no matter how demanding our job at hand is. But there is more to life than just toiling away, day after day. Relaxing may not come easily, but we will need to shut off our urge to stay busy, now and then, so that we can prevent undue nervous stress from exhausting us.

Too Skeptical?

Having several planets in this rational sign suggests that we may assess situations with a level-headedness that doesn't leave much room for fanciful speculation or abstract theorizing. This orientation is fine, when appropriate, but it can also lead to a dull, conservative outlook that squelches imagination and even discounts spiritual awareness. Mismanaged Virgo energy suggests that we're too intellectually earthbound, and that we use our acute powers of reason to dismiss otherworldly possibilities. We're skeptical about anything that defies the established laws of physical nature. Demanding rock-solid evidence and infallible proof, we have a harder time believing in invisible worlds of an extrasensory nature.

It will be important to have a broad education if we have planets in Virgo. We are likely to learn a lot on our own, even if we also collect several academic degrees. Like Gemini, Virgo is strongly curious about the workings of anything—it's just apt to stay with its subject matter longer than do the Twins, and thus Virgo develops a more thorough knowledge. The Analyzer also likes to break down information into smaller parts, while designing its own methods of organizing detailed data. We'll probably want to educate ourselves forever, even as we age, since our minds must always stay busy. Productivity is a big theme for Virgo planets; nobody could ever accuse them of mental laziness.

All Work, No Play?

Planets in Virgo believe in simplifying matters. We find we don't wish to indulge in an extravagant lifestyle, nor do we relish involvement in situations that require high levels of maintenance (perhaps once we try that, we'll conclude, "Never again!"). It's important to us that we don't fritter away our time on frivolous pursuits. Still, we'll need to be careful not to deprive ourselves of recreational activity that could actually recharge our mental batteries and work like a health tonic. All work and no play is not how we're going to stay in tip-top shape. Much of our life may be dedicated to all forms of self-improvement— but we'll need to let our hair down and enjoy living, rather than forever try to fix imperfections in people and circumstances in our life.

Our Future Prospects

Even if we don't have any planets in Virgo at birth, someday a planet— at least the Moon—will move into this fastidious sign by secondary progression or solar arc. That's when we're more motivated to get ourselves in excellent condition by organizing our life in better, smarter ways. We learn to eliminate what no longer works for us, thereby creating order that's beneficial to our ongoing growth.

PLANETS IN LIBRA

Sharing the Stage

Having planets in Libra is a mixed blessing. On one hand, they greatly help us make our mark in social spheres, whereby doors of opportunity open for us, due to the charm and sophistication we may exude. Our friendly ways and our show of consideration for others can make us popular—we're also very agreeable and thus likeable. On the other hand, Libra forces us to occasionally deal with tension-producing partners who have contrasting temperaments and needs. This invites varying levels of open competition and confrontation into our lives that we'd normally avoid.

Libra defines a point in the zodiac where we realize that others will sometimes need to come first—we are not always to have our way in relationships. We are learning to be more aware of how those we love need as much praise and attention as we do. We are realizing how important a healthy sense of give and take is in such unions. Usually, our Libra planets suggest that we're willing to share the stage and take turns enjoying the spotlight. We really do want others to look good and be at their best, and we'll find ourselves to be actively supportive along these lines. But we'll also need the same level of support in return.

Our Libra Planets

The **Moon** and **Venus**, when in Libra, are perfect examples of planets that are sometimes too diplomatic for their own good. They also have a hard time saying "no" to pushy people who ask for favors. For the Moon, it's mostly a case of wanting "other-approval" a little too much, and maybe for the wrong reasons. This planet hates to make waves and get people all upset. A Libran Moon can be very accommodating, avoiding emotional clashes whenever possible. Yet, in this sign, the Moon will fight against injustice. Although it, too, values fairness, Venus in Libra may try to appease others in ways that appear too ingratiating to seem sincere. Actually, its need to act as a peacemaker is real, but the way this Venus prevents conflict can look more like an attempt to "kiss up" to others, just to be liked (or to elevate one's social standing). Otherwise, Venus' graceful manners and congeniality are assets that improve the quality of our social relations.

The **Sun** and **Jupiter** do very well in Libra. This sign enhances the good things that these fire planets are all about; it tries to showcase their energies in a positive light. The Sun adds an element of self-pride that keeps Libra from yielding to the unreasonable demands of another, just to keep a union alive (the Sun won't play that degrading game forever). We can also feel like an authority when it comes to understanding people's motives, especially concerning close partnerships. We are confident that we can appreciate both sides of an issue. Jupiter, already a gregarious planet, is even more good-natured and amiable when in Libra. With this placement, we can be quite charismatic in an appealingly social sense. However, there is also a legalistic mind found here (as both planet and sign are associated with the law). We probably have lofty ideals concerning justice. We advocate fairness regarding social issues that affect those treated unfairly by the System.

Mercury and **Mars** learn that Libra's talent for making social connections means a lot to how one succeeds in life. Mercury is glad that Libra's polished presentation makes whatever comes out of our mind and mouth sound pleasing to others. Our powers of persuasion are very strong. Still, we can be too complimentary of people and things, in ways that at times sound phony. However, we'll strategically use our sharp intellect to score key points in relationships that can advance our ambitions. Any Libran assertiveness is less obvious, since we communicate with a charm that encourages others to help us attain our objectives. Mars in Libra has mixed feelings when in this sign. Libra encourages cooperation and a sharing of power. Mars is never going to have the complete freedom to run the show. Actually, this is a shrewd Mars that works to fire people up and get them engaged in our personal projects. But if we're angry about how things turn out as a result, we seldom point the finger of blame at ourselves. It's always someone else's fault!

Saturn admires Libra's impartiality, since this planet is also about serving justice well. Libra even has a sense of decorum and civility that Saturn appreciates. Both planet and sign are sticklers for adhering to appropriate behavior, especially in public situations. They dread social embarrassment. Libra likes to deliberate before making its moves, which suits Saturn's disposition well (this is not an impulsive planet). Actually, Saturn can be a little rough around the edges—being so earthy—but Libra does add a touch of sophistication that helps this reserved planet feel less awkward and out of place in lively social situations. Saturn's composure combined with Libran finesse make for a favorable presentation that rarely ruffles feathers.

Unfair Play?

Problems occur when we expect others to reciprocate fully by giving us the same courteous, encouraging treatment we typically give them. What happens when they don't deliver the goods, not because they can't, but because they refuse to? There is a side to us, then, that—in the name of fair play—will face off with another and argue for our right to be respected and treated evenhandedly. We may not actually have the guts to confront someone when we should, but a slow-building, righteous anger churns inside, once we've suffered a major injustice in any close partnership, and eventually the time for a showdown comes.

A prime lesson found with Libra planets has to do with how we squarely get our hurt and anger out and onto the negotiating table. Our dialogues, with those who've managed to thwart us, must be based on being straightforward and clear about defining mutual needs. Libra has a horror of offending people. It thus searches for soothing words to use, while trying to get its point across—call it tact—without inflaming others. Yet, a more forceful and direct approach may be required if we are truly to be heard.

An Eye for Beauty

Having Libra planets suggests we'd do well channeling our talents into artistic projects, or whatever else brings a measure of loveliness and refinement to our surroundings (Libra's the sign of architecture and design). Objects of beauty help us balance our energies in ways that leave us feeling relaxed and even-tempered. Ugliness and discord have opposite effects. The more Libra we have natally, the more upset we become when our delicate sensibilities are jarred. Our Libra planets suggest that we need peaceful conditions within which to operate, which is not always realistically accomplished—but still, let's try our best to bring serenity to any environment.

We'll also need to overcome our bouts of indecisiveness if we really want to get anywhere in life in a timely fashion. Libra usually stalls because it waits for the perfect moment to take action. Many missed opportunities may occur instead. Heavily Libran types—often concerned about the consequences resulting from any moves they make—need to learn to relax, try their best, and then maturely accept what results, with a measure of composure. It's much better in the long run to do this than to remain noncommittal and thus ineffective.

Our Future Prospects

Even if we don't have any planets in Libra at birth, someday a planet— such as the Moon—will move into this perspective-enhancing sign by secondary progression or solar arc. That's when we can learn to better understand the many sides of our relationship issues, and insightfully so. Partnership concerns that may come to the fore require our honest evaluation; how can our intimacy needs best be fulfilled in ways that are mutually agreeable?

Planets in Scorpio

Depths of Passion

Seeing many planets in Scorpio in someone's chart shouldn't automatically make us shudder, although they can evoke that sort of gut reaction. We quickly suspect that there's more going on here than meets the eye. What secrets are kept well hidden, and why? Actually, it's Scorpio who's an expert at playing the role of ace detective. These planets, certainly intense in expression, often are only scary to those who are not used to such passionate depths—yet nobody witnesses that level of emotional fervor until such planets are duly provoked. Most of the time, Scorpio has such enormous self-control that it seems more a strange enigma than a potentially dangerous threat. (Still, Scorpio can be "silent but deadly.")

Scorpio planets symbolize where we can be hard on ourselves psychologically. We don't seem to process our life experiences the easy way, which we'd have a better chance of doing if we took them at face value. Instead, we probe below life's surface, where things can get darker and more complex. Scorpio makes sure we come equipped with a special radar system that picks up on powerful but invisible forces, especially those percolating inside people's psyches. Our biggest concern, however, is finding effective ways to navigate our own underground world. What are our deeper motives for our involvement in intimate relationships?

Our Scorpio Planets

The **Moon** and **Venus** aren't necessarily sweet-natured when in Scorpio, since their behavior sometimes borders on cruel, calculated responses designed to "get back" at the ones they supposedly love, but also hate. At least the potential for that dynamic exists. Astrologers prefer to say that these planets are fond of Scorpio's desire to transform unions for the better. The Moon, however, can be very self-protective when in this sign, yet not obviously so. Both planet and sign are good at putting up protective shields to guard against the exposure of vulnerabilities. This passionate Moon feels so strongly about its emotional attractions that it possessively holds on to others too tightly. Obsession may be a problem. Venus in this sign is loaded with seductive allure and palpable sex appeal. Yet this is a Venus that shows a concentrated strength, allowing it to endure much turmoil in a relationship before calling it quits. Love is never a frivolous pursuit; in fact, it can help motivate us to reexamine emotional values needing an overhaul or a rebirth.

The **Sun** and **Jupiter** don't like to sneak around or conceal their intentions, but Scorpio does—and will—when it must. Yet, working through these upfront fire planets, this sign is encouraged to reveal its profound insights. Our penetrating observations about life can be a source of strength and understanding. For the Sun, self-esteem is tied to having a profound awareness of human psychology—we pride ourselves for not being superficial in our evaluations. Jupiter capitalizes on Scorpio's steely courage to confront whatever the future unfolds. Jupiter believes the future to be brighter, and with more expansive options, than Scorpio usually imagines. Our greatest blessings come from any honest self-investigation that helps effectively tap our latent sources of power.

Mercury and **Mars** are stimulated by Scorpio's driving need to uncover what's hidden. For Mercury, curiosity is heightened and is only relieved when this planet plays the bloodhound on the trail, sniffing out information. Awesome intellectual stamina is found here. Scorpio despises censorship, and thus Mercury insists on being exposed to things that others find provocative or controversial. It'll probe as deeply as necessary, if necessary, to uncover "the ugly truth" about certain situations. Mars loves knowing that brave, no-nonsense Scorpio is willing to use its stinger, when in battle mode, without remorse. Tremendous fortitude allows this Mars to take action, even under grueling conditions. Sometimes a sneak attack is most tempting, but Mars works best when it's out in the open, wielding Scorpio's power tools in honest, healthy ways. Still, this Mars may sabotage itself when frustration can no longer be tolerated.

Saturn accentuates the control factor within Scorpio, yet self-discipline may be taken to the extreme, as an inborn ascetic quality turns compulsive and rigid. This sign nonetheless greatly admires Saturn's ability to focus on its tasks at hand, since Scorpio also has excellent powers of concentration. Still, Scorpio may intensify Saturn's repressive nature, and thus, much of what this sign could uncover about our inner mysteries may instead be blocked—by fear, by doubt, or by shame. Saturn builds walls and dams to keep from being flooded by unwanted emotions. Nevertheless, as Scorpio won't tolerate needless detours, this single-minded Saturn fulfills its ambitions through a display of incredible dedication and determination.

Nasty Complications?

Planets in Scorpio are sources of self-renewal. Here we have underground resources that can further enrich our life, once we become better acquainted with them. The urge to dig within to discover our inner power is strong. It's always good to have a keen, psychological grasp of who we are if several of our natal planets fall in this sign. The unhappiest among us are those who refuse to look inside ourselves for answers. Nasty complications also await us when we use our Scorpio energies to manipulate others against their will, and it gets even worse when revenge is on our mind—that's when life can dramatically turn the tables on us.

Scorpio is a sign of punishment, the kind that sometimes mixes justice with twisted emotions. With many Scorpio planets, we will need to be careful not to be overbearing with others, or heavy-handed in our management policies. Control is something we feel we must exert, but do we know why we distrust letting nature take its course, without our willful intervention? Probably not, yet life will let us know when we've gone too far with our coercive tendencies. It's much better to use our Scorpio strengths to reformulate ourselves, working from the inside out. We need to show interest in others without being intrusive (this is a highly nosy sign, but usually not obviously so).

Mapping the Psyche

Since we are insightful in our comprehension of human behavior, it would be good for us to think of doing something with our lives in the area of analyzing people's internal worlds. Any field that provides a detailed map of the psyche or soul would be appealing, even if our interest is in only observing the more pathological bumps in the road. Actually, one standout talent of ours is the ability to provide people with the healing skills needed to rejuvenate self-respect and a restoration of confidence, so that barriers to achieving emotional peace within are eliminated.

We can be uncannily astute in our silent observations of others, but we usually need to wait to be asked before we enter someone else's private world (although the more troublesome Scorpio types simply trespass at will, and in an intimidating manner). Delving into the mysteries of the so-called paranormal might also be intriguing, as unnerving subjects like death (or even terminal diseases) capture our full attention. Scorpio has less trouble handling life's more disturbing features than do the other signs. That doesn't mean we will have more than our share of traumas, but that we have a knack for navigating our way through life's darker passages, while able to keep our wits about us. We even remain cool-headed during emergencies.

Our Future Prospects

Even if we don't have any planets in Scorpio at birth, someday a planet—at least the Moon—will move into this psychologically life-altering sign by secondary progression or solar arc. That's when we learn to reclaim any power we have given away and thus to potently reinvigorate our ourselves. This is a great time to tackle long-term problems and resolve them for good.

PLANETS IN SAGITTARIUS

Glorious Tomorrows

Planets in Sagittarius enjoy one another's company, due to this gregarious sign's "the more the merrier" philosophy. (Actually, the nature of the planets best determine if that's true.) The more Sagittarius is emphasized in our chart, the fewer petty gripes we probably engage in (we mainly get riled about global-scale problems that cry for enlightened social remedies). For the most part, we have the flexibility needed to ride the waves of change; not much about life dampens our spirit or makes us bitter. Sagittarius is a firm believer in glorious tomorrows to be had, as long as we never abandon our faith. We believe—sometimes naively—that there's a fundamental goodness to be found in most people, once we reach out to befriend them. The Archer also wants us to become better acquainted with a diversity of cultural backgrounds.

Sagittarian planets set their sights on high-minded goals, idealistic in tone, that keep us feeling optimistic about where we and everyone else are headed in life. What, spiritually, is the right path for us to be on? For the Archer, life is eternal and ultimately full of meaning, even during those most mundane of moments when our day-to-day existence seems to be totally uninspiring. How we manage to keep hope alive is very important for our evolutionary growth (Sagittarius enjoys thinking of our development in such terms). The future that calls for our enthusiastic attention is abundant with possibilities that both enrich our spirit and widen our mental perspective.

Our Sagittarius Planets

The **Moon** and **Venus** in Sagittarius aren't all that sentimental—or even cuddly—since this sign reserves its strongest feelings for its abstract ideas and universal ideals. The Archer, while very friendly, is transpersonal in nature; it won't allow these two planets to become too dependent or clingy. The Moon in this sign may not seem to be sensitive to the emotional needs of others—it's not a soothing hand holder—but it does know how to uplift people who've been deflated by disappointments. It's a cheerful Moon that doesn't believe in wallowing in sadness or despair. Venus enjoys Sagittarius' good-natured, sociable disposition and its eagerness to meet strangers (it's not the shy type). Even a measure of Venusian security comes from our opportunities to meet and greet people everywhere, rather than remain isolated and socially disconnected (Sagittarius likes being around people).

The **Sun** and **Jupiter** are fiery enough to suit Sagittarius. The Sun here dreams big and fully trusts the Cosmos. What seems to be "plain ol' luck" often enters our life to sweeten it. Our faith alone can move mountains and win jackpots! We also abide by our own code of living, based on elevated moral and ethical principles dear to us. At times, a Sagittarian Sun or Jupiter is guilty of overreach, as sensible boundaries are ignored. We can also sound pompous when taking on a "know-it-all" stance. Jupiter loves Sagittarius' lack of restrictions. Here it can expand all it wants. Sharing many of the qualities of the Sun in this sign, Jupiter adds an almost prophetic sense of future happenings. Seeking spiritual truths results in illuminating travels, on all levels.

Mercury and **Mars** accelerate their speed while in peppy Sagittarius, a sign with little regard for applying the brakes. With Mercury, our thoughts also travel far and wide, and are attended by bursts of Sagittarian exhilaration, due to mind-expanding revelations. We can also talk up a storm, while on our soapbox, as we preach to the world and sell our beliefs with conviction. Our ability to promote anything in which we have faith is powerful. People enjoy hearing our testimonials, as long as we don't sound fanatic. Mars in Sagittarius is hopefully an example of inspired impulse; otherwise, we burn a lot of fuel too quickly by running around in circles and get nowhere, due to our lack of patience or strategic planning. We can also be bluntly opinionated in our all-out attack against hypocrisy and phoniness. Our actions may seem brusque and tactless when we run roughshod over people's feelings. Feisty and fearless, we can boldly spearhead worthy causes that jolt society's awareness. We have a crusading spirit.

Sagittarius tones down its energies when filtered through sobering **Saturn**. Its capacity for wisdom is accented (Sagittarius is the sign of the wandering sage). Saturn admires Sagittarius' legalistic mind, and thus its attention is put on the nature and validity of laws (from civil to cosmic). Serious pursuits of the "higher mind" are thus suggested, even those of the scholarly kind. Still, there is much about Saturn that squelches pure Sagittarian enthusiasm, since this sign is much too adventurous for a planet as cautious and distrustful as Saturn. Yet as long as this planet is operating in its typically dutiful and conscientious way, Sagittarius' notorious irresponsibility and carelessness are less of a problem.

Free as a Bird?

Our Sagittarius planets are eager to show us how vast the field of consciousness can be. We benefit by learning all that we can about not only this world, but also those more awesome realms beyond—especially from scientific, religious, or metaphysical perspectives. Our mind searches for sweeping overviews that explain more to us. We love being on far-reaching mental journeys, even if we don't get all of life's biggest questions satisfyingly answered.

Sagittarius shies away from making emotional commitments. It's a sign that's hard to pin down when it comes to long-term involvement in close relationships. What intimacy requires seems stifling to Sagittarius, and a bit of a trap. This sign is more relaxed when it keeps things loose and casual (it doesn't enjoy overly structured unions). Its need to remain "free" can pose problems in unions that demand steady, responsible involvement (plus an adherence to routine). It's paradoxical that Sagittarius, while loving to embrace the concept of humanity in altruistic terms, is nonetheless uncomfortable in close, one-on-one arrangements that require real emotional interaction—the kind that, while not always uplifting, are very human and bonding. The Archer's urge is to run away from all this and not look back.

A Holy Path

When we have many planets in Sagittarius, it's hard for us not to contemplate the universe from vast perspectives, and to wonder about the nature and purpose of life's overall design. For those of us who are less scientifically inclined, we'll find ourselves on a long-term quest to discover God and other realms of sacred experience. Sagittarius can act as a conventional but enthused member of any established religious congregation that seems to have all the answers spelled out. We may thus interpret our role here as someone who's committed to dispersing vital knowledge and wisdom regarding holy matters. We feel driven to teach and preach what we believe to be the Truth, rather than keep all such awareness exclusively inside ourselves.

Yet there is another Sagittarian path that some of us may take, one that respects the diversity of spiritual expression found in the many systems of faith that exist in various cultures worldwide. We seek to embrace the essential truths that all such serious belief systems share. We have our own strong beliefs, yet we allow others the right to pursue their chosen paths, knowing that we'll all arrive at the same destination point someday in the future.

Our Future Prospects

Even if we don't have any planets in Sagittarius at birth, someday a planet—such as the Moon—will move into this upbeat, broad-minded sign by secondary progression or solar arc. That's when we're ready to further explore what life is all about in a more mentally exuberant manner. We feel an urge to open our heart and mind to different lifestyles that could happily broaden our understanding and acceptance of the world at large.

PLANETS IN CAPRICORN

Compelled to Excel

Planets in Capricorn have a lot going for them, as this sign is prominent in the charts of those likely to do important things in the world. There will be many dues to pay, at first, and even a few frustrating delays and denials to experience (since little in the Goat's world happens overnight). These planets—and our enduring patience—are continuously put to the test. As a result, we eventually utilize our expert abilities in a mature and purposeful manner, and thereby excel in worldly accomplishment. Even early on, we start to develop commendable traits and excellent work habits that later ensure such levels of high achievement (we grow up very quickly, but unfortunately, we may never have known a truly carefree childhood).

Capricorn is a sign that doesn't believe in rushing the process that leads to ultimate greatness. Every step along the way is timely and absolutely necessary, according to the Goat. Shortcuts to success, while tempting, are to be avoided. In Capricorn's way of thinking, we have to earn our long-sought attainments by hard work and dedication. Thus, expect planets in this sign to appear—in the beginning—as if they are not having all that good a time in life. Although serious and level-headed, they're almost too self-controlled to enjoy themselves.

Our Capricorn Planets

The **Moon** and **Venus** feel that Capricorn provides a safe but sometimes chilly atmosphere for them. The Moon wants unconditional love and caring, yet little about Capricorn is unconditional. We absorb the message here that nurturance is offered only to those who are well deserving. Capricorn Moons find greater security coming from their fulfillment of ambition. We hide our emotional vulnerabilities behind a self-reliant, businesslike demeanor. Venus, gracious and well polished when in Capricorn, is often only interested in pleasing the "right" people (it is status-conscious, but perhaps too afraid of being socially rejected to really relax). Love takes a lot of careful planning; sensible choices are to be made. This conventional Venus—seldom carried away by intoxicating romance—is a firm believer in dutifully upholding its marital vows, even if true, everlasting love is hard to find or feel.

The **Sun** and **Jupiter** act with integrity in Capricorn. Although these planets in this sign seek prominence and prestige, they are honorable in their pursuit of such social recognition. These two can act like "big shots," yet Capricorn only elevates those to higher ranks who persevere through steady effort and a willingness to perfect their skills. Fame is otherwise fleeting when we try to bypass the years of required preparation that Capricorn demands. Both the Sun and Capricorn reinforce a sense of dignity and responsibility and the urge to take charge of affairs. Jupiter's exuberance is less spontaneous in Capricorn. Sheer luck doesn't enter the picture as much, since opportunity is tied to hard work and true expertise. Realistic Capricorn also adds a welcome dose of common sense, enough to keep Jupiter from overestimating its potential. Perhaps this sign's organizational skills improve our chances for Jupiterian prosperity in our later years.

Mercury and **Mars** know they'll stay busy in Capricorn, since this sign tries to make every minute a productive one. The Virgo side of Mercury is easily evoked, as the Goat supports pragmatic and sensible thinking. It also likes to plan things out with care—nothing is to be rushed or done haphazardly. Here's a shrewd, business-minded Mercury, blessed with the ability to concentrate on its objectives without getting restless. The power to deliberate before making major decisions is strong. Mars doesn't care for restraining measures, but Capricorn makes it clear that acting without sufficient self-control leads to ineffective results. Ambition is underscored, although impulsive Mars will sometimes learn the hard way about proper timing. Capricorn admires this planet for its courage and its willingness to mow down obstacles that try to block success. (Capricorn hates quitters who give up too soon!)

Saturn and Capricorn have a lot in common, except that the Goat is more eager for the limelight and public notice than reclusive Saturn. Still, Capricorn likes this planet's ability to stay on course—even when the going gets tough—and to not bail out on its duties and obligations. The Goat knows a lack of such determination invites failure. Saturn is as conservative as Capricorn, and likes to make safe choices in life that allow for predictable results (only "calculated" risks appeal to Capricorn, not wild and crazy gambles). It's possible that both planet and sign are too worldly and earthbound in orientation, and need to develop an awareness of less physical realms of reality. Still, they each have a well-deserved reputation for being reliable and trustworthy—they'll deliver the goods as promised, and on time!

Better with Age

Capricorn planets get better with age, as long as cynicism doesn't creep into the picture too early on in our lives (as those disappointing delays we experienced can sour our outlook on our future). Wherever we have Capricorn emphasized, getting older can indeed mean getting wiser, especially after enough "dues have been paid." The road here is typically bumpy at first for us, even a bit of an ongoing strain, before things finally smooth out.

Our life improves once we assume only those responsibilities that are rightfully ours, and not those obligations that are truly someone else's burden. By becoming discriminating about where our duties lie, we'll stop unnecessarily putting extra weight on our shoulders. We also succeed sooner when we focus on doing what is within our grasp, even if our objectives take much time to unfold. If a goal is impossible or inadvisable for us to tackle, due to unrealistic expectations, Capricorn will make sure we're thwarted by a series of unrelenting setbacks, if need be. At least we won't waste too much precious time going down the wrong road in life, unless other parts of our chart suggest we are too thickheaded to heed the Goat's warning—repeated delays here mean we're to head down a different and less self-defeating path.

Rising in Rank

Planets in Capricorn give us clues about our professional leanings. They come alive when we're involved in an active career in which we are motivated to rise in rank. We are keenly attentive to the rules of

the game when it comes to achieving success, and we are most interested in making business contacts that can pay off for us in the future
(Capricorn's a long-range thinker and an opportunist who knows the
value of making the right connections early on). Folks with Capricorn
highlighted need to develop healthy attitudes about hard work, otherwise they run the risk of feeling crippled by chronic failure due to un-
derachievement (and can be left depressed as a result).

Sometimes ruthlessness is an issue, but more often, Capricorn
planets quietly take on roles of duty without much fanfare. They
climb high up the career ladder due to their steadfastness and even
their loyalty to the company (or to their own professional vision, if
self-employed). Such dedication eventually bears fruit, as long as we
keep our integrity intact and act with dignity, rather than claw our
way to the top and not care about who we displace in the process. If
karmic backlash is a reality, then Capricorn is one sign to watch for
evidence of such repercussions in the lives of those who ignore ethics
in self-serving ways.

Our Future Prospects

Even if we don't have any planets in Capricorn at birth, someday a
planet—at least the Moon—will move into this realistically focused,
highly goal-oriented sign by secondary progression or solar arc. That's
when we're able to take on authoritative roles that call for an inner
strength and an organizational ability that earn the respect of others.
We learn to coordinate our life in a timely manner that helps us clarify our most important priorities.

PLANETS IN AQUARIUS

The Friendly Sort

Having several planets in Aquarius may symbolize a mixed bag of energies. Some of these planets may resonate with Saturn, the Water Bearer's old-time ruling planet, while the others are more attuned to Uranus, Aquarius' modern-day agent. Just by looking at the chart alone, we can't tell which is which (except for cases where Saturn *is* in Aquarius). Still, this planetary dichotomy partly explains this sign's paradoxical nature. Aquarius' temperament is also defined by its placement on the zodiac wheel. It's at a latter stage, in the circle of signs, where we are to shed our socially programmed roles in favor of experimenting with untapped human potential. We are also learning to see life in more transpersonal terms—a purely egocentric perspective must make way for a more compelling and liberating collective vision, one that unites progressive thought with altruistic concern.

Aquarius is known for being friendly, as are all the air signs. Yet it lacks warmth and emotional depth. Careful not to overly personalize an interest in any one individual, Aquarius instead focuses on humanity as a whole. Aquarian planets enable us to step back and mentally establish the distance needed to broaden our outlook on life—we cannot afford to get too close to what we're observing if we want to see things with crystal clarity. Nor can we can become too emotionally involved and still remain objective. Thus, it's no wonder that Aquarius seems to be cool and detached when dealing with ordinary human affairs that play on most people's feelings.

Our Aquarius Planets

The **Moon** and **Venus** appreciate how Aquarian friendliness makes it easy to connect socially. It's not afraid to make the acquaintance of strangers, and does so quickly, even if not assertively. The basically shy Moon is thus encouraged to accept new people into its life without feeling insecure. Still, Aquarius' cerebral disposition ensures that rational, intellectual responses supercede reactions based on gut emotion. However, there is an intuitive streak in operation that seems almost like pure instinct at work, since both are equally fast. Being sociable, Venus has less trouble with Aquarian energy—it enjoys this sign's wide interest in people. Yet, when it comes to romance and sensuality, Aquarius lacks the chemistry needed to inspire Venusian passion. Still, there is an open and honest nature here that makes this a well-liked Venus, although one who's nonetheless awkward in more intimate situations.

The **Sun** and **Jupiter** make use of their nobler, idealistic qualities while in humanitarian Aquarius. Here these fire planets burn with zeal regarding social progress. They support honesty and integrity, and are eager to promote social enlightenment. An Aquarian Sun finds its self-esteem by opening people's minds to unusual ideas, as if on an exciting expedition. Mental explorations of the unconventional sort feed us vital energy. We may resist outside authority, yet we will allow our intuition to guide us. Jupiter in Aquarius has an above-average interest in futuristic enterprise. It has an inventive spirit that seeks to better society. Humanitarianism is strong, as is a fiery urge to rebel against anything that limits the mind's potential. This Jupiter fully embraces the wonders of technology. It also believes in raising social consciousness.

Mercury and **Mars** do very well in Aquarius. Mercury especially likes this sign's ability to process information rapidly, thanks to ingenious Aquarian shortcuts that help Mercury sort things quicker and smarter. Here's a mind that can be brilliant in a farsighted manner. Futuristic concepts revolutionize standard systems of thought, or they can simply defy established procedure and cause social disruption. Usually, we educate ourselves in all sorts of interesting ways, and are not afraid to explore controversial subject matter—we sometimes shock others to educate them, not offend them. Mars in Aquarius, assertive when it comes to doing things differently, doesn't like following "the rules" and will blatantly ignore them. A headstrong willfulness can have us clashing with authority. Our sudden bouts of rebellious anger surprise others, as well as ourselves. Still, Aquarius triggers Mars' daring and courage. We may take galvanizing action within group efforts that support community needs, as the spirit of volunteerism is strong.

We act as fervent reformists who'll energetically work to awaken society in progressive ways.

Saturn in Aquarius evokes the side of this sign that is oddly conservative. The Water Bearer is sometimes willing to faithfully submit to a group's ideology, even when facets of such a thought system go against the rights of individual freedoms. Saturn here cautions Aquarius to build its ideal societies with care, and with an adherence to law and order (it's the Uranian element of this sign that flirts with anarchy). Aquarius is a fixed sign, and thus appreciates Saturn's ability to steadily structure a better world for all (since fixity respects endurance). However, Aquarius still needs its "wild and crazy" moments, those that Saturn may frown upon. Aquarius likes to suddenly switch gears and experiment by going down different paths that Saturn may not condone. Yet Aquarian unpredictability should not be stifled, as it can lead to major breakthroughs in thought.

Team Spirit

Planets in this sign are tailor-made for relevant group involvement and for generating the spirit of teamwork needed to help society advance. We may show a talent for coordinating various social units that must creatively work together as a whole (Aquarius has an ability to interact with people of all ranks, and manages to treat them as equals). We may land positions on committees and boards that teach us about the importance of achieving democratic cooperation, especially when all members are *not* in agreement about timely collective issues. Aquarius can either symbolize the disruptive agent who refuses to go along with a majority consensus—it can be aggravatingly contrary—or the one who mediates differing viewpoints with fairness and clarity, often leading to an innovative resolution (Aquarius is one to break deadlocks because of its out-of-the-ordinary negotiating power).

Sometimes Aquarius intellectually rejects the importance of acting independently—such as the way Leo acts—especially from an individualistic perspective that shuns peer-group identification. Not all in life has to focus on collective needs to be relevant, a lesson Aquarius planets must learn. We're not here just to fight for important social causes, at the expense of our personal development. (Actually, Aquarius sees itself as a staunch individualist who just chooses to participate in groups efforts, when sparked by pressing concerns that involve the welfare of many. It advocates organized social participation as the best way to enforce major reform.)

Freedom Lover

As long as we engage in consciousness-raising pursuits aimed to make society more humane and even interesting, we should be entitled to unconditional personal freedom—at least that's what Aquarius theorizes. Being free to reinvent ourselves is important. Doing what's socially expected of us—predictable, appropriate behavior—often rubs the Aquarius in us the wrong way, triggering us to go in the opposite direction. We'll have to apply common sense when such rebellious urges act up, as undisciplined Aquarius energy can also be socially alienating. But within reason, we can develop our own one-of-a-kind, offbeat style of living, and we can do it in a manner that others find refreshingly original.

Our Future Prospects

Even if we don't have any planets in Aquarius at birth, someday a planet—like the Moon—will move into this idealistic, social-minded sign by secondary progression or solar arc. That's when we're more ready to play an active role in social progress, especially the kind that advances the collective mind. We'll also be ready to break out of old shells of conformity and begin to experiment with exciting and novel formats of self-expression.

PLANETS IN PISCES

Nourishing Our Spirit

Planets in Pisces need delicate handling, since they represent emotionally impressionable parts of us that are highly sensitive to the psychological currents in which we swim. If our environment is warmly supportive of Pisces' creative, healing inspiration, then such planets help us create a special magic that nourishes souls everywhere (Pisces can be a very spiritually uplifting sign). Yet if our surroundings are harsh, difficult, mean-spirited, or chaotic, such planets can easily be led down paths of despair and hopelessness. Here we soak in the invisible waves of darkness around us, often without realizing how they further feed our secret fears or inner pain.

Piscean planets ideally allow us to feel so unbounded, ego-wise, that we are willing to risk failure and social ridicule just to pursue an illuminating life quest that nurtures our spirit. We can follow an inner dream with great faith and hope, as if guided by an unseen, benevolent presence. These less-worldly planets are dedicated to universal causes that help humanity feel unified and at peace. Yet there's a problem with a lack of discrimination—are we really in touch with a divine vision, or is our path illusionary and filled with pitfalls that we're too blind to see?

Our Pisces Planets

The **Moon** and **Venus** easily absorb the compassionate energy of Pisces. These planets like close involvement with others, so that they can feel a comforting sense of belonging. Pisces is inclusive by nature, and thus wants all of life to feel interconnected. A problem these planets have revolves around the risk of losing one's identity in others. We may also dedicate our time and energy to those who do not want or even appreciate our devotional or sacrificial efforts. Pisces Moon folks can deny themselves proper emotional attention, as they focus energy on helping people through difficult life predicaments. We can be charitable, but also too giving in ways that reflect poor judgment. Finding the time to quietly reflect—perhaps to gain insight on how best to heal our own wounds—is vitally important. Venus in Pisces loves in unselfish ways, yet if we ignore our own affectional needs too often, we end up feeling empty and even numb inside. We'll need to form unions in which we don't feel victimized or used. We also have unrealistic, romantic yearnings that others find impossible to fulfill.

The **Sun** and **Jupiter** are probably too ego-driven and adventure-seeking, respectively, to fully appreciate the quiet, reflective ways of Pisces, a sign that avoids the limelight. Still, these planets are capable of generosity of spirit, something that Pisces also excels in. They are big-hearted planets that encourage this sign to give its inner resources freely to the world. The Sun also demands that Pisces honor our individuality. Our ego is fed well when we exercise our powerful imagination and tap deeply into rich veins of creativity. We are to bring out our soul strengths with much color and dramatic flair, rather than to submerge our being in the murky waters of self-denial. Jupiter loves the unconditional faith that the Fishes possess. Pisces trusts the world as much as this outgoing planet does. Yet this sign also helps soften Jupiter's nature, allowing it to not only be giving to others, but to be more receptive of people's inner worlds—this Jupiter gains wisdom by listening to what other's feel deeply. Its nonjudgmental nature helps elicit such private feelings.

Mercury and **Mars** are sometimes too busy and on the go to effectively handle Pisces' sublime energies, especially those that require more contemplative states of stillness to realize. Mercury is flexible and curious enough to try to go with Pisces' unusual, meandering flow. Our mind is stimulated by our imagination and even by our psychic sensitivity, as long as Mercury doesn't use its logic and reason to devalue these Piscean gifts. Hopefully, we'll conclude that a higher level of intelligence is at work here, one that runs on intuition. This Mercury doesn't always apply common sense; impractical thinking leads to inefficient results.

Mars in Pisces is fueled by emotional triggers that are not always understood; something deep within us pushes our buttons, sometimes irrationally. Inspiration is quite motivating when a sweeping social project needs our dedicated attention. But let's not pretend that any unresolved personal anger or jealousy no longer really exists within us.

Saturn admires Pisces' willingness to serve society's pressing needs, which sometimes means doing the necessary hard work it takes to keep humanity from getting sick or going crazy. Pisces can help restore cultures back to spiritual health, that is, if this sign's unifying collective visions are taken seriously. Yet Saturn is distrustful of intangible realms that defy solid structure. It doesn't put much stock in Pisces' invisible worlds. Both planet and sign, however, recognize human pain and suffering; they also value humility. If anything, skeptical Saturn will need to refrain from robbing Pisces of its wondrous dreams of universal love and peace.

Unearthly

With planets in Pisces, we often feel out of sync with the norms of everyday living. We're not always grounded in ways that the mundane routines of life demand. We may be less aware of the passage of time than are those who have little trouble being punctual or efficient. We may not pay attention to practical details if we're too caught up in our internal world (daydreams, fantasies, musings, and such may instead capture our attention, leading to absent-mindedness). Pisces planets indicate that we follow our inner voice for guidance, yet we'll need to be careful not to misjudge outer situations due to personal blind spots that contribute to a muddled outlook.

A Pisces emphasis may make some of us feel like we're from a different planet, or from a bygone era (ancient times), and thus, we suffer a peculiar sense of time warp when living in the here and now. We're not very earthbound, and may sense that our soul longs to return to a higher dimension, its true spiritual home. This is unconscious in most cases, but it may explain why we feel discontent in the material world and are susceptible to escapist pursuits—but as long as our grand escapes are of the highly creative kind, we're in good shape.

Wise Soul

Pisces planets are blessed with a "knowing" when it comes to people's hidden lives. We easily pick up on the pain and unspoken sorrows that others feel, and instinctively want to minister to their special needs. We're sensitive to the emotional world of those who feel shunned by mainstream society (we somewhat identify with such rejection). We feel a longing to ease their plight. Pisces energy supports less self-indulgent lifestyles, those that are more in touch with humane endeavors that attempt to heal collective wounds. Helping those less fortunate feels rewarding to us. It will still be important to know when to pull away from the neediness of others, and instead to restore our energy. Practicing spiritual techniques in quiet, peaceful surroundings helps us replenish our soul resources and thus feel more at one with the Universe.

Our Future Prospects

Even if we don't have any planets in Pisces at birth, someday a planet—like the Moon—will move into this compassionate, unity-conscious sign by secondary progression or solar arc. That's when we're more moved to do good works in society that help those who may have reason to feel hopeless about their lives. We feel an urge to contribute to collective development in emotionally enlightened ways.

Note

1. For more detailed interpretations about Saturn's natal signs, house positions, and natal and transiting aspects, please read my book *Twelve Faces of Saturn*, a 1997 Llewellyn publication.

Chapter Nine

Signs on House Cusps

A sign on a natal house cusp determines those attitudes and outlooks that we will need to embrace and develop, if we are to psychologically knock on the door of that house, enter its domain, and learn to adapt to its circumstantial affairs. Life programs us to experience the various situational challenges of any house, in part, according to the qualities of its cuspal sign (as well as from the perspective of any natal planets found therein). The sign on the cusp thus describes the types of people and external conditions we'll attract while trying to handle the life themes of that house.

In some charts, a house may also contain an intercepted sign—sandwiched in between two house cusps—whose energies may at first appear to be less operative on a typical, day-to-day level. Our intercepted signs are of more subjective value to us. This condition either deepens our understanding of such signs or further complicates our inner life, when we cannot find suitable ways to allow such energies to surface and ventilate (the way the signs on our house cusps do). A house with an intercepted sign is certainly complex, suggesting a life zone where we can seem at odds with ourselves (the two signs involved with that house form a semisextile relationship, suggesting contradictory behaviors and contrasting needs at work).

The sign on any house cusp is also influenced by the sign on the opposite house's cusp (these two polar opposites are able to work in a complementary manner). When we are having trouble satisfactorily expressing a house's sign, we may be able to tap into the traits of the opposite house's sign in order to introduce factors that help balance our expression, thereby providing needed relief. There is always a constructive partnership going on between opposing signs, as well as opposite houses.

It seems that in present-day astrology, houses are home not only to our daily circumstances, but to facets of our inner self (at least some houses are commonly portrayed in such a manner). In the past, before astrology was ever used as a psychological tool of self-analysis, houses strictly represented our worldly surroundings, but less so today. The boundary line separating our inner and outer world is no longer as sharply defined.

For example, the First House deals with our self-image and any personal mannerisms that easily identify us; our Second House relates to our self-worth issues and the nature of our security instincts; our Fifth House is associated with "the child within" us and the will to be creative; our Eighth House deals with hidden psychological dynamics of all sorts, as does the house of our most unconscious yearnings and outpourings, the Twelfth—and so on.[1]

Thus, house matters are not exclusively concerned with our life conditions on the outside. Our subjective world is also reflected in our situational affairs, and vice versa. The signs on the cusps of houses therefore symbolize internal states of being, as well as the external conditions we attract that involve the people and events of our world.

For further information, astrologers not only look at a house cusp's sign, but also its associated planet, which is often elsewhere in the chart, in another sign and house. If that planet is not undergoing multiple stress aspects, the sign it rules works more smoothly with the house cusp it occupies; the constructive attributes of the sign come into play more easily during the unfoldment of circumstances we attract.

Let's now look at each sign's influence on our natal houses.

OUR ARIES HOUSE

Our Outer World

Aries enlivens the house it rules in our chart with an extra shot of "get up and go" enthusiasm. Here we are encouraged to move forward into our immediate environment, actively and courageously, to grab for what we want—as long as we're not too inconsiderate or reckless in the process. The situational circumstances of this house allow us to "do our thing" in ways most natural to our instinctual self. Spontaneous impulses are permitted freer release here than in most other houses, since taking action "in the now" helps us develop a healthy sense of self-will.

Should we instead feel trapped in this area, unable to act autonomously, it's a warning that we're not fulfilling our Aries needs properly (we're snuffing our fires out too often). One result of this is that we attract those who become too assertive and even aggressive with us, or who are snappish and impatient in irritating ways (this occurs when we project less attractive Aries tendencies onto our environment). We are easily overcome by dominant forces that no longer allow us to feel independent and in charge of our lives. Outer situations become increasingly uncompromising—actions taken, that personally affect us, are not of our own choosing.

In such situations, we may sit on our unspoken anger—as it builds up further in force—until agitated conditions, in our surroundings, finally pressure us to strike out explosively at whatever we find oppressive. Aries does much better when it gets things directly off its chest, before matters become too hot to handle (that way, things may only get "ugly" for short while, as we let others know exactly what inflames us the most). Learning to nip things in the bud is always smart advice, regarding how to best deal with the burning issues of our Aries house. Let's not allow congested energies to fester from a lack of open, honest self-expression.

This is a life sector where, if our actions are to prove successful, we had best not mull things over too much. We'll get nowhere when we deal with this house's affairs too slowly or cautiously, plus we *really* defeat ourselves when we act solely to please others, and not us alone. Here's instead where we're to focus on more self-preoccupied desires (few other houses allow us that privilege, without guilt or backlash). If our self-absorption goes too far, others will let us know about it in direct terms (let's hope we're strong enough to listen to their valid complaints about us).

Situations here can turn out to our personal advantage, as long as we don't try to arm-twist or bully people, just to satisfy our needs—otherwise, our selfish motives may quickly backfire. In this house, we're basically trying to determine what potentials can come alive and serve our needs. Others aren't supposed to make things happen for us. We are to initiate these matters on our own terms. Our Aries house is all about how we embrace newness, innocently but eagerly. We do not have a lot of built-in wisdom here to draw upon, when tackling the challenges immediately thrust upon us. We learn—sometimes the hard way—what to do as we go along, and usually without the ongoing support of others.

Actually, other people's constant involvement in our personal affairs could, unfortunately, sidetrack us. It's better not to seek such assistance. If left alone, we can develop needed self-reliance. We're free in this house to create our own successes, and even our failures—action is taken without regard for achieving secure end results. Still, our Aries house supports all bold, enterprising efforts that pump vital energy into our emerging life situations. Let's not act like a coward in this area of our chart. Life here says, "Go for what you want with no regrets!"

Our Inner Life

On an internal level, our Aries house shows us where we need to overcome a potential fear of the unknown, which is something that could stop us from confidently making new starts in life. It's not easy to act spontaneously on our desires when we're worried about the potential risks to face that could thwart such intentions. Yet Aries urges us here to develop inner strength, rather than to cave in to self-doubt or vague uncertainties. Courage and determination are what we gain when we absorb the Ram's energy and let it take us where it will.

Otherwise, inner frustration builds when we stifle our impulse to do something that inwardly feels so right (tension headaches reportedly come from holding back on taking desired action, even if someone else is the one blocking us). We can become testy and on edge when we unwisely hinder our Aries potential in this house. Actually, if we overcompensate for our fear to act, we may jump into situations with blinders on, boldly but thoughtlessly. The results could blow up in our face.

Aries, on an inner level, is also teaching us to see the expression of anger has a healthy way to clear the air, when faced with potential opposition (I'm talking about justified anger—not irrational rage). If we instead always choose to "bite our tongue," and silently swallow our resentment, the accumulative results could be damaging to our body (a little inflammation here, a little acid build up there . . .). We can also sabotage our energy levels in ways that leave us feeling listless and anemic—we cannot get our fires burning. We need to embrace our Ariesness to remain high-spirited and loaded with vitality. If letting off steam now and then helps us achieve this, so be it. It's not the worst thing in the world to let others know when they're stepping on our toes or cramping our style.

OUR TAURUS HOUSE

Our Outer World

Taurus brings a calm steadiness to the affairs of the house it rules in our chart. Things unfold at a slower pace that enables us to build the solid support we need over time. We learn to value gradual development in this life sector, which thus allows any benefits that emerge to be savored—we're less prone to move on quickly to new experiences, since the pleasures and comforts we enjoy here are long-lasting. In our Taurus house, coping with existing realities requires practical deliberation and sensible handling (plus what we see is usually what we get—here's where our first impressions seldom deceive us). We learn to assess current conditions accurately, as we evaluate these matters with care and clarity.

Others may see us here as being stuck in habitual patterns, whereby we resist viable options that could alter our life for the better. Instead, we stubbornly cling to what's familiar. Although such fixed behavior seems self-limiting, we personally find much contentment in knowing that this house symbolizes one facet of our life that, thankfully, is less subject to change. The crazy ups and downs of modern living have little effect on us. We become increasingly determined to keep things sane and predictable in this house, even if others find that approach to be a bit dull. A state of permanent stability is what we want, although we realize that such a state of permanency cannot be guaranteed.

Our Taurus cusp describes where we learn to value and apply our common sense, which for us acts as a reliable instinct that we'll need to employ whenever we're sizing up a situation involving our time and effort (two things that the Bull refuses to waste). We usually don't care to get involved with that which is needlessly complex, exhausting to undergo, or made aggravating by too many ambiguous features. We hate playing guessing games here, and we certainly don't welcome the surprises that can occur when life matters get out of hand. Keeping things clear and simple appeals to us in this house.

Actually, if we are less in touch with our Taurus energy, others we attract are then the ones who routinely balk at the complexities that we may unwisely bring to this house's affairs. They are also the ones who can't handle too much confusion; they make impractical attempts to tackle this house's here-and-now issues. Perhaps, in this case, we could feel hampered by someone else's lack of imagination or daringness (someone else's conservative nature may feel suffocating to us). Yet, since this is *our* house pattern (not theirs), we are more the ones who patiently need to take down-to-earth approaches to getting our objectives met.

Our Taurus house shows where we tend to possess things that we then persistently hang on to. What we accumulate is emotionally of true worth to us (although Taurus also has an eye for material goods that have great resale value). In those houses that put us in touch with life on more tangible terms, Taurus operates in an acquisitive manner (we have a temptation to hoard here). The very earthy appetites we seek to fulfill are sometimes purely sensual, not just material. Here's where we attract pleasurable experiences that comfort and soothe us. Manifestations of beauty are important to us, as are harmonious surroundings. We're quick to enjoy any comforts this house can offer. Here is where self-gratification comes easily.

Wherever Taurus' house cusp falls natally describes an area where we can make money, if desired. Circumstances allows us to profit financially in this sector. The Cosmos here seems to promote and protect our material interests, but we'll need to value our resources enough to then capitalize on them. We're challenged to avoid letting our assets go unpaid on some level. Talents are not to be undervalued—they instead are to be well appreciated and nicely rewarded.

Our Inner Life

On an internal level, our Taurus house is where challenges to our sense of personal value are often found. Feelings of self-worth are important to the Bull, yet because resistance can be a problem wherever Taurus is found, we may not always allow ourselves to feel good about who we are—we could have a problem appreciating ourselves in this house. Yet healthy self-acceptance is important for steady growth in this life zone. In whatever house Taurus is found, we'll need to learn how to be more content with ourselves and our activities in the world.

Possessiveness can pose problems in our relationships, especially if the house involved is predominantly a "people-oriented" one (such as the Fourth or Seventh House). The less secure we feel within, the more we may tightly grasp onto people and things that we hope will provide us with lasting stability. However, it's more appropriate to actually "own" a physical object than an actual person. We'll need to make that distinction, since turning people into our possessions can lead to frustrating power struggles that destabilize our union—just what we were trying to avoid. Taurus' opposite sign, Scorpio, plays a key role in this hard lesson—and if we don't get the message, then the relationship dies. Let's instead strive to love and share intimacies without becoming so attached that others feel oppressed and are left gasping for air.

We can appear solid and grounded in the affairs of our Taurus house—partly because the stable nature of experiences here gives us little reason to feel otherwise—but we still may be so one-track-minded that we have trouble expanding our potential by trying out different routes available in life. If we're hung-up on something, we can remain in a rut for quite a while. Flexibility, often sorely lacking, could help us make more of this house's potential—bullheadedness only limits our progress. Let's learn to value adapting to life's changes with an understanding that they'll only help nourish our inner growth in the long run.

OUR GEMINI HOUSE

Our Outer World

If circumstances emerge slowly in our Taurus house, they certainly speed up in Gemini's life department. In this busy area, little stays quiet and still for long (unless Saturn is also in this house); constant activity keeps us alert and energized. The environment encourages us to go down many roads, each equally stimulating, yet none will guarantee us security. Gemini's mission is only to provide us with the newness and excitement that fresh alternatives offer. Here is where we're learning to be multifaceted. Although our surroundings bombard us with almost too much information at times, they also force our mind to dart here and there, and take it all in. Yet, that's also what makes this house fun to explore; we're never made to feel trapped by doing the same old thing, since this house elicits our versatility.

Life teaches us here to utilize the power of our intellect. This is an area where we can benefit from—and enjoy—an ongoing education in the matters associated with this house. We're probably highly curious, so why not let that prompt us to know more about how things work in this sector? It wouldn't hurt to be open to the various opinions of others, as long as we don't end up feeling scattered, as a result. Hopefully, we gain insights that help us in our understanding—maybe not deep insights, but knowledgeable ones that satisfy our questions for the moment.

Communication is vital to the workings of our Gemini house. What we know, and how we go about expressing it, plays a key role in our development. This is a life zone where we are learning to be expressive with our thoughts. We have budding opinions that need to be heard (we're urged to test out our developing ideas on others and then to observe their reactions). Yet, in this house, we're less willing or able to draw firm conclusions (perhaps we sense that all the facts are not in—there's still plenty more to study or to inquire about). It's also important that we be allowed to change our minds frequently and not feel pinned down by anything (although if we overdo this, problems can occur due to our inconsistent frame of mind; even the environment reflects our changeability and thus becomes unreliable). On the other hand, becoming fixated on certain ways of looking at life deprives us of stimulating options that otherwise await our eager minds.

In some cases, our siblings may be involved in the external affairs of our Gemini house, and sometimes even our neighbors are indicated. The relationships that Gemini describes are not to be approached in a heavily emotional manner. The Twins need space to breathe and cannot endure any union where somebody's dependency needs are overemphasized. We thus are challenged to communicate clearly to others—without seeming unsympathetic—the reasons why we don't want companionship that comes with heavy psychological baggage. We instead desire social contacts that involve a lighter touch, a sense of humor, and lively verbal exchange. We may also find ourselves having to explain our ideas a lot, in our Gemini house. Here's where we even get to hear ourselves think out loud.

Our restless need for change can be one reason that explains any missed opportunities, since we are likely to quit projects too soon, perhaps due to boredom, before the fruits of our efforts have had sufficient time to ripen. We get detoured by new events that pop up and momentarily capture our interest. Remaining grounded and determined to finish what we start becomes unappealing. Our outer world provides short-lived stimulation that proves too distracting to resist—or maybe we try to juggle too many things at once. Learning to stay focused will be important, should we find ourselves squandering our time and talent on activities that arouse only our brief enthusiasm, not our enduring commitment.

Our Inner Life

On an internal level, our Gemini house is where we experience a duality that often pulls us in contradictory directions. Yet, our conscious mind is well exercised by such observations of life's contrasting features; they initially grab our attention, probably because of their obvious dissimilarities. Perhaps such duality also explains why we don't easily make up our mind in our Gemini house; little here seems cut-and-dried to us. In this life sector, we'll question existing conditions, realizing that more explanations are needed to satisfy us. One result of all this is that we'll find ourselves mentally pulling back and emotionally detaching, as we cool-headedly observe the people and things of this house.

Sometimes our intellectual detachment gets in the way of forming close, intimate bonds. Gemini, although friendly and full of smiles, can still approach others in a somewhat disengaged manner, as if its mind is elsewhere. Connection on a purely feeling level is nearly absent, or perhaps we relate emotionally to people in ways that seem insincere. We may even become chatty or overly animated, as our unconscious way to keep others at a safe distance (although our informal style of relating may fool people into thinking that we're chummier than we really are). Staying in motion, due to ever-changing circumstances, is also another way to avoid more in-depth encounters. We'll have to monitor ourselves in our Gemini house to make sure we're not becoming superficial in our dealings with the world. Hopefully, we remain alert enough to catch ourselves when we're acting phony or shallow.

In our Gemini house, we'll need to have internal dialogues, where we can toss our ideas back and forth to evaluate them objectively. We'll also need to find time to slow down our mental processes so that we give our nervous system a break. Too much thinking here can wear us—and others—out. Let's work on being quiet more often, so that we can be better listeners.

OUR CANCER HOUSE

Our Outer World

Cancer's house cusp symbolizes where we have powerful gut feelings about the people and life affairs of that house. It also describes where our vulnerability can be so strong that our instinct is to shield our emotions from potential threat. We're wrapped up in our feelings and how people respond to us, more than we may appear. Still, our environment coaxes us to expose our caring, maternal side. Who or what we attract triggers our subjective nature, for better or worse. It's usually best for us to reveal what we're feeling inside, rather than to keep everything hidden (since water energies, when pent-up, can later explode in irrational ways).

Cancer provides us—in life areas governed by the house it rules—with a marvelous opportunity to embrace deeper parts of ourselves that operate on pure instinct, which in itself is blessed with a special intelligence all its own. We can sense what's going on in this house without actually having factual knowledge at hand—our inner radar automatically tells us what's up. Yet, if we live in a culture that openly ridicules the existence of psychic sensitivity—and even flat-out dismisses it—our ability to tune in consistently to our surroundings is probably underdeveloped in this house (since it's been drummed into us how illogical it is to "know" unrevealed things about others, just by "feeling the vibes" they supposedly send out).

Perhaps out of fear or frustration, we're likely to develop a hard, defensive shell that won't allow us to penetrate life beyond our own limited internal boundaries, especially if we've been duped into believing that there's no reliable way to read hidden signals in people—so why bother? Yet perhaps, on deeper reflection, we'll confidently reject the false assumption that we read too much into people as a result of their body language or tone of voice. In truth, we're highly receptive to such subtle indicators. Let's vow to keep the intuitive waters of this natal house flowing freely, even if being keenly responsive means our feelings get hurt now and then. It's worth the risk. Cancer teaches us that there's more to gain than lose when we sincerely trust our gut intelligence and let our sensitive impressions guide us through life.

Family issues are usually connected with our Cancer house, and typically our experience with our mother—or a mother figure—is emphasized. This can either be seen as a welcome, nurturing influence or as an unwanted interference. Since we struggle with feelings of immaturity in this area of our chart, we may grow to resent having parental types in our life who unwisely prevent us from fully growing up. Thus, while we appreciate any maternal attention we can get, we also need to manage our security issues on our own, without undue family support or intrusion. It's truly better for us not to encourage another's overprotectiveness here, no matter how such insulation is provided; being too dependent and sheltered handicaps us in this house.

It has been observed that our Cancer house, in general, can be where we may have dealings with anything that serves the public. Here is where we receive great emotional satisfaction for helping those in need, or for giving something our nourishing support. We approach our environment sympathetically. If our energies are in a state of balance here, we also receive kind encouragement from our surroundings. We attract those who are willing put us under their wing, when necessary. They help foster our growth and emotional maturity in ways that enable us to feel anchored inside.

Our Cancer house is also where we surround ourselves with security symbols, usually possessions saved from long ago, that warm our emotions. Cancer—a sentimental sign—urges us to collect nostalgic reminders of the past (perhaps odds and ends that others call junk). Having them around, filling empty space, comforts us, even during our moodiest of times.

Our Inner Life

Our mother—or our family in general—unconsciously shapes our emotional outlook and our expectations in this house. It's here that we carry—even into adulthood—programmed messages from our early childhood; we are highly susceptible to parental conditioning in this life sector, since here we absorb things that make a lasting emotional impression on us. Part of our ongoing development in Cancer's house involves learning to deprogram negative influences from our past, especially in those areas where unexamined, subconscious fears prevent us from attaining our desires. We need to outgrow these parts of ourselves, yet it's difficult to let them go. Many of our ingrained safety needs—those that we sometimes defend against all logic or reason—are also attached to the matters of this house.

Our Cancer house also describes where we can't take much criticism (we're quite self-protective and thin-skinned here), yet where we nonetheless may need to hear a few objective insights about us from others. Once we sense that someone might expose a hidden weakness we've normally managed to cover up, it's into our thick shell that we retreat, like a turtle; or perhaps we blindly lash out at others instead, in an uncalled-for state of overreaction. We may have a few prickly, infantile traits that need to be examined, so that we can free ourselves of such immature, knee-jerk responses. Yet, with cardinal Cancer, we are more apt to push people away who dare to invade our private space; we don't want our hidden problems brought to light.

However, we do respond well to tender loving care from those who are gentle with us and considerate of our feelings. We need to know that others can truly relate to what we've been through in this house; they're not just giving us lip service or brusquely telling us to "get over" our hang-ups here. They'll listen to our complaints, once we have the guts to reveal them. Of course, we'll only open up when we sense we're in a safe space where we won't be attacked.

OUR LEO HOUSE

Our Outer World

Our Leo house cusp symbolizes an area of our chart where life can treat us very well, as long as we retain a healthy sense of pride and a good feeling about displaying our ego. This can also be a fun place to develop our recreational side, that part of us that wants to feel like a kid forever, enjoying life in a carefree manner. As the Sun represents our main objectives in life—our central purpose for living—its associated sign, Leo, thus describes a house where we can fulfill much of our life's primary mission (along with the house in which our Sun falls natally). Here, the spotlight can unabashedly be on our glowing achievements (realizing that it is actually our dedication and our faith in ourselves that help make these achievements shine).

Developing self-confidence is one of the challenges of this house, but also found here is a measure of luck (as also seen in our Sagittarius house). Perhaps the Cosmos has a special regard for those who bravely take the risks and gambles in life that Leo does, based on its passion for living and its innocent love affair with itself. This kind of luck is thus deserved and may actually result from not acknowledging obstacles in life. In our Leo house, pessimism only hurts our chances to make something big of our special abilities—our ambitions will never get off the ground if we lack self-assurance. We also may not capitalize on what good fortune brings our way when we don't inwardly feel deserving—but thankfully, Leo almost always feels it deserves special privileges in life.

Leo points to where we can shine and stand out as being special in some way. Our environment supports our urge to showoff a bit—to strut our stuff—mainly because we'd probably do it in an interesting, individualistic way. This is where we can show a degree of flair and pizzazz, once we convince ourselves that we have a right to be seen and heard. Since we are apt to be less plagued by fear and doubt, we tend to expend our resources vigorously here, and without fear of being unable to resupply them later. It's thus no wonder, at times, that our behavior can be extravagant and even wasteful (Leo doesn't foresee deprivations in its otherwise rosy future). We need to learn how to protect our assets against unanticipated losses during those less glorious, rainy days that may await us. Financial self-discipline is a must.

Sometimes we may attract Leo types in this house who may overwhelm us with their larger-than-life personality. If we haven't allowed ourselves to take center stage often—maybe we're riddled with insecurities—then we won't enjoy the performances of the "ego freaks" we keep running into; we find their blatant attempts to grab attention to be obnoxious. Yet, they are partly the unconscious creations of our own projections, and thus should be studied as potential role models (needing some adjustments, here and there). We shouldn't be so quick to reject these folks, since they are showing us, in an exaggerated form, how we can better deal with this house. If we cannot occasionally allow ourselves to roar like a lion and be colorfully expressive in this house, something is very wrong—and we're missing out on a lot of enjoyment to be had.

Situations involving children (not just our own kids) may be tied to this house. They'll teach us how to stay young at heart. There is something about dealing with children that puts us in direct touch with the part of us that is still looking for a fun time. Kids are willing to engage in awesome adventures and to allow their imaginations to run free (they allow for more possibilities in their world than most stuffy adults do). This kind of youthful spiritedness can be ours, in our Leo house, provided that we're able to become less self-conscious about how we look when being fully entertained by life. What emerges from us during such times comes straight from the heart, so let's give it all we've got!

Our Inner Life

Although Leo's a very self-involved sign, it's less interested in internalizing its energies in the subjective manner that Cancer does. Still, the Lion gets us in touch with our "inner child." The results of this often depend on how free we actually were to be childlike—even childish—when we were young. We adults who are on good terms with Leo energy were often exuberant kids—filled with passion and excitement— although perhaps we also were a bit too wired-up and self-willed. We nonetheless made our childhood a robust experience. We may still desire to relive parts of it, as a preventative way to avoid feeling old and tired.

If we had a miserable childhood, where harsh realities squelched that happy kid inside us, then it'll take some time to warm up to our Leo house. We are less able to reach out and grab for whatever could provide us with joy. Our self-esteem may be low, and we may lack a sense of wonder about life. We instead dread having attention thrown our way, especially in public, and would rather disappear into the backdrop. Yet, learning to accept the spotlight confidently is crucial to our development in our Leo house. We are not to underplay—due to false modesty or a distorted sense of humility—our potential for greatness. We also shouldn't have to ask for permission to let our hair down; our need to come alive here includes spontaneous self-expression.

Fortifying ourselves with courage and determination is also important in this life sector. We're challenged not to just boldly take our chances, but to be ourselves authentically and live a life free of social intimidation. Leo does care about the bad reviews it might get, but not so much that it won't even go on stage and try to win over its audience with show-stopping talent and charisma. By following our heart and dreaming big, we have a great opportunity to succeed in our endeavors in this house. Yet, we cannot reach the heights if we don't have a high regard for who we are as creative, worthy human beings.

OUR VIRGO HOUSE

Our Outer World

Our Virgo house may not be the most popular sector of our chart, since here is where life puts us to work, like it or not. This house runs best when efficient methods of operation are set into motion. Learning how to get organized is our challenge. However, where Virgo is found, we also tend to receive criticism whenever we don't do a great job handling our tasks. Life points out what we've done wrong, but also teaches us how to correct our mistakes. If we slip up in any way, we're sure to hear about it from the fussy folks we attract in this area. Circumstances here leave little room for error.

It's thus harder to feel secure and confident, knowing that critical eyes are taking note of our every move and are evaluating our performance. Our fear is that those we meet in this house will be impossible to please. Yet, Virgo energy goads us to do our best work; getting everything right is often the result of much trial and error. Here's where we'll need to be patient and attentive to detail. Working long and hard, to perfect something meaningful to us, is to be deemed a good thing, not a punishment. Work only becomes drudgery when we're slaving away at something that doesn't stimulate our mind. If things start to become tedious, we're not making the best use of our Virgo energies—we're probably getting too caught up in minor or irrelevant issues.

This house is also about learning to discriminate. We'll need to recognize which obligations in life are truly ours to fulfill, versus those that someone else should rightfully be shouldering alone. If we don't learn to be choosy in this regard, we'll end up doing other people's messy little jobs, often under strained conditions, and then wonder why we're so irritable and exhausted. We'll need to analyze the real motives behind our compulsion to serve, since it's not always done just to be helpful. The servile roles we play, uncomplainingly, could also suggest underlying issues that underscore hidden feelings of inferiority—do we subconsciously struggle with a low opinion of ourselves?

Virgo's clarity and practical level-headedness help bring matters into sharp focus. We must not be confused when handling this house's affairs. We cannot afford to waste energy on momentary, incidental interests that sidetrack us. Here's where we'll be tested to stay on track and to keep busy (Virgo cannot tolerate idleness). We like to know how things work. Our analytical powers help us unlock the detailed information that we must have in order to function in this life zone. We learn the hard way that being careless, or too lazy to do things right, encourages life to penalize us in some irksome manner. So, let's "get with it" in our Virgo house, and pay careful attention to what we're doing, step by step.

This is a life department where we can be all business and no play (unless heavy labor brings us joy). Emotionality is less apt to get in our way, and this alone can help us get things done effectively. Still, we may come across as too cool and crisp in our dealings. Remember, we're humans, not machines. Thus, taking a highly intellectualized or mechanical approach to whatever we're doing may lead others to assume that we are low on passion and sensitivity. We instead seem motivated by a need to be functional and by a nagging drive to do our work expertly, without flaws. Yet, if too caught up in perfectionistic behavior, we can appear to be dull and lacking in personality when engaged in the more social affairs of this house.

Moderation allows us to get those jobs done that matter the most, but let's also find quality time to attend to any neglected parts of ourselves. They'll only grow properly once care is taken to avoid making our work routine our sole priority. Virgo can show us were we have practical talents that can bring us much enjoyment, if we make a conscientious effort to develop them further.

Our Inner Life

Virgo may seem like a very industrious sign, always preoccupied with doing useful things in the day-to-day world (with no time to slow down and rest). It would thus appear to be too busy with mundane affairs to turn its energies reflectively within, but this just isn't so. The

Analyzer prompts us to look at ourselves as if under a microscope. We dissect the circumstances we undergo until they are spread out in many pieces before us; we then scrutinize every piece to determine its essential purpose and how we've contributed to its current condition. Virgo's inner life is not on the turbulent side (unlike Scorpio's). This sign's tries to keep its internal world as orderly as Virgo likes to appear on the surface—maybe a little too orderly at times.

We may actually fear chaos, in our Virgo house, and thus refuse to open ourselves to the depths of our unconscious. We're also uneasy with emotional displays and are determined not to let our own feelings spill out in irrational ways (our Virgo house is where we least wish to appear crazy to others). We keep a tight lid on those facets of ourselves that otherwise would expose our more private self. Yet if we're too concerned with controlling our emotions, they can nevertheless manifest as body symptoms. Health issues can tie in with our Virgo house, especially if we've long repressed our feelings. We'll need to find healthy ways to vent the anxieties that often build within.

Although Virgo likes to instruct people, it doesn't care to get too close to them. In our Virgo house, we may need to work harder at showing a little affection, to offset the appearance of being a touch-me-not. Our responses to matters of this house may seem emotionally flat (of course, having "water" planets in our Virgo house—the Moon, Neptune, or Pluto—helps dispel this impression). Here, our goal is to improve our functioning on all levels. Sustaining psychological health requires that we not inhibit our feelings or rationalize them away.

OUR LIBRA HOUSE

Our Outer World

In our Virgo house, we sometimes feel that we've got more serious things to do than fritter away the hours socializing (in general, light-hearted activities are of less interest to the Analyzer). Yet Libra helps us realize the importance of having quality, face-to-face, human contact. In this sign's house, we wish to attract those who share similar tastes and values. While they don't have to be exactly like us, we'll enjoy their company even more if they have complementary traits that sweetly harmonize with ours.

Wherever Libra is in our chart, we'll seldom tolerate stressful partnerships for long. Initially, we may try to adjust to another, if doing so reduces tension; but when that fails, we'll break off the relationship without lingering regret (air emotionally detaches and moves on, rather than remain in a stifling, no-win situation). Libra's ideal is to unite sincerely with partners it appreciates, primarily to co-create unions of dynamic interchange, based on fairness and mutually founded on love. The Balancer is careful not to provoke discord that leads to separation.

Our environment here will send cordial, cooperative, and even cultured people our way whenever possible—in fact, all those who help make our relationships pleasurable experiences. We also learn to be nicer to others and even to help folks feel good about themselves; we'll need to be equally receptive to their attempts to do the same for us. This house believes in benefiting both sides of any alliance. Yet, at times, our Libra house is also where we learn to fight for our own rights within social arenas of all sorts (it's even where we see the positive side of being competitive). Sometimes, pressing issues here take a legal turn, allowing us our day in court. But usually, most minor disputes result in amicable settlements, although if matters are indeed to end smoothly, we'll need to brush up on our diplomacy and show a willingness to concede. If we opt to take the stubborn, selfish route, we'll needlessly prolong existing conflicts (and blindly see our adversary as the sole source of our problems).

Our Libra house is not where we benefit from lone-wolf behavior or "me-first" attitudes. Let's learn to look at situations from other people's perspectives and meet them halfway in most instances. This house is where we are less able to fulfill our ego-driven urges without first considering their impact on others. Here, we are to pause and deliberate—weighing the pros and cons—before taking action. However, the people we attract are likely to be reasonable and considerate of our needs.

Libra deals with a comfortable, intimate sharing that is found in healthy marriages. In this house, we are to discover how to "give-and-take" effectively with others. Too much giving or too much taking throws our unions off balance (we're usually the ones who give more than we get—we'll need to learn how to be fair with ourselves by being more assertive; we shouldn't always try to please others at our own expense).

Indecisiveness can sometimes be a problem. Situations here may not move at the pace required for optimum results. When action is needed, we sometimes stall instead. We may be reluctant to stir things into motion, even when that is the only way for positive change to occur. So even if our situation looks steady and tranquil on the outside—poised Libra does give that impression—there may be a sense of unrest, on deeper levels, that is only aggravated by our reluctance to make decisions that could alter our circumstances (maybe for the better). We'll have to evaluate all sides of any issue in question, up to a point; but then, if we do not come to a firm conclusion about what to do, life instead will forcefully usher in necessary changes that can seem uncompromising. It's always better if we commit ourselves to some sort of action.

Our Inner Life

It may seem odd to think that we'd first need to make "a marriage within ourselves" to be truly happy, yet this is an inner lesson Libra teaches us. It would seem more likely that finding the "perfect partner" is all we'd need to feel complete, but folks who are out of sorts with themselves wouldn't even know how to relax around such "ideal" partners. Attaining internal balance in this house also means we are to find an appropriate time to express anger, assertiveness, or an urge to act independently—all Aries-sounding traits—along with all those other Libra qualities that make us agreeable and easygoing. Libra, a sign of both love *and* war, suggests we'll need to acknowledge our contrasting drives and urges before we can act on them.

Thus, wherever Libra is, we do not always have to be at our best, socially speaking. We must allow ourselves to express our darker moods, as well, even in front of others. Why wait until we're home, alone, before we dare to show our true colors? If we have something to get off our chest, we need to give ourselves permission to say it to somebody's face, while our feelings are strong (if we wait too long to confront, we may chicken out and say nothing). Astrology doesn't emphasize enough how explosive our pent-up Libra energy can be, once finally released (all that surface "niceness" may be our attempt to suppress less pleasant feelings that eventually must vent, in the direct and forceful ways that only outraged cardinal energy can).

Once we realize that not everybody has to like us, we can stop trying so hard to gain people's acceptance. Actually, here's where we attract relationships that we'll find to be generally congenial, yet during those times when we do meet up against the hard-to-please types, it's best to stop bending over backwards to try to appease them. Our Libra house is where feeling at peace with ourselves, regardless of our social circumstances, is more important. Internal balance permits us greater clarity regarding our underlying motives in existing relationships.

OUR SCORPIO HOUSE

Our Outer World

Whatever goes on in our Libra house is at least out in the open. But in Scorpio's life sector, external appearances can be misleading. Things may seem calmer and more stable than they really are. We'll only know what's actually going on with the affairs of this house by digging below the surface. It'll take time to unravel matters here, since we'll need to work through many psychological defenses to get to the heart of any conflict found. The environment doesn't make things any easier for us, yet perhaps that's precisely what forces us to turn within to tap into those inner resources that enable us to attain powerful self-knowledge.

Little about our Scorpio house is spelled out in superficial terms. Situations presented to us stimulate us to probe such life matters cautiously (since we sense there is more here than meets the eye, we can become suspicious). Life is teaching us to sniff out the hidden facets at work in this sector, which means we'll take little for granted. Digging deeply into the affairs of our Scorpio house allows us to unearth valuable assets that can empower us. With this comes a challenge to our ethical framework, since here we may uncover things about people and circumstances that we shouldn't be so quick to disclose—especially if others may be injured in the process. Our Scorpio house's experiences are teaching us when to remain silent about the complex conditions we sometimes observe or find ourselves in.

If self-mastery is our goal—since Scorpio drives us to conquer our inner weaknesses—it may come at a price. We'll find ourselves embroiled in circumstances that call for emotional resilience, yet our typical response is one of willfulness. We may even fixate on our desires in ways that further complicate this house's affairs. We could try to force issues, when it would be wiser and more advantageous for us to just let things naturally fall into place, without our manipulative ploys. Scorpio is a sign with many shadowy elements that instinctively resist exposure, and so, we may likely project many of this sign's less-desirable qualities onto those we attract in this house.

As a result, some people to whom we're magnetically drawn may seem power-hungry and too eager to force a makeover on us; we may resent being handled in such a heavy-handed manner. These folks can also seem maddeningly secretive, the types who deliberately conceal exactly what we most want to know (of course, the real experts at doing this are so subtle about being inscrutable that we may not even suspect they are hiding anything from us). When it comes to communicating, our relationships here seldom resemble free-flowing, two-way streets of open exchange. And when we do have a candid dialogue, it's typical that at least one of us is erupting in flames and showering the other with heated words that trigger a release of feelings from that person's hidden depths. While this won't be a common occurrence, it is memorable when it happens—and hopefully therapeutic in a cathartic way for all involved.

How finances are managed in a relationship is often a big issue wherever Scorpio is found. A major test in partnerships is the shared handling of whatever is deemed valuable or powerful. Matters of ownership can turn complex in this area of our chart—who is in charge of what? Battles can be fought over territorial rights, brought about by feelings of being intruded on or invaded. We may seek privacy here, but feel our space has been violated by another. We can react intensely and with a surprising amount of hostility when we feel dominated by dictatorial types. Confrontations, as a result, can be fierce, or slow grudge matches may occur, where nobody tries to remedy the conflict. Matters instead boil away for long periods of time. Yet, at some point, Scorpio insists that we permanently let go of all issues that cannot be willingly resolved.

Our Inner Life

Scorpio is one sign whose active inner life calls for periodic self-examination. We can let resentments silently build, deep inside, that may eventually poison our attitudes about the people and things related to this house. If we do not air our grievances, because we are so reluctant to share our private feelings, bitterness and even hatred can result. We can become so paranoid in this life sector that we don't trust a soul with our thoughts. However, the less we claim power from within, the more we sense a hostile power coming from sources in the outer world and threatening our autonomy. While we seldom openly fight the forces that we feel endanger us, we can turn icy and unapproachable as our way of defending our vulnerability. Nobody gets to enter our inner realm, unless invited—and nobody gets invited until passing a rigorous inspection!

By emotionally closing off all paths leading to our inner self, we can end up feeling isolated and too remote to be effective in the world. Luckily, Scorpio insists that we do not remain in this state for long, yet until we undergo the transformations required to dynamically reemerge in the world, the affairs of this house can remain a thorn in our side, constantly reminding us of the depths of our pain. Our difficulties may compound, should we turn cynical about any matters that frustrate us in Scorpio's house.

When we begin to consciously reclaim our power, this house becomes a source of constant rejuvenation. The environment impels us to undergo many needed rebirths that leave us only feeling stronger about ourselves in very healthy ways. We let go of whatever has weighed us down with heavy emotional baggage for too long, and as a result, we approach the matters of this house as if we have a new lease on life. Psychologically, we begin to feel we can handle anything that comes our way, without allowing fear to bind us in its tight grip. We thus can become a source of healing for people needing to be revitalized by our potent energies.

OUR SAGITTARIUS HOUSE

Our Outer World

In our Scorpio house, we can obtain in-depth awareness due to our curiosity about life and how well we observe others (especially if Scorpio planets are also in this house). We quietly build inner strength and emotional stamina, while enduring the complexities of this life sector. Yet, wherever Sagittarius is found, little stays quiet for long. This is an energized area where we can receive a broader education about society and the world at large. Our surroundings show us how much better relationships can be, once we learn to trust others. We happily discover that people can be honest and good, in ways that uplift our spirit. The environment warmly embraces us with open arms and inspires us to achieve high-minded goals, according to the affairs of this house.

Being moody or secretive in behavior goes against the nature of the Archer. In this house we learn to be forthright in our thoughts and actions; we're not to deliberately hide our intentions or slyly calculate our moves. Situations work better for us when we take an upfront approach. This is also a stimulating area where mind expansion is encouraged. We get to contemplate various life issues from wide perspectives that help us develop liberal, tolerant outlooks. Some of the social circumstances we meet in our Sagittarius house may sharply contrast our early family conditioning, yet these unfolding situations can be eye-opening for us. We may find ourselves looking at such thought-provoking issues from philosophical angles that make us question our former assumptions of what is "right" versus "wrong" or "true" versus "false."

Although Sagittarius is sometimes convinced that it gets its information directly from God, it is not a sign that has "the last word" regarding knowledge of the spiritual mysteries of the Universe (Pisces has a better shot at that). In this house, we may search for answers to life's biggest questions, only to find we're left with even more questions. Still, the journey on which our seeking takes us leads us to an awareness of vaster fields of consciousness that require deeper contemplation.

Adventures of the mind and soul are what Sagittarius provides us with, not just geographical travels. Our Sagittarius house is where we look forward to the prospects of an auspicious future, and with a degree of optimism which, in itself, helps us attract the best circumstances that this life sector can provide. We'll just need to venture forth in good faith to discover what opportunities will cross our path and further enlighten us.

In our Sagittarius house, we probably don't like to feel tied down by obligations or be restrained by rules and regulations. Yet by adhering to sensible limits and by using good judgment, we can keep ourselves from needlessly wasting time, energy, and resources. We learn to aim our sights toward realistic objectives. We may overextend ourselves here, since this sign puts us in touch with the expansive principle of life. We'll need to apply moderation, from time to time, but not to the degree that it cramps our potentially freewheeling style. We generously share our energies here and are apt to advocate or promote social causes that are beneficial to our community. This is not where we are close-minded or silent in our opinions.

Our Sagittarius house is where we expect truthfulness from others, since we also are upfront with our intentions here. Sometimes we're too honest for others to bear. Yet, as long as we're not being brutally blunt, it is best to be straightforward with the people symbolized by this house, and not worry about the consequences of being so direct. Let's just apply a little tact where needed, since we can respond to conditions in a fiery way that does not regard the emotional sensitivity of others. We'll need to be careful that we don't speak first and think second in this area of our chart, as not everyone appreciates our frank declaration of the plain truth.

Our Inner Life

Sagittarius is not a sign that goes inward too much to attain self-understanding. It shows more the daredevil spirit of an intrepid explorer seeking to voyage to outer worlds unknown. Yet it's also very intellectual in its search to find life's greater meaning. The Archer views the human condition in transpersonal terms, meaning that it believes our collective purpose for existence includes more than the gratification of our worldly desires. Sagittarius intuits that we are connected to a divine, cosmic framework of possibly infinite proportions. How we discover more about our true place in the Universe will come from a mental willingness to move up and away, beyond the familiarities of our mundane circumstances. Faraway destinations of the soul await those of us who are not afraid to take the required leaps of faith needed to broaden our awareness.

Thus, in our Sagittarius house, we can only help ourselves grow in mind and spirit when we look at human nature as rich in untapped potential waiting to emerge. Exposing ourselves to as much about life as we can is one way to stretch our minds. We don't even have to know the finer details of the wide range of subjects we study—having a general knowledge of things or an informed overview will satisfy Sagittarius. Therefore, it is important that we open ourselves to all beliefs and theories that help us reconsider what life is all about, even on abstract levels. We should never become too comfortable with narrow, uninspiring interpretations of reality.

How we choose to connect to the divine, via systems of faith that typically involve ceremony and ritual aimed to strengthen our devotion, is part of the life experience of Sagittarius. Not all houses are conducive to this spiritual quest, although on some level, we do tend to worship and glorify the matters associated with this sign's house. We are urged to find a higher purpose for undergoing the life-improving situations we attract.

OUR CAPRICORN HOUSE

Our Outer World

In our Capricorn house, what the future may have in store for us—if we get lucky—is less important than here-and-now opportunities to advance our social position, thanks to our steady ambitions and smart connections. Actually, the Goat does think ahead regarding where it wants to be someday, professionally speaking, yet it has the patience and organizational skills needed to slowly build a reliable power base. After many years of dedicated effort and hard work, we may finally achieve our goals and make our mark in society here. In our Capricorn house, our outlook is typically mature and pragmatic. We realize that self-discipline is required of us in order to succeed in the world. We learn to make our moves carefully and strategically.

Wherever Capricorn is found, delays to achieving our goals are common. Our environment forever seems to test our mettle by putting roadblocks in our path, specifically designed to promote determination and build character. At first, we can feel frustrated by our circumstantial affairs in this house, since here we have to wait longer than others do to get what we most want. Capricorn is teaching us to stop complaining, stay focused, and get on with the business at hand in this house. The more proficient we become, as we continue to plug away, the easier things get. In the end, our steadfast efforts will pay off, provided that our goals are realistic and our striving has been honorable.

Gaining maturity, a major theme wherever Capricorn falls in our chart, implies sound judgment and a level-headed acceptance of one's limits in life. In this house, we eventually learn what we can and cannot achieve or control, and it's best that we make peace with that fact. In our Capricorn house is where we cannot afford to suffer chronic discontentment, which can otherwise happen should our "great expectations" be based on self-delusion. We'll have to stay quite grounded here if anything big is to happen for us. Our environment brings people and events that test our honesty and integrity. This means we won't get away with much, in the affairs of this house, if our attempts to elevate our status are devious and unethical (which is how we can behave if we apply Capricorn's energies in a cold and ruthless manner). A sense of duty, leading to responsible and timely action, is to be instilled. We'll just need to know when to stop weighing ourselves down with too many obligations, since that's when various situations in this house start to become burdensome.

Wherever Capricorn is in our chart, we can be highly accomplished at some point. Years of hard work and dedication result in expert abilities that help us rise to the top of our professional field of interest. Such expertise can attract the positive attention of those in prominent and powerful social positions who'd like to see us advance further. Ambition is thus a good thing to have in our Capricorn house, since here it spurs us to admirably bring out our best. Since Saturn rules this house, we will always be reminded that humility is also important, no matter how distinguished we become. Still, it's comforting to know that, due to our self-discipline and perseverance, we get ahead in life and reach our concrete goals because we've earned the right to do so—dumb luck plays less a role in our ultimate destiny.

Capricorn is a sign of our experiences with our father and other authority symbols. Its house is where we will confront others who try to supervise us on some level. Do we lock horns with those in charge of us, or we will cooperate and learn that being an authority means first being willing to accept authority? Those who have power over us usually lead us in a direction we may be forced to follow, for a while, until we've had enough experience in the real world to manage ourselves and call the shots.

Our Inner Life

Capricorn is not a superficial sign, although it is tempted by the trappings of material power in ways that can block deeper self-reflection. Trying to control or conquer the world is a very external preoccupation, involving little time for quietly going within. Yet the Goat is very sensitive on the inside and ponders life's serious matters more than is visibly apparent. In our Capricorn house, we can feel defensive, knowing that things do not unfold for us quickly or easily here. A sense of struggle is involved, if we are to achieve our objectives; this is not an area of instant gratification. As a result, we may not trust the world to be good to us—it certainly does not indulge our wishes until certain dues have been paid.

Any long-term denials we undergo in this area may nonetheless help us build backbone. Due to such fortitude, we learn to endure life's ups and downs better. A calm, internal strength emerges when we're masterfully in touch with our Capricorn consciousness. We thus realize that we will prevail in our ambitions, and that time is on our side. Delays are not punishments, but are how the Cosmos best prepares us for the results of achieving our much-desired goals.

In our Capricorn house, we feel concerned about our place in the world. How do we fit socially into the larger scheme of society? Being status-conscious, however, has its drawbacks, especially if we feel we're on the lower end of the social totem pole. If we are overly concerned about class and rank, we may also be fearful of being judged by others. Capricorn secretly worries that it won't make the grade in the eyes of those it tries to emulate. We'll need to watch out about beating ourselves up too much, in our Capricorn house, for not being a model of social success (here's where we can loathe ourselves for underachieving). We're also subject to attacks of guilt and remorse when we perceive we're not always trying our hardest to be our best. Let's learn to lighten up and be reasonable in our demand to excel in all that we do.

OUR AQUARIUS HOUSE

Our Outer World

Our Aquarius house is where we're less driven to make a name for ourselves in society, since the Water Bearer is not interested in conventional social climbing. While we tend to mindfully monitor our public behavior in our Capricorn house, some of us give in to the Uranian urge to jolt others with our rebellious attitudes in our Aquarian life sector. Here, we're allowed to push the envelope by experimenting with progressive modes of collective interaction—we can break a few time-honored rules in favor of doing things in uncommon, nontraditional ways.

Actually, Aquarius is so futuristic, at times, that its natal house may be where we prefer to act conservatively, even while we remain curious about the colorful folks and unusual situations that our environment unexpectedly thrusts onto our path. We are learning how to broaden our definition of social tolerance. Here's also where we're kept alert to lifestyle trends in society that shake up the status quo. Yet, since this house is influenced by an impersonal air sign, we may find—while in a state of mental detachment—that we're content to sit back and watch what transpires "out there" on the evolving cultural landscape. Let others dare to defy society's mainstream mindset, not us (this is Aquarius' Saturnian side talking).

Still, it's probably better for us to directly activate some of the reformative energies that Aquarius liberally offers those bold enough to buck the System, now and then. We won't truly know what greater freedom of thought and action feels like until we personally liberate ourselves from certain predictable routines and habits. This house thus encourages us to become receptive to the possibilities of living our life differently than do many folks in our community. Let's make a few waves by disregarding conventional behavior, and then see what comes of it—it'll probably be a mixed bag of reactions: some will admire our guts for being a free spirit, while others will feel we're too odd to ever be accepted by their tribe. Our originality can even seem threatening to such people.

This is a house where we surprise others with our attitudes, since we often do not look like the type who would advocate the unusual things we do. Much of what we espouse revolves around a "live and let live" outlook. We don't like to feel hemmed in by the narrow or biased notions of others, who feel we have no business thinking differently than they do. Our independent and sometimes intuitive mind feels impelled to march off defiantly in the opposite direction, rather than mindlessly join the crowd.

Therefore, in this house, we can get caught up in controversial, polarizing issues, as we show a determination not to be dictated by anybody who has the gall to tell us how to think or live. And if they try to, we'll give them exactly what they don't want instead. Thus, here's where we can indulge in willful, uncooperative behavior just to make social statements on behalf of freethinkers everywhere. In this house, we do seem to be drawn to group activity—i.e., people who share common ideals that they'd like to see implemented in society. We may have little in common with other members of the club, society, or organization to which we belong, besides our shared passion for the social principles that we all agree would enlighten others. (Aquarius also deals with special-interest groups who believe that the timely but radical causes they fight for will theoretically benefit everyone, especially in ecological ways.)

In general, our Aquarius house is where we can dare to be different and get away with it—we can happily reinvent ourselves here. Let's not be afraid to resist conventional wisdom, in favor of following our intuitive urge to bravely head off in new directions. We may even show a genius ability to brainstorm ideas quite unlike what anyone else had thought of before.

Our Inner Life

Aquarius is not an introspective sign, but it does have an exciting inner life, based on its lightning-fast intuition. However, our thoughts regarding our Aquarius house are often on the abstract side, plus they may be so avant-garde that few people understand or appreciate them. In this life sector, we can harbor idealistic or innovative attitudes that are way ahead of their time. They may be about how to establish a perfect society by correcting long-time social injustices as well as eliminating other defects (Aquarius does lean toward utopian communities where all inhabitants are on equal footing; the Water Bearer seeks to abolish all social class systems).

Depending on the condition of Uranus, the ruler of this house, our ideas can be brilliant and progressive, or just plain eccentric and ungrounded. We do tend to look at life from peculiar angles in our Aquarius house, but so have all intellectual trailblazers throughout history. It is probable that we are restless with the standard way things are typically done in this house. We want change to occur at a more dramatic and rapid pace, and can feel boxed-in when things remain too predictable. We seem to crave periodic excitement, an occasional thrill to stimulate and spark us to experience the affairs of this house in new ways (as this may not always be a conscious need, it involves an element of surprise and sometimes shock).

Because of a rebellious quality within, even if not completely acknowledged by us, we conduct ourselves in ways that allow the unexpected to enter our world and break up any monotonous patterns that we secretly find intolerable. Aquarius will do whatever is necessary to prevent boredom (the same goes for our Gemini house). Still, the solutions that the Cosmos provides us with can seem a bit extreme at times. This is probably why it's best not to take an emotional slant on whatever happens in our Aquarius house; since our security and stability are often challenged, we'll need to exercise mental detachment when life demands sudden changes.

OUR PISCES HOUSE

Our Outer World

In our Pisces house, we have the option to pull away from the mundane affairs of our day-to-day world and instead retreat into our psyche's most private realm, where we can meditatively reflect on our deeper yearnings. This house is not where we are all that worldly, to begin with; we may have to struggle to stay grounded in sensible, realistic ways—yet we also need to keep the waters of our imagination flowing. Here's actually a house that urges us to release our soul's energy so that it will spread out into the world and do some good.

Yet, problems can occur here when we fail to realize that our most basic needs to be met are spiritual, not material. Typically, we may remain confused and unfulfilled in our Pisces house, as long as we assume that the peace of mind we yearn for will come from possessing power in the outside world. If we deprive ourselves of meaningful contact with our spiritual self—perhaps by creating a lifestyle where there is no time for such delving—we may find we become exhausted and disillusioned from chasing rainbows that fail to materialize satisfactorily for us in the tangible world. Even when our worldly dreams do manifest, we find it's not enough to appease our inner feelings of emptiness or pain. Let's thus find quieter moments to care for our soul's development—something very deep inside us needs special nurturing here.

This is also a house where the environment encourages us to be less ego-guarded. As a result, we may not have well-constructed boundaries to keep unwanted intruders from invading our space (this is quite a different situation from what we find in our Taurus or Capricorn house). Our instinct is to help those in need, since here we can be empathetic to their suffering, but we must be careful not to abandon common sense or critical judgment in our dealings with others. If we do so, we are subject to attracting people and conditions that rip us off on some level, that at least drain us of our energy. What's worse, we may passively allow this to happen without realizing how unfair and demeaning it is to us. Perhaps we'll learn the hard way here that having an ego and a strong will are assets that will protect us, when we find ourselves swimming with the sharks and barracudas of the world.

Practicing moderation is a smart way to navigate our Pisces house, but the Fishes are instead more prone to surrender themselves totally to any experience, and indiscriminately so. We can go overboard in our emotional response to life. Obviously, other more practical facets of our astrological makeup may come to our rescue, once we've had enough of being taken advantage of in this life sector by those who manipulatively pull at our heartstrings, or who instead deal in insidious, guilt-producing tactics designed to bend our will. How can we truly be doing spiritual good works when we let ourselves be undermined in this fashion? Let's stay alert to the threat of those who engage in subtle sabotage games at our expense in this house.

Meanwhile, we can use our strongly sympathetic Piscean nature to work little miracles in our environment; life allows us our moments of bringing a ray of hope to those who seem disenchanted or bitter about life. It is exceedingly hard to remain self-preoccupied in our Pisces house, when there are so many folks out there who have been wounded by life (and even injured by they own negative self-images). Where this sign is found in our chart, we have a spiritual duty to contribute to the dream of unifying consciousness for all beings on the planet. Troubled humanity needs our unselfish contributions in this life sector. As long as we don't fall into the trap of becoming a messiah or a martyr, we are free to follow our hunches and to comfort those in need. We will also benefit from associating with others who share our ideals and who are compassionately willing to help society heal wherever it must, for the betterment of all.

Our Inner Life

Pisces is one sign whose inner and outer realities easily merge. Our external circumstances uncannily tend to reflect our unconscious hopes and fears, and vice versa. We become strongly reflective of archetypal forces that dwell inside us (this could be said of any sign on any house cusp, but it emphatically applies to our Pisces house, where our situational affairs symbolically resonate deeply within us). In this house, we must find quality time, alone, to explore our boundless imagination. The inner world of the Fishes is rich in wondrous imagery. Besides a host of techniques available to center ourselves spiritually, there are also the beautiful worlds of art, music, and dance in which to immerse ourselves. How can we effectively combine our sensitivity to aesthetics with the everyday affairs of our Pisces house? We enjoy gravitating toward highly creative surroundings that lift our spirit and bring us inner peace.

It's also true that where we have Pisces, we can be fooled by the people associated with that house, yet not always deliberately so. We're sometimes duped here because we don't want to see the truth, since it can crush our cherished illusions. We blindly assume things that aren't really happening. We fail to look into matters level-headedly, and later we may suffer the consequences. Such self-deception also leads to feelings of victimization. Let's get real with ourselves in this house and deal with life in more practical terms.

Let's hope that we never feel disconnected from humanity in our Pisces house, even if we otherwise enjoy a private life involving minimal socializing. In this life sector, we don't need a lot of attention and praise (our Leo house takes care of that desire). But what we do need is to feel universally associated with others, almost in a mystical sense. It thus is important that we don't feel sadly isolated from our surroundings. Let's reach out and establish some meaningful degree of human contact in this area, so that we can feel we belong to something bigger than just ourselves. Others can be healed by their contact with us, once we surrender to the power of universal love.

SIGNING OFF

Now that you've finished reading *All Around the Zodiac*, I hope you'll agree that knowing more about what makes the twelve signs tick provides another level of vital information that helps you better understand the dynamics of any birth chart. If it's true that planets most strongly indicate our psychological drives and needs, then what motivates us to find suitable ways to channel our basic planetary urges—even on circumstantial levels—is determined by the signs. It would thus be a mistake to ignore or minimize their impact.

For example, just knowing that Aries is on our Sixth-House cusp tells us that here is an area of our life where we are learning how to "productively" and "efficiently" assert our will and show a spirit of independence, but it's also where we may behave antagonistically and create friction. As the Sixth House points to our workplace, here we may appear self-reliant but seldom appreciative of unsolicited advice, assistance, or criticism—or maybe our forceful Ariesness pops up while we are in the doctor's office (thanks to a case of pounding headaches) and are demanding that our physician be straightforward and quick in his or her assessment of our symptoms (we're typically impatient patients who balk at having a lot of time-consuming medical tests done—we just want fast relief).

We obviously will learn, firsthand, the pros and cons of engaging in various Arien behaviors, most particularly so in this work/health sector of our life. Therefore, let's not get too hot under the collar on the job or become the ambitious go-getter who's insensitive to other employees. Let's not even argue with our healthcare provider for daring to suggest that dietary changes or less strenuous exercise is in order. Astrology warns us that wherever we have Aries emphasized, we can unwisely lock horns or butt heads with others in a battle of wills. Yet losing our cool and flying off the handle is seldom a smart idea, especially in the office. So, by realizing just this one fact about our chart—that Aries rules our Sixth House—we can learn that this a situational area that doesn't require us to be overly assertive in temperament, just moderately alert and energized (and maybe it's our Arien aggression, when thwarted or unacknowledged, that causes frustrations and explains why we're prone to tension headaches or even spats with coworkers, who become fighting rams in our eyes).

By knowing more about a sign's astrological makeup, we can take advantage of a wider range of behavioral options when dealing with any planet or house in question. After all, signs offer specialized solutions that enable us to better apply a planet's energies, or to better manage the environmental pressures common to any house. Our job here is to find out what works best for us. We do that by accentuating the qualities of any sign in ways that help us become increasingly self-aware. Overdoing or underdoing this sign's traits can lead to frustration and unhappiness. It may take many years of trial and error before we finally establish a happy balance that results in self-fulfillment.

I do encourage you to refer to *All Around the Zodiac* again and again—for example, during those occasions when you discover that someone you're romantically attracted to has Mars aspecting your Venus—especially if you're feeling a great amount of physical chemistry, but are also wondering if the sparks ignited will be short-lived or long-lasting. The signs involved, and the nature of the aspect these planets make, can give you the clues you seek.

You'll also need to review what I've said about signs that square or oppose one another, since you probably have a few natal planets in this condition and will need to know how to handle any tensions implied, without becoming your own worst enemy. Try to focus on any common denominators you can find in this challenging pairing of signs (and planets). Can these energies be used in complementary ways? If not, you may feel continually torn in two conflictive directions. Find sensible ways instead to pull the energies of these signs together and make them sources of strength, instead of sorry excuses for why you fail to satisfy your needs.

It also doesn't hurt to read as many other resources about planets in signs and signs on house cusps as you can, even if that means buying astrological "cookbooks" (i.e., texts that describe specific planet/sign and planet/house combinations, albeit in terms a little too cut-

and-dried for some astrologers). If the cookbook writer's "recipes" look interesting, by all means, use them to learn more about the various astrological "ingredients" combined, and then maybe improvise by attempting to cook up a fine meal of your own. For beginning students, this cookbook approach is a good way to get further into a chart, as long as the interpretations dished up are not too "lite" in calories (go for the more full-bodied fare).

Well, letting you in on what I know about the zodiac has been my pleasure. I'm sure you'll come across additional tendencies and traits for each sign, as you continue in your explorations of astrology (whether through books, classes, workshops, conferences, Kepler College, or online surfing). The lists of keywords associated with each sign seem almost endless, but you will also enjoy discovering some of these associations on your own—such as when you enter a tastefully decorated restaurant, quickly soak in the rich atmosphere, and say, "My, what a lovely Libran ambience!" It's at wonderful moments like this that you are no longer just learning astrology by reading about it—you are now inhaling it as it exists in its many manifestations around you!

Note

1. Here are further elaborations of how houses do not strictly represent the concrete facets of our outer environment:

   The **Third House** deals with the intellectual workings of our mind, something not ordinarily considered to be a byproduct of our external world, although local experiences in our day-to-day surroundings provide us with the variety of stimuli we mentally need to perceive ordinary reality.

   Apart from our normal domestic conditions and family affairs, the **Fourth House** also symbolizes our subjective security needs; here is where interior, emotional undercurrents and even deep soul memories dwell.

   The **Sixth House** of work and health implies that, while poor health may be the result of environmental germs and toxins, it can also be due to how we react inwardly to stress on the job and even to being overworked. How we cope or struggle internally with the imperfections of life plays a big role in this house.

   While the **Seventh House** describes the people with whom we want to share an intimate life commitment, it is also home to some of our strongest psychological projections, those unrecognized inner qualities that we project onto others, who then act out such traits. Thus, we expect to find some of our unresolved inner factors at work here.

The **Ninth House** is more than long-distance travel; it's the realm of our superconscious mind, sometimes referred to as our Higher Self. Even when we are able to contact preexisting spiritual dimensions, the experience can feel as if it is coming from an internal source, in an almost mystical sense. Personal issues of faith and belief in something higher also relate to the inner revelations we have in this house.

The **Tenth House** is a very concrete, external life zone, but also found here is the concept of *dharma*, which roughly means an inner recognition of our social duty in the world, based on our acceptance of divine law (thus, it's the fate we're eager to fulfill). Also, our internal urge to contribute something important to society is found here in this house of inner callings (something more than just a career).

The **Eleventh House**, besides being home to our friendly associations and our social-activist pursuits, has long been linked with our "hopes and wishes," which sounds rather abstract and intangible. Yet, it means our personal vision of progress, for both ourselves and our culture. How we dream of a better future for all is part our altruistic yearnings stimulated here.

Bibliography

Books

Casey, Caroline. *Making the Gods Work for You: The Astrological Language of the Psyche.* New York, NY: Harmony Books, 1998.

Chambertin, Ilya. *How to Astro-Analyze Yourself.* New York, NY: Lancer Books, Inc., 1972.

Erlewine, Stephen. *The Circle Book of Charts.* Ann Arbor, MI: Circle Books, 1972.

Forrest, Steven. *The Inner Sky.* New York, NY: Bantam Books, 1984. (The 1998 edition is available from ACS Publications.).

Hand, Rob. *Horoscope Symbols.* Rockport, MA: Para Research, Inc., 1981.

Kriyananda, Swami. *Your Sun Sign as a Spiritual Guide.* Nevada City, CA: Ananda Publications, 1971.

Jocelyn, John. *Meditations on the Signs of the Zodiac.* Blauvelt, NY: Rudolf Steiner Publications, 1970.

Moore, Marcia and Mark Douglas. *Astrology: The Divine Science.* York Harbor, ME: Arcane Publications, 1971.

Oken, Alan. *An Astrological Guide to Living in the Age of Aquarius.* New York, NY: Popular Library, 1971.

Parry, Robert. *In Defense of Astrology.* St. Paul, MN: Llewellyn Publications, 1991.

Powell, Robert. *The Zodiac: A Historical Survey.* San Diego, CA: ACS Publications, 1996.

Reid, Vera W. *Toward Aquarius.* New York, NY: Arco Publishing Company, 1971.

River, Lindsay and Sally Gillespie. *The Knot of Time.* New York, NY: Harper & Row, 1989.

Rodden, Lois M. *Profiles of Women (Astro Data I).* Tempe, AZ: AFA, 1979.

———. *The American Book of Charts (Astro Data II).* San Diego, CA: ACS Publications, 1980.

———. *Astro Data III.* Tempe, AZ: AFA, 1988.

———. *Astro Data IV.* Tempe, AZ: AFA, 1990.

Rogers-Gallagher, Kim. *Astrology for the Light Side of the Brain.* San Diego, CA: ACS Publications, 1995.

Watters, Barbara. *What's Wrong with Your Sun Sign?* Washington, D.C.: Vahalla Paperbacks, Ltd., 1970.

Wolfe, James Raymond. *Astrology and Your Secret Self.* New York, NY: Popular Library, 1970.

Internet Websites

www.metamaze.com

www.mrshowbiz.com

Astrological Computer Software

Cochrane, David. *Kepler 4.6.* Gainesville, FL: Cosmic Patterns, 1999.

☽ REACH FOR THE MOON

For readers of

All Around the Zodiac

only

FREE Natal Chart Offer

Thank you for purchasing *All Around the Zodiac*. There are a number of ways to construct a chart wheel. The easiest way, of course, is by computer, and that's why we are giving you this one-time offer of a free natal chart. This extremely accurate chart will provide you with a great deal of information about yourself. Once you receive a chart from us, *All Around the Zodiac* will provide everything you need to know to gain a deeper understanding of how each sign emphasized in your birth chart motivates you to grow and evolve in consciousness.

Also, by ordering your free chart, you will be enrolled in Llewellyn's Birthday Club! From now on, you can get any of Llewellyn's astrology reports for 25% off when you order within one month of your birthday! Just write "Birthday Club" on your order form or mention it when ordering by phone. As if that wasn't enough, we will mail you a FREE copy of our fresh new book *What Astrology Can Do for You!* Go for it!

Complete this form with your accurate birth data and mail it to us today. Enjoy your adventure in self-discovery through astrology!

Do not photocopy this form. Only this original will be accepted.

Please Print

Full Name:_____

Mailing Address:_____

City, State, Zip:_____

Birth time:_____ A.M. P.M. (please circle)

Month:_____ Day:_____ Year:_____

Birthplace (city, county, state, country):

_____

_____

Check your birth certificate for the most accurate information.

Complete and mail this form to: Llewellyn Publications, Special Chart Offer,
P.O. Box 64383, 1-7387-0111-4, St. Paul, MN 55164.

Allow 4–6 weeks for delivery.

Alive and Well with Neptune

Transits of Heart and Soul

BIL TIERNEY

This book is a fascinating look at a planet that astrology associates with emotional highs and lows. Sometimes pain and sorrow are part of this learning experience, but so is our ability to fully embrace joy and ecstasy—and passion. Our life would be colorless and dull without Neptune's magical make-overs.

This book focuses on the themes of transiting Neptune that take into account our capacity for ongoing spiritual development, our psyche's power to entrap or liberate us, and the fact that our imagination and sense of self are our two greatest resources for attaining our goals.

Much of what Neptune represents is truly not of this world. During our Neptune transits, we have opportunities to discern the real from the unreal. Often, we dismiss our inner voice that attempts to nudge us in the right direction. This book emphasizes the importance happily letting Neptune guide our inner radar systems so we can achieve a little heaven on Earth in the process!

1-56718-715-3, 264 pp., 6 x 9   **$12.95**

Alive and Well with Pluto

Transits of Power and Renewal

Bil Tierney

Pluto's path of deeper self-understanding is not an easy one, and its rewards do not come quickly. But when you learn to consciously confront this dynamic part of your psyche that otherwise remains dark and intimidating, you'll find a gold mine of psychological strengths that can help you face the world and maybe even transform it.

Learn how to better master the most complex areas of your life. Pluto's energy is intent on having us overcome our fears and self-doubts in favor of finding bolder and more passionate ways to express who we really are deep down inside. *Alive & Well with Pluto* offers new ways of looking at any personal life-dilemma you may fear is impossible to resolve—and does so in ways that will both entertain and enlighten you.

1-56718-714-5, 264 pp., 6 x 9 $12.95